POLICIES TO COMBAT DEPRESSION

NATIONAL BUREAU OF ECONOMIC RESEARCH

Special Conference Series

Policies to
Combat Depression

A CONFERENCE OF THE

UNIVERSITIES–NATIONAL BUREAU COMMITTEE

FOR ECONOMIC RESEARCH

A REPORT OF THE

NATIONAL BUREAU OF ECONOMIC RESEARCH, NEW YORK

PUBLISHED BY

PRINCETON UNIVERSITY PRESS, PRINCETON

1956

338.54

U 58

Printed in the United States of America
by Vail-Ballou Press, Inc., Binghamton, N.Y.

CONTENTS

CONTENTS

POLICIES TO COMBAT DEPRESSION

INTRODUCTION

HERBERT STEIN, COMMITTEE FOR ECONOMIC DEVELOPMENT

The papers published in this volume were presented at two conferences held in Princeton, New Jersey—the first on October 30–31, 1953, and the second on May 14–15, 1954.

The purpose of the conferences was to survey the existing state of readiness to deal with the problem of depression, in terms both of understanding the problem and of the availability of instruments to deal with it. The conferences were not called in the expectation that the United States was about to encounter a major depression, although there was a feeling, in early 1953, that we were entering a period of increased vulnerability to an economic decline.

There were two main reasons why the conferences were called when they were. First, there had been a number of important developments in the economy in the preceding fifteen years or so which would affect its ability to resist a depression. The change in the size and character of the federal budget and the alterations in the banking structure are outstanding examples. While these developments were widely recognized, attempts to assess their significance had been fragmentary. It seemed timely to try to obtain a more systematic quantitative appraisal of their importance. Second, the depression problem had slipped far from the center of attention it formerly held in the work of economists. This was natural and, to some extent, a move in the direction of better balance. But there was a possibility that the appeal of more fashionable subjects was causing undue neglect of still-vital problems. It seemed desirable to see whether aspects of the depression problem would emerge which deserved more attention than they were getting.

Even in four days of conference it was not possible to cover all phases of antidepression policy. The selection of subjects reflects, in part, the planning committee's estimate of relative importance. But this was not the whole explanation of the selection. One area—the contribution of private business—was excluded because it had been thoroughly discussed in a recent Universities–National Bureau Conference on Regularization of Business Investment. In one or two cases the choice of subjects was influenced by the possibility of getting constructive papers written in the time available.

I shall not attempt here to summarize the papers or to deduce their

3

net conclusion about our ability to deal with the depression problem. There are, however, a few observations that should be made to place the papers in perspective.

For the past twenty years or so the question of what causes business depressions has seemed not to be importantly involved in the question of how to prevent, check, or correct depressions. "Raise total money spending" was all we needed to know; the cause and specific location of the deficiency in spending did not matter. Now both Mr. Gordon's paper and Mr. Boulding's paper present the possibility that depressions differ in specific causes and in other respects in ways that call for different policies to deal with them. This view certainly has great appeal. Its acceptance, however, requires us to face two problems. First, we must learn what measures are appropriate to each of many possible kinds of depressions. Second, we must learn to identify the kind of depression we confront in time to select the appropriate policy. On the first point the Gordon and Boulding papers are highly suggestive, but their authors would probably not regard them as definitive. On the second point neither the papers nor the discussion are encouraging.

If we must be able to detect specific economic imbalances or deficiencies in order to deal with the depression problem satisfactorily, we probably have a long way to go. But this may imply too stringent a standard of what is satisfactory. We may be able to improve greatly on our past record in combating depressions without knowing a great many things that we should ideally know.

Mr. Roosa's paper on monetary policy deals with an aspect of the problem of detecting and responding to specific qualitative features of business declines. Is it sufficient to say that we will ease bank reserves when business is too low and tighten them when busines is too high? Or is the specific point in the capital markets where reserves are injected or withdrawn a matter of primary or at least important concern?

Somewhat similar questions about what we need to know are raised by Mr. Caplan's paper on the recession of 1948–1950. There were, and still are, apparently substantial differences of opinion about what was going on in the economy at that time. There were disagreements about whether we were going to have a recession, whether it would be deep or long, what might be responsible for it. We know from subsequent revisions that many of the statistical series studied at the time were seriously in error.

Nevertheless the policy followed seems to have been about right. How can this be explained, and, more important, can we count on a repetition of this fortunate outcome? Was it just luck? Did the policy reflect an equilibrium between budget balancers and tax cutters, between all-outers and stand-patters—and is that equilibrium likely to persist? Or is it sufficient for most practical purposes to be able to make certain gross distinctions about the economic situation —as between rampant inflation and reasonable stability or between moderate recession and deep depression?

The papers by Miss Merriam and by Messrs. Lusher, Cohn, Fox, Heer, Goode, and Pechman are important contributions to the evaluation of various aspects of the built-in flexibility of government finance. From this portion of the conference's work we can get good estimates of what may be called the first-round effects—the extent to which government receipts, expenditures, or deficits will be influenced by certain assumed changes in income or employment. This brings us to the borders of another problem, namely, How will the economy respond to the operation of the built-in stabilizers? The Lusher and Fox papers make some approach to answering this question, in addition to measuring the first-round effects.

To make progress in appraising the built-in stabilizers we must test them—on paper—in a variety of models of possible economic declines. The effectiveness of the stabilizers will depend upon the relative weight of autonomous initiating factors and of multiplying factors in the decline as well as upon other specific features of the situation. This is not a matter only of the extent to which the decline will be cushioned by built-in stabilizers. In some models of economic declines the built-in stabilizers will stop a decline and initiate an upturn.

The development of realistic models of cyclical responses is, of course, a difficult task and one that is receiving much attention. I wish to point out only that appraisal of the strength of built-in stabilizers depends upon fairly specific assumptions about the response pattern, even when the first-round effects are known.

At many points in this volume we are evaluating as antidepression instruments programs that have important objectives other than preventing depressions. This is conspicuously true of the papers on public works, housing, international commodity programs, and international monetary arrangements by Messrs. Owens, Grebler, Johnson, and Triffin. This volume can present only part of the evidence that is needed for policy judgments on these matters.

In a broader sense, a conference on antidepression policy deals with an abstraction. We want not merely to prevent depressions but to do so while doing certain things about economic efficiency, economic growth, price levels, economic freedom, and other objectives. The limitations that these other objectives might impose on anti-depression policy were not much discussed at the conferences, perhaps because there is so much implicit agreement to accept these limitations. But the question would undoubtedly have been more prominent if the conferences had tried to arrive at a Program for Action.

Our authors were given a relatively short time for preparing the papers contained herein. On behalf of the planning committee I wish to thank the authors and discussants for their cooperation throughout. I also wish to express our thanks to Messrs. Charles T. Broderick, Grover W. Ensley, and Irwin Friend, who participated in a panel discussion, not reproduced here, on signals for action to prevent depression. Also distributed to members of the conference were selected portions of two studies under way at the National Bureau of Economic Research—John Firestone's "Cyclical Behavior of Federal Receipts and Expenditures, 1879–1949" (mimeographed, NBER, 1955), and Daniel Creamer's *Personal Income during Business Cycles* (Princeton University Press for NBER, 1956).

The services of Mr. Daniel M. Holland of the National Bureau in organizing the meetings and guiding the production of this volume were invaluable. Members of the National Bureau's editorial staff performed the indispensable tasks of bringing order and finally print out of a welter of manuscript.

Mr. Donald H. Wallace served as chairman of the planning committee for the conferences until his death on September 19, 1953. In this project, as he had in many others, he displayed that competence and generosity that so endeared him to all his colleagues.

The other members of the planning committee were:

> Lester Chandler
> Gerhard Colm
> Melvin G. de Chazeau
> Daniel M. Holland
> Geoffrey H. Moore
> Lawrence H. Seltzer
> Arthur Smithies

I am grateful to them all for guidance and support.

TYPES OF DEPRESSIONS AND PROGRAMS
TO COMBAT THEM

R. A. GORDON, UNIVERSITY OF CALIFORNIA, BERKELEY

History tells us that no two business cycles are alike. While there are essential features that we expect to find in all cycles, we know that past cyclical contractions (and expansions) have varied widely in amplitude and duration,[1] and even cursory study of past periods suggests that the causal factors at work in different cycles have also varied.

If business contractions can vary widely as to duration and amplitude, important questions for policy obviously arise. What causes these differences in cyclical behavior? How can we predict in advance or identify at an early stage the kind of downswing inherent in a particular situation? And what bearing do the answers to these questions have on the kinds of stabilization measures which are likely to be most effective in combating an incipient depression?

The most recent theoretical literature—with its emphasis on simplified models—provides us with but limited help when we try to classify and explain these differences in behavior from cycle to cycle. Recent theoretical models have been of much too simple a form—too few variables and equations, too simple a system of lags, and too much dependence on unchanging relationships—to reproduce the wide diversity of cyclical experience that we find in practice.

There is, however, a moderately large body of literature on the possibility of different kinds of cycles. Without attempting to be exhaustive, we may mention Schumpeter's three-cycle model, several variants of the major-minor cycle hypothesis, the view that the character of major cycles is influenced to an important degree by the course of the long building cycle, and the work done on the interrelation between secular trends or "long waves" on the one hand and business cycles on the other. Perhaps mention should also be made of the older view that some but not all booms lead to

---

I am indebted to the Bureau of Business and Economic Research of the University of California for assistance in the preparation of this paper.

[1] Cf. Arthur F. Burns and Wesley C. Mitchell, *Measuring Business Cycles*, National Bureau of Economic Research, 1946, Chaps. 9–12.

financial and monetary "crises" that generate unusually severe depressions.[2]

I do not think it is necessary to review this literature here. Instead I shall take the liberty of merely stating several conclusions that I have drawn from these writings and from a fairly intensive study of American business cycles since World War I. (1) There is considerable justification, both in theory and on empirical grounds, for a flexible version of the major-minor cycle hypothesis; and this distinction, if carefully drawn and applied, can help us in interpreting past and current fluctuations in economic activity. (2) The empirical evidence does not lend much support to rigid multi-cycle models, such as Schumpeter's. (3) Even those writers who use some variant of the two-cycle hypothesis have not drawn an adequately careful distinction between major and minor cycles. Too often in applied work the distinction rests merely on differences in statistical behavior (particularly the amplitude of downswings), although the basis of the distinction is supposed to be a difference in causation. (4) Not enough attention has been paid to the possibility of mixed or hybrid types which combine some of the characteristics of both major and minor cycles. (5) And, finally, there is some reason to believe that the effectiveness of various types of stabilization measures depends in part on the type of boom or downswing they are intended to combat.

In the pages that follow I shall attempt to develop an analytical framework that permits a more precise (and I think more useful) differentiation of cycles than is involved in the usual formulation of the two-cycle hypothesis. In the concluding sections of the paper I shall consider some of the implications of my analytical scheme for the formulation of an effective stabilization program.[3]

[2] Detailed references to this fairly familiar literature are scarcely necessary. See, however, Burns and Mitchell, *op. cit.*, Chaps. 10 and 11, for discussion of some of these views and an attempt to apply statistical tests to them. The best source for Joseph Schumpeter's exposition of his three-cycle model is his *Business Cycles*, McGraw-Hill, 1939, Vol. I, pp. 161–174; see also his essay "The Analysis of Economic Change," reprinted in *Readings in Business Cycle Theory*, Blakiston, 1944, esp. pp. 12–16. Alvin Hansen's position regarding different kinds of cycles is summarized in his *Business Cycles and National Income*, Norton, 1951, Part I. See also Moses Abramovitz, *Inventories and Business Cycles*, National Bureau of Economic Research, 1950, Chap. 21, and R. A. Gordon, "Cyclical Experience in the Interwar Period: The Investment Boom of the 'Twenties," in *Conference on Business Cycles*, National Bureau of Economic Research, 1951, pp. 163–168. Some of these sources contain references to earlier writings on the subject.

[3] The next three sections are reproduced here only in summary form. For a more detailed presentation, representing a revision of these sections as originally presented at this conference, see my "Investment Behavior and Business Cycles," *Review of Economics and Statistics*, February 1955.

Minor Cyclical Movements

We know from past experience that, even without significant fluctuations in long-term investment, we can get mild cyclical movements in income and employment. It is not difficult to construct a dynamic model that will generate fluctuations in income, employment, prices, etc., even in the absence of fluctuations in long-term investment. If production plans are made in advance of sales and in response to factors partly different from those determining the subsequent demand for the planned output, businessmen will experience price changes or unplanned changes in inventories. As a result, production plans are subject to continuous revision; and, depending on the nature of the assumed relationships, cumulative movements result. Production plans may also need to be revised because of cyclical instability in the relation between consumption and income and because of induced changes in cost-price relations and in businessmen's attitudes toward liquidity.

Thus minor cyclical movements may occur even without fluctuations in long-term investment. Such fluctuations will tend to be of moderate amplitude and short duration; they will be reflected in fairly narrow fluctuations in consumption but in wide movements in inventory investment.

Investment Opportunities

We now turn to the determinants of investment behavior (exclusive of inventories). We begin with a distinction between "underlying investment opportunities," on the one hand, and inducements to exploit these opportunities, on the other. The *stock* of investment opportunities at any moment may be defined as the difference between the existing capital stock and that which businessmen would find it most profitable to have if they were well informed regarding all relevant cost and demand relationships and the forces making for long-run growth in the economy. Thus we may speak of an "appropriate" level *and composition* of the capital stock, and we may look on all investment (not based on mistaken expectations) as an attempt to modify the existing capital stock in the direction of what is appropriate.

The appropriate capital stock is always changing, thereby creating new investment opportunities. Investment opportunities arise because of technological change, population growth, changes in taste, governmental intervention, and other forces which may be considered exogenous from the point of view of the cycle. Investment opportunities are further widened or narrowed by purely cyclical changes, e.g. through innovations induced by changing cost-price relations, through movements in interest rates and prices of capital goods, and, most important, by the rate at which existing opportunities are exploited through current investment.

If investment opportunities were perfectly known, there would be, for any appropriate capital stock, an equilibrium rate of investment per time period, determined in effect by certain lags and the elasticity of supply both of loanable funds and of capital goods output. Actually, investment opportunities are not known with certainty. The inducement to exploit a given stock of investment opportunities varies with the cycle; it depends primarily upon profit and sales expectations and current attitudes toward liquidity. Thus the volume of current investment is a function of the (changing) state of investment opportunities, of other variables which also influence profit and sales expectations, and of the variables influencing liquidity attitudes.

Total investment is not a homogeneous aggregate with respect to the ways in which investment opportunities arise. One useful classification divides total investment into the following groups: (1) replacement expenditures, the opportunities for which are created by wear and tear and obsolescence (replacement because of obsolescence perhaps belongs in our third category); (2) expansions in capacity induced simply by a rise in aggregate income in the economy as a whole (this occurs particularly in older industries not subject to important technological changes); (3) net investment intended to exploit new opportunities which come about for reasons other than an increase in aggregate output (new processes, new products, changes in tastes, etc.); (4) residential building, which has a particularly high capital-output ratio and is intimately related to population growth and migration; and (5) inventory investment.

Three Types of Contraction

The cyclical forces described in the preceding sections can lead to different sorts of cyclical contractions, which we can conveniently group into three broad types.

First, we have the case of the "pure" minor recession, in which the cyclical response mechanism operates without affecting long-term investment. The downturn comes because of a downward revision of short-period production plans. The stock of investment opportunities remains large, and there is no significant deterioration in the inducements to exploit these opportunities. The necessary adjustments are brought about through moderate price declines, some contraction of short-term debt, and the curtailment of production in order to reduce inventories. Examples of minor-cycle contractions of this sort are those which occurred in 1923–1924, 1927, 1949, and 1953–1954.

The "pure" minor cycle becomes less pure as changes in production plans lead also to changes in investment plans. This brings us to our next case, which results in sharp but relatively short cyclical contractions. We may call this the "hybrid" case, intermediate between the pure minor and the pure major cycle.

A hybrid contraction may occur for either of two reasons. In the first place, once a downswing begins for any reason, the deterioration in short-term expectations may affect long-term expectations, even though investment opportunities remain large enough to support long-term investment at its previous peak rate. The second possibility is that, at the end of a particularly vigorous boom, a cyclically induced monetary or real capital shortage may temporarily reduce the stock of profitable investment opportunities.

What is important about this hybrid case is that the revival of long-term investment is brought about endogenously through the operation of the cyclical response mechanism: as soon as excess inventories are liquidated, prices stop falling, interest rates and capital goods prices fall to lower levels, etc. Thus while contractions which arise in this way may be quite sharp, they are not likely to last very long. It is more useful to think of the depressions of 1907, 1937–1938, and (with some qualifications) 1921 in these terms, as hybrid contractions, rather than as "major" depressions.

Finally, we have the case of the major cycle proper, in which a high level of investment has been maintained for a long enough time so that long-term investment opportunities become seriously impaired, even without the advent of a capital shortage. When a depression develops for this reason, the forces making for revival that gradually emerge from the contraction will not be enough in themselves to restore the stock of investment opportunities. The severity of the depression will depend particularly on how much overbuilding went on during the preceding boom, on the strength of the forces making for further growth which open up new investment opportunities, and on the nature of the financial maladjustments resulting from earlier speculative excesses. To this category of prolonged (and usually severe) major depressions belong the depressions of the 1870's, 1890's, and 1930's and probably also that of 1882–1885.

Stabilization Policy

Let us turn now to a consideration of some of the apparent implications of the preceding analysis, so far as it is valid, for business cycle policy. Several rather obvious implications immediately emerge from the argument of the preceding sections. (1) There is no one kind of program which would be equally effective against all cyclical contractions. (2) An effective stabilization program needs to be flexible, and its details should to some extent be tailor-made to fit the changing character of the cycle. (3) Therefore, an essential requirement is continuing and careful diagnosis of current cyclical developments, both in order to influence the current phase of the cycle (if that is desired) and as preparation for prompt action in the most effective way if future developments should take an unfavorable turn. (4) A further conclusion, derived from the preceding ones, is that an effective stabilization program cannot rely exclusively on automatic stabilizers. Discretionary action, extending beyond the field of merely monetary policy, is necessary in all except relatively pure minor cycles.[4]

While I think we need to re-evaluate some of the conventional instruments of stabilization policy in terms of the types of depression they may be aimed at, certain minimal techniques are appropriate regardless of the type of instability anticipated. This is particularly true of the so-called automatic stabilizers and of monetary policy.

Two essential and familiar features of all cyclical contractions are the multiplier process whereby a decline in spending reduces incomes and therefore leads to still further reductions in spending, and the effect of the increased desire for liquidity on production and investment plans.

The automatic stabilizers—by reducing tax receipts and increasing transfer payments as the national income declines—moderate the cumulative contraction in disposable income and in consumers' expenditures. Undoubtedly, the effectiveness of the present stabi-

---

[4] Perhaps it is unnecessary for me to add that these conclusions follow only if the stabilization objective is paramount—or at least sufficiently so to outweigh objections that might be raised on other grounds to discretionary government intervention.

lizers could be improved,[5] but any retardation in the decline in disposable income and consumption will have some influence, in a degree depending on the circumstances, in ameliorating the deterioration in profit expectations and in liquidity attitudes and will reduce the decline in production necessary to bring about a given decrease in inventories. Some favorable effects on long-term investment, again in a degree depending on the circumstances, may also be expected.

The principal role of monetary policy, regardless of the type of depression, is to combat the increased desire for liquidity. To the extent that it is successful in doing so, it will hold back the liquidation of inventories and the consequently exaggerated decline in output, ameliorate the decline in commodity and security prices and the resulting further deterioration of expectations, and lend some support to the inducement to exploit existing investment opportunities. It is likely also to have some beneficial effect on consumers' expenditures, particularly for durable goods.

Let us now look at our three main types of depression to see what additional measures are best suited to each. A "pure" minor recession, with little or no decline in the sum of private long-term investment and government expenditure, does not, of course, cause a great deal of damage. For such mild and short-lived deflationary episodes, one might argue that no correctives are needed beyond the mechanical working of the automatic stabilizers and a prompt and strong dose of an easy money policy. The stronger the underlying trend toward secular inflation, the stronger the argument against going farther than this if one is confident that only a minor recession is involved.

Since we can never feel perfectly sure of our diagnosis, and particularly if the community is not prepared to tolerate an unemployment rate higher than, say, 5 per cent even for a short period, additional discretionary action might be taken to ameliorate a minor recession and hasten revival. "Formula flexibility" might be introduced into the system of unemployment insurance, so that payment provisions become more liberal as the unemployment rate rises. Expenditures on the lighter types of public works, which could be started quickly and completed within a short period, could be accelerated. It does not seem to me, however, that this sort of minor recession is the time for discretionary tax cuts, to be reversed later, or for an elaborate public works program.

[5] A. G. Hart offers some suggestions for improvement in *Money, Debt, and Economic Activity*, Prentice-Hall, 1948, pp. 480 ff.

In all probability, something can be done to eliminate or offset the specific maladjustments that might bring on a minor downswing. Let me suggest one or two illustrations. Assume that consumers' stocks of durable goods rise to the point that sales of such goods decline and initiate a general downswing, the underlying investment situation, however, remaining favorable in these and other industries.[6] Special credit facilities can be extended to the affected industries to permit easier credit terms to consumers, to assist these industries in carrying inventories, and to reduce the rate of repossessions. Efforts might also be made to bring about significant price reductions. Or to take another example, if the major difficulty seems to be the impact of a drop of wholesale commodity prices on short-term expectations and production plans, government purchases of strategic and farm commodities could be accelerated to the extent permitted by legislative enactment, and, within the framework of an easy money policy, special efforts could be made to encourage bankers to help business firms carry their existing inventories.

Let us now look at our second and more interesting type of contraction, the "intermediate" or "hybrid" case. I think most discussions of depression policy envisage this sort of recession—i.e. a contraction of considerable amplitude, associated with a fairly sharp drop in private long-term (as well as inventory) investment, but with no significant impairment of underlying investment opportunities. Under these circumstances the right kind of expansionary measures can well have the desired pump-priming or "leverage" effects.

Clearly, the measures suggested above for a minor recession are suitable here also. The more successfully income and consumption can be maintained through the operation of the automatic stabilizers and a discretionary increase in government expenditures, the less serious will be the impairment of inducements to exploit existing investment opportunities. In this type of sharp contraction, also, it is particularly essential that everything possible be done to combat the rapid and cumulative deterioration in attitudes toward liquidity.[7] A vigorous use of the conventional instruments of

---

[6] I suspect that periodic saturation of consumers' demands for durables and perhaps semidurables will play a more important role in creating minor fluctuations in the future than it did before World War II.

[7] To the extent that capital shortage was responsible for the downturn, the contraction process will provide an automatic correction; but it then becomes imperative to combat a new deflationary force—the recession-inspired scramble for liquidity.

14

monetary policy can flood the system with excess reserves, the purpose being not only to reduce interest rates but, more important, to minimize the increase in credit rationing resulting from the reevaluation of risks by lenders and to satisfy the increased desire for liquidity by business firms. One result I think it is important to aim at is the maintenance of replacement demand. In a depression this demand is likely to be sensitive to an increased desire for liquidity. An easy money policy, particularly if promptly initiated, should also help to hold back the decline in security and commodity prices and therefore further bolster business confidence.[8]

Beyond these minimal measures, something can be done directly to stimulate the inducements for exploiting existing investment opportunities and possibly, also, to create new opportunities. Lower interest rates will obviously help. A proposal frequently suggested is some form of tax remission or direct subsidy for private investment undertaken during periods of depressed activity.[9] While I have no great confidence that this could be done promptly and and without great friction, government-induced reductions in the prices of capital equipment and building materials, beyond what can normally be expected in a cyclical decline, would provide some additional stimulus to investment, chiefly by leading some firms to maintain or increase expenditures and to anticipate future investment needs. It is not clear that a moderate cut in this category of prices would have a bad effect on short-term expectations, but I suspect that it might create some difficult wage problems in these generally highly organized industries.[10]

[8] The need, through both general monetary policy and more specific measures, to increase the availability of funds for investment in depression periods is emphasized by N. H. Jacoby and J. F. Weston in their paper "Financial Policies for Regularizing Business Investment," in *Regularization of Business Investment,* Princeton University Press for National Bureau of Economic Research, 1954.

[9] For some discussion of the possibilities here see E. C. Brown, "Business Income Taxation and Investment Incentives," in *Income, Employment, and Public Policy: Essays in Honor of Alvin H. Hansen,* Norton, 1953, pp. 300–316; H. M. Groves, *Postwar Taxation and Economic Progress,* McGraw-Hill, 1946; R. S. Brown, Jr., "Techniques for Influencing Private Investment," in *Income Stabilization in a Developing Democracy,* Max Millikan, editor, Yale University Press, 1953, pp. 416–432; and J. P. Shelton and G. Ohlin, "A Swedish Tax Provision for Stabilizing Business Investment," *American Economic Review,* June 1952, pp. 375–380. These sources contain references to other literature on the subject. This topic is also touched on in some of the papers in *Regularization of Business Investment,* as cited.

[10] For further discussion of what might be done to maintain private investment in (by implication) our intermediate type of contraction, see the papers in *Regularization of Business Investment,* as cited. A good many of the authors were pessimistic as to the possibilities unless aggregate demand could first be supported through general monetary-fiscal measures. The chief grounds for pessimism were

In general, it is this "hybrid" type of depression which offers the fullest scope for the conventional instruments of stabilization policy because, by vigorous and prompt action, we can hope to bring about a revival in private spending without undue delay. The more successfully aggregate demand is maintained, the more willing will businessmen be to exploit existing investment opportunities. A combined monetary and fiscal policy can slow down the decline in private spending; fiscal policy working through increased government expenditures and reduced tax receipts can partially offset the decline in private investment; and the specific measures previously mentioned, as well as others, can be used to stimulate private investment.

Perhaps it is superfluous to add that the hybrid case, even more than a minor recession, may require measures aimed at specific types of maladjustment. Prompt action may be necessary to control liquidation in the commodity and security markets. Agriculture may need special help. It may be possible to stimulate the demand for consumers' durables or to increase the availability of mortgage credit. And so on.

The hybrid case shades into the more serious situation of a major depression, in which there is a significant impairment of underlying investment opportunities. Reference to reduced investment opportunities does not necessarily mean secular stagnation in a really long-run sense. The impairment of investment opportunities may be and in the past has been temporary. But, while this situation lasts, measures aimed at maintaining or reviving disposable income and consumption will not be enough to restore private investment to the level needed for full employment. In short, this is the case in which pump priming will have only limited success and the "leverage effects" of expansionary measures will be disappointingly small.

The types of policy already discussed should also be appropriate in a major depression; but, if these restorative efforts seem to have only limited effect and if private investment continues to decline, further steps can be taken. The public works program can be expanded, with particular attention being paid to those types of construction and those geographical areas which have been hardest

---

(1) that the present value of investment made in slack times is less than in booms because the higher earnings of prosperity must be discounted for a longer period, (2) that the risks of anticipating future needs are considered too great both because of possible obsolescence and because of depression liquidity attitudes, and (3) the reduced availability of funds in depression, particularly from retained earnings (see, for example, the paper presented by Joel Dean).

hit.[11] Efforts can be intensified to stimulate investment by monetary policy and by tax and other investment incentives. In addition, lower interest rates and reduced prices for capital goods will extend the margin of profitable investment opportunities in some directions.

It should, however, be possible to go farther than this in accelerating the expansion of investment opportunities. Political and administrative problems might well arise, and it would probably be quite difficult in some cases to secure the detailed information necessary for effective action. In addition, the stabilization authorities might run into a special problem of timing and diagnosis. Vigorous application of the measures already mentioned might well stop even a major downswing and bring about a substantial revival in activity. After all, a considerable stock of investment opportunities always exists. It may well be that a new upswing will begin which will peter out too early, because the stock of investment opportunities is not yet sufficient to maintain for long, if at all, a satisfactorily high level of employment. Hence, mistaken or incomplete diagnosis of investment prospects might lead to deferment of some kinds of action until a second downswing had occurred.

What are some of the ways in which the stock of private investment opportunities might be expanded? I have not tried systematically to explore the major possibilities, but the following cursory suggestions may provide a basis for discussion. Also, I shall not consider whether any of these suggestions might entail a greater degree of detailed government intervention than a large section of public opinion would be prepared to accept.

Lower interest rates and prices of capital goods have already been mentioned. Special aid might be given to relatively young industries which perhaps had become temporarily overbuilt but which had considerable growth ahead of them—for example, financial assistance to firms in difficulties and technical help in accelerating the reduction in cost and improvement in product. Tax incentives and other government help could be offered generally to stimulate industrial research and modernization. Public expenditures might be made with a view to expanding particular industries. Thus road and street improvements might stimulate the automobile and house-building industries; construction and improve-

---

[11] The more important literature on the countercyclical use of public works expenditures is familiar enough not to require extensive citations here. For one recent useful contribution see M. L. Colean and Robinson Newcomb, *Stabilizing Construction: The Record and Potential*, McGraw-Hill, 1952, esp. Appendix Z.

17

ment of airports would help the aircraft and related industries; government assistance in the exploration for new oil reserves might result in a substantial increment of private investment in the important oil industry; and so on. Undoubtedly there are many other ways of helping private industry to develop new opportunities for expansion of which it is not yet aware.[12]

Particularly difficult problems are created when a major depression is brought on or intensified by the downswing of a building cycle, particularly in residential construction. This may well be a problem that the American economy will have to cope with sometime during the 1950's. In recent years nonfarm residential building has amounted to half or more of new private construction activity, and the latter has been nearly half of gross private domestic investment excluding additions to inventories. In the last few years we have been adding new dwelling units at a rate of better than a million a year, which is considerably higher than the rate of new-family formation that we can probably expect during the middle and late 1950's.

A serious decline in residential building is likely to mean that there has been a decline in the stock of investment opportunities in one or both of two ways. There may have been overbuilding, so that the current stock of housing is too large, given the size and other characteristics of the population and given also current incomes and prices. Second, and less serious, there may not have been any overbuilding, but the past rate of building (which brought the stock of dwellings up to the appropriate level) may have been larger than that called for by current and expected future increments of demand. If the stock of housing does become excessive, particularly if a general decline in income and a deterioration of liquidity attitudes also occur, the supply of mortgage funds may dry up, thereby reducing the level of building activity still further.

These considerations suggest the general lines along which attempts to revive residential building activity might proceed. I should prefer to leave the details to the experts, and I note that Mr. Grebler is contributing a paper on financial aids to housing. Perhaps the following suggestions, however, can at least be noted. Slum clearance and other forms of subsidized demolition can contribute to reducing an excess stock of housing. Special tax and financial inducements can be offered to private builders of housing for low

---

[12] Special mention should probably be made of the whole field of foreign investment, where undoubtedly much could be done to stimulate the flow of private capital to other parts of the world.

and middle income groups. Special efforts can be made to bring down building costs and to stimulate the maintenance and improvement of existing dwellings. Public works can be undertaken in part with a view to stimulating residential and commercial building—for example, improvement of streets and roads and public transportation systems, and the opening up of potentially attractive new suburban areas.[13] Government efforts that stimulate internal migration—for example, through decentralization of industry and government—may also tend to stimulate construction activity. It goes without saying that, from the point of view of a coordinated stabilization program, the time for accelerating the construction of public housing projects is during depression rather than boom periods—and particularly during periods of depressed building activity.

On the financial side, mortgage credit regulations can be relaxed, particularly if they had been tightened during the preceding boom. Unfortunately, American policy since World War II has been to stimulate the flow of mortgage credit in boom periods also, except for a short period after the outbreak of the Korean crisis.[14] Increased government support of the secondary mortgage market might be helpful during a period of depressed activity, as would steps to relax unduly tight credit standards applied by institutional lenders.

The measures discussed in the preceding pages can do some good, but undoubtedly they cannot *prevent* a major depression. Delays in diagnosis and the inevitable political and economic problems involved in putting any large-scale discretionary program into effect mean that, if a serious impairment of investment opportunities were to occur, steps could not be taken in time to prevent a business contraction of considerable magnitude. But perhaps I am more pessimistic than I should be.

Concluding Remarks

I have had little to say about wage-price policy and how it should be applied in the different kinds of contractions, largely because I am not at all sure I know the answer. A few sketchy observations

[13] It has been suggested that for every dollar spent in improving the Long Island Railroad, several dollars of additional demand for suburban housing on Long Island would be created.

[14] Cf. Leo Grebler, "Stabilizing Residential Construction—A Review of the Postwar Test," *American Economic Review*, September 1949, pp. 898–910, and Colean and Newcomb, *op. cit.*, pp. 145–147.

will have to suffice. I see little reason for tampering with the wage-price structure in minor recessions. Wages would certainly decline little if at all; a moderate decline in flexible prices would probably do more good than harm; and by definition the moderate decline in prices relative to wages that would be associated with a minor recession would not seriously impair long-term profit expectations.

In the hybrid case, exaggerated liquidation in commodity and security markets should obviously be prevented, if possible. Perhaps I am too confident that a vigorous easy money policy would help in this respect. Beyond this, we can assume that a farm price-support program would hold within moderate limits the decline in domestic agricultural prices. In the international sphere I should be happy to see an established, adequately financed buffer stock scheme. Something might be done to bring about some reduction in the prices of capital goods, through consultation with industry leaders. But since I suspect that the hybrid case is not the time for government pressure on wage rates, I have some doubts about pushing reductions in industrial prices to the point where we risk serious wage-price distortions and a further deterioration in business confidence.

In a prolonged major depression, downward pressure on prices and wages will, of course, be stronger than in the milder types of contraction. And the creation of some needed new investment opportunities may well require substantial changes in prices and costs in particular sectors. I have no great confidence that a stepped-up antitrust program will help reduce inflexible prices; government-industry cooperation may do a bit more; government and private measures aimed at stimulating greater efficiency in order to reduce costs may do a little more. Widespread wage cuts should not be pressed until fairly late in the downswing, and then the government might make a contribution by helping to bring about the reductions considered necessary in a few key industries. I share the view expressed by others that wage reductions should not be dragged out over a long period. A once-for-all cut relatively late in a contraction is probably better.

I do not think that either an effective or a practicable stabilization program can rely on a combination of the "castor oil treatment" (sharp downward revision of the cost-price structure and widespread bankruptcy of weak firms) and the "Pigou effect" (the stimulus given by the increased real value of cash balances to an increase in spending in relation to income). At the same time, efforts to bolster every weak spot that develops to the point of preventing needed price and cost adjustments can seriously delay recovery.

Probably the most important problem I have ignored is the one of diagnosis. Granted there is something in the sort of distinction I have tried to draw, how do we recognize the kind of contraction being presaged by a downturn in the more important business indicators? Perhaps empirical research will eventually tell us that certain constellations of behavior among various time series at cyclical peaks are associated with particular types of depression.[15] One difficulty is that the early stages of a contraction may look entirely like a minor recession and, indeed, be preceded by a minor boom. Only as the downswing develops do businessmen come to reevaluate long-term investment opportunities.

So far as I know, the only way out is careful analysis of the unfolding business situation, done in considerable detail and on the basis of a continuously improving body of information. In particular, we need more and better information on the factors influencing the production and investment plans of business firms and the spending plans of consumers. Needless to say, the time to start preventing a depression is during the preceding expansion. And when the beginnings of a downturn are recognized, the answers to three questions should be ready so far as it is possible to obtain them. What minor maladjustments need to be corrected, and how serious do they seem to be? To what extent do the speculative characteristics of the preceding boom suggest the imminence of a substantial secondary deflation? And, in many respects most important, what seem to be the long-term prospects for each important category of private investment? It is the answer to the third question which is likely to determine how intractable a depression will be.

Government commitments to spend belong in our concept of investment opportunities. Today government expenditures are considerably greater than gross private investment, and it does not seem likely that their total will fall below the level of private investment in the near-term future. As a result, a given percentage decline in private investment would mean less than half as great a relative decline in total nonconsumption expenditures, even without any contracyclical increase in government spending. This can be bad enough, but it suggests that for this reason alone "major depressions" are a somewhat less fearsome possibility than they have

---

[15] In this connection, note the interesting experiments reported by Geoffrey H. Moore in "The Diffusion of Business Cycles," in *Economics and the Public Interest*, Robert A. Solo, editor, Rutgers University Press, 1955, pp. 35–64.

been in the past. And, so far as the troublesome hybrid type of depression is concerned, we can safely assume that, in the absence of a philosophy of "balanced budgets at any cost," this type of "investment" (i.e. government spending) would be in any event well maintained. Unfortunately, this still leaves us with plenty of potential instability to worry about.

COMMENT

Elmer C. Bratt, Lehigh University

The difficulty of distinguishing the various types of contraction, which Gordon describes, might be partially remedied by a different kind of classification of depressions. He holds that "the only way out is careful analysis of the unfolding business situation, done in considerable detail and on the basis of a continuously improving body of information." If the attempt were to differentiate the business cycle from the long cycle, this prescription might be considerably modified.

A shrinkage in investment opportunities is a notable characteristic of the peak levels of the long cycle. The seriousness of a subsequent depression is directly dependent upon the extent of the shrinkage which has taken place, and the latter can often be determined by a study of approaching saturation in growth industries, made industry by industry.[1] I believe that a stage is reached at which most of these industries experience, or are about to experience, a marked shrinkage in new-owner demand.

This is only one of the ways of predicting the continuation of the fundamental factors on which the high level of the long cycle rests. A study, industry by industry, of the development of new companies also offers promise in this respect. Department of Commerce studies under the direction of Lawrence Bridge indicate that new companies account for a large percentage of total investment. It may be possible to show that a point is reached, while the long cycle is still at a high level, at which the promise of new-company formation significantly declines in a predominant group of industries.

A study of the changing need for replacement is another promising area. Studies are needed of the changed age distribution of the

---

[1] A list of rapidly growing industries is given in two Department of Commerce publications: *Markets after Defense,* pp. 66–71, and the *Survey of Current Business,* January 1953, pp. 5–10.

stock of commodities in various durable industries. It appears likely that usually the average age comes to be abnormally low in the majority of durable industries when the long cycle is near its highest level.

There are no doubt other methods of throwing light on the fundamental conditions of the long cycle. Shifting debt obligations might be indicative. Grebler's suggestion that we need data on the combined housing and consumer durable debt obligations of individual consumers in relation to their income is interesting in this connection. Also, some method is needed to represent the changing pressure of business debt obligations. The combined movement of several aggregative variables—population changes, family formation, changes in business population, and others—must be considered, although work done so far indicates that chief reliance cannot be placed on aggregates.

Special conditions existing at any given time must be carefully weighed. The large demand for educational, commercial, and public utility construction is a current illustration. The reasons for the level of demand in each of these three major cases differ substantially, and, with the exception of public utility construction, they appear to center on forces that the techniques suggested above would not be likely to uncover. For example, wartime material shortages created a backlog of demand for commercial and educational construction. I believe that serious depressions occur only at low levels of the long cycle. If this is true what we need to forecast is the imminence of such low levels.

A study of the unfolding of the business situation offers little promise in classifying recessions because the unfolding is quite similar in early recessions. From the point of view of indication of needed early action, a classification into concomitant long cycles and business cycles offers substantially more promise than Gordon's classification.

MAURICE W. LEE, Washington State College

The principal papers presented at this conference were concerned with national fluctuations and with national policies to combat them. They did not explore intranational fluctuations, the transmission of intranational fluctuations from region to region, and the possibility that a first line of national policies to combat national depression might well take the form of policies designed to isolate and prevent the transmission of subnational fluctuations.

Intranational fluctuations might well be a suitable area of inquiry for subsequent meetings of this group. Among others, the following questions might be explored:

1. *Intranational Fluctuations.* What evidence do we have either confirming or negating the concept of subnational fluctuations? Many studies, some published, some in thesis or manuscript form and not otherwise widely known, have dealt with regional fluctuations. As a first step a bibliography of known studies of this sort might be prepared and circulated to members of this conference, with a request for the addition of any other known titles. On this basis, a paper might be presented to a future session of the conference dealing with a "survey of contemporary knowledge of intranational fluctuations."

2. *The Transmission of Intranational Fluctuations.* To the best of my knowledge, this subject has been little explored by existing studies. Most regional cycle studies have suggested some fairly obvious relationships between the timing of regional vs. the timing of national turns, and that has been the end of the matter. A much more penetrating study dealing with the mechanisms by which fluctuations in one region are transmitted to others is required. We may borrow heavily from the techniques of international economic analysis. We need information upon regional trade balances, upon interregional capital and money flows. There is a clear use for input-output analysis.

3. *National and Intranational Fluctuations.* Are there any identifiable intranational fluctuations that have shown a consistent lead relation to national fluctuations? Presumably no such consistent relationships will be disclosed. But national fluctuations will be preceded by fluctuations in some subnational regions and the identification of such patterns may provide a helpful guide to the early perception of developing national trends.

4. *Intranational Fluctuations and Policies to Combat Depression.* Any cycle turning point for the national economy will be preceded by turns in some subnational units and followed by turns in others. Most of our antidepression policy is directed to the national level. It is possible that we can construct policies designed to offset regional declines before their effects are transmitted elsewhere within the national economy.

5. *Variations in Vulnerability of Subnational Units.* We know in a general way that different regions show differing degrees of vulnerability to different kinds of national depressing forces. A general decline in farm prices will have much greater impact upon the

24

total economy of the Great Plains–Intermountain region than upon the New England economy. The application of selective countering measures in the more vulnerable regions may discourage the development of secondary repercussions that will transmit the regional depression to a broader market.

6. *Policies for Combating Intranational Depression.* While national depressions quickly develop to a stage requiring national action, there are still wide intranational differences in the magnitude of such depressions. And, as suggested above, appropriate subnational measures may contribute to the preventing or mitigation of national depressions. Among the many measures that might be considered are: (1) Development of public works programs with known variations in regional impact. This will require a considerable advance preparation of input-output data. (2) Policies for greater variation in regional credit and loan policies.

A CASE STUDY: THE 1948–1949 RECESSION

BENJAMIN CAPLAN, WASHINGTON, D.C.

Introduction

Great significance has been attached to the 1948–1949 recession because it appeared to be the first postwar test of the basic strength of the New Economy equipped as it was with a whole array of built-in stabilizers. In retrospect it is clear, I believe, that it was scarcely such a test. The 1948–1949 recession seems to have been hardly more than a warning signal that such a test could occur. The episode was far more significant as a test of what might be called the New Political Economy, viz. the capacity of government to fulfill its obligations under the Employment Act of 1946 with respect to the furtherance of "maximum employment, production and purchasing power." Even here it was a limited test with rather mixed results. But it was significant in the sense that though the problems which had to be faced were relatively minor in character they were of the same type which would have to be faced whenever the problem of recession recurred.

To understand why so much interest has been given to the 1948–1949 episode it is well to recall briefly the climate of opinion following the ending of the war. There were two main features of the 1946–1948 period, the first economic, the second psychological. There was first the boom in the economy and there were also widespread doubts as to the solidity of the boom. To paraphrase a famous remark, many felt that "Depression was just around the corner." The reasons for this uneasiness are not far to seek. For one thing, there was the carry-over of the deflationary psychology of the thirties. This found its immediate expression in two perhaps closely related events: the predictions of massive unemployment as a consequence of reconversion from war to peacetime production, and the passage of the Employment Act of 1946 enunciating the responsibility of government for maintaining a healthy and stable economy.

Even though the immediate postwar fears proved groundless, the uneasiness, though perhaps subdued, persisted. This was based on two facts: the recognition that major elements in the postwar demand were the backlogs built up during the war both at home

The opinions expressed herein are solely the personal views of the writer.

and abroad, and the sharp inflationary developments which marked the period. These were, of course, to a major extent opposite sides of the same coin. The doubts ran as follows: Once the postwar backlogs of demand for construction and durables were satisfied, would the "normal" levels of demand be adequate to maintain full employment without massive programs by government? Did not the inflationary developments intensify the seriousness of this problem by creating major maladjustments between prices and purchasing power, between prices and costs? Moreover, did not past experience indicate that major periods of inflation generally lead to major collapses in prices and production? It was true that new elements of long-run strength had been built into the economy during the thirties. But were the new shock absorbers or stabilizers sufficiently strong to minimize the degree of readjustment that would occur? No one thought that we could avoid readjustments, but could we hold such readjustments to relatively minor declines in production and employment?

Although we have not yet had a definitive answer to these questions—and they are as current now as they were then—the mildness of the 1948–1949 experience in the minds of many seemed for a time to be conclusive. In fact, the apparent success of that experience led to the development of a new state of mind: the Age of Inflation thesis. This is the notion that the long-run propensity of the economy is inflationary. As I have pointed out elsewhere, this state of mind seems to represent a typical lag reaction to developments, and such theses are generally developed on the eve of a major change in the opposite direction. There were the New Era economics of the late twenties, the Secular Stagnation thesis of the latter part of the thirties, and the Age of Inflation thesis of the early fifties.

It will be interesting to see whether the Age of Inflation thesis like the others is followed by its Hegelian antithesis. But such far-ranging speculations are beyond the scope of this paper. To keep the paper within manageable limits, I have selected as my primary focus the adequacy of the response of government to the problems created by the recession. It will, however, be necessary to sketch briefly and selectively some of the salient economic features of that experience as indispensable background to the main discussion.

In what follows I therefore concentrate on three questions: What kind of a recession was it? How adequate was the response of government? and What are the lessons of that experience? This paper does not contribute any fundamentally new answers to these questions. But perhaps in the perspective of 1954 the whole experience will appear in a clearer light.

What Kind of a Recession Was It?

The commonly accepted view is that it was an inventory recession. What this means is that the forces which initiated the downturn had their major impact on the accumulation of inventories. These initiating factors have been well summarized by Professor R. A. Gordon,[1] as follows:

1. The increasing availability of goods both at home and abroad exerted increasing downward pressure on prices, particularly on farm prices.

2. The postwar abnormal expansion in consumers' demand began to level off. This resulted from the satisfaction of the most urgent backlogs of demand, the rise in consumer credit, and increasing price resistance, all leading to a more normal rate of saving.

3. Private fixed investment failed to maintain its rate of expansion and, on the contrary, developed a slight declining tendency.

The 1948 drop in the rate of growth of demand at the same time that supply capacity continued to expand was only temporary. It was only a brief pause in the postwar boom. It did not take long to complete the relatively small market readjustments called for, such as price and inventory declines. Because of that fact, the recession turned out to be very mild.

What may be a matter of interest, however, is the fact that every revision of the Department of Commerce estimates of gross national product for the years 1948 and 1949 increasingly indicates the mildness of the downturn. Thus, on the basis of yearly data, the decline between 1948 and 1949 was estimated in 1950 at $4.5 billion; at $1.7 billion in the 1951 revision of the data; and at $0.8 billion in the latest publicly available. No doubt the gap will be further narrowed if not eliminated when the results of the revision currently under way are published next July.[2] In real terms the data as of May 1954 indicate that the 1949 GNP was slightly above 1948. This is a sufficient commentary on how mild the recession was in terms of total output.

It is interesting, however, to note that the various revisions of the data have not altered the basic pattern of the changes between

---

[1] See his *Business Fluctuations,* Harper, 1952, p. 440.
[2] The July 1954 revision published by the Department of Commerce shows that the 1949 GNP was at about the same level as the 1948 GNP.

quarters. GNP reached a peak in the fourth quarter of 1948 and its low point a year later. It reached a new peak in mid-1950. The various revisions in the data have reduced the decline from peak to bottom from about 5 per cent to about 4 per cent. On the other hand, the rise to the second quarter of 1950 has become progressively steeper.[3]

Based on the latest data as of May 1954, the pattern of changes in GNP between quarters for the period 1947 to mid-1950 was that shown in the accompanying table.

Quarterly Changes in Gross National Product,
First Quarter 1947 to Second Quarter 1950

(annual rate in billions of dollars, seasonally adjusted)

| | GNP CHANGE FROM PRECEDING QUARTER | |
| | *Including* | *Excluding* |
YEAR AND QUARTER	*Inventory Changes*	*Inventory Changes*
1947		
1Q	+3.6	+6.6
2Q	+7.7	+7.3
3Q	+1.4	+4.9
4Q	+11.2	+7.3
1948		
1Q	+3.9	+2.0
2Q	+9.6	+7.3
3Q	+5.4	+4.2
4Q	+4.0	+3.5
1949		
1Q	−6.4	−.4
2Q	−2.0	+2.2
3Q	−1.7	−2.3
4Q	−.1	+2.7
1950		
1Q	+8.2	+1.1
2Q	+15.3	+7.7

Source: Department of Commerce data.

The pattern indicated by the table is as follows: (1) the quarterly changes in total output including inventory change were not markedly different in most of 1948 from those in 1947 except for the fourth quarter; (2) however, sales to final users increased at

[3] These constant revisions, undoubtedly inevitable, do raise serious questions for the forecaster and policy maker. So long as the basic pattern is unaltered, their usefulness is unimpaired as part of the economist's tool kit for discerning changes in the economy. But large changes in the level do create serious problems in trying to assess the quantitative significance of any change or of any policy proposed to deal with such change.

a fairly steady rate in 1947, whereas the 1948 rate of increase lagged behind the 1947 rate and definitely turned down in the second half of the year; (3) the 1949 decline in total output was concentrated in the first half of the year and then mainly in the first quarter; (4) sales to final users were on the average unchanged during the first three quarters of 1949 and thereafter began to increase; (5) in terms of total output, the second half of 1949 was a leveling-out period while the first half of 1950 marked a vigorous resumption of the upward movement. Because of the Korean outbreak, we cannot know whether and to what extent the rise would have continued beyond the first half of 1950. It seemed clear then that it would continue at least until the end of 1950, but whether 1951 would have been another period of contraction or of expansion can only be speculated upon.

Preceding the decline in total output, there was thus a weakening in the rate of growth of final sales. When the downturn got under way, final sales did not decline but tended to level out for a while before resuming their upward progress. Consequently, the fluctuations in GNP were primarily in that part of output which does not go to final sales, viz. inventory. Thus, between the fourth quarter of 1948 and a year later, the decline in GNP was $10 billion, annual rate, while business inventories declined about $12½ billion and nonfarm inventories about $10 billion. (See Table 1 for details.) There were, in addition, declines in the consumption of nondurables, producers' durables, and net foreign investment, but these were more than offset by increases in the consumption of durables and services and in government purchases of goods and services. The decline in consumers' nondurables seems to have been largely a price phenomenon, but that in producers' durables probably represented some hesitation in investment activity due perhaps to the need for reassessing the long-range outlook.

The preceding description covers the 1948–1949 recession in broad strokes. We shall now summarize briefly some of the salient points of the economic scene in 1948 as a prelude to the discussion dealing with the response of government, subsequently picking up additional details about the course of economic developments as the narrative requires. Unless specified, the reference to economic series will be to the latest available as of May 1954.

New orders, business sales, and business inventories reflected the weakening of the expansion of demand in 1948. In terms of new orders, sales, and inventories, the following facts are important: (1) new orders reached their peak in June 1948 over-all and for durables and nondurables; (2) over-all business sales reached their peak in August 1948, for durable manufacturers in December 1948, for nondurable manufacturers in June 1948, and for both types of retailers in December 1948; (3) the rise in sales in 1948 was at a lower rate than in 1947; (4) total business inventories (book value) increased steadily through 1948, reaching their peak in February 1949. The rate of increase was lower than in 1947 but represented

TABLE 1

Changes in Gross National Product, Selected Quarters, 1948–1950
(*billions of dollars, annual rates, seasonally adjusted*)

Component	Fourth Quarter 1948	Fourth Quarter 1949	Second Quarter 1950	Change from 4Q 1948 to 4Q 1949	Change from 4Q 1949 to 2Q 1950
Gross national product	267.0	256.8	280.3	−10.2	+23.5
Personal consumption	179.8	183.0	189.7	+3.2	+6.7
Durable goods	22.5	25.0	26.8	−2.5	+1.8
Nondurable goods	101.4	99.1	100.7	−2.3	+1.6
Services	55.9	58.9	62.2	+3.0	+3.3
Gross private investment	45.7	31.0	52.0	−14.7	+21.0
New construction	17.8	18.2	22.0	+.4	+3.8
Producers' durables	20.7	18.2	21.7	−2.5	+3.5
Change in business inventories	7.2	−5.4	8.3	−12.6	+13.7
Nonfarm only	5.6	−4.2	7.3	−9.8	+11.5
Net foreign investment	1.2	−.5	−1.6	−1.7	−1.1
Government purchases of goods and services	40.3	43.3	40.3	+3.0	−3.0
Federal	23.6	24.5	20.7	+.9	−3.8
State and local	16.7	18.8	19.5	+2.1	+.7

Source: Department of Commerce, latest published estimates as of May 1954.

a substantial build-up in real inventories, while the 1947 increase had been primarily the result of price changes. The build-up took place in manufacturing and retailing and was relatively larger in manufacturing than in retailing, relatively larger in durable goods than in nondurables. It was mainly a build-up in finished goods inventories. Durable manufacturers reached their peak level in February 1949, nondurable manufacturers in October 1947, durable retailers in December 1948, nondurable retailers in September 1948.

What was also important in 1948 was the sluggish behavior of industrial production compared with 1947. At the end of December 1947 the index was 103, and it reached a peak of 105 in July 1948. For manufacturers the rise was from 103 in December 1947 to 104 in January 1948 and oscillated back and forth until October when it began its decline. Durable manufactures were somewhat more vigorous than nondurables, rising from 104 at the end of 1947 to 106 in July and August 1948. Nondurables in 1948 did not exceed the peak level of 103 reached in November 1947 although they hovered about this level until June 1948. This accords with the relative build-up in durable goods inventories. At the time the behavior of industrial production was thought to reflect the fact that the increase in total production necessarily had to be small—a few per cent a year—if output were already close to capacity. In retrospect it is clear that the behavior of industrial production was due to the lessening pressure of demand. The proposition would have been correct if we had really been pressing up against the capacity ceiling.

In the investment field the most important development in the second half of 1948 was a weakening in the housing market. Housing starts fell below the level of the previous year. This fact was duly noted at the time. It was largely due to uncertainties connected with changes in housing legislation and to the fact that, with the demand for higher-priced houses largely met, demand shifted to lower-priced ones. In 1949 the housing industry, aided by new legislation, shifted to the lower-priced market, and housing starts exceeded 1 million for the first time in history.

In the case of consumers the following are the outstanding features: (1) Disposable income grew more rapidly in 1948 than in 1947, largely because of the reduction in taxes which became effective July 1, 1948. (2) The rate of growth of consumption decreased. In fact the process began in the latter half of 1947. (3) Consumers were, therefore, devoting a large part of their additional disposable income to building up savings so that the savings rate rose from the postwar low of 2.5 per cent of disposable income in 1947 to 5.6 per cent in 1948. (4) The demand for nondurables tapered off in the second quarter of 1948; for durables in the second half of the year. Re-imposition of consumer credit controls limited the demand for durables in the fourth quarter.

Price developments during the year were of major importance. Following the lifting of price controls, there had been a sharp advance on all fronts in the second half of 1946, some hesitation early in 1947, and a new considerable advance in the second half of 1947. In 1948 important divergencies in trend began to appear. Farm prices reached a peak in January 1948, broke sharply in February, and then recovered most of the loss by June. Thereafter, they began a new decline which gathered momentum. Processed foods followed much the same pattern except that they reached a new 1948 high in

August and then began their decline. Industrial commodities hesitated slightly in the first quarter of 1948, then advanced steadily under the impetus of metals and metal products to a new postwar high in November 1948. Consumers' prices under the influence of foods declined in the first quarter, rose to their high for the year in August 1948, and thereafter declined.

On the labor front, unemployment in 1948 averaged slightly less than in 1947, about 2.0 million or 3.4 per cent of the labor force compared with 2.1 million or 3.6 per cent of the labor force. At the same time the civilian labor force expanded by over 1.3 million in 1948 compared with 1947. However, in the fourth quarter of 1948, layoffs began to appear in nondurable industries and in some consumer durable industries.

In retrospect, of course, the signals of a decline seem quite clear in the second half of 1948. But that is because we have the benefit of 1949 to verify the correctness of these signals. It was not so clear to those watching the scene then and responsible for recommending appropriate policy. We turn now to the principal portion of this paper, in the course of which we shall refer to additional data on economic developments where pertinent.

How Adequate Was the Response of Government?

The new charter of government responsibility contained in the Employment Act of 1946 set forth "that it is the continuing policy and responsibility of the Federal Government . . . to coordinate and utilize all its plans, functions and resources . . . to promote maximum employment, production and purchasing power." This was to be done "in a manner calculated to foster and promote free competitive enterprise and the general welfare."

The problem of carrying out this responsibility is aptly characterized by the following quotation from *The Testament of Beauty*, by Robert Bridges: [3a]

"Mortal Prudence, handmaid of divine Providence,
  hath inscrutable reckoning with Fate and Fortune:
  We sail a changeful sea through halcyon days and storm,
  and when the ship laboureth, our stedfast purpose
  trembles like as the compass in a binnacle.
  Our stability is but balance, and conduct lies
  in masterful administration of the unforeseen."

[3a] Oxford, 1929, p. 9.

To see how "masterful" was the "administration of the unforeseen" by government during the 1948–1949 recession the subsequent discussion will revolve around the following key questions: How effectively did government diagnose the change in the trend of the economy? How effectively did it appraise the seriousness of the change? How effectively did it prescribe for the malady? and How consistent were government actions in achieving the desired goals? In speaking of government I mean, under the first three questions, the Administration position as expressed principally in the President's Economic Reports and by the Council of Economic Advisers, and, under the fourth question, all the agencies of government including Congress.

To anticipate, the record of government was poor on recognizing the turning point, very good on appraising and prescribing for the malady, and fortunately quite inconsistent on actions to implement the desired policy.

The failure to pick the turning point was a blot on an otherwise good postwar record. The Council, for example, while warning about the dangers of inflation, had maintained a generally optimistic view on the ability of the economy to maintain full employment in the postwar period at a time when unfounded pessimism was quite rife. It had rendered a signal service by popularizing the notion of an expanding economy.

Before beginning the analysis of the factors responsible for the Council's failure to recognize the turning point, we shall summarize the major steps taken and proposed by government to deal with the postwar problem of inflation. This is necessary to recapture the climate of opinion of the period.

INFLATION CONTROL POLICY: 1946–1948

Following the collapse of price controls after mid-1946, there was a sharp upsurge in prices in the second half of the year. There was little government effort to deal with this problem then. Little action to cope with inflation seemed needed in the first half of 1947 although there was some government concern in the spring about price and wage developments.[4]

The picture changed dramatically in the second half of 1947 with the resurgence of inflation. The mounting public concern with this problem led the President to call a special session of Congress in November 1947 to deal with inflation and European aid. It will be recalled that at that time there was great fear of the inflationary

[4] E. G. Nourse, *Economics in the Public Service*, Harcourt, Brace, 1953, p. 177.

35

implications of a substantial foreign aid program. In preparation for the President's message, the Council was asked to submit suggestions on the control of inflation. These suggestions stressed a budget surplus and restraints upon credit expansion as "the policies which should now be adopted," but they also included extension of export controls and selective stand-by price and wage control.[5]

The Board of Governors of the Federal Reserve System also advocated a strong anti-inflationary program with a somewhat different emphasis. The Board was caught in what appeared to be a very difficult situation. Consumer credit controls had expired on November 1, 1947. The Board had begun to tighten up short-term rates in mid-1947 but in November it had entered the market to support the price of long-term government bonds. Consequently, it was extremely concerned with the inflationary implications of this problem. It recommended: (1) increased productivity; (2) suspension of wage demands; (3) the largest possible surplus to pay off government-held debt; (4) legislation granting the Board the authority necessary to restrict further expansion of bank credit including a device such as the special reserve plans; and (5) expansion of the Savings Bond campaign. Price controls were regarded merely as curbs and not as cures.[6]

The President in his message to Congress set forth a ten-point program which largely embodied the recommendations of the Council. It included, in addition to the items mentioned above, requests for authority to impose rationing, to bring about the efficient use of grains in marketing livestock (this appeared then as an acute problem), to impose allocation and inventory controls, to control the commodity exchanges and some others.

Congress, then controlled by the Republicans, granted the President only three of his ten points, the less important ones: an extension of export controls, extension of allocation authority over transportation facilities and equipment, and expansion of the agricultural conservation program. It also granted him authority to make voluntary allocation agreements and for the voluntary regulation of commodity exchanges. These agreements when approved by the Attorney General would be exempt from antitrust laws. In addition, the Board of Governors of the Federal Reserve System issued a statement asking bankers to "exercise extreme caution in their lending policies." Thus the President's basic anti-inflationary program was not passed.

---

[5] *Ibid.*, p. 211.

[6] Statement by Chairman Eccles before the Joint Committee on the Economic Report, November 25, 1947.

I have recited this program in some detail because it was, with some modifications, the same program the President presented to Congress up to and including January 1949.

The President repeated his request for his anti-inflationary program in January 1948. The Economic Report emphasized strongly that Public Enemy Number One was inflation. It stated, "The first objective for 1948 must be to halt the inflationary trend." This report was published on the eve of the great break in agricultural prices. Congress ignored the President's request in the first half of 1948 but did take certain actions that seemed to increase the inflationary dangers: it reduced taxes by $5 billion; it passed the Marshall Plan; and it provided for a step-up in defense spending. The cut in taxes weakened what had been the major weapon against inflation in 1947 and 1948, the accumulation of a substantial cash surplus.

By midyear an upward movement in prices and the development of a third round of wage increases were under way. The President, in what has been regarded as one of his shrewdest political moves, called a special session of Congress in July to deal once again with his anti-inflationary program. This time he was more successful. Temporary authority was granted for the reimposition of consumer credit controls and to increase reserve requirements. Consumer credit controls were reimposed on September 20, 1948. The Board had in February and June of 1948 raised reserve requirements at New York and Chicago. With the new authority all reserve requirements were raised 2 percentage points on demand deposits, and 1½ points on time deposits, about half of what was permitted by law.

Thus, just when the boom in the economy was tapering off and the trend changing, new anti-inflationary controls were imposed. It was a case of locking the barn after the horse was stolen. It should not be thought that the Board accepted its new responsibilities with dismay. It had been keenly concerned about its yardstick of inflationary pressure, the large rise in bank credit in the postwar period. It had not lost its concern by the summer of 1948. An article in the August 1948 *Federal Reserve Bulletin* declared: "In view of the current tight situation in supplies of labor and materials, further expansion of installment credit can neither increase output nor put more people to work. It can only add more purchasing power to the already swollen spending stream and reinforce inflationary pressures. International developments, moreover, inevitably cause added pressures in the market for consumers' durable goods." [7] This

[7] Page 903 of that issue.

certainly indicates that in August 1948 the Board regarded the economy as being stretched as tight as a drum and extremely sensitive to any additional purchasing power.

The final attempt of the President to have his anti-inflationary program passed was in his State of the Union Message of January 1949. The portion asking for his anti-inflation program was much more moderate than in the past as to the dangers of inflation. He dropped his request for rationing but added a request to deal with inadequate capacity in basic industries such as steel. He also asked for $4 billion in additional taxes, mainly corporate, to provide a substantial surplus to offset inflationary pressures. Shortly after this message went to Congress, the country became much more concerned with deflation than with inflation.

THE FAILURE TO DIAGNOSE THE CHANGE IN THE ECONOMY

The most interesting and paradoxical phase of the record is the first one: that dealing with the faulty diagnosis of the situation. This is all the more paradoxical because of the repeated warnings by the Administration that the end result of inflation could well be a downturn. Yet signs of weakening were discounted throughout 1948 even as the signs of a turn became more numerous, particularly in the second half of the year; warnings against the dangers of inflation continued into the first half of 1949.[8] Perhaps even more incredible at first sight to some—an additional anti-inflationary program was instituted just as the postwar round of inflation was uttering its last gasps in the fall of 1948. Yet it was not until the spring of 1949 that the anti-inflationary program began to be eliminated. This was obviously an intriguing but not a unique episode.

What makes it more intriguing is that a rereading of the Economic Reports for January 1948, July 1948, and January 1949 makes clear that the lessening impact of inflationary pressures through the year was clearly recognized. In January 1949 the divergent trend in price movements was duly noted as was some weakening in consumer demand and some softening in investment. This was in sharp contrast to the July 1948 Report. However, government was

---

[8] Mr. Nourse reports that in the April 1949 Quarterly Report to the President, the Council considered that another spurt of inflation was one of three possibilities, although the least likely. Another possibility was a serious downturn, but the most likely was the "process of price readjustment in a manner to facilitate the clearing of markets with only moderate temporary departure from maximum levels of employment and production." Nourse, *op. cit.*, pp. 237–238. This was a very good forecast but it is interesting to note that there was still some concern with the problem of inflation.

seen as further contributing to expansion of demand. Inflationary pressures were seen as active in only a few sectors. It was quite a *non sequitur* to infer from that the need for a rather drastic anti-inflationary program. Yet there seems to have been no dissent in the basic diagnosis of the continuing danger of inflation.[9]

There were differences in the second half of 1948 as to degree or as to control methods but not as to the nature of the disease. The misjudgment developed out of a series of factors that put the error in a more reasonable light. The fact that, almost a year after the beginning of the current downturn, there is still no consensus as to whether we are witnessing the same kind of downturn as the 1948–1949 recession or something more serious should incline us to be charitable toward the earlier experience. It merely confirms the validity of the Hegelian dictum, "Was wirklich ist, ist vernuenftig." This may be freely translated as "That which happens has a rational explanation." The cynic may retort that Freud taught us that the irrational, which also happens, has a rational explanation. But the error may be adequately explained by simpler, more obvious reasons than the dark subtleties of Freud and therefore is preferred by Occam's razor.

Through mid-1948 few would have said that the diagnosis of inflation was incorrect and that strong measures were not needed. I have already quoted a Federal Reserve statement made in August 1948. The business analyses of the period that I have read in the main took the same position. But increasingly after mid-1948 there were signs of a tapering off in the economy. Increasingly, skepticism grew with respect to inflationary pressures, particularly in the fourth quarter. I wrote a memorandum on September 21, 1948, to the Council with the title "No More Inflation in 1948." In dealing with the outlook for the next six to nine months, I wrote: "Since the end of price control in 1946, there have been three successive major waves of price increases, each subsequent wave diminishing in intensity . . . the outlook for the next six to nine months is for no further significant advance in over-all wholesale prices but rather for some slight downward trend. Subject to the qualification that no one at this point can predict the trend of armament expenditures or the crops of 1949, one can go further and state that the postwar inflation is over." Others, including some members of the Council staff, shared my view. It was based on three factors: the easing of supply in major markets; the divergence in trend between farm

[9] See Mr. Nourse's discussion of his role as chairman of the Cabinet committee for an anti-inflation program in November 1948. Nourse, *op. cit.*, p. 228 *et seq.*

prices and industrial prices on the one hand and between non-durables and durables on the other; and the obviously smaller degree of price rise in 1948 than in earlier years, although there were some exceptions. However, it is important to note the qualifications I added to my forecast.

But the enunciation of this view did not necessarily make it correct. It depended on a particular evaluation of the outlook, which happened to be correct although that could not have been known at the time. Moreover, certain important prices, particularly for metals and associated products, continued to advance through most of the fourth quarter.

There are, it seems to me, three major reasons that account for the failure to recognize the change in the economic climate: historical, international and budgetary, and political. These reasons would not all be considered applicable by all the major policy makers, nor am I sure to what extent they would accept any of them.

The influence of history lay in the continued frustration of the millennial expectation of an immediate severe downward readjustment. I have referred to this earlier. The sharp rise in prices in the second half of 1946 led in many quarters to the expectation of a downturn in 1947. (This was not, however, the position of the Council, which was optimistic although it recognized the unfavorable factors in the situation.) There was some hesitation in the pace of economic activity in the first half of 1947. But then there followed a new wave of inflation in the second half of the year. (Significantly enough, although its importance was not then fully appreciated, the intensity of this wave was considerably less than in the second half of 1946.) In February 1948 the break in farm prices took place. Surely, if the downturn were to come, this was the signal. (It was, but the reaction was delayed.)

On the contrary, after some delay a new and, as it subsequently developed, moderate price rise took place, sparked by a rise in steel prices. There were many efforts by business to keep prices down but these efforts increasingly failed, particularly as the third postwar round of wage increases got under way. By midyear the whole process seemed to be in full swing. These developments led to wrong interpretations. The repeated postponements of the expected decline created a false sense of security. Yet this danger too was recognized. The President's Economic Report of July 1948 warned: "I must emphasize that the course of inflation does not run according to any set schedule. Until the very eve of an economic collapse many people are apt to grow more and more confident about the soundness of the economy and the indefinite continuance of the boom." These were prophetic words indeed! But the same document saw the current danger to be still the strength of the inflationary pressures.

The second factor lay in the international and the budgetary realm. This was most significant for the situation at mid-1948. It will be recalled that 1948 was a year of great international tension. There was the setting up of a Greek Communist government. There was the Communist coup in Czechoslovakia. There was the problem of the outcome of the Italian election. There was the great conflict over Germany leading to the blockade of Berlin and the airlift, which began at the end of June. The great uneasiness of the period brought pressure for an expanded defense program, particularly for a much larger air force. How would these events affect government spending?

In addition to these potential influences on government policy a number of important actions were taken in the first half of 1948 that affected the budgetary picture for fiscal 1949. These were, as pointed out earlier: some step-up in defense spending; the adoption of the Marshall Plan; and, most important in its immediate impact, the $5 billion tax reduction made by the Republican Congress, overriding the veto of President Truman.

Thus federal government expenditures were to rise in the coming fiscal year at the same time that government receipts due to tax reductions were to decline. The net effect of these budgetary changes, as it was then estimated, brought about a decline in the federal cash surplus from $12.6 billion, annual rate, in the first half of calendar 1948, to $3.9 billion in the second half, a decline of $8.7 billion.

It should be remembered that in 1947 and the first half of 1948 the major defense against inflation had been substantial federal cash surpluses. Now this defense was being seriously breached. Even had it not been thought that the basic situation was still inflationary, a shift of this magnitude by itself would strike most people as creating substantial inflationary pressures.[10]

[10] Parenthetically, I might remark that the experience of the economy then in the face of the tax reduction and recently in the face of another tax reduction suggests that for effective countercyclical action against even minor changes in the trend, we must think in terms of net budgetary changes in excess of $10 billion. This, I suspect, applies when the action is taken by government at about the time private market forces are turning from expansion to contraction. If, however, government is able effectively to forecast the turning point well in advance and

Certain other factors connected with the fiscal 1949 budget were matters of concern at mid-1948. Although the expansion in the defense program would not have too much impact in fiscal 1949, it did provide for a rising trend over the next three years. This was important, because, as pointed out earlier, 1948 was generally regarded as a year when, with the economy at full capacity, expansion in real output must therefore be limited to a few per cent each year. Given the notion that the basic situation was still inflationary, any expansion in demand from the side of government would increase the degree of excess demand and therefore accentuate the inflationary situation.

Moreover, the new government measures would have disproportionate effect upon that sector of the economy which seemed most clearly to be working at capacity, viz. the metals sector. There was to be a step-up in the stockpiling program, and the direct defense and foreign aid programs would also put pressure on the supply of lead, copper, zinc, steel, and aluminum. There would be collateral effects on electric power and the general availability of consumer supplies. In mid-1948 it was estimated that the supply of steel outside certain essential categories would be less in fiscal 1949 than in fiscal 1948. Given the strategic importance of steel in the economy, a new spiral could, it was thought, easily develop. Witness the situation in early 1946 and that in early 1948. Some of the predicted consequences did take place in the second half of 1948, e.g. the rise in the prices of metals and associated products, but these events did not have a cumulative impact on the economy.

The consequences of a rise in government spending and the mounting pressure for an expansion in the defense program following the Berlin airlift led the then Chairman of the Council to advocate, in a widely discussed talk delivered at the Pentagon in November 1948, a $15 billion ceiling on defense spending compared with the then $11 billion of spending. The alternative, he warned, was an imposition of wartime controls to suppress the inevitably large inflationary pressures.

But however valid the position at midyear may have been, why was it maintained in January 1949 when, as mentioned earlier, the

takes action at the time of the forecast, smaller changes should suffice. But such a policy suffers from an obvious defect: it implies that government should appear to be following an inflationary policy at a time when the economy appears to be suffering too much from inflation. On the other hand, it would probably not be politically acceptable to advocate at least a $10 billion decline in the surplus (or increase in the deficit) at a time when the economy is turning down though the extent of the decline is still uncertain.

Council analysis clearly showed that weakening signs in the private economy were numerous? One plus factor was the estimated shift in the federal government's cash account from a surplus of $4 billion, annual rate, in the second half of 1948 to a slight deficit in calendar 1949. But this was not such a large factor in the face of the declining trend in other factors. There were, however, large uncertainties still about the international situation.

This leads to the third major factor that played a role: the political one. I do not mean that the Council played politics. It should be emphasized, however obvious it is, that poor forecasts leading to inappropriate policies are the poorest kind of politics. In politics, particularly, Oscar Wilde's dictum is most appropriate: "Nothing succeeds like success." The political factor is something more subtle and more fundamental. It raises one of the most difficult problems that confronts government. Its essence resides in the question, How quickly can government, having taken a position publicly, admit that circumstances have changed? As one member at that time of the Council put it to me, Can government change its position every time there is some minor change in the economy? Such minor changes are always occurring. Can government policy be shifted about month by month? Given the great uncertainties that exist, government must wait until it is clear that the situation has really changed. There is also an important technical consideration. To implement a policy takes a considerable period. There are three stages: formulation of a policy by the Administration, its acceptance by Congress, and its implementation by the Administration. There is thus always the danger that a conflict will arise between short-run changes and longer-run policy. But this underscores the need for better and better forecasts. Unfortunately, if policies are to be accepted, the current situation must plainly require them, but by that time the underlying factors may already be changing. This is an unresolved dilemma of democratic society.

One other aspect of this period should be covered: the inappropriateness of the proposed anti-inflation program, particularly the direct controls feature. The postwar inflationary problem, as I see it, was not to prevent a price rise but to prevent the development of a serious inflationary spiral. A postwar price rise was inevitable for a number of reasons: (1) By keeping prices down more successfully than incomes, the wartime system of controls had created a relationship between incomes and prices that was not viable for a full employment peacetime economy. (2) The deferred demands and accumulated purchasing power would inevitably impose upward pressure on prices. (3) The return to a normal workweek, the loss of overtime, and the chafing of the trade unions under wage controls meant pressure for higher wage rates. (4) Finally, overseas demand was abnormally great.

In my opinion, and with the advantage of hindsight, the only major way to mitigate the postwar price rise while keeping the economy fully employed would have been to continue price control through mid-1947. Another year of expansion in production would have brought the supply-demand relationships to the point where the subsequent price rise, while substantial, would not have been as great as that which actually took place. I mean, of course, a liberalized and looser type of price control than in wartime. This would have permitted moderate price and wage increases. If you will, I am suggesting a policy of controlled inflation as the appropriate anti-inflation control for the postwar period.

Once, however, price controls were dismantled, the only real alternative was a vigorous budgetary policy of accumulating cash surpluses. This was in fact the basic policy that was pursued, but it was largely accidental, thanks to the effects of inflation, and least significant in 1946 and 1947 when it was needed most. The surplus was largest when the need for it was declining, i.e. in 1948.

But consider the course of postwar inflation: before 1949 there were two short but vigorous spurts of inflation. By the time government could be prepared to deal with them, they were over. Any attempt to reconstitute a price control system was a will-o'-the-wisp policy because it could not be rebuilt on a short-time basis, and by the time the system could be reconstituted, the need for it was over. A price control system can only be justified, it seems to me, for war or near-war conditions where the period of the emergency is long enough and the nature of the emergency is serious enough to warrant such controls.

But even the policy of accumulating a budget surplus has dangers of its own. There is the danger, graphically illustrated by the previous discussion, of inflexibility in changing the course of action. It was very fortunate that Congress voted a $5 billion reduction when it did. It did not stave off the downturn but it helped to mitigate it. Its effects were offset to some extent by the credit controls imposed in the fourth quarter. The melancholy conclusion must be that we are still a long way from having developed the flexibility in our policies to meet adequately the short-run problems of inflation. We can deal with longer-run problems of inflation, but other difficulties arise.

There is, however, at least one optimistic conclusion which some have drawn from our postwar inflationary experience. This is the thesis that the degree of inflation has been remarkably moderate considering the strains that have been put upon the economy. Without the impact of war, our economy when operating with full employment would show remarkably little propensity to inflation. I have a great deal of sympathy with this thesis but its test is yet to come.

THE SALIENT FEATURES OF THE DECLINE

The year 1949 was one of recession, although as pointed out earlier, the major impact on gross national product came in the first quarter while the second half of the year was primarily a leveling-off period. Let us now examine, still briefly, but in more detailed fashion, the salient features of that decline.

The percentage declines from respective peaks to respective bottoms for selected series were: GNP, 4; consumption, less than 1; consumers' durables, 5; nondurables, 3; gross private domestic investment, 32; producers' durables, 12; new construction, 8; total business sales, under 10; manufacturers' sales, 13; retailers' sales, 4; manufacturers' new orders, 18; total business inventories (book value), 7; manufacturers' inventories, 11; retailers' inventories, less than 4; industrial production, 10.5; manufacturing, 9; durable manufacturing, 13; nondurable manufacturing, 6. On the income side the percentage declines were: national income, 7; private wages and salaries, 5; personal income, 4; disposable income, under 4; personal savings, 71; corporate profits before taxes, 29. In prices the percentage declines were: all wholesale prices, 8; farm products, 22; processed foods, 14; industrial prices, 5; consumers' prices, 4; retail food prices, 10. (See Table 2 for additional details.)

Unemployment averaged slightly over 2 million in 1948 or 3.4 per cent of the civilian labor force, 3.2 million in the first half of 1949 or 5.2 per cent, 3.6 million in the second half of 1949 or 5.7 per cent, and 3.9 million in the first half of 1950 or 6.2 per cent. In February 1950 it reached 4.7 million or 7.6 per cent of the civilian labor force. Non-agricultural employment declined about 3.1 million or about 6 per cent between August 1948 and May 1949. The decline in manufacturing employment was 1.8 million or 11 per cent between September 1948 and July 1949. (These figures are not seasonally adjusted.)

Since this was an inventory recession, let us look more closely at what happened in that area. The bulk of the change in inventories

TABLE 2

Peaks and Lows of Selected Economic Indicators in the 1948–1949 Recession

Indicator	Peak Level	Low Point	Per Cent Decline	Peak Period	Low Period
Gross national product (billions quarterly)	$267.0	$256.8	3.8%	4Q '48	4Q '49
Consumption	179.8	178.7	.6	4Q '48	1Q '49
Durable goods	23.5	22.4	4.7	3Q '48	1Q '49
Nondurable goods	101.4	98.1	3.3	3Q '48	2Q '49
Gross private domestic investment	45.7	31.0	32.2	4Q '48	4Q '49
New construction	18.2	16.8	7.7	3Q '48	2Q '49
Producers' durable goods	20.7	18.2	12.1	4Q '48	4Q '49
Change in business inventories—total	7.2	−5.4	—	4Q '48	4Q '49
Nonfarm only	5.6	−4.2	—	4Q '48	4Q '49
Government purchases of goods and services	44.5	40.3	9.4	2Q '49	2Q '50
Federal	26.6	20.4	22.3	2Q '49	3Q '50
National income (billions)	229.7	212.7	7.4	4Q '48	4Q '49
Wages and salaries	138.1	132.8	3.8	4Q '48	3Q '49
Private	118.3	112.0	5.3	4Q '48	4Q '49
Farm income	18.8	11.8	35.2	2Q '48	4Q '49
Corporate profits before tax	34.8	24.7	29.0	3Q '48	2Q '49
Corporate profits after tax	21.3	14.8	30.5	3Q '48	2Q '49
Disposable income	193.0	186.1	3.6	3Q '48	3Q '49
Personal saving	13.3	3.9	70.7	3Q '48	4Q '49
Total business sales (billions monthly)	37.1	33.5	9.7	Aug. '48	Dec. '49
Manufacturers' sales	18.0	15.6	13.3	Sept. '48	Dec. '49
Durable	8.1	6.3	22.2	Dec. '48	Oct. '49
Retailers' sales	11.1	10.7	3.6	Dec. '48	Jan. '49
Durable	3.7	3.3	10.8	Dec. '48	Jan. '49
Total business inventories (book value, billions monthly)	55.8	52.1	6.6	Feb. '49	Dec. '49
Manufacturers'	32.1	28.7	10.6	Feb. '49	Nov. '49
Durable	16.2	13.9	14.2	Feb. '49	Nov. '49
Retailers'	15.8	15.3	3.2	Dec. '48	June '49
Durable	6.8	6.4	5.9	Feb. '49	Dec. '49
Manufacturers' new orders (billions monthly)	18.4	15.0	18.5	June '48	July '49
Durable goods industries	8.2	5.9	28.0	June '48	July '49
Manufacturers' unfilled orders (billions)	29.8	20.0	32.9	Aug. '48	Aug. '49
Durable goods industries	26.2	17.6	32.8	Aug. '48	Sept. '49

(continued on next page)

TABLE 2 (continued)

Peaks and Lows of Selected Economic Indicators in the 1948–1949 Recession

Indicator	Peak Level	Low Point	Per Cent Decline	Peak Period	Low Period
Index of industrial production					
(1947–1949 = 100)	$105.0	$94.0	10.5%	Oct. '48	July '49
Manufacturers	104.0	95.0	8.7	June '48	May '49
Durables	107.0	93.0	13.1	Oct. '48	May '49
Nondurables	103.0	97.0	5.8	Nov. '47	Apr. '49
Index of wholesale prices					
(1947–1949 = 100)	106.2	97.7	8.0	Aug. '48	Dec. '49
Farm products	113.4	88.8	21.7	Jan. '48	Jan. '50
Processed foods	109.4	94.0	14.1	Aug. '48	Jan. '50
Industrial	105.5	99.8	5.4	Nov. '48	July '49
Index of consumers' prices					
(1947–1949 = 100)	104.8	100.4	4.2	Aug. '48	Feb. '50
Food	107.3	96.5	10.1	July '48	Feb. '50
Index of spot market prices					
(1947–1949 = 100)	113.5	77.6	31.6	June '48	June '49

Note: Price indexes and unfilled orders are not seasonally adjusted. Where the series reached a peak or low more than once, the first period was selected.

was in the manufacturing field both in terms of book values and even more so after allowing for the inventory valuation adjustment. In fact, after allowance for the IVA, there was virtually no change in retailers' real inventories between 1948 and 1949, and an actual increase for wholesaling.

In manfacturing, two-thirds of the decline was accounted for by the durable goods segment. The largest drops took place in the fabricating industries, particularly machinery and motor vehicles and equipment. In nondurables, textiles and chemicals showed important drops. By stage of fabrication, the greatest relative drops were in purchased materials and goods in process. Finished goods inventories evidenced little drop. It is, however, interesting to point out that in 1947 and 1948 the greatest relative gains were in finished goods inventories (see Table 3).

To a large extent, the relative stability of finished goods inventories during the recession is accounted for by the fact that as supply becomes easy the customer shifts the burden of carrying the inventory to the supplier. The latter, to be able to ship promptly, therefore accumulates inventories. In the battle for sales, the order will go to the supplier who can, other things being equal, deliver the most promptly. To some extent also, the relative stability of fin-

47

ished goods inventories is accounted for by the unwillingness of the producer to dump goods on the market and by his inability to cut production fast enough to offset the decline in sales.

TABLE 3

Declines in Book Value of Manufacturers' Inventories, February 1949– November 1949

(*dollars in billions*)

Category	Dec. 1948 Level	Dec. 1949 Level	Dollar Decline	Per Cent Decline
All manufacturing	$32.1	$28.7	$3.4	10.6%
Durable goods industries	16.2	13.9	2.3	14.2
Fabricated metals	1.8	1.5	.3	16.7
Electrical machinery	1.9	1.5	.4	21.1
Machinery (except electrical)	3.6	3.2	.4	11.1
Motor vehicles and equipment	2.1	1.6	.5	23.8
Other durables	6.8	6.1	.7	10.3
Nondurable goods industries	15.8	14.9	.9	5.7
Food	2.7	2.6	.1	3.7
Textile mill products	2.2	2.0	.2	9.1
Paper and allied products	.8	.7	.1	12.5
Chemicals and allied products	2.2	2.0	.2	9.1
Petroleum and coal products	2.4	2.2	.2	8.3
Other nondurables	5.5	5.4	.1	1.8
State of Manufacturing				
All industries				
Purchased materials	$13.0	$11.1	$1.9	14.6%
Goods in process	7.7	6.7	1.0	13.0
Finished goods	11.6	10.8	.8	6.9
Durable goods industries				
Purchased materials	5.9	4.6	1.3	22.0
Goods in process	5.4	4.6	.8	14.8
Finished goods	5.0	4.4	.6	12.0
Nondurable goods industries				
Purchased materials	7.2	6.5	.7	9.7
Goods in process	2.2	2.1	.1	4.5
Finished goods	6.6	6.3	.3	4.5

Note: Stage of manufacturing series not adjusted for seasonal variation.

The chronology of 1949 goes as follows: Retail sales reached their low point in January and for the rest of the year fluctuated within a narrow range. Total consumption and consumers' durables reached their low points in the first quarter and thereafter rose. In the second quarter, housing starts began to shoot up very markedly although the low point for construction was in the second quarter.

Construction then moved only slightly in the third quarter and thereafter rose vigorously. The second quarter also saw the low point of corporate profits before taxes, but the recovery in the second half was only moderate. In April, nondurable manufacturing reached its low; it bumped along at that level until September, when it rose moderately. In May, total manufacturing and durables reached their lows, but they did not rise until September. The steel strike interfered with the upward movement in the fall but undoubtedly boosted the vigor of the recovery in the first half of 1950. In June, retail inventories reached their low point; thereafter they rose, especially the durables.

The third quarter witnessed further turnarounds. New orders bottomed in July, thereafter turning up again. Unfilled orders reached their low in August and rose gradually for the rest of the year. Industrial prices reached a low in July and were virtually unchanged for the rest of the year. They rose moderately in the first half of 1950. Personal income bottomed in the third quarter and rose slightly in the fourth.

The fourth quarter saw the low points for GNP, gross private domestic investment, total business and manufacturing inventories, total business and manufacturing sales, national income, private wages and salaries, personal savings, industrial production, and wholesale prices. Wholesale farm and processed food prices reached their low point in January 1950, all consumers' prices and retail food prices in February 1950.

Unemployment increased steadily from October 1948 to July 1949, declined thereafter until December although remaining well above 1948, rose sharply in the first quarter of 1950, and then declined substantially.

Government purchases of goods and services rose steadily throughout 1948 and the first half of 1949. They then declined steadily and moderately through the second quarter of 1950. Thus, while the private economy was declining, the government sector was rising, and when the private sector began to recover, the government sector began to decline.

Certain government actions in 1949 had an important bearing on economic developments. In March and April the Board of Governors of the Federal Reserve System eased consumer credit control, lengthening permissable lending periods and reducing the scope of this control. On June 30 Regulation W expired.

At the end of March, stock margin requirements were reduced from 75 to 50 per cent. At the end of April and again in August, reserve requirements were lowered, more than wiping out the previous increases. Certain actions were also taken in the housing field; these actions provided federal aid to localities for low income housing, increased the amount of mortgages that could be bought by the government from $1 billion to $1½ billion. This led to substantial purchases and aided the market for housing. In addition, during fiscal 1950 the government distributed about $2.6 billion in National Service Life Insurance dividends.

The process of decline was substantially over by midyear. The recovery was initiated by the consumer sector of the economy and by that part of investment connected with consumers, i.e. housing. The business sector of the economy, producers' durable and inventory accumulation, lagged behind. This raises the interesting question of what the recession would have looked like had there been no Regulation W to inhibit the use of installment credit and no increase in reserve requirements which probably tightened funds for residential housing.

THE RESPONSE OF GOVERNMENT TO THE RECESSION

Unlike its poor record in diagnosing the turning point in the economy, the record of government was very good during this phase of the recession. I have already quoted from the Council's April 1949 Quarterly Report to the President. In the mid-1949 Report by the Council, there was a generally optimistic note about the outlook and the capacity of the economy to work its way out of the recession. The factors of strength which bred this confidence were: the orderly character of the readjustment; the fact that consumption was outrunning production, which meant that production would have to rise to be in balance with recent sales; coupled with the last item, the sales success which attended aggressive merchandizing efforts; the strength displayed by housing starts; the relatively favorable level of investment; the ample character of bank credit and the contribution of government through its budget expenditures, unemployment compensation, and other built-in stabilizers.

But the future was not wholly assured. The downturn had not yet been reversed (as of June 1949), and there was always the danger that public confidence might become impaired, leading to a panicky downward spiral. On this the Council said: "The weight of evidence as we see it does not support so gloomy an outlook. But we may still face an unsatisfactory alternative. While the decline may be halted or even reversed, a satisfactory expansion

50

might not follow. Our real need is for industrial production not only to rebound to the level of present consumption but also for both production and consumption to continue to rise sufficiently to absorb a labor force which is both growing in size and increasing in productivity per man."

As aids to recovery, the Council laid great stress on proper price and wage adjustment, on the recognition by business of the need to maintain a high rate of investment, and on the maintenance of government spending without any attempt to raise taxes to balance the budget. The President presented a program which was in sharp contrast to his anti-inflationary program. It proposed measures to strengthen purchasing power by improving the unemployment compensation system, to improve social security, to encourage advance planning of public works, to increase the minimum wage, to improve farm supports, to improve the tax system without any major increase in taxes, and to promote foreign aid and trade.

The response of government to the recessionary phase was good. It saw the root cause in the liquidation of inventories; it saw from the behavior of markets that this was being done in an orderly fashion; and it concluded that there would not be a serious downturn. The downturn, it was believed, could be handled primarily by market forces; or, to put it differently, market forces should be given the major responsibility for the time being to work out the readjustments. These worked out about as anticipated.

Lessons of the Experience

It would be pleasant if we could prescribe a simple method for avoiding the difficulties of the kind of period I have been describing. But that experience can easily happen again. It is true that better forecasting will be helpful, if we are able to devise such improvements. But that happy day is still a long way off. The era of scientific forecasting is still ahead of us. Until then our knowledge will have to be supplemented by the judgments, intuitions, and general good sense of those charged with making basic decisions.

The problem lies deeper than the improvement of scientific method. It is nothing less than the problem of historical development. Let me put it this way: Has our postwar economy taken on a significantly new character that renders it less susceptible to the likelihood of severe fluctuations? While my feeling is that it has, I would be hard put to justifying it, for the definitive answer to such a question always lies ahead. Even if we could answer definitively that the economy, *qua* economy, is hardier and more shock-resistant than in the past, the fact is that we are living in a world where international developments have had and will continue to have major repercussions on the economy. How can these contingencies be provided for?

The review of the 1948–1949 episode makes clear certain basic difficulties. In the first place, there is the inflexibility which tends to be built into a position publicly taken by government. As I have said earlier, it is a fundamental question as to how rapidly a government can change its position. Governments like to appear in firm command of the situation, and nothing would weaken that appearance more than frequent changes in position. It is no answer to say that government should not take a position—it must do so. The whole machinery of government grinds too slowly for changes to be made quickly. Even in emergencies where basic changes in policy can be taken quickly, the implementation is frequently agonizingly slow.

Another basic difficulty lies in the confusion of short-run with long-run problems. I think it is fair to say that, on the whole, we have not really been able to develop any satisfactory short-run policies other than our built-in stabilizers. The advocates of monetary policy may disagree on this point, but I am not personally convinced. The non-automatic types of policies we can formulate are basically longer-run in their implications. The postwar spurts of inflation have been extremely short-run in character. The result has been that by the time a program can be put into effect, a new situation has emerged. But this problem is really a facet of the problem I earlier posed: What is the long-run character of our new economy?

The public and Congress are generally aroused by short-run situations. The government, under pressure, can only propose to kill flies with heavy artillery. This is an exaggeration, of course, but the essence is correct.

The answer must lie in the continual improvement of basic long-range policies on the part of government, business, labor, and the public generally. The better those policies are—and they have been improved—the less significant may become the short-range fluctuations.

The above discussion has concentrated on the problems of inflation. The experience of 1948–1949 does not provide much of a clue to the capacity of the economy and government to handle the more serious problems of recession. It does indicate, however, that once the problem was recognized, government proved to be quite flexible in readjusting its policies. The policies proved to be adequate mainly because of the inherent strength of the economy. But that raises another question: Had the downturn proved more serious than it actually was, would the response of government have been adequate? It is to be hoped that it would have been, but the 1948–1949 recession throws little light on that question.

COMMENT

MARTIN BRONFENBRENNER, University of Wisconsin

Caplan accepts the majority opinion among American economists that 1948–1949 was entirely an inventory depression or "Kitchin" cycle, and a mild one at that. Minority opinion in this country, expressed for example by Daniel Hamberg,[1] ascribes the recession largely to underconsumption. But this, I believe, is the majority view in Britain and elsewhere in Europe, and I wish Caplan had said a little more about it.

My personal analysis is a compromise one, which seems to fit the current (1953–1954) recession as well as the 1948–1949 recession, which is under discussion. I believe with the underconsumptionists that we should go beyond the record of accumulation and decumulation of business inventories to its cause, and that in general we can find the cause in the changing rate of growth in aggregate personal consumption. But I believe with the orthodox that the recession cannot be traced yet further back, to any shortage in purchasing power. For, indeed, consumption seems to have recovered without the stimulus of massive additions of purchasing power, and apparently only because the temporary satiety of 1948–1949 wore itself off. Perhaps the recovery came about because consumers' own inventories of soft goods were exhausted. Would it be amiss to combine the two strands of thought (inventories and underconsumption) to suggest that perhaps in this case at least we may have a fluctuation explainable in terms of inventories, yes, but of consumer rather than business ones?

The figures which lead to this viewpoint are presented on the next page. They are from the 1954 National Income Supplement to the Department of Commerce *Survey of Current Business*. The

[1] Daniel Hamberg, "The Recession of 1948–49 in the United States," *Economic Journal*, March 1952, pp. 1–14, and "1948–49 Recession Re-examined: A Rejoinder" (to Bratt and Ondrechen), *ibid.*, March 1953, pp. 104–110.

quarterly figures are seasonally adjusted, and at annual rates in billions of current dollars. Note how the rate of change in consumption leads the inventory cycle downward and again upward by two or three quarters.[2]

Year and Quarter	GNP (gross of inventory accumulation)	Invest- ment	Con- sumption	Increase in Con- sumption	GNP (net of inventory accumulation)	Invest- ment	Inven- tory Accumu- lation
1948— I	247.9	38.6	174.1	3.4	244.9	35.6	3.0
— II	255.5	41.2	176.8	2.7	251.2	36.9	4.3
—III	261.9	42.5	179.5	2.7	257.5	38.1	4.4
—IV	264.0	42.4	180.1	.6	259.1	37.5	4.9
1949— I	259.9	37.0	178.4	−1.7	258.4	35.5	1.5
— II	257.2	32.1	180.4	2.0	260.3	35.2	−3.1
—III	256.5	32.0	180.1	−.3	259.5	35.0	−3.0
—IV	255.5	29.1	183.5	3.4	261.8	35.4	−6.3
1950— I	264.9	39.9	185.2	1.7	262.4	37.4	2.5
— II	275.9	49.0	189.1	3.9	268.6	41.7	7.3
—III	294.4	53.4	202.9	13.8	289.6	48.6	4.8
—IV	305.0	62.6	198.8	−4.1	290.3	47.9	14.7

In addition to consumption and its growth rate, I wish Caplan had given more attention to two other factors. One is international

[2] It is interesting to compare corresponding figures for the 1953–1954 recession. The pattern seems quite similar to that of 1948–1949.

Year and Quarter	GNP (gross of inventory accumulation)	Invest- ment	Con- sumption	Increase in Con- sumption	GNP (net of inventory accumulation)	Invest- ment	Inven- tory Accumu- lation
1952—IV	358.5	54.4	225.3	7.1	351.0	46.9	7.5
1953— I	361.8	51.9	228.6	3.3	359.0	49.1	2.8
— II	369.9	55.9	230.8	2.2	364.5	50.5	5.4
—III	367.2	52.4	231.2	.4	365.2	50.4	2.0
—IV	360.5	45.5	229.7	−1.5	364.7	49.7	−4.2
1954— I	355.8	44.5	230.5	.8	360.0	48.7	−4.2
— II	356.0	45.6	233.1	2.6	359.8	49.4	−3.8
—III	355.5	45.3	234.8	1.7	360.3	50.1	−4.8
—IV	362.0	49.5	237.7	2.9	363.3	50.8	−1.3

Among writers using change in consumption as an economic forecaster (and therefore implicitly as a causal factor in their cycle theories) I am impressed particularly by Stahrl Edmunds, "Plant Capacity: Too Much or Too Little?" *Harvard Business Review*, vol. 30 (July–August 1952), pp. 82–85. Edmunds' key variable is the short-term inter-temporal marginal propensity to consume, or (change consumption)/(change in income). He interprets changes in this variable from quarter to quarter as expressing changing "willingness to consume."

trade—in particular, the course of United States exports. The other is public fiscal policy. There was a $5.5 billion increase in 1949 expenditures over 1948, with a $9 billion decline in aggregate surpluses, which may have been instrumental in bringing about recovery. I share what I believe to be Caplan's doubts that these are the crucial pieces of the puzzle, but it seems necessary to dwell on them if one is to meet squarely the opinion of the man on the street, particularly on the left side of the street. The majority of the thinking public, certainly abroad and perhaps also at home, believes the 1948–1950 recession was caused by cuts in exports and military spending, and believes it was cured by the revival of exports and military spending. The public is largely unaware of the recovery that occurred in the first half of 1950, and believes implicitly that the recession would have become a major depression but for the Korean war. One cannot combat fallacies so widespread as these by ignoring them.

Caplan's discussion of the federal government as forecaster and adviser relies heavily on a few selected excerpts, not all published, mainly from the Council of Economic Advisers. These selected excerpts indicate that someone in the Council was right all the time. The staff (but not the three Council members) forecast the recession correctly. The Council members (but not the staff) called the turn on the recovery. What follows from this? With selected excerpts, one can prove almost anything, and sellers of forecasting services often do just that in reconstructing their past records. It would have been more interesting (at least to this reader) had Caplan compared the over-all forecasting record of the government (or of the Council) with the records of some of the private forecasting agencies, particularly those that were right when official Washington was wrong in 1946–1947.

It is less easy to agree with Caplan on the general conclusions he draws from the 1948–1949 episode than on his analysis of the episode itself. He is correct when he ascribes the mildness of the recession largely to fortuitous circumstances (like the Eightieth Congress tax cut and the pent-up demand for housing). He is also correct in his belief that recovery came about as rapidly as one could have hoped from monetary and fiscal policy (indirect controls). But his resulting skepticism regarding indirect controls in general, in both inflation and recession, needs somewhat more support to be acceptable.

Caplan uses $10 billion as the minimum year-to-year budgetry change that can be effective in the short period. If the figure really

55

is that large, fiscal policy against an economic recession is like the proverbial peashooter against a tank. But I wonder whether Caplan is not neglecting multiplier effects in setting so large a figure. Perhaps the target figure might be set as $10 billion, to be reached within approximately a year by the operation of the multiplier process. Furthermore, if sufficient powers are delegated to monetary and fiscal authorities, either fully discretionary or limited by statistical indexes, the authorities can act more quickly than Caplan implies, and likewise reverse themselves more quickly if they go too far. This is not to say that they always *will* act promptly and reverse themselves promptly—but merely that they *can* and *may*.

The 1946–1948 inflation came in three short spurts, as Caplan says, but could not the last two of these have been choked off in advance had the Board of Governors of the Federal Reserve System been granted wider controls over primary and secondary bank reserve ratios, and had the Board not been committed to support of the government security markets? As to the Korean war boom, the tight-money policies of 1953 came too late to check it when it should have been checked, and it is fashionable to make fun of these policies in the light of the subsequent recession.[3] But would Caplan go so far as to deny that these same measures might not have done some good if they had been introduced during the fall and winter of 1950–1951? (Incidentally, the rapidity of their reversal during 1953 belies Caplan's thesis that reversals always come too late.)

Caplan's iconoclastic strictures against depression controls are correct for those controls which require detailed Congressional legislation to implement them, or the recruiting of large staffs to administer and enforce them. Price control and rationing, for example, seem to fall under Caplan's ban, unless they are to become permanent features of our economy. But whether monetary and fiscal policy fall likewise under the ban depends not on their nature but on the power which Congress chooses to delegate to administrative agencies and on the agencies' ability to use it with wisdom and with consistency.

Caplan does not spell out his objections to the thesis of secular inflation, although it is perfectly clear that he objects to it. This thesis is that our pressure-group-dominated "New Political Economy" lets prices rise when times are good, and then keeps them from falling to anything like the same extent when times are bad. The 1948–1949 recession is often cited as a case in point, but Caplan

[3] See, for example, Bertram Gross and Wilfred Lumer, *The Hard Money Crusade*, Public Affairs Institute, 1954.

shows that the support of the price level during the recession was fortuitous rather than intentional. In this he is correct, and he has made a contribution to our understanding of the cycle. But unless I misunderstand him, he does not deny that support would have been forthcoming fairly early in 1950 had it been required to keep the price level up. Nor does he deny that the business, agricultural, and labor communities were counting on such support in some form (just as they seem to be counting on it again in 1954). These potential matters are fundamental to the secular inflation thesis, perhaps as much as the actual record of prices and price movements.

I may be another of the economic sheep whom Caplan decries, but despite his objections I remain convinced that the trend of the American price level will continue upward for good or ill, until the New Political Economy is supplemented either by the Old or by some Newer Political Economy which includes some forthright redistributionism of a quasi-Socialist variety to keep wage and farm price increases from passing through to the consumer level.

WESLEY LINDOW, Irving Trust Company

Caplan's use of statistics in analyzing the 1949 recession raises a number of questions.

Should public policies of the past be judged on the basis of revised statistics only or also on the basis of data actually available to public officials at the time? Revisions in both gross national product and industrial production tend to show smaller declines in 1949 than the original figures indicated.

Caplan does not use industry statistics which were available for analytical purposes at the time, and which have not been extensively revised. Public officials must have been reassured by the fact that steel production rose successively in January, February, and March 1949 to new all-time highs, and by the fact that automobile production continued to rise to record levels well into the summer of 1949.

On the other hand, a slowing up of the rate of growth in certain aggregate figures might have suggested to public officials the possibility of emerging economic weakness even in 1948. For example, business loans of reporting banks were running 25 per cent ahead of 1947 in the early part of 1948, but by the end of 1948 were running only a few percentage points above the corresponding months of 1947, and early in 1949 began to show actual declines in comparison with the figures of the year before. The trend here gave some early suggestion of changing inventory momentum. Similarly, employment figures also indicated some weakening momentum in 1948. The average workweek declined in the fore part of 1948 and then leveled out in the latter part of the year when it usually rises seasonally.

The statistics cited by Caplan on saving are incomplete and point to misleading conclusions. It is true that personal saving as a whole rose sharply in 1948 as compared with 1947, which led to Caplan's conclusion that consumers were saving more. A breakdown of the saving figures, however, indicates that the entire change was due to business (unincorporated and farm) saving, which is included in the personal saving aggregate. Nonbusiness saving was 3.3 per cent of disposable income in 1947 and 3.4 per cent in 1948, indicating virtual stability.

Even if perfect forecasting were possible, should government endeavor to forestall minor corrections like the 1949 downturn? The arguments in favor would presumably hinge on the basic point that preventative action might keep a small recession from cumulating into a big depression. The arguments against would be concerned with the need, first, to let natural market forces come into play to permit corrective actions to take place in the interest of stronger markets, and, second, to let downswings in prices counteract upswings in order to avoid a cumulative upward trend over a long period of time.

With regard to the potentialities of central banking I am much more hopeful than Caplan. Monetary action is no panacea, but I believe that it can play an important role in conjunction with such other activities as fiscal policy and debt management.

STRUCTURE AND STABILITY:
THE ECONOMICS OF THE NEXT ADJUSTMENT

K. E. BOULDING, UNIVERSITY OF MICHIGAN

I am going to begin with some elementary propositions, which may seem too familiar and obvious to be worth stating. Nevertheless, it is the obscurities at the heart of the obvious which cause the most trouble.

The first proposition, then, is that underemployment of resources, undercapacity use of an economic system, or, more plainly if less exactly, depression, is the result of an inability of the system to "absorb" or dispose of as much output as will be produced at "full" or optimum capacity. There are only two ways in which output can be absorbed. It can be consumed, in the literal sense of the word—that is, it can be destroyed and cease to exist—or it can be held willingly. "Willing holding" implies that at the existing structure and level of prices people can be found who are willing to hold the present stock of goods of all kinds. If, therefore, at capacity or optimum [1] output the institutions and the desires of the members of the system together do not suffice to absorb it all, there will be "unwilling accumulation."

Actual accumulation in a period is always equal to the total output of the period less its consumption, for whatever has been produced must either have been consumed or is still around somewhere. Put into the form

Accumulation = production — consumption

and expressed in value terms, this identity is seen as the famous savings-equals-investment identity of Keynes' *General Theory*. The value of accumulation is one important meaning of investment, the value of production is one important meaning of national income, and income minus consumption is an important meaning of saving.

---

[1] "Optimum" output is likely to be less than output at physical capacity because of the desire for leisure and nonmarket activities. The vagueness of this concept in no sense detracts from its importance.

Flexibility of the Price System

The critical question now is what happens when actual accumulation is greater than "desired" accumulation, that is, when there are "unwanted" stocks of goods. The answer depends largely on the flexibility of the price system. If the prices of these goods are flexible, the appearance of unwanted stocks (at the existing price level) will drive down the prices to the point where people willing to hold the goods can be found. If *all* prices are flexible, the appearance of unwanted stocks will cause a general deflation of the price level to the point where holders can be found. This in essence is the famous "Pigou effect." It assumes of course that the stock of money has a degree of inflexibility in it, so that a decline in the general price level will not reduce the money stock proportionally. As prices fall, therefore, the value of the money stock rises relative to the value of the stock of goods or real assets; hence the willingness of people to hold *physical* assets should increase. The prospect of a future rise in price will of course make people even more willing to hold goods. It is thus clear that the Pigou effect *can* operate merely by increasing the community's willingness to invest—that is, to hold stocks of goods that otherwise it would not wish to hold.

Deflation also may operate on the level of the consumption function. It may do this partly by a simple liquidity effect, in that the rise in value of household balances may induce households to consume more at given levels of real income. The most important effect, however, is likely to be through the redistribution of income. Deflation redistributes income toward the recipients of fixed money incomes—*rentiers,* pensioners, etc.—and away from profit makers. Insofar as the *rentiers* are low savers and the profit makers are high savers, the redistribution of income itself will raise the level of the consumption function. This assumes, of course, that the *marginal* propensity to consume is higher among those who gain by the deflation than among those who lose by it. If the reverse is the case— a situation which cannot be ruled out as impossible—this effect of deflation will be perverse and will lead toward a fall rather than a rise in the consumption function.

Price flexibility may also lead to dynamic instabilities of the system, familiar to most economists. The "Pigou effect" depends on low, not on falling, prices. A falling price level in itself tends to have a perverse effect. It discourages investment, for when prices are falling it is more profitable to hold assets in the form of cash and bonds, which are appreciating in value, than in the form of goods, which are declining. It is true that the losses of deflation are in part fictitious, because of an almost unavoidable defect of the accounting system which records a decline in the dollar value of assets as a loss in net worth, even though the purchasing power of these assets in terms of other things may not have changed. Even fictitious losses affect behavior, however, and the losses are not wholly fictitious in that the purchasing power of cash and bonds does increase more rapidly than that of real goods, so that those who hold cash and bonds do better than those who hold goods, conduct business, and give employment. A falling price level may even have an adverse effect on consumption, if people regard it as a sign to wait until prices have reached bottom. This merely reflects the impact on households of the fact that with a falling price level "idle money" bears a real rate of interest in terms of purchasing power.

In addition to these weighty theoretical objections to flexible prices as a cure for underemployment, there is of course the very practical objection that general price flexibility is not practicable in a highly organized economy, as least by any institutions which can easily be visualized. Under deflationary pressure those who can hold up the prices of what they sell, whether they are manufacturers, farmers, or laborers, do so, believing, not unreasonably, that even if the pie is smaller their share will be larger. One certainly cannot visualize in our society the destruction of the labor movement, the abolition of agricultural price support, and the ruthless antitrust activity or even the "counter speculation" (in Lerner's language) that would be necessary to make prices flexible in private markets. We can perhaps visualize a price control in reverse, beating down the price-wage structure by setting legal maximums well below existing levels. This may not be absurd, but it is certainly visionary, and of dubious value even if it could be achieved.

We must therefore reconcile ourselves to a substantial degree of price inflexibility, especially downward. If, however, prices cannot be lowered, the result of unwanted accumulations is an immediate cutback in output, and therefore in employment. In the case of a single firm, unwanted accumulations of inventory usually involve unwanted decumulations of liquid assets, for unsold goods and depleted money balances tend to go hand in hand. The usual response to this situation of firms selling in an imperfect market is to cut back output and lay off men, this being the only practicable way of restoring their liquidity and diminishing their inventory. The decline in output, employment, and income, however, diminishes consumption, leading to further unwanted accumulations, and the economy will slide back along the total absorption curve until the decline in output overtakes the decline in consumption and the decline in the willingness to accumulate, and temporary equilibrium is reached at levels of output low enough to eliminate involuntary accumulation. This melancholy situation can be eliminated only through spontaneous upward movements of the consumption and investment functions brought about, for instance, by a decline in stockpiles or the wearing out of fixed capital, or through a deliberate increase in absorption performed by or engineered by government.

Positions of Equilibrium

By the "precariousness" of an economy I mean the extent to which a given change in the position of the total absorption curve changes the position of equilibrium. Equilibrium in this connection implies having no unwanted accumulations. Precariousness as defined above is a matter of comparative statics—a comparison of two positions of equilibrium with different parameters for the determining functions. There may also be dynamic precariousness if the dynamics of the system are perverse, in the sense that a movement toward equilibrium itself will change the parameters of the determining equations in such a way as to move the equilibrium still farther away from the actual position of the system. Thus a dog is precarious in the sense that the appearance of a rabbit makes him want to be where the rabbit is. This is comparative statics. This system, however, is also dynamically precarious—the act of chasing the rabbit generally removes the rabbit still farther from the dog's old position of equilibrium.

A simple output system is statically precarious if the propensity to absorb is close to 1, that is, if a change in output produces an almost equal change in consumption plus willing accumulation. It is dynamically precarious if the adjustments forced upon the system by unwanted accumulations (or decumulations), whether in the form of price changes or output changes, themselves lower (or raise) the level of the total absorption function. These concepts are illustrated in Figure 1. OY measures output or real income, OA real absorption. N_1P_1 is a total absorption curve which intersects the 45° line OP_1 at a "high level" equilibrium with output at OM_1. If the absorption curve is close to the 45° slope, a relatively slight shift in its position, say to N_2P_2, causes a large shift of the

Figure 1

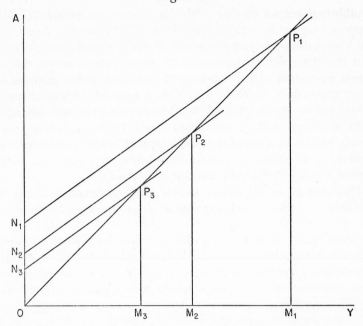

Figure 2

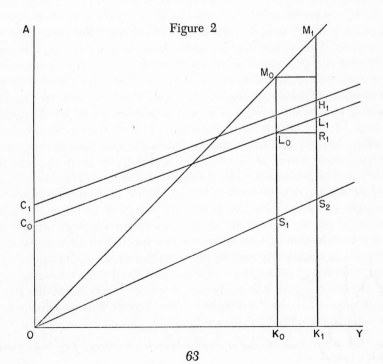

equilibrium output to OM_2. This is "static precariousness." Now suppose that the movement from M_1 to M_2, however contrived, itself lowers the absorption curve to N_3P_3 : output will go on declining past the static equilibrium point M_2 to M_3, or to where this dynamic movement peters out. Once the movement has stopped, the curve moves back to N_2P_2, say, and an upward movement pushes output up to M_2 and beyond till the movement peters out again, from which point the cycle repeats itself. Dynamic precariousness clearly results in a cyclical movement, which may be damped, explosive, or of stable amplitude depending on parameters of the system. It is most likely in practice to be damped.

This simple model shows clearly the difference between the problem of cycles, which are due to dynamic precariousness, and the problem of the "general equilibrium" of the economy in its static state. The static equilibrium may be one of stagnation below full capacity, with unemployment relieved only by dynamic movements above the equilibrium position, or it may be a "pressure economy" with constant inflationary pressure relieved only by downward dynamic movements.

I have dwelt at some length on this simplest of all models of a macroeconomic system, familiar as it is, because it illustrates so well the dilemmas of policy that face us at the present time. It is not always realized that the problem of moderating the amplitude of dynamic fluctuations may be quite different from the problem of shifting the position of static equilibrium of the system and may require quite different kinds of measures. If we are suffering from excessive dynamic instability, the remedies would seem to lie along two possible lines. The first would be to damp the cycle itself by identifying and correcting those factors in the system which lead to perverse dynamic reactions. The "100 per cent reserve" plan, aimed at preventing a shrinkage of bank deposits in deflation of prices, would be a remedy of this type. The second line of attack on dynamic instability would be to introduce into the system counterfluctuations which are designed to offset the perverse dynamic movements of the absorption function. Monetary policy, reduction of interest rates when investment lags, adjustable tax plans, commodity reserve plans, public works cycles—these are all examples of counterfluctuations. The difficulty of counterfluctuation policy is that it must be timed properly and be of the right intensity; otherwise, as Friedman has shown,[2] it may actually intensify the amplitude of the cycle.

[2] Milton Friedman, *Essays in Positive Economics*, Chicago University Press, 1953, pp. 117–132.

The Stagnation Thesis

If, however, the problem is not so much one of dynamic instability as of stagnation, or undercapacity equilibrium, measures with different ends in view are necessary, measures to be conceived not as countercyclical but as directed toward shifting the "level" of the cycle—i.e. the range within which the cyclical forces move the essential variables. This is not to say, of course, that measures which may be useful in combating dynamic instability may not also be useful in shifting the level of the cycle itself, but in principle the two problems must be kept distinct. The long war and postwar prosperity has made the secular stagnation doctrines seem very out of date. Nevertheless, it is possible that the long period of almost continuous full employment from 1941 to the present is a reflection of the size of the war economy rather than of any sufficient long-run forces in the civilian economy, and it is worth glancing at the stagnation thesis again in case there should be an outbreak of peace.

The stagnation thesis is simply that the level of investment (i.e. the willingness to accumulate) is inversely related in any given state of techniques to the amount previously accumulated, and that hence the process of accumulation itself destroys further opportunities for accumulation. Opportunities are, in a dynamic culture, constantly recreated by discoveries and inventions; but even this source of dynamism must eventually wear itself out, and the shadow of the stationary state falls across the march of events. The notion of a stationary state was, of course, familiar to Adam Smith and Ricardo; in their view, however, there would still be full employment in the stationary state because consumption would rise to fill the gap left by the decline in accumulation, and when the stationary state was reached consumption would be equal to production and there would be no further accumulation or saving. In the Malthus-Keynes-Hansen version, the consumption function fails to rise sufficiently to take care of the decline in investment, and the stationary state is reached only at the cost of unemployment and undercapacity output.

The stagnation thesis has been confused by the failure to distinguish clearly between the "real" and the monetary aspects of the models—an unfortunate characteristic of Keynesian theory. If the model is formulated clearly in "real" terms, it becomes apparent that the stagnationists have left out of account a very important variable in the consumption function: the stock of capital itself. If we think of consumption as the destruction of capital, it includes depreciation, and we can suppose that there is a certain "fixed consumption" which is independent of income but which depends on the size and on the durability of the stock of real capital. The larger the capital stock and the shorter its average period of production (if I may use an old-fashioned but useful concept) the larger will this "fixed consumption" item be. Thus the basic assumption on which, for instance, the gloom of the Harrodian system is founded—that consumption is a constant proportion of income—seems to me quite indefensible.

These principles are illustrated in Figure 2, where the axes have the same meaning as in Figure 1. We suppose C_0L_0 to be a consumption function at time t_0. OC_0 is the "fixed consumption," assumed to be dependent on the capital stock.[3] This is the amount of consumption even at zero income. Now let us suppose that the "ideal" or full employment output is OK_0. If this output is to be stable, an amount L_0M_0 must willingly be added to total capital. This addition to total capital, however, increases the capacity of the system, which in the next period is OK_1. The ratio L_0M_0/K_0K_1 is the accelerator coefficient required for continuous full employment, or Harrod's "capital requirement." If the consumption function does not change in the period t_1, the amount of investment required to give full employment is L_1M_1. If, however, as a result of the rise in the stock of capital the consumption function rises from C_0L_0 to C_1H_1, the amount of investment required for full employment in the period t_1 is only H_1M_1, not L_1M_1. The question of stagnation in the stationary state then depends on whether the rise in "fixed consumption" with increasing capital stock will be enough to compensate for the decline in willing accumulation (investment).

Let m ($= R_1L_1/L_0R_1$) be the marginal propensity to consume; c the "capital coefficient," L_0M_0/L_0R_1; and f the fixed consumption coefficient, L_1H_1/L_0R_1. Then

$$H_1M_1 = L_0M_0 + L_0R_1 - L_1H_1 - R_1L_1$$

whence

$$\frac{H_1M_1}{L_0M_0} = 1 + \frac{1}{c} - \frac{f}{c} - \frac{m}{c} = 1 + \frac{1-f-m}{c} = 1 + e$$

[3] It should be observed that the volume of "fixed consumption" depends on the stock of human capital as well as the stock of material capital. Thus in a society in which a high level of skill and education is maintained, a considerable portion of the output consists of the replacement of the depreciation of the human population through death and aging by child rearing and education. Here again the volume of fixed consumption depends on the period of production; if the average expectation of life is high, less will have to be expended in maintain-

where e is the "warranted rate of growth" of investment—i.e. the rate of growth necessary to maintain stable full employment. In the Harrod system, of course, $f = O$ and $1 - m = s$, the "average propensity to save," as Harrod assumes a consumption function like OS_1S_2. In Harrod's system, therefore, there is practically no chance for e to be zero or negative. In the extended model, however, it is quite possible for $f + m$ to be greater than 1, in which case a declining level of investment will still yield full employment. The value of f depends on the average length of life of additions to the stock of capital. If these additions are short-lived, f will be large. In view of the problem of the *structure* of the populations of goods we cannot assume a simple relation between the length of life and f, but in an equilibrium population the relationship would be $f = 1/L$, where L is the average length of life of additions to the stock of capital. Thus if the additions to the stock of capital have a life expectancy of five years, the addition to consumption in the form of depreciation, reflected eventually in maintenance expenditures, will be one-fifth of the total investment.[4]

The weakness of these aggregative models as a means of identifying the strategic factors in antidepression policy is their neglect of the more intricate structural problems of the economy. Capital and income, in real terms, are not homogeneous aggregates, but highly heterogeneous aggregates of large numbers of different commodities —vectors that cannot be reduced to a single linear dimension without doing serious violence to reality. This is important for policy questions because difficulties that arise as a result of strains in the structure and composition of the aggregates may not be suitably resolved by methods, such as tax or government expenditure changes, that operate on the economy as a whole, or at least on its various sectors more uniformly than the structural situation may require.

---

ing the population. The output involved in population *growth* should properly be regarded as investment, but a considerable proportion of this can also be regarded as independent of income.

[4] Recent studies indicate that there has been a sharp downward trend in the capital/output ratio in recent years. According to Daniel Creamer (*Capital and Output Trends in Manufacturing Industries, 1880–1948,* National Bureau of Economic Research, Occasional Paper 41, 1954) the ratio of capital to value added in manufacturing (in 1929 prices) fell from 2.555 in 1929 to 1.655 in 1948. A recent (unpublished) calculation by L. R. Klein indicates a similar decline for the whole economy from around 3.5 before 1929 to about 2.5 in 1950. If this can also be regarded as indicating a similar fall in the marginal capital-output ratio, there must have been a considerable increase in the consumption coefficient f, which will make the task of maintaining full employment with constant or even declining rates of investment much easier.

Possible Structural Difficulties

An example will clarify the point. I have recently made a projection (*Kyklos*, August 1955) of automobile population and production on various highly simplified assumptions for the next fifteen years. On almost any assumptions there seems to be trouble ahead for the automobile industry on a strictly structural basis, because we are now approaching the period when the non-existent cars of the war years would have been in those age groups with the highest "death rates." Because of this serious distortion in the age structure of automobiles it seems certain that if automobile production is to be maintained between now and 1960 at present levels, the total population of cars will have to rise much more rapidly than it has been rising. If the population merely continues to rise at present rates the annual production will fall from over 5 to a little over 4 million by 1958—a serious prospect not only for the automobile industry, but for the whole American economy. There may be similar structural difficulties ahead in other consumer durables, for similar reasons, but unfortunately we know nothing about the age composition of consumer capital beyond the happy accident of the information provided by automobile registrations. There may be similar structural difficulties ahead in residential housing, as a result of a decline in the number of new families because of the low birth rates of the thirties and the inevitable cessation of the decline in the age of marriage.

There is also a strong possibility of serious structural difficulties in agriculture, always the sick sector of a progressive economy. In part, overproduction in agriculture is a result of foolish policies in the past, but it is also a recurrent structural difficulty in a society like ours, simply because the amount of rural migration necessary to maintain a proper balance between agricultural and industrial output seems to require almost a condition of inflation and hyper-employment in industry. When industrial employment is "normal" the job opportunities in the cities are not plentiful or attractive enough to create the necessary rural exodus, and agricultural surpluses begin to pile up. Agricultural surpluses, however, especially in a free market, have a strongly depressive effect on the price level of agricultural commodities, and even on the price level in general. I am in the middle of a study of the relation of commodity stocks to prices which suggests—in spite of the limited information available —that there is a strong inverse relation between commodity stocks and the price level, as we should expect from market theory. Therefore, a disproportionality in the structure of industry involving an excessive amount of resources in the raw material industries and a deficiency in services and processing near the consumer end increases "unwanted" accumulations and thereby sets off a process either of deflation of prices or of contraction of output, or both. This structural difficulty may have nothing to do with any deficiency in money supply or even in aggregate demand; there may be "shortages" of services at the same time that there are surpluses of commodities. Nevertheless, it creates a strong deflationary force in the economy, which is almost certain to cause trouble. We have managed to avoid this particular difficulty in the war and postwar years largely by subsidized exports, first through lend-lease and later through the Marshall Plan. This policy is not well adapted, however, to a more "normal" world when the deficiencies in the domestic production of other countries have been remedied.

Information and Effector Channels

Getting a little closer now to the policy issues facing us, we must raise the difficult and largely unexplored problem of the nature of the economic *information* required to operate a successful antidepression policy. In their theoretical constructs economists have been curiously indifferent to the information concept and to learning processes. This perhaps is because of the long predominance of the perfect competition model, where the price system itself provides, in simple and accessible form, all the information necessary to describe economic behavior. As soon, however, as we take imperfect markets into account, and as soon as we begin talking about stabilization policy on the part of government, we must face the questions of *what* information is necessary for appropriate action and how this information is obtained. In stabilization policy especially, what we are proposing is the setting up of a servomechanism for the "governing" of certain critical economic variables. Such an apparatus always involves devising information channels from the system to the "executive" or controller, and channels of effect from the controller to the system. If systems of this kind are set up too clumsily, they may even generate wider fluctuations, especially if there are serious lags in the effector apparatus or in the information system.

Several problems involved here have received far too little attention. One is the problem of "signal detection"— How do we distinguish a signal from "noise," i.e. purely random, or at least non-significant, events, changes, or positions of our sensitive variables? All economic variables are subject to fluctuations; the question is what changes are significant, in the sense that they require action, and what changes are not significant and can be regarded as "random." Recent work on the theory of signal detection has shown that the *criterion* for selection of doubtful signals depends on the penalties for false alarms and missed signals and the rewards for correct perception of either the presence or the absence of a signal. Thus if the penalties for false alarms (saying there is a depression when in fact there are only random fluctuations) are light, and the penalties for missed signals (saying there is no depression when in fact there is) are heavy, the criterion for detection will be set at a point where there is a likelihood of a considerable number of false alarms but very few misses. This is a possible explanation for the tendency of all advanced societies to inflation in the absence of strong taboos against it in the form of artificial false alarm penalties, such as those involved in the maintenance of a gold standard.

The behavior of a servomechanism depends in part on the time lags involved in the information and effector channels, and these may be serious in the case of the economic system. If information regarding the state of the economy only reaches the controller with, say, a six months' time lag, and if his decision to act on this information only takes effect in another six months, the danger that his action will augment instead of diminish cycles is a real one. Fortunately, much has been done in recent years to speed up the transmission of information. We should be unwise, however, to assume that this problem is solved, particularly where action involves cumbersome governmental and Congressional procedure.

Perhaps the most serious of all the problems involved in the control of depressions, however, is that of the appropriateness of the "effectors." If the action of the controller affects many variables, and especially if it affects them with a time lag, the attempt to stabilize one variable or set of variables may result in the destabilization of others. In any antidepression program, therefore, it is necessary to look at the structural problems as well as the aggregative measures of the economy, with a view to improving the *specificity* of the action taken. Thus suppose unemployment develops in the automobile and perhaps a few other industries as a result of the structural difficulties peculiar to these industries outlined above. This will be reflected in a rise in the over-all unemployment figures. A rise of this kind, however, concentrated in a few industries, constitutes a very different kind of "signal" from a rise uniformly spread over the economy. In recent years economists have rightly criticized a "piecemeal" approach to problems of economic stability, as reflected, say, in agricultural policy, and have emphasized the importance of looking at the economy as a whole. The ease with which the macroeconomic variables can be manipulated has reinforced this tendency. Nevertheless, it is now time, perhaps, to point out that although the economy is a whole it also consists of parts, and that even though we must look at the effects of policy as a whole, this does not mean that actions taken should be only those which spread their influence uniformly over the whole economy.

There is a case, therefore, for "structural policies," directed at those parts of the economy where difficulties are arising. This is the case for specific agricultural policies directed toward the removal or prevention of surpluses. It is a little odd, though no doubt explicable on political lines, that agriculture is almost the only sector for which specific policies are suggested. There is a good case, for instance, if my projections of automobile population are correct, for helping the automobile industry over the expected trough by deliberately withdrawing automobiles from the road, either by more stringent licensing provisions or by a program of the purchase and scrapping of obsolete vehicles. The case for public works in a trough of the building cycle is of course a familiar one and is part of this same argument for "structural" policy. There is no absolute reason why tax policy and even monetary policy should not be "structural" in the sense of having an uneven incidence in different sectors of the economy. Traditions of equity in fiscal and monetary affairs, however, are strong—and rightly so—and make it difficult to impose frankly discriminatory taxes or loan policies.

All this in a sense is merely introductory to the main theme of this conference. I shall be glad, however, to leave the practical application to hornier statistical hands than mine, and I shall end with a brief recapitulation of what I conceive the present problem to be.

Seeing the Whole and the Parts

We are now in the thirteenth year of virtually full employment, beginning with 1941. In the attainment of this happy state, however, we have endured one major and one minor war, an arms race, and an inflation. The critical question for our society is whether this association between war and full employment is an accident or a necessity. If the latter, then I think we can write our society off as a failure, with all its accomplishments. War is not only an outrageously high price to pay for full employment, but is a most unreliable means of payment, for wars are created much more by political than by economic breakdowns, and nobody in his senses is going to go to war in order to get full employment. Fortunately, I think it can be shown that the connection between war and full employment is *not* a necessary one, though it is by no means accidental. What gives us full employment is not war itself, but the expansion in government absorption which it entails, coupled with inflationary finance and price-wage stickiness or control. It is clear, therefore, that one recipe for full employment is a sure thing—large government expenditures, a budget deficit, and suppressed inflation —and that this remedy is good no matter what the government expenditure is on: an $80 billion budget is likely to yield full employment *and* inflation whether it is spent on the means of death or on the means of life.

This remedy, however, is not acceptable, for good and proper reasons. It is still too high a price to pay for full employment, even though it is a much more agreeable price than war. Our instructions are therefore to think again and come up with peacetime full employment at cheaper rates, with less government and no inflation. I am not altogether sure that the article we want is in the window with this price tag on it. Nevertheless, it is worth asking for; it may be hidden in the back of the store.

The broad outlines of the problem are clear. If government absorption declines, and if private domestic investment declines, there must be a corresponding increase in household absorption or in net foreign investment, if capacity output is to be maintained. The details, however, are difficult. We have first to inquire whether there are "legitimate" expansions in peacetime government activity that can take the place of military expenditures. A moderately affirmative answer can surely be given to this question, especially if state and local governments are taken into account. One of the contributing factors to the Great Depression was that the decline in state and local government activity more than compensated for the expansion in federal activity. There seems to be a real weakness in our overall governmental structure at this point, and we should explore methods of expanding state and local government expenditures which are consistent with a federal system. Certainly the economic needs are there—in roads, in education, in the beautification of towns and cities, in slum clearance, and so on. It would be tragic if the federal nature of our Constitution imposed quite unnecessary

72

financial barriers to the satisfaction of these legitimate needs in a time of threatened depression.

The center of the problem, however, lies around the level of the consumption function and the trend in this level. If we may look at the bright side of things for a moment, there are reasons to suppose that the consumption function is higher than in the threadbare thirties and is likely to remain so. One reason is the change in the age distribution of the population. In the thirties an abnormally large proportion of the population was of working age. This meant a low consumption function, for it is those in the middle years who produce more than they consume and those at the extremes, both children and old people, who consume more than they produce. It also meant that the labor force itself was abnormally large, so that even had the proportion of the population employed been normal for an undistorted age distribution, there would still have been a gap between the labor force and the employed force, creating a social problem of unemployment. Now, on the other hand, we are in a period where the rise in the proportions both of the aged and of children may lead us to a situation with a relatively smaller proportion of people in the labor force and in middle life, so that we shall have high consumption functions and a low labor force.

The introduction of social security, insurance of bank deposits, agricultural income-maintenance programs, and other legacies of the depression also give us a certain amount of "built-in flexibility" that we did not have in the thirties, which should serve to protect us against some of the worst aspects of "perverse dynamics." Nevertheless, we cannot assume any necessarily automatic adjustment. An economy as "precarious" or sensitive as ours can go bad fast if conditions favor a general decline in the absorption functions, as they did for instance in the 1937–1938 episode. The situation may be all the more dangerous, potentially, if the perverse dynamic reactions have a "threshold" so that hope suddenly turns to despair on a large scale at some critical point on the downward path.

It is easy to think of drastic and wholesale remedies for an obvious crisis—wholesale remission of taxation, budget deficits, public works, and so on. What is difficult is to design a policy that will interpret small signals correctly and will be sensitive to the structural dislocations of the economy. Thus if we seek to use a general remission of taxation to counteract a depression in automobiles caused by age-structure factors, the result may be inflation in the economy as a whole without much effect on employment in the automobile industry. Many of these difficulties arise because economic signals are significant not by themselves but only in conjunction with others. Thus a decline in agricultural prices may mean that adjustments are necessary in the proportion of resources going into the production of the storable crops and not enough into other things, even within agriculture. Or it may mean that the banking system is failing to provide increments of money supply sufficient to take care of increasing population and income. Or it may be the result of a pure speculative movement of a "self-justifying" nature. Each of these conditions may require different policies.

Thus the time may now be ripe for a new generation of economists to turn their attention to the structure of the economic aggregates, with a view both to elucidating what subaggregates are essential parts of the economic information system and to collecting information about them. The pre-Keynesian type of business cycle theory can be justly accused of never seeing the wood for the trees. Keynesian theory is open to the opposite accusation—that of never seeing the trees for the wood. In this generation we may well set ourselves the task of seeing both wood and trees, returning, with the Keynesian vision of the whole firmly in mind, to the renewed study of the parts in the light of their contribution to, and significance for, the general system.

COMMENT

GERHARD COLM, Chief Economist, National Planning Association

Without judging the usefulness of Boulding's basic concepts for economic analysis in general, it seems to me that they are not suitable for business cycle analysis. Boulding asserts that economic theory has overlooked an important fact by not counting depreciation, "which is independent of income but which depends on the size and on the durability of the stock of real capital," as consumption. He does not explicitly recognize, however, that this "fixed consumption" is a kind of consumption which in itself does not affect the level of economic activity and that of employment. It affects these only to the extent that actual replacement of worn-out plant and equipment takes place, and replacement is not a "fixed" element of demand.

I agree with Boulding's main point, that we are facing a double precariousness, namely, a dynamic instability and the possibility of an undercapacity equilibrium—or, we may say, a cyclical problem and a structural one.

There are, of course, interrelations between the cyclical and structural problems. Because of structural, and in part institutional, changes in our economy, the nature of the cyclical processes has changed. Other papers in this conference discuss a number of the structural and institutional changes that have made the American economy more shock-resistant. But I agree with Boulding that we have no assurance of stability. Some reduction in incomes and spending may still cause further reductions in income and spending. Also, an undercapacity equilibrium—that is, a "sidewise" movement of the economy—if continued for some time, is likely to result in a curtailment in investments for expansion and thus may cause a cyclical disequilibrium.

The initial reasons for the recent downturn and the possibility of a "sidewise" movement below the full employment level are likely to lie in structural changes in the economy now taking place. One of the structural changes is that national security expenditures have recently been leveling off and that, under present programs, they are expected to be further reduced. The problem that we are facing can be expressed in simple quantitative form as follows: At the present time, economic activity is moving at an annual rate of about $15 billion below the full employment level. Because of the increase in productive capacity and in the labor force the full employment level itself increases by $10 to 15 billion over the period of a year. Thus a year from now a full employment level will be $25 to 30 billion above the present level of activity. Furthermore, if national security expenditures should be reduced in accord with present plans by about $5 billion over a year, it follows that private demand and demand for government nondefense services should increase by at least $30 billion during the same time to permit full use of available resources.

In this needed expansion of private demand, consumer demand will probably have to rise more than investment demand. During the three-year period of the build-up in national defense, the ratio of consumer demand to total demand was reduced (even though the absolute level of consumer expenditures continued to rise). If national security expenditures should level off or contract, consumer expenditures would have to rise not only in proportion with the needed rise in total demand but, in addition, enough to increase

75

their ratio to total demand. This is a problem of structural adjustment which, if not taken care of, may lead to a cyclical downswing.

"The economics of the next adjustment" in my judgment centers around the question as to how, through the forces of the market supported if necessary by government policies, this rise in active demand and these structural changes can be made.

THE STABILIZING EFFECTIVENESS
OF BUDGET FLEXIBILITY

DAVID W. LUSHER, COUNCIL OF ECONOMIC ADVISERS

1

Such terms as "budget flexibility" and "built-in stabilizers" have come to be accepted currency in economic discussions, particularly in the purchase of freedom from recession. As often as not, however, the currency engraving is fuzzy and ill defined. And, most generally, the currency circulates without established values.

The study reported on here attempts, first, to disclose and measure those segments of federal budget revenue and expenditure programs which are flexible and which change automatically in response to changes in gross national expenditures and income: that is, built-in movements within previously defined programs, as opposed to changes in programs that require explicit, new administrative or legislative action. Second, estimates are made of the extent to which these induced budget changes act as stabilizers, in that they, in turn, have a repercussive, determining influence on the amount of change in gross national income and expenditures.[1]

2

The broad method used is suggested by the purpose of the study. A clearly defined federal budget, with all its attendant revenue and expenditure programs, was established, and definite patterns and rates of economic change were postulated.

1. When the study began, there was some uncertainty as to

This paper draws on a number of basic studies and estimates contributed by Benjamin Caplan, Sam Cohn, Thomas Leahey, Robert Masucci, Karl Nygaard, Louis Paradiso, and Carl Winegarden. The paper has benefited, especially, from suggestions made by Mr. Caplan. The treatment of the subject, however, is the responsibility of the author alone, and does not necessarily reflect the views of the organization with which he is associated.

[1] In order to identify the flexible components of the federal budget and to estimate their degree of flexibility and stabilizing effectiveness with the greatest possible thoroughness and accuracy, it has been necessary to use rather elaborate assumptions, procedures, and calculations. These details, clearly relevant to an appreciation of the estimates, cannot be dealt with here in any extended form. This paper must of necessity be little more than a partial summary of the study and its findings.

how the federal tax system would be altered. It was decided to use the then-existing tax law with certain modifications recommended by the President on May 20, 1953; namely, that:

    a. The excess-profits tax would be removed on January 1, 1954

    b. The reduction in the regular corporate tax rate from 52 to 47 per cent, scheduled to go into effect on April 1, 1954, would be rescinded

    c. The reductions in excise taxes, which would take place April 1, 1954 under present law, would be rescinded pending the development of a better system of excise taxation

This modified tax system was assumed to continue in effect through fiscal years 1954 and 1955.

2. On the expenditure side, the programs contained in the August 27 review of the 1954 budget were taken for fiscal 1954. In the absence of an official budget for fiscal 1955, we arbitrarily settled on an expenditure level of $66 billion. These expenditures were regarded as taking place under conditions of an expanding high-employment economy, with prices stable at the level of the first half of 1953.

3. The revenue and expenditure estimates, translated into national income account equivalents, were incorporated in three models of gross national product designed to trace high-employment, moderate downturn, and recession conditions. In the case of the last two models the government revenue and expenditure estimates were adjusted to reflect the postulated economic conditions. The adjustments, however, were regarded only as first approximations to the induced movement of revenues and expenditures. These comprehensive models served as the basis for more exhaustive and accurate estimates of revenues and expenditures. The models, in turn, were then recast to include the more accurate estimates of government transactions, and to reconcile all other expenditure and income calculations.

4. Flexible expenditure programs were defined and classified as follows:

    a. Appropriations or major programs in which changes in expenditures could occur without requiring either action by Congress or the exercise of administrative discretion. This type of flexibility is exemplified by permanent, indefinite appropriations, such as interest on the public debt, expenditures from the social insurance trust funds, and programs in which suppliers could change delivery schedules for goods under contract.

b. Programs which would require supplemental appropriations by Congress in order to carry out expenditure commitments made under existing policies and enabling legislation. It was assumed that such additional authorizations would be enacted to meet the requirements resulting from additional case loads or other factors in "open-end" programs, such as public assistance grants to states and veterans' pension and readjustment benefits.

c. Programs financed by public debt authorizations, whether or not additional borrowing authority would be required to make expenditures under existing policies and enabling legislation. It was assumed that additional authorizations would be made as required. This applies to farm price support operations (Commodity Credit Corporation) and to the mortgage purchase program (Federal National Mortgage Association).

d. Programs in which changes could occur as a result of administrative discretion, to the extent that funds were available without further Congressional action. This would include a speedup in letting contracts, an increase in the rate of construction on river, harbor, and reclamation projects, or other changes in existing policies (including policies mentioned in b and c above).

e. Programs in which expenditure levels could be changed by changes in the prices of goods and services purchased.

5. The gross national product models were not derived from any fixed set of economic relationships, but were built up on a step-by-step judgment basis. In the case of the recession model, we attempted to surmise just how the general economy and its components might move, time- and amplitudewise, and what other characteristics the recessionary development might have. This was done, however, with the fullest possible regard to past experience and relationships and to the peculiarities of the economy at the onset of the hypothetical recession. It cannot be stressed too strongly that all models are regarded as purely hypothetical parts of a technical study, and not in any way as suggesting possible future developments. The more basic assumptions and characteristics of the recession model are:

a. Unemployment is assumed to reach 8.0 million over a two-year period.

b. Labor force growth is assumed to slow down, with a net reduction in the participation rates of teen-agers, elderly men, and adult women. The labor force, at the end of two years, is put at 68.1 million, compared with 67.2 million in the first half of 1953.

c. Farm employment is assumed to rise from 6.3 to 6.8 million farm workers.

d. Factory hours fall about 5 hours to a below-standard workweek (i.e. from 41.0 to 35.9 hours) and overtime virtually disappears. The private nonfarm workweek is assumed to fall 3.2 hours (from 39.8 to 36.6 hours).

e. The growth in private nonfarm product per man-hour is kept at about .5 per cent per year (i.e. from an index of 100.0 to 101.8 in two years).

f. Despite sharply decreased hours of work, the foregoing assumptions entail a net reduction of 5.7 million private nonfarm jobs (from 49.1 to 43.4 million).

g. The consumer price index is assumed to show an average decline of ⅜ per cent per month, or an over-all 9 per cent decline for the two-year period. The post-1929 fall was at the rate of .5 per cent per month during the first 24 months.

h. Wholesale prices are assumed to fall at a rate 1½ times that of retail prices, or 12 per cent over the two-year period. The post-1929 fall in wholesale prices was at twice the rate of consumer prices.

i. Farm prices are assumed to fall 14 per cent over the period.

j. Private wages and salaries per man-hour are assumed to fall at half the rate of consumer prices.

k. Corporate profits plus inventory valuation adjustment are assumed to move with the private nonfarm gross national product, at a marginal rate of roughly one-fourth.

l. At the onset of the recession, dividends are less than one-half of corporate profits after taxes. They are assumed to rise to about three-quarters of profits by the end of the period.

m. The personal saving rate, out of disposable income, is assumed to fall to roughly 4.0 per cent.

n. Farm and government gross products were estimated separately, and added to the private nonfarm gross product, derived on the basis of the assumptions listed above, to yield a total gross national product.

o. Personal consumption expenditures were estimated from an income account consistent with the estimated gross national product and other assumptions listed.

p. With estimated government and consumer expenditures, gross investment outlays were obtained, residually. Inventory changes were estimated on the assumption of keeping the ratio of total inventories to sales or gross nonfarm product roughly the same as in the first half of 1953. The remaining sum of gross private domestic investment was distributed over construction and producers' durable goods on what appeared to be a most reasonable basis.

3

The concept of flexibility in budget revenue and expenditure programs can be clearly and meaningfully defined in a number of alternative forms. It may be expressed as the amount of induced, absolute dollar change in a given revenue or expenditure program following an absolute dollar change in some external variable, such as gross national expenditures. Alternatively, it may be measured in elasticity terms: the percentage change in revenue, for example, relative to a percentage change in gross national expenditures. Or budget flexibility may be stated in terms of change in the average effective tax rate in response to a change in the external variable.

Similarly, the notion of the stabilizing influence of budget flexibility can be given reasonably clear alternative definitions. But these alternatives include arbitrary elements and differences in meaningfulness which make the selection of one definition a matter of some moment. In testing the stabilizing effectiveness of flexibility, the calculation is basically in terms of what the gross national expenditure level would be with a given budget flexibility, as compared with what the level would be in the absence of the given flexibility, or with some other degree of flexibility. This, however, at once suggests measurement against some assumed bench-mark dependent upon the definition of flexibility employed. To illustrate with the case of revenue flexibility, the test involves comparing gross national expenditures under the actual tax system with what such expenditures would be if some other, hypothetical tax system were in existence.

Thus the income or expenditure level obtained with an actual tax system may be compared with the income level that would result under a hypothetical tax system designed to keep total revenues completely unchanged or inflexible. In terms of the alternative definitions of flexibility described above, this hypothetical tax system would have zero absolute, zero elasticity, and perverse effective-rate flexibility in response to changes in the external variable. Another hypothetical tax system may be one in which the average effective tax rate remains unchanged with changes in income. That is, effective-rate flexibility is zero, absolute flexibility is positive, and elasticity flexibility is equal to one.

Instead of using such hypothetical tax systems as bench-marks for testing the stabilizing effectiveness of the present tax system, it has been suggested that some other actual tax system, such as that in effect in 1929, or 1937, or 1948, might be used as a bench-mark. Some technical difficulties arise in this sort of calculation, but, more important, the approach involves a conceptual difficulty which militates against its use. Apart from differing general levels of economic activity, which is a relevant consideration, the structural and interrelationship pattern of an economy is clearly influenced or shaped by the particular, existing tax system. It seems awkward, at the least, to place the present tax system, for example, into the economic environment of 1929, which was shaped in some degree by the actual tax system of that year.

The bench-mark used in this study is that given by assuming zero effective-rate flexibility, which is equivalent to the unit elasticity flexibility of a proportional tax system. That is, the stabilizing effectiveness of the present tax system is tested by comparison with what, say, the effect on income would be if tax revenues changed in direct proportion to changes in gross national income.

The detailed, precise definition of stabilizing effectiveness used here is most readily given in algebraic form.

With all values expressed in current prices, let

Y = gross national expenditures or income

C = consumption expenditures

I = investment expenditures

G = programed government expenditures for goods and services

G_f = flexible government expenditures for goods and services

Y_d = personal disposal income

R = total tax revenues

T = government transfer payments; broadly interpreted to include interest and subsidies minus current surplus of government enterprises

S_b = business savings; including capital consumption allowance, undistributed corporate profits, corporate inventory valuation adjustment, excess of wage accruals over disbursements, and the statistical discrepancy

(1) $$Y = C + I + G + G_f$$

(2) $$Y_d = Y - R + T - S_b$$

(3)
$$C = a + c(Y - R + T - S_b)$$

where c = marginal rate of change in consumer expenditures relative to disposable income

a = constant in the consumption function

Setting

$R = rY$ where r is the average effective tax rate, measured as the ratio of revenues to gross national income

$T = tY$ where t is the ratio of transfer payments to gross national income

$S_b = d + sY$

$G_f = gY$ where g is the ratio of flexible government expenditures to gross national expenditures

then

(4) $Y = a + c(Y - rY + tY - d - sY) + I + G + gY$

(5) $Y = \dfrac{a - cd + I + G}{1 - c(1 - r + t - s) - g}$

The initial gross national expenditure, before a change in investment and/or programed government expenditures, would be

(6) $Y_1 = \dfrac{a - cd + I_1 + G_1}{1 - c(1 - r_1 + t_1 - s) - g_1}$

With a change in investment and/or government programed expenditures,

(7) $Y_2 = \dfrac{a - cd + I_2 + G_2}{1 - c(1 - r_2 + t_2 - s) - g_2}$

where the change in "autonomous" expenditures induces a change in r, t, and g. If r, t, and g are assumed to remain unchanged, the hypothetical gross national expenditure would be

(8) $Y_{12} = \dfrac{a - cd + I_2 + G_2}{1 - c(1 - r_1 + t_1 - s) - g_1}$

The actual change in gross national expenditures would be $Y_1 - Y_2$. If the average rates r, t, and g had zero flexibility, the hypothetical change would be $Y_1 - Y_{12}$. And, the difference between the hypothetical and actual changes may be expressed in the form

$$(Y_1 - Y_{12}) - (Y_1 - Y_2) = Y_2 - Y_{12}$$

This difference, the amount of further change in expenditures which is prevented by the built-in flexibility other than zero, may be measured relative to (a) the original level of expenditures

$$\frac{Y_2 - Y_{12}}{Y_1}$$

(b) the new actual expenditure level

$$\frac{Y_2 - Y_{12}}{Y_2}$$

(c) the hypothetical expenditure

$$\frac{Y_2 - Y_{12}}{Y_{12}}$$

or (d) the full, hypothetical change that might have taken place

$$\frac{Y_2 - Y_{12}}{Y_1 - Y_{12}} \text{ (see footnote 2)}$$

This last, which shows the degree to which the built-in flexibility offsets the change in investment and/or programed expenditures, is calculated for the present study.

Since

$$(9) \quad Y_1 - Y_{12} = \frac{\Delta(I + G)}{1 - c(1 - r_1 + t_1 - s) - g_1}$$

and

$$(10) \quad Y_2 - Y_{12} = Y_2 \left[\frac{c(r_1 - r_2) - c(t_1 - t_2) - (g_1 - g_2)}{1 - c(1 - r_1 + t_1 - s) - g_1} \right]$$

the stabilizing effectiveness of built-in flexibility, or the degree to which automatic flexibility offsets a change in investment and/or programed government expenditures, is shown by

$$(11) \quad \frac{Y_2 - Y_{12}}{Y_1 - Y_{12}} = Y_2 \left[\frac{c(\Delta r - \Delta t) - \Delta g}{\Delta(I + G)} \right]$$

This expression is identified as ϕ—the coefficient of stabilizing flexibility, or the flexibility offset to change in investment and/or

---

[2] This is equivalent to the measurement used by Richard A. Musgrave and Merton H. Miller in their article on "Built-in Flexibility" (*American Economic Review*, March 1948, pp. 122–128). In that article, which deals essentially with revenue flexibility, the hypothetical decline is taken as that associated with a tax system which has zero absolute and elasticity flexibility, rather than zero effective-rate flexibility, assumed here. The relation between the two approaches is shown in the appendix to this paper.

programed government expenditures. The coefficient has boundary values of zero, when there is no change in the sum of average rates; and one, for perfect stabilizing flexibility or offset. Negative values may also be obtained, reflecting destabilizing or perverse flexibility.

In the case of a fall in investment and/or programed government expenditures, a decrease in the average tax rate and increases in the average transfer and flexible government expenditure rates (measured relative to gross national income) provide offsets to the deflationary change in outlays.

4

As is apparent from equation 11, separate, additive subcoefficients of stabilizing flexibility can be calculated for the tax, transfer, and expenditure programs; and for components within each major program. The preliminary estimates available at this time are presented in Table 1. Coefficients are shown for half yearly changes in the recession model, for successive yearly changes in the period 1929–1932, and for the 1937–1938 change. All government expenditures for goods and services, in the latter historical periods, were taken as programed.

Though the figures are still tentative, their general magnitudes are probably accurate enough to permit evaluations; however, we are unable to undertake this evaluation in the present paper. This deficiency is partially remedied by the comments that follow.

Appendix

The relation between the approach used here and that employed by Musgrave and Miller may be shown as follows:

Summarizing the Musgrave and Miller method, using their notation and equation numbering,

$$(1) \qquad \Delta Y = \Delta I + c\Delta Y - c(r_1 Y_1 - r_2 Y_2)$$

"The income elasticity (E) of the tax yield (T) is"

$$(2) \qquad E = \frac{\Delta T Y_1}{\Delta Y T_1}$$

Solving equation 2 for ΔT and substituting for $(r_1 Y_1 - r_2 Y_2)$,

$$(3) \qquad \Delta Y = \Delta I \frac{1}{1 - c + cE\dfrac{T_1}{Y_1}}$$

TABLE 1

Stabilizing Effectiveness of Budget Flexibility

		Hypothetical			Actual			
	Expression	"1953"—II to "1954"—I	"1954"—I to "1954"—II	"1954"—II to "1955"—I	1929 to 1930	1930 to 1931	1931 to 1932	1937 to 1938
Change in investment and/or programed government expenditures for goods & services								
		Billions of Dollars						
	$\Delta(I+G)$	13.6	14.4	14.3	5.0	5.3	5.6	2.9
		Percentage Offset						
Revenues								
Personal tax & nontax receipts	ϕrp	.0811	.0600	.0672	−.0351	.0403	−.0038	−.0192
Federal	ϕfrp	.0879	.0646	.0802	−.0053	.0578	.0190	−.0028
State & local	ϕlrp	−.0068	−.0046	−.0130	−.0300	−.0176	−.0228	−.0164
Corporate profits tax accruals	ϕrc	.2094	.1138	.1998	.0680	.0354	.0003	.0606
Federal	ϕfrc	.2068	.1114	.1917	.0628	.0344	.0002	.0572
State & local	ϕlrc	.0026	.0024	.0082	.0053	.0012	.0001	.0034
Indirect business tax & non-tax accruals	ϕri	−.0603	−.0721	−.0890	−.1861	−.1495	−.2091	−.0892
Federal	ϕfri	−.0125	−.0100	−.0106	−.0002	−.0035	−.0332	−.0067
State & local	ϕlri	−.0478	−.0621	−.0784	−.1860	−.1460	−.1760	−.0960
Contributions for social insurance	ϕrs	−.0809	−.0186	−.0257	−.0072	−.0087	−.0108	−.0460
Federal	ϕfrs	−.0769	−.0131	−.0189	−.0028	−.0034	−.0042	−.0410
State & local	ϕlrs	−.0040	−.0056	−.0068	−.0044	−.0053	−.0064	−.0047
Subtotals								
Revenues	ϕr	.1493	.0830	.1524	−.1606	−.0824	−.2233	−.0936
Federal	ϕfr	.2053	.1530	.2424	.0545	.0853	−.0182	.0201
State & local	ϕlr	−.0560	−.0699	−.0900	−.2151	−.1677	−.2052	−.1137

CALENDAR YEAR

TABLE 1 (continued)

		Hypothetical			Actual			
	Expression	"1953"—II to "1954"—I	"1954"—I to "1954"—II	"1954"—II to "1955"—I	1929 to 1930	1930 to 1931	1931 to 1932	1937 to 1938
Transfer payments								
All governments	ϕt	.1690	.2152	.2366	.0581	.2572	.0224	.1355
Federal	ϕft	.1452	.1916	.2031	.0316	.2133	−.0287	.0960
State & local	ϕlt	.0238	.0237	.0335	.0265	.0439	.0511	.0396
Subtotals								
Revenues and transfers	ϕrt	.3183	.2982	.3890	−.1025	.1748	−.2009	.0419
Federal	ϕfrt	.3505	.3446	.4455	.0862	.2986	.0468	.1162
State & local	ϕlrt	−.0322	−.0462	−.0565	−.1886	−.1238	−.1541	−.0741
Flexible expenditures for goods and services								
Federal	ϕfg	.0053	.0319	.0123	⋯	⋯	⋯	⋯
Programs (see pp. 78–79)								
4a	ϕfga	−.0017	−.0020	−.0025	⋯	⋯	⋯	⋯
4b	ϕfgb	.0009	.0009	.0010	⋯	⋯	⋯	⋯
4c	ϕfgc	.0113	.0116	.0128	⋯	⋯	⋯	⋯
4d	ϕfgd	.0784	.0802	.0895	⋯	⋯	⋯	⋯
4e	ϕfge	−.0836	−.0588	−.0885	⋯	⋯	⋯	⋯
Total								
Revenues, transfers, & expenditures		.3236	.3301	.4013	−.1025	.1748	−.2009	.0419
Federal	$\phi frtg$	.3558	.3764	.4578	.0862	.2986	.0468	.1162
State & local	ϕlrt	−.0322	−.0462	−.0565	−.1886	−.1238	−.1541	−.0741

Note: Preliminary estimates. Details will not necessarily add to totals because of rounding.

Substituting r_1 for $\dfrac{T_1}{Y_1}$,

(4)
$$\Delta Y = \Delta I \, \frac{1}{1 - c(1 - Er_1)}$$

"As a convenient measure for the compensatory effectiveness of 'built-in flexibility' we may then write

(5)
$$a = 1 - \frac{\Delta Y}{\Delta Y_a}$$

where ΔY refers to the change in income in the particular tax system under discussion (with its specific positive value for Er_1) and ΔY_a refers to a system where (E) is set equal to zero."

Substituting equation 4 in equation 5,

(6)
$$a = 1 - \frac{1 - c}{1 - c(1 - Er_1)} = \frac{cEr_1}{1 - c + cEr_1}$$

Continuing now to establish the relation between the above approach and that used here, equation 2 may be stated as

(7)
$$E = \frac{r_1 Y_1 - r_2 Y_2}{\Delta Y} \cdot \frac{Y_1}{r_1 Y_1} = 1 + \frac{\Delta r Y_2}{r_1 \Delta Y}$$

so that

(8)
$$E - 1 = \frac{\Delta r Y_2}{r_1 \Delta Y} = \Gamma$$

If now ΔY is taken to refer to changes in income in a particular tax system with a flexible average effective rate (i.e. Δr has a value other than zero), and ΔY_a refers to a system where $E = 1$ or effective-rate flexibility is zero (i.e. $\Gamma = 0$, rather than $E = 0$), equation 6 becomes

(9)
$$\phi = 1 - \frac{1 - c + cr_1}{1 - c + cEr_1} = \frac{cr_1(E - 1)}{1 - c + cEr_1} = \frac{cr_1 \dfrac{\Delta r Y_2}{r_1 \Delta Y}}{1 - c + cEr_1}$$

or

(10)
$$\phi = \frac{c\Delta r Y_2}{\Delta Y(1 - c + cEr_1)}$$

which, from equation 4, is

(11)
$$\phi = Y_2 \left[\frac{c\Delta r}{\Delta I} \right]$$

As to the comparative values of ϕ and a, equation 9 may be written

$$(12) \qquad \phi = \frac{cEr_1}{1 - c + cEr_1} - \frac{cr_1}{1 - c + cEr_1}$$

And, since $a = \dfrac{cEr_1}{1 - c + cEr_1}$, from equation 6

$$(13) \qquad \phi = a - \frac{cr_1}{1 - c + cEr_1}$$

where ϕ is clearly less than a.

The change in the government deficit associated with the flexibility offsets may be shown in the following manner:

The government surplus (S) may be defined as

$$(1) \qquad\qquad\qquad S = R - (G + G_f + T)$$

$$(2) \qquad\qquad\qquad \Delta S = \Delta R - \Delta G - \Delta G_f - \Delta T$$

which can be expressed in the form

$$(3) \quad \Delta S = s_1 \Delta Y + \Delta s Y_2 = (r_1 \Delta Y + \Delta r Y_2) - (n_1 \Delta Y + \Delta n Y_2)$$
$$- (g_1 \Delta Y + \Delta g Y_2) - (t_1 \Delta Y + \Delta t Y_2)$$

where s and n are the ratios of the surplus and nonflexible government expenditures, respectively, to gross national expenditures. Equation 3 can be written as

$$(4) \quad \Delta S = s_1 \Delta Y + \Delta s Y_2 = Y_2 (\Delta r - \Delta t - \Delta g - \Delta n)$$
$$+ \Delta Y (r_1 - t_1 - g_1 - n_1)$$

If $S_1 = 0$, $s_1 = 0$, and $r_1 - t_1 - g_1 - n_1 = 0$, so that

$$(5) \qquad \Delta S = \Delta s Y_2 = Y_2 (\Delta r - \Delta t - \Delta g - \Delta n)$$

then with a decline in gross national product, a decrease in r ($\Delta r = r_1 - r_2 > 0$) and increases in t, g, and n ($\Delta t = t_1 - t_2 < 0$; $\Delta g < 0$; and $\Delta n < 0$) reduce the government surplus or increase the deficit.

Let $F = Y_2 [c(\Delta r - \Delta t) - \Delta g]$, which is the offset to the decline in investment and/or programed expenditures ($\Delta (I + G)$ in equation 11 of the text).

$$(6) \quad \Delta S - F = Y_2 [(\Delta r - \Delta t - \Delta g - \Delta n) - (c\Delta r - c\Delta t - \Delta g)]$$

$$(7) \quad \Delta S - F = Y_2 [(1 - c)(\Delta r - \Delta t) - \Delta n]$$

In ratio form

$$(8) \qquad\qquad \frac{\Delta S}{F} = \frac{\Delta r - \Delta t - \Delta g - \Delta n}{c(\Delta r - \Delta t) - \Delta g} > 1$$

with a decline in expenditures.

COMMENT

Samuel M. Cohn, Bureau of the Budget

Lusher's interesting paper provides one possible measure of "budget flexibility"—a measure of the offset provided by "built-in stabilizers" to programed declines in investment and government purchases. The estimates he provides for ϕ, measuring the stabilizing effectiveness of built-in budget flexibility, are indeed interesting, and provide a base from which further analysis could lead to policy conclusions and decisions.

However, these estimates of ϕ and the conclusions derived can be no better than the underlying data and the estimates which were made to measure the responsiveness of the federal budget to assumed changes in economic activity.

The study of budget responsiveness that provides the basic figures for Lusher's paper includes only those government programs for which federal receipts or expenditures would change appreciably with a change in economic activity. In other words, it excludes the effects of government programs which do not currently influence the federal budget; for example, bank deposit insurance, mortgage insurance, savings and loan insurance, and loan guarantee programs. It also excludes the economic effects of a flexible monetary policy.

In summary, therefore, we have examined the changes in receipts and disbursements of the federal government which would occur with certain assumed changes in the economy, without adding any new antirecession programs. Estimates of the changes in some government programs were relatively easy to make. In other cases, however, many auxiliary assumptions and judgments were necessary, and these assumptions and judgments—although reasonable —are certainly debatable. I shall try to mention the important ones as I describe the estimates.

First, however, several general observations are in order. The estimates in my discussion are based on fiscal years; thus the fiscal year 1953 is the year that ended on June 30, 1953. They have to do with the federal budget, and are conceptually different from the income and product accounts of the federal sector which form the basis for Lusher's calculations. For example, my revenue estimates are in terms of collections and therefore lag the tax liabili-

The estimates and opinions presented are my judgments and are not necessarily the same as those of the Bureau of the Budget.

ties (accruals) which are included in the income and product statistics. It is by looking at the federal budget, rather than the national income accounts, that we can obtain a background against which political and administrative decisions would have to be made in response to various kinds of economic change. Quantitative changes in the federal budget are computed in terms of the consolidated cash statement, or receipts from and payments to the public. At the end of the discussion I shall reconcile the figures to show the change in the deficit of the conventional or so-called administrative budget.

My discussion will be limited to the fiscal year which Lusher has called, in quotation marks, 1955. Institutionally, present laws and government programs pretty much tie down the period of time to the actual fiscal year 1955. Lusher described the assumptions we made with respect to changes in present tax laws and with respect to the total of budget expenditures. Within limits, other assumptions could be made which might be just as reasonable. On the expenditure side of the budget, however, the limits are such that other reasonable assumptions for the fiscal year 1955 would not have appreciably altered the dollar estimate of the change in government expenditures due to the assumed change in economic conditions.

In discussing the change in the cash surplus (or deficit) resulting from the assumed change in economic conditions, I shall group the federal programs involved into five categories. These categories indicate differences in the degree to which the budgetary changes are really "built-in," and also indicate differences in the kinds of judgments which must be made in preparing the estimates. The five categories are (1) truly automatic changes—those occurring without the necessity for any executive or legislative decisions; (2) changes arising from needed supplemental appropriations—here executive and legislative decisions are required, but the area of discretion is very limited; (3) changes arising in programs financed by public debt authority—mostly government enterprises—where market conditions make for special problems; (4) changes resulting from price declines, and here very definite administrative decisions are required; (5) changes which can be accomplished by administrative discretion—within already appropriated funds and without changing program objectives—the administrative decisions required here might be more difficult to make than those in the fourth category.

In total the estimates show that under the assumed recession conditions the consolidated cash deficit for the fiscal year 1955 might be

Summary of Changes in Cash Surplus or Deficit between Expanding Economy
and Recession, "Fiscal Year 1955"

(*billions of dollars*)

Category	Increase in Cash Surplus (+) or Deficit (−)
1. Automatic	−19.2
2. Supplemental appropriation requirements	−1.2
3. Programs financed by public debt authorizations	−2.7
4. Effect of price declines	+3.2
5. Administrative discretion	−4.0
Total	−23.9

1. *True Automatic Changes.* As shown in the summary below, over 80 per cent of the estimated automatic increase in the cash deficit results from a decline in budget revenues.

Type of Automatic Change	Increase in Cash Surplus (+) or Deficit (−) (*billions of dollars*)
a. Decline in trust fund receipts	−1.2
b. Rise in trust fund expenditures	−2.5
c. Decline in budget receipts	−15.7
d. Decline in budget expenditures	+.6
e. Increase in cash payments, not elsewhere classified	−.4
Total	−19.2

$23.9 billion greater than under conditions of an expanding economy.

a. Most of the change in trust fund receipts, taken as a whole, results from reduced payroll tax collections, which are the major source of receipts of these funds. With a decline in employment and in wages and salaries, "covered" payrolls would decline, thus lowering tax collections, primarily in the old age and survivors' insurance, railroad retirement, and unemployment trust funds. A small decline would also occur in the interest received on trust fund investments, since worsening economic conditions would reduce the amount available for investment or—in the case of the unemployment trust fund —necessitate the liquidation of investments to pay current benefits.

b. The increase in trust fund expenditures consists almost entirely of increased benefit payments from the social security trust funds. These would occur because of the greater number of persons who would be eligible and who could be expected

92

to apply for benefits under existing laws. By far the largest increase is in the unemployment trust fund.

c. Estimates of budget receipts were based on the President's tax proposals of May 1953, which would rescind the reductions scheduled to occur April 1, 1954 in corporation income taxes and in excise taxes.[1] Since tax collections lag tax liabilities, the full impact of the economic change is not apparent in these estimates. Thus if economic conditions were to stabilize at the assumed recession level, tax collections in the fiscal year 1956 would be lower than in 1955. This is pointed out because the corresponding 1955 estimate on the national income and product basis is in terms of accruals (or liabilities) and is substantially lower.

d. Most of the automatic decline in budget expenditures under recession conditions is estimated to result from a slowdown of deliveries of military goods, despite attempts that might be made by the Department of Defense to keep military procurement on schedule. Estimates of such a slowdown were based on the *assumption* that most military contractors would try to stretch out this federal contract work under recessionary economic conditions so that they could maintain a nucleus of key technical and skilled personnel and thus improve their competitive position when civilian demand began to rise. This assumption was made after lengthy discussions with government experts in this field, but it is certainly debatable, since any contractors pressed for cash might tend to speed up deliveries in order to receive final contract payments earlier.

e. The increase shown above for "cash payments not elsewhere classified" consists largely of interest on redeemed savings bonds and of redemptions of notes of the International Bank and International Monetary Fund. Under recession assumptions it is estimated that there would be a rise in cash redemptions of savings bonds, particularly Series E bonds. As a result, interest paid out would increase. The increased interest payments (but not the repayment of borrowing) are considered cash expenditures. It is also expected that member nations of the IMF would have balance of payment difficulties requiring a greater supply of dollars, and we therefore estimated

[1] After this study was prepared Congress deferred the scheduled reduction in corporation income taxes for one year. However, excise tax rates were reduced (resulting in an estimated revenue loss of $1 billion) and the internal revenue code was revised; these actions differed from the basic assumptions made in preparing the revenue estimates for this study.

that there would be net redemptions of IMF notes of $300 million under recession conditions, while no net redemption was estimated under the expanding economy assumption.

2. *Expenditure Changes from Supplemental Appropriations.* The programs included in this category are those in which a worsening of economic conditions would cause increases in the number of persons applying and qualifying for benefits under present law, thereby raising the financial requirements of the programs in terms of both benefit payments and administrative workloads. These programs differ from the trust fund programs mentioned under "true automatic changes" since appropriations for the latter are "indefinite," the amount available depending on the program requirements, while appropriations for the programs in this category are enacted in specific amounts. To meet the increased financial demands under the assumed recession, administrative and legislative actions would be required to obtain supplemental appropriations. Some time lag in obtaining the necessary actions might occur, but the supplemental appropriations would undoubtedly be enacted because the funds required to meet the increased program requirements are in effect legal and moral obligations of the government.

Program or Agency Requiring Supplemental Appropriation	Increase in Cash Surplus (+) or Deficit (−) (billions of dollars)
a. Veterans' compensation, pensions, unemployment benefits, care, etc.	−.9
b. Defense Department drill pay	−.1
c. Public assistance grants	−.1
d. Post Office deficit	−.1
e. Other	a
Total	−1.2

a Less than $.1 billion.

a. Veterans' programs account for three-fourths of the estimated increase in expenditures under supplemental appropriations. The specific programs involved and the assumptions used are: (1) education and training benefits are expected to rise because the number of Korean veterans going to school would increase with a decline in employment opportunities; (2) eligibility under the compensation and pension program is determined in part by the annual income of veterans or their dependents— with declines in employment and income under recession conditions, the average number of newly eligible veterans would be expected to rise and additional currently eligible veterans would undoubtedly apply for benefits; (3) unemployment compensation payments to Korean veterans would increase in the event of an economic decline; and (4) expenditures for the loan guarantee program would be expected to rise because defaults on loans would increase under the assumed recession.

b. The increase estimated for drill pay is based on the expectation that attendance of reservists would rise as employment and income fell.

c. With increased unemployment, expenditures for public assistance are also expected to rise.

d. Postal volume and postal revenue are estimated to fall somewhat faster than expenditures under recession conditions, thus increasing the postal deficit—which must be met from general revenues.

3. *Expenditure Changes (Net) in Programs Financed by Public Debt Authority.* Programs in this category are financed through enacted "authorizations to expend from public debt receipts" and are mainly carried out by wholly owned government corporations. Because these programs are of a business character, regular appropriations have been considered too cumbersome and inefficient for their ordinary operations. Therefore, the government agencies involved are usually authorized to conduct their activities on a "revolving fund" basis—i.e. they may spend their operating receipts as well as additional funds to the extent that their outstanding liabilities at any one time do not exceed the amount of the available public debt authorizations. Such authorizations are usually enacted in relatively large amounts, so that the agencies can carry on their activities for several years without the necessity for returning annually to Congress for additional funds. To the extent that this is true, the net expenditure changes estimated are somewhat similar in nature to the "true automatic" changes already discussed. They are grouped here, in a separate category, because (1) the estimates are much more difficult to make than those in the "true automatic" category and (2) there is some degree of administrative discretion involved unless one assumes that present program objectives are rigidly defined and will remain unchanged.

With changing economic conditions, changes would occur in the various markets in which these government enterprises play a role. The expenditure estimates, therefore, are based on a number of specialized assumptions and judgments about these markets. In addition, they assume no change in present laws and program objectives.

Program or Agency Financed by Public Debt Authorization	Increase in Cash Surplus (+) or Deficit (—) (billions of dollars)
a. Federal National Mortgage Association	—1.0
b. Agricultural price supports	—.5
c. Export-Import Bank	—.5
d. Low rent housing	—.2
e. Defense Production Act	—.2
f. Insurance of housing mortgages and savings and loan deposits	—.1
g. Reconstruction Finance Corporation	—.1
h. Other	—.1
Total	—2.7

a. The Federal National Mortgage Association is authorized to purchase FHA- and VA-insured mortgages of face value up to $10,000 so long as the Association's total holdings do not exceed $3,650 million.[2] FNMA net expenditures reflect sales and purchases of such mortgages plus earnings and repayments. It was assumed that under recession conditions, private lenders would be more reluctant to invest in mortgages and that therefore the FNMA would be called upon to provide mortgage funds necessary to meet housing demand not supplied by the private market, and to encourage private mortgage investment by providing a secondary market.

b. Expenditures by the Commodity Credit Corporation for agricultural price supports (including the International Wheat Agreement) are determined by the level of price supports and the factors affecting supply and demand for the commodities under price supports. Assuming effective marketing quotas and acreage allotments, it is estimated that expenditures of the CCC would rise in a recession due to (1) a drop in cotton exports, (2) an increase in the subsidization of wheat export under the International Wheat Agreement, and (3) an increase in expenditures for the support of nonbasic crops. However,

[2] Under the Housing Act of 1954 enacted during the Eighty-third Congress, second session (after this study was prepared), the FNMA is authorized to purchase FHA- and VA-insured mortgages of face value up to $15,000 and the limit on its total holdings has been changed.

it should be pointed out that expenditure estimates for this program are difficult to make under any conditions.[3]

c. The Export-Import Bank is authorized to make loans to foreign countries in order to facilitate and assist the export and import trade of the United States. Operating within its lending authority limit of $4.5 billion,[4] the Export-Import Bank could expand its loan program in response to increased need for funds by foreign countries in the event of a recession. In addition, decreased repayments on loans now outstanding might be expected. Thus net expenditures of the Bank might be expected to increase substantially over the level assumed in an expanding economy.

d. Most of the estimated net increase in expenditures for the low rent housing program results from an assumed increase in the ratio of government to private financing under recession conditions.

e. The rise in net expenditures under the Defense Production Act reflects increased purchases of aluminum, copper, titanium, and other materials for the stockpile as private consumption declines. Such purchases would, of course, be limited by stockpile objectives and the availability of funds.[5]

f. A recession could also be expected to produce additional defaults of mortgages insured by the government.

g. Net receipts of the Reconstruction Finance Corporation are estimated to fall as the liquidation of RFC assets might be hampered by the assumed economic recession.

4. *Expenditure Change Due to Price Declines.* Price declines during the assumed recession would result in lower costs to the government for many of the goods and services it purchases. Under present law the President (through the Bureau of the Budget) may establish budgetary reserves out of savings made possible after an appropriation becomes available. It was assumed that the President (through the Bureau of the Budget) would place savings

---

[3] New farm price support legislation, recently enacted by the Congress, is not expected to affect expenditures until 1956.

[4] This authority was increased by $500 million during the second session of the Eighty-third Congress.

[5] Since this paper was prepared, the President has approved a new long-term stockpile policy, which is being reflected in additional procurement and stepped-up deliveries for the stockpile. To finance increased procurement, a supplemental appropriation of $380 million was approved by the Eighty-third Congress, second session. These changes were not taken into account in the estimates presented here.

due to price declines in such reserves. Possible expansions of program objectives through the use of these savings is included in the next category, "administrative discretion."

Program or Agency Affected by Price Declines	Increase in Cash Surplus (+) or Deficit (−) (billions of dollars)
a. Defense Department	+2.4
b. Mutual Security Program	+.4
c. Atomic Energy Commission	+.1
d. Stockpiling of strategic materials	+.1
e. Various grants to states	+.1
f. Other (including civil works)	+.1
Total	+3.2

a. About three-quarters of the expenditure reductions due to price declines are estimated to be in the Department of Defense, resulting in large part from the assumed declines in the wholesale prices of metals, metal goods, and construction materials. Costs of procurement of major equipment and construction would be particularly affected.

b. In addition, it is estimated that expenditures for mutual security—representing in large part heavy (including military) equipment—could drop considerably in the event of a recession, as a result of declines in both foreign and domestic prices.

c–f. Expenditures for other agencies and programs would be affected, but to a smaller degree.

5. *Expenditure Changes through Administrative Discretion.* The estimates in this category are based largely on the following considerations: (1) Congressional appropriations are sometimes enacted for one year, sometimes for two years, and sometimes without any specific time limit; thus government agencies have some discretion with respect to the speed with which they undertake

Program or Agency Affected by Administrative Discretion	Increase in Cash Surplus (+) or Deficit (−) (billions of dollars)
a. Defense Department	−.8
b. Mutual Security Program	−2.8
c. Various grants to states	−.1
d. Farm programs	−.1
e. Stockpiling of strategic materials	−.1
f. Other	−.1
Total	−4.0

authorized programs and objectives. (2) The budgetary reserves established because of price declines could be made available to expand or expedite projects within the limits of the legislation authorizing and financing the work, the feasibility of management and administration, and the objectives of the particular activity.

  a. The estimated increase in Defense Department expenditures results from an assumed administrative decision to initiate construction of projects already authorized and funded, but deferred because of general budgetary restrictions. An expansion would also be possible without additional appropriations in the Defense Department's industrial mobilization program, which provides for the building of additional plant capacity.

  b. The program for which the largest change is estimated as a result of administrative discretion is the Mutual Security Program. For several years various factors have contributed toward keeping expenditures for military assistance below previously agreed-upon objectives. These factors include the imperfect availability of productive resources to meet program goals, budgetary restrictions, and the inability of foreign countries completely to absorb the military shipments (i.e. to support operating and maintenance costs). With a worsening of economic conditions, it would be reasonable to expect that more productive resources would be available to meet existing program goals and that budgetary restrictions would be eased, thus permitting a step-up in the foreign aid program within available funds. In making our estimates for this program, we assumed that the recipient countries would be able to absorb the additional aid sent to them. It is possible, however, that this would not be the case and that our estimates of increased expenditures are thereby overstated.

  c–f. Discretionary expansions are possible in several other government programs, but the amounts involved are substantially smaller than in the Defense Department and the Mutual Security Program.

Almost all of the changes discussed above affect the budget surplus or deficit as well as the cash surplus or deficit. Only three of all the items mentioned do not affect the budget deficit. These three are in the category of "true automatic" changes, and are (1) trust fund receipts, (2) trust fund expenditures, and (3) cash payments, n.e.c. Together, they were estimated to increase the cash

99

deficit by $4.1 billion. Thus the increase in the budget deficit would be $19.8 billion ($23.9 minus $4.1) from the assumed expanding economy conditions to the assumed recession.

It is against the background of a deficit of this size that the political feasibility of the $4 billion increase in expenditures through administrative action (category 5) would be decided. There might well be serious opposition to such an increase in federal expenditures. On the other hand, pressing for increases would be the political, social, and economic effects of the unemployment that would accompany the assumed recession. These same factors would also influence the adoption of new legislation providing pump-priming antirecession expenditures. We have made no estimate for any such legislation.

BENJAMIN CAPLAN, Washington, D.C.

My discussion will concentrate on what might loosely be called the dynamics of the recession model from which Lusher derived his estimate of the coefficient of flexibility.[1] Clearly, the estimates as to the effectiveness of budget flexibility are no better or, perhaps more accurately, no worse than the reasonableness of the design of the basic model. As a problem in methodology, model building has great instructional merit, but we are primarily interested in its heuristic value—that is to say, we are interested in the model not as a dialectical exercise but as a guide to policy. Model making is no longer a novel exercise. The model must depict a realistic contingency that prudent policy makers should take into account.

In discussing the dynamics of this particular recession model, one obvious approach is to consider the dynamics of the individual assumptions, e.g. specific assumptions as to the behavior of wages or prices, or investment, or consumption over the time period postulated given the primary changes postulated. Equally obvious are some of the points that can be made, e.g. that the rate of decline in the individual variables would not take place in the even fashion postulated. But such questions, while important, are not basic unless it can be shown: (1) that the set of assumptions and interrelationships is internally inconsistent so that the model is fundamentally self-contradictory and therefore meaningless, or (2) that the degree of weakness postulated by the recession model is unrealistic.

The views expressed here are solely the personal views of the writer.
[1] The model was the joint product of a group of economists.

On the first point, those of us who prepared the model obviously did not think it was self-contradictory. We believe it depicted a possible situation in terms of assumed changes in the primary factors and historically reasonable interrelationships.

There was, however, vigorous debate in the group over the second point: the realism or timeliness of such a model. The debate was reminiscent of the one which raged over the ill-fated postwar forecasts of a deflation. We, of course, have learned our lesson. The model was not intended as a forecast. If, however, the model is to help as a guide in formulating policy, the model should be realistic in terms of current and foreseeable trends even though it is not intended as a forecast. For this purpose no one would build a model showing a decline of about the same magnitude as that which occurred between 1929 and 1932. The arithmetic could be done but it would be irrelevant for policy purposes. (Parenthetically, I might add that the group prepared two other models: [1] of a more moderate downturn, and [2] of an expanding economy.)

The realism, and therefore relevance, of the recession model is important for another reason. As Cohn has pointed out, budget flexibility is a function of the composition of the particular government program in existence at a particular time. The effectiveness of budget flexibility is geared to the kind of forces in operation at the time it is needed, and the nature of the forces is partly dependent upon the kind of budget flexibility available at the particular time. There is a mutual interaction that is dependent on the historical conjuncture. Hence it is important to determine whether, with existing budget flexibility, it is still realistic to think in terms of a possible 8 million unemployed.

The criticism of the relevance of the recession model has a threefold aspect: the historical position of the economy, the structural problem, and the stabilizing influence of market forces and liquidity factors. There is obvious overlap between these three categories but it will aid the analysis to separate them.

On the first point, the historical position of the economy, the argument runs along the following lines: The economy has been enjoying virtually uninterrupted full employment since 1941. More important, this has been true throughout the postwar period. In such a situation some easing is possible—witness 1949 and the current signs (1953). But the postwar momentum is still great—investment intentions still remain high, consumption should remain high, there is a scheduled decline in taxes, and any programed decline in government spending will be moderate. Hence any decline in the economy at this stage would at worst be moderate and in no event as serious as the decline postulated by the recession model. Perhaps at some future time there will be a decline as serious as that postulated, but not now.

On the second point, that dealing with structure, a number of basic issues are raised: (1) High, relatively inflexible government expenditures for goods and services are strengthening the economy. In 1929 the ratio of such expenditures to gross national product was about 8 per cent, in 1937 about 13 per cent, in 1952 about 22 per cent, and in the first half of 1953 somewhat higher. We did not have this tremendous anchor before the war, when most economists would probably have predicted perpetual prosperity if the government accounted for over 20 per cent of the GNP at levels of high activity. Even with the estimated declines in programed federal expenditures, their level would still be high. (2) The economy is also being supported by built-in stabilizers such as revenue flexibility, transfer payment flexibility, and the familiar list of supports: deposit insurance, farm supports, FHA and VA mortgage insurance (which also permits flexible downpayment requirements), etc. (3) Many believe that psychological attitudes have changed, that continuous high-level prosperity has bred behavior patterns tilted toward higher minimum levels of investment and consumption than in the past. (4) Stronger unions will be able to prevent excessive cumulative downward price changes by maintaining stickier wage rates than in the past.

The final point which the critics of the recession model make deals with the strength of market forces and the influence of liquidity. These critics say that the market is strong because: competitive development of new products is encouraging higher investment and higher consumption; firms are watching inventory-sales ratios with greater care; moderate price reductions are proving effective in encouraging demand; the greater stickiness of wage rates is increasing the pressures to cut costs by new techniques of production.

In discussing the liquidity factor, some make great point of two items: the high level of liquid assets in the hands of individuals and business; and the expansion of such assets as a result of the substantial deficits which will occur in a downturn, on the reasonable assumption that monetary policy will then be geared to increasing the economy's liquidity. The combination of these two items plus the increase in real value of liquid assets resulting from some decline in prices would tend to lower liquidity preference and to stimulate spending by both business and consumers. On the basis of these factors, it is believed that endogenous stabilizing factors will set in at an early enough stage of the downturn to prevent the type of recession postulated by the model.

Thus, while it is realistic to expect some weakening—indeed, the signs of such a weakening in economic activity are already clear—the stabilizing forces are, it is contended, strong enough to limit it to far less than 8 million unemployed and probably strong enough to initiate an early reversal and a further resumption of expansion.

In all this we are, of course, abstracting from that exogenous stabilizer, the Congress.

The list of potential stabilizing forces is indeed impressive, but it would be a mistake to ignore the possibility depicted by the recession model. I believe that the recession model is not an unreasonable possibility in the light of current forces. I detect too much reliance in the discussions on the 1949 experience, which was primarily an inventory readjustment. The present situation appears to differ radically from that experience. For the first time since the end of the war we are approaching a situation in which several basic demand factors seem to be turning down simultaneously. These are: consumer demand for durables; plant and equipment; residential housing; and government spending. Individually, the changes appear quite small, but that could be only the first impact. In addition, inventories are very substantial and could quickly become out of line with some further weakening of sales. Finally, we have had a very large increase in manufacturing capacity. The combination of all these factors adds up, in my opinion, to a situation potentially more serious than 1949.

I have dwelt overlong on this debate for one major reason: it is clear that the policies needed to combat a downturn must be geared to the particular kind of downturn that may be coming. Of course, insofar as we can improve our automatic stabilizers, so much the better. But it seems clear to me that the trouble with them is that they are *ex post* and not *ex ante*, and that if a downturn is substantial other specific policies will be necessary. We make a great point of revenue flexibility, for example, but all it amounts to is that when my income goes down, my taxes go down more than proportionately but I still have less income than before. Compared with some worse system of taxation, I am better off, but that is not my yardstick. I prefer to compare my position with where I was when I was *actually* better off.

Since policies must be related to the character of the anticipated downturn, governments cannot avoid the frustrating experience of having to appraise current and foreseeable trends. If, for example, the recession model appears the more realistic, then government policies stronger than those needed to deal with a moderate downturn will be called for. All this is obvious, but it is why I thought it important to discuss the reasonableness of the recession model.

In all of this we must rely upon judgments, intention, and flair as well as scraps of data. This is unsatisfactory, but I suppose that it is the penalty we must pay for disobeying the commandments enunciated by W. H. Auden: "Thou shalt not sit / With statisticians nor commit / A social science." [2]

GERHARD COLM, Chief Economist, National Planning Association

David Lusher has done all of us a great service by suggesting a precise formulation of what built-in stabilizers may mean in the budget area and by following his concept through with computations.

What Do His Computations Tell Us? In case of a recession the decline in GNP will be mitigated by 30 to 40 per cent because of the stabilizing effect of revenues and expenditures of the federal government and state and local governments. This means that the actual decline in GNP will be 30 to 40 per cent less than it would be without the stabilizing effect of the budgets. Under conditions as they prevailed at the beginning of the depression of the thirties, government budgets aggravated the downturn by 10 to 20 per cent. What a stabilizing or aggravating effect is can best be seen by stating what in Lusher's approach would be a neutral revenue or expenditure system. If taxes and expenditures were to move exactly in proportion with GNP they would have neither a stabilizing nor an aggravating effect on the economy.

The fact that we had a 10 to 20 per cent aggravating effect in 1929–1930 and can expect a 30 to 40 per cent stabilizing effect under the present tax and expenditure system is quite reassuring. The only warning which must be expressed is this: These percentages are calculated to the last decimal, but we don't know what the 100 is to which these percentages refer. In other words, we do not know what the total decline would be if government expenditures and revenues were to fall in proportion to the drop in GNP. Even if the decline were only 60 percent of what it would

[2] "Under Which Lyre, A Reactionary Tract for the Times," in his *Nones*, Random House, 1939, p. 70.

be without the built-in stabilizers, it could still be very discomforting. Half as big as big can still be very big!

We cannot apply these percentages to any of the current recession models because these are designed to take the stabilizing effect of the budget into consideration.

What Are the Respective Contributions of Government Revenues and Expenditures to the Stabilizing Effect of the Budget? Looking at Lusher's figures in detail, it is surprising to see that the stabilizing effect of expenditures for goods and services is negligible compared with that of revenue and transfer expenditures. It is .5 to 3 per cent compared with a 30 to 33 per cent combined effect of revenue and transfer expenditures.

This unexpected result occurs, I believe, because flexible expenditures for goods and services are defined in a particular way in the budget study which Lusher used in his computations. If I understand it correctly, those expenditure programs were regarded as flexible in which a change of $10 million or more can be expected in response to a change in business conditions. As some of these so-defined expenditure flexibilities are up, and others are down (because of assumed price declines), their net stabilizing effect is negligible. Lusher considers the stabilizing effect of "programed" expenditures as a factor influencing economic conditions as they would be without budget flexibility. This is an entirely possible approach, but it results in a treatment of expenditures different from that used on the revenue side. It explains why Lusher's computations show expenditures for goods and services to have only a negligibly stabilizing effect.

Assume that government expenditures for goods and services remain entirely stable measured in absolute dollars. Then their proportion in a declining GNP would go up—they would be flexible if the same concept of flexibility were used that Lusher uses with respect to revenue. If, for instance, expenditures for goods and services of the federal government and state and local governments should remain stable at a level of $85 billion while private expenditures contracted, they would make a very considerable contribution to stabilization. Without going into the details of computation it follows that approximately stable expenditures for goods and services would contribute perhaps 20 to 25 per cent to relative stability. Using a comparable approach for all elements of the budget, it appears that revenues, transfer expenditures, and expenditures for goods and services would make approximately the same contribution to stability.

Is Use of a Uniform Multiplier Justifiable for All Parts of the Budget? Lusher's computations imply that every unit of budget flexibility—whether taxes of various kinds, changes in transfer expenditures, or changes in expenditures for goods and services—has the same stabilizing effect. He knows, of course, that an increase in unemployment benefit payments has probably a greater relative effect than a reduction in profits taxes of the same amount. It is entirely justifiable in a first approach to neglect these differential effects. However, it is necessary to be aware of this simplification. In a refinement of the study an attempt should be made to consider the differential effect of various kinds of budget flexibility.

A. G. HART, Columbia University

The volume includes two papers on the measurement of "built-in flexibility" in fiscal arrangements. But it still seems necessary to ask why we want such measurements, and how our mode of measurement can be linked to our objects.

Policy Context. The term "built-in flexibility" has a touch of paradox. It aims to express the fact that the skillful introduction of automatic-stabilizer characteristics into standing policy arrangements is up to a point a substitute for policy flexibility.

I doubt that any serious advocates of built-in flexibility have much hope of designing a policy that can make discretionary stabilization measures superfluous in all conditions. We are talking about arrangements that can *reduce the amplitude* of downswings or inflationary upswings set up by uncontrolled forces elsewhere in the economy (or by errors in discretionary policy!). In terms of the categories used in R. A. Gordon's paper, such arrangements may suffice in depressions where underlying investment opportunity is unimpaired. In such cases (as in 1949) the presence of built-in flexibility can enable business to sell more than it produces long enough to generate an inventory shortage—and without such deep price cuts to move stocks threatened with obsolescence as to make it impossible to move newly produced goods at remunerative prices. But in more deep-seated depressions the most we can expect of built-in flexibility is that it will limit the spread of depression from its original focus and keep the depression tolerably mild long enough so that some favorable development can pick us up—whether it be good discretionary policy or good luck.[1]

[1] Extreme advocates of price flexibility can reasonably claim that the monetary effects of built-in flexibility in fiscal policy should reduce the amplitude of price swings and (where they recognize such a thing) the time needed for prices to flex sufficiently.

I infer that we want essentially a measure of the ability of automatic stabilizers to reduce the amplitude of fluctuations. The question is whether to prefer measurements that are characteristics of complex economic models (involving a good deal in the way of assumptions about behavior of various sectors of the economy), or more naïve measurements that are more purely descriptions of the fiscal sector.

Naïve Measurements. For many purposes we are best off with measures that do not involve too many assumptions.[2] Here we want something that registers both the income elasticity of the magnitude we are studying (tax liability, or unemployment compensation, or whatever it may be) and also its large or small size relative to the total economy.

Mindful of the amplitude-reducing function of built-in flexibility, we can have recourse to what I hint at in *Money, Debt and Economic Activity:* [3] a coefficient that measures the extent to which the arrangement in question shifts the government budget toward deficit. For each arrangement we can set up a fraction of the dimensions

$$\frac{\text{Dollar increment of deficit}}{\text{Dollar increment of GNP}}$$

and these fractions can be added up.

This type of measurement leads to an argument a fortiori. If the fractions add up to .35 (to illustrate with a figure which seems to me of the right order of magnitude), this implies that investment can drop relative to saving by $3.5 billion without carrying GNP down by *over* $10 billion. Another way to put this is to take the reciprocal of .35 (that is, 2.86) as a multiplier, and say that a given drop in investment will not reduce GNP *by more than* 2.86 times the drop in investment. Implicitly, we assume that a drop of GNP will *lower or at least not raise* private saving.

Estimating Components of the Naïve Measurement. The worst of the problems of gauging built-in flexibility are evaded by this technique of naïve measurement. But serious difficulties remain. A few notes on the main components will map these difficulties.

Personal income tax: Joseph Pechman's estimates rely on time series analysis (see paper following). He shows clearly that the only aspect of progression markedly affecting the outcome is the jump

---

[2] I still shiver over the reaction of the Congressman who wanted to know "whether a revenue estimate was based on assumptions, because if so, I don't believe it"! Obviously, without assumptions we can reach no conclusions; yet we must prefer estimates whose assumptions seem reasonable to the layman.

[3] Second edition, Prentice, Hall, 1953, p. 462.

from a zero rate on income covered by exemption to 20 per cent or so on surtax net income. We may agree with Pechman that tax liability works out much as if a flat tax applied to surtax net income —at 1954 rates, about 24 per cent. On historical grounds we may take it that adjusted gross income is a fairly uniform proportion of GNP—around 70 per cent.[4] But the relation of surtax net income to adjusted gross income is open to argument, and it must be analyzed in terms of the structure of the tax base. Pechman's marginal co-efficient of .6 to .7 for the proportion of variations in adjusted gross income that will show up in surtax net income seems too low from his own data if we allow for population growth.[5] On the other hand, to get this marginal coefficient as high as .7, we must apparently assume a larger relative variation in the incomes of those who remain taxable throughout an income fluctuation than in the incomes of those who are not taxable at all or are taxable only part of the time.[6] If we call the coefficient .69, the marginal relation of the tax to GNP is (.24) (.7) (.69), or about .116 ($\pm$.01).

Most estimates of the built-in flexibility of this tax run in terms of annual data. I have tried to use Department of Commerce quarterly figures on personal income and tax liability, with inconclusive

[4] Applying such a uniform proportion, however, implies that the sum of indirect taxes, corporate taxes, and corporate savings—less government transfers and interest—is also a uniform proportion of GNP—an assumption which cannot fit situations where drastic reshaping of the tax structure is considered.

[5] We want to compare alternative situations that might exist at a given date (population constant). If we reduce Pechman's figures for adjusted gross income and surtax net income at 1953 exemptions and deductions (Table 4) to a per capita basis, and then take the increments, the ratio of increase in surtax net income to increase in adjusted gross income in Table 5 will range from .64 to .80 instead of from .61 to .68, the 1946–1953 over-all change shows a ratio of .70 instead of .63, and the 1948–1949 decrease shows a ratio of .74 instead of 1.20.

[6] We may look at taxpayers in two groups. A group that is pretty sure to remain taxable can be marked off by using the data for adjusted gross income (AGI) and exemptions by marital status and sex for taxable returns covering the 1950 tax year (Treasury Press Service Release H-266, October 8, 1953, Table 3). In each status-and-sex group we can mark off the income classes for which AGI was at least double the exemptions. The group of taxpayers so defined reported .680 of all AGI, and with rough allowance for deductions seem to have enjoyed .87 of all surtax net income. On a slump of income the exemptions and *itemized* deductions would be unimpaired. Their standard (presumptive) deductions averaged about 6 per cent of their AGI. Since their AGI must slump by some 43 per cent to render them nontaxable, we may suppose that for moderate fluctuations of income their surtax net income (SNI) will vary by about 94 per cent of the variation in their AGI. If their AGI varies in proportion to total AGI, therefore, their SNI will fall by about .64 (i.e. .94 × .68) of the fall in AGI. The SNI of the remaining taxpayers amounts to only about 6 per cent of AGI, so that if most of it is wiped out, a general slump of AGI will reduce SNI by a trifle less than .70 of the fall in AGI.

results.[7] Quarterly data on withholding in relation to civilian wages and salaries seem to offer better holding ground, since we are able to adjust for changes in withholding rates and blow the receipts up into a withholding tax base by quarters since the spring of 1948. But here again the shape of the figures is not very illuminating—presumably largely because of difficulties in timing adjustments.[8] It should be noted, however, that if we blow up *Statistics of Income* figures on the amount of tax withheld each year, we find a withholding base equal to over 90 per cent of surtax net income for most years. In short, almost all of the built-in flexibility of the income tax is reflected in withholding and may be presumed to take hold currently.[9]

For the corporation tax we are probably well advised to ignore the progression of the tax at low levels of corporate income and to treat it (after the termination of the excess profits tax) as a flat rate on corporate profit. The prosperity level of corporate profit, in a noninflationary situation, may be put at .12 ($\pm$.01) of GNP. But the marginal relation to GNP depends on the situation in view. In Gordon's frame of reference a short slump arising in business policy toward orders and inventories, for example, implies allowance at the trough for the tax effects of inventory losses. On the other hand, if we got into a stabilized depression because of a flagging of investment opportunity, we would want to compare profits *not* much affected by inventory losses with prosperity profits. For

[7] On a seasonally adjusted basis the Commerce figures show a decline of personal tax liabilities from the last half of 1948 to the last half of 1949 amounting to about one-fifth of the $6.3 billion decline in the average level of GNP. On a seasonally unadjusted basis, however, Commerce shows no drop in personal taxes between these two half years. Similar oddities appear for other periods we might compare.

[8] The dates when withheld taxes enter the Treasury Daily Statement (or the Internal Revenue reports) are not tidily related to the dates of withholding. Treasury reports funds as they reach Treasury depositories—largely in the month of withholding, but with a lag of one to three months for amounts withheld by smaller employers. The Bureau of Internal Revenue reports funds as the Bureau gets *either* checks *or* deposit receipts for sums placed earlier in Treasury depositories.

On the whole a two-month lag of collections behind withholding seems the best simple adjustment. But on this basis, if we blow up receipts to a withholding base and subtract from civilian wages and salaries, we get a residue (approximation to withholding exemptions) which as late as early 1952 shows no growth over 1948! There are also some suspicious quarter-to-quarter jumps. The drop from the second half of 1948 to the second half of 1949 in civilian wages and salaries fails to show up in the withholding-base series.

[9] The timing of effects depends significantly on the time of year at which incomes slump, in view of the concentration of tax refunds in February through May of the ensuing year.

the first problem I would be inclined to put the marginal propensity of profits to slump at about .3 of any fluctuation in GNP, suggesting a tax-flexibility coefficient of, say, .135 ± .015. For the second I would be inclined to put the marginal propensity of profits to slump at .2, suggesting a tax-flexibility coefficient of .09 ± .01.

With unemployment compensation, again, the type of fluctuation affects the outcome. A fall in insured payrolls is likely to approximate half of any fall in GNP. But if the fall in payrolls represents reduced hours of work, it will lead to virtually no unemployment compensation; while if it represents layoffs with working hours of those still on the payroll little affected, compensation will be substantial. If we want a single-valued coefficient, we must give it a wide margin of error—say, .065 ± .020. By good fortune, this source of error is partly hedged by an offsetting error in estimating personal income taxes.[10] Social security contributions run around .025 of GNP and may be assigned a marginal coefficient of .025.

Commodity taxes may be assigned an income elasticity on GNP of around .8 (about half that of the personal income tax); property taxes and the like, an income elasticity for short fluctuations close to zero. For taxes other than income taxes, taken as a whole, we may write a flexibility coefficient on GNP of about .06 ± .01. While the built-in flexibility of government outlays seems doubtful, we may add up these coefficients for the whole fiscal system:

Personal income tax	.116 ± .010
Corporate tax	.090 ± .010
Unemployment compensation	.065 ± .020
Social security contributions	.025 ± .002
Commodity taxes	.060 ± .010
Sum of coefficients	.356 ± .052

In view of offsetting errors, we may write .36 ± .04. For an inventory fluctuation we would write .40 ± .04.

Full-Model Estimates. A more interesting but less secure way of estimating built-in flexibility is to think of fiscal instruments as part of a general equilibrium model, and to ask how much of the prospective amplitude of a fluctuation would be removed by a given policy change. This view is essentially relative; it would yield, for example:

[10] In the case where unemployment takes the form of short hours, most of the reduction of pay will come out of the withholding base and SNI; so that the contingency that points to the lower limit of the estimation range for unemployment compensation points to the upper limit for the personal tax.

$$\text{Flexibility of personal income tax relative to sales tax} = \frac{\text{amplitude of fluctuation arising from a given disturbance with sales tax in force}}{\text{amplitude of fluctuation arising from same disturbance with income tax in force}}$$

Alternatively, it can be looked at as a comparison of Keynesian multipliers (treated as derived magnitudes rather than assumptions) under two policy setups. The setup with the lower multiplier has the higher built-in flexibility (greater stability in face of a disturbance).

This way of looking at things calls for explicit assumptions about two main problems—saving patterns and tax shifting—on which economists cannot feel too confident. I have amused myself, for all that, by setting up three illustrative models bearing on the income tax–sales tax comparison. In Model A, I assume roughly present taxes; in Model B, I assume the personal income tax to be replaced by a sales tax 100 per cent shifted to consumers; in Model C, I assume the personal income tax to be replaced by a sales tax absorbed 100 per cent by corporate and unincorporated profits. Model A yields a multiplier of 1.84, Model B a multiplier of 2.09, Model C a multiplier of 2.24. A comparison works out as follows:

Model	A	B	C
Multiplier	1.84	2.09	2.24
Forecast level of output (per cent of full employment GNP) if investment falls 10 per cent of full employment GNP	81.7%	79.2%	77.6%
Index: ratio of slump under Model C to slump under model in question	1.22	1.08	1.00

MELVIN I. WHITE, Brooklyn College

A procedure like that developed by Musgrave-Miller and Lusher seems to me indispensable to any attempt at assessing the automatic contribution of alternative fiscal structures to economic stabilization. By making the fiscal structure—characterized by the income elasticities of its components—an explicit variable in an income determination model, the effects of changes in the fiscal structure on other variables can be isolated. The Musgrave and Lusher measures of the contribution of automatic, or "built-in," flexibility isolate the effects on aggregate income, given a fixed decline in autonomous ex-

111

penditures and assuming constant consumption and business savings functions.[1]

I think, however, that the use of declines in aggregate income as the measuring (or dependent) variable does not yield the coefficient that is always the most useful for policy purposes. Certainly if there is any stabilization goal on which there is professional and lay consensus, it is that some policy must be adopted to prevent aggregate income from ever falling below a figure that is within a moderate range of the full employment level. Formulating the stabilization goal in this way implies that if built-in flexibility alone is sufficient to maintain aggregate income at or above the "floor" level, no other immediate fiscal action will be required. But if it is not, then supplementary action to offset or reduce the decline in autonomous expenditures will be necessary—such as deliberate expansion of public works, tax rate reduction in the low income brackets to stimulate consumption, etc. Thus in evaluating the effectiveness of the flexibility built into alternative fiscal structures, the relevant question may frequently not be how much aggregate income will fall in response to a given decline in autonomous expenditures, but rather how much supplementary action will be required to maintain an acceptable floor under aggregate income. This suggests that the effectiveness of built-in flexibility be measured in terms of the maximum decline in autonomous expenditures that ultimately can be permitted, given an acceptable maximum decline in aggregate income from an initial level.

Specifically, as an alternate to Lusher's coefficient, I propose the following measure, which can be identified as F:

$$F = \frac{(A_1 - A_2) - (A_1 - A_{12})}{(A_1 - A_{12})}$$

A, autonomous expenditures, is equal to the sum of Lusher's $I + G$. $(A_1 - A_2)$ is the maximum drop in autonomous expenditures consistent with a decline in gross national expenditures from their initial level, Y_1, to the floor level Y_2. (Since Y_2 is set in relation to the

---

[1] Actually, of course, their coefficients refer directly only to the differential results of shifting between a given structure and a hypothetical one. As Lusher points out, the hypothetical system in and of itself is of significance mainly as a bench-mark, and therefore it is the comparison of coefficients for the prevailing structure and for proposed modifications that will be of practical interest.

It is true that zero elasticity implies perverse changes in effective tax rates, which may be too unrealistic even for a bench-mark, except perhaps for excises. However, it may be noted that the bench-mark which Lusher has used, unit elasticity, implies that transfer payments and the flexible component of government expenditures are actually reduced when income falls.

full employment income, it would rise secularly as the full employment output of the economy expanded.) $(A_1 - A_{12})$ is the maximum hypothetical drop in autonomous expenditures consistent with the decline in gross national expenditures from Y_1 to Y_2, but with the bench-mark fiscal structure assumed in effect. Thus the expression F represents the percentage additional decline in autonomous expenditures that can be permitted under the actual fiscal structure over that permitted under the bench-mark structure.

Lusher's first three equations can be solved for $A = I + G$ as follows:

$$(1) \quad A = Y - C - G_f = Y - [a + c(Y - R \\ + T - sY - d)] - G_f$$

$$(2) \quad A = (1 - c + cs)Y + cR - cT - G_f - (a - cd)$$

Defining elasticity in the usual fashion:

$$E_R = \frac{\Delta R}{\Delta Y} \cdot \frac{Y_1}{R_1} \text{ or } \frac{\Delta R}{\Delta Y} = E_R r_1$$

similarly,

$$\frac{\Delta T}{\Delta Y} = E_T t_1 \text{ and } \frac{\Delta G_f}{\Delta Y} = E_G g_1$$

(E_T and E_G normally being negative).

The actual decline in autonomous expenditures can then be expressed as:

$$(3) \quad (A_1 - A_2) = (Y_1 - Y_2)(1 - c + cs + cE_R r_1 - cE_T t_1 - E_G g_1)$$

The hypothetical decline in A can be given either by setting the E's equal to zero, as in the Musgrave-Miller bench-mark:

$$(4) \quad (A_1 - A_{12})_M = (Y_1 - Y_2)(1 - c + cs)$$

or by setting the E's equal to one, following Lusher:

$$(5) \quad (A_1 - A_{12})_L = (Y_1 - Y_2)(1 - c + cs + cr_1 - ct_1 - g_1)$$

and the final form of the coefficient becomes: [2]

$$(6) \quad F_M = \frac{(A_1 - A_2) - (A_1 - A_{12})}{(A_1 - A_{12})} = \frac{cE_R r_1 - cE_T t_1 - E_G g_1}{1 - c + cs}$$

[2] For comparison, reference can be made to Lusher's equations 6 and 9, recalling that, for those equations, T, G, and S_b are not independently defined variables. For comparison with Lusher's first formulation, his equation 11, my expression can be reduced to:

$$\frac{Y_2(c\Delta r - c\Delta t - \Delta g)}{(Y_1 - Y_2)(I_1 + a - cd)}$$

or

$$(7) \qquad F_L = \frac{cr_1(E_R - 1) - ct_1(E_T - 1) - g_1(E_G - 1)}{1 - c + cs + cr_1 - ct_1 - g_1}$$

Either of the final forms of F would vanish should the elasticities of the actual structure reach the values of the respective bench-mark elasticities. The value of F varies directly with the effective rates at the initial level of income and with the degree of elasticity in the fiscal structure—the latter, of course, being greater the larger the figure for E_R is and the larger the negative figures for E_T and E_G are.

The relative advantage (or disadvantage) of any contemplated modification of the prevailing fiscal structure, so far as built-in flexibility is concerned, can be given by the formula

$$\frac{F_m - F_p}{1 + F_p}$$

where F_p is the coefficient for the prevailing structure and F_m the coefficient for the structure after modification. For example, if the prevailing structure has a coefficient of .30 and the suggested modifications would result in a coefficient of .43, then the modification would increase the permissible decline in autonomous expenditures by 10 per cent. Thus the coefficient can be construed—perhaps more readily than Lusher's—as measuring the relative built-in capacities of fiscal structures to *offset* the declines in autonomous expenditures.

It can be noted that for policy-making purposes, when absolute magnitudes—current and anticipated—are of immediate interest, equation 3 may become more useful than equations 6 and 7. If a decline, say, in autonomous private investment were anticipated for a forthcoming year, the difference between the amount of the anticipated decline and the expression $(A_1 - A_2)$ indicates directly the amount of offsetting expansion of autonomous government expenditures, or of induced rise in consumption resulting from tax reduction, that would be necessary to maintain the "floor" level under aggregate income.

C. HARRY KAHN, National Bureau of Economic Research

Lusher's discussion raises a question as to the meaning of his coefficients. His method of measuring the stabilizing flexibility of budget revenues and expenditures against an assumed bench-mark brings up the problem of when changes in the government budget are stabilizing and when not. No objection can, of course, be raised against the use of a bench-mark per se. It is only when this bench-mark is taken as the dividing line between what is stabilizing and what is destabilizing, or "perverse," that there arises ground for concern.

Lusher's coefficient of flexibility, ϕ, would indicate a neutral budget when the average rates of taxation and government expenditures relative to the gross national product each remain constant. If his coefficient, ϕ, has a positive value it merely indicates that the ratio of government expenditures to gross national product rose and/or the ratio of revenues to gross national product fell. What we have, then, is an assumption that the effect of governments' budgets on gross national product is neutral if the absolute amounts of both expenditures and taxes fall in proportion to the national product. This implies that any budget deficit will decline in size as gross national product declines. An initially balanced budget will be balanced at a lower level after the decline in gross national product. However, unless specific assumptions as to the behavior of investment have been made and unless government expenditures are assumed to consist entirely of transfer expenditures, considerations arising from the balanced-budget theorem suggest that an equivalent fall in government expenditures and taxes, such as occurs under the proportional tax-expenditure system used as a bench-mark by Lusher, is not neutral in its effect on the level of gross national product. Even when Lusher's ϕ has a positive value it does not rule out a declining level of government expenditures *and* a declining deficit.

To repeat, it is not my intention to question the use of a bench-mark and the logic underlying the coefficients derived therefrom. I believe, however, that Lusher's coefficients may lend themselves to misinterpretation, and I am concerned because Lusher himself appears to have taken his bench-mark to be the dividing line between stabilizing and destabilizing budget effects.

DANIEL M. HOLLAND, National Bureau of Economic Research

I am not sure that Lusher's claim that "Though the figures are still tentative, their general magnitudes are probably accurate enough to permit evaluations" can be strongly put forward. In particular, I find difficulty in evaluating the ϕ found for the corporation income tax.

One of Lusher's most startling findings is the very high coefficient of stabilizing effectiveness of the federal corporation income tax. In every period of the hypothetical recession the corporation income tax has a stabilizing effectiveness at least twice as great as the federal personal income tax. This is an important conclusion, and one that is not completely expected. How firmly can it be held?

As I understand his procedure, Lusher measures the stabilizing effectiveness of the components of our revenue system by applying the same c (marginal rate of change in consumers' expenditures relative to disposable income) to each component of the tax system. The use of this technique means that the greater stabilizing effectiveness of the corporate income tax as compared with the personal income tax is to be found in greater rate flexibility of the former.

But, as Richard Goode points out elsewhere in this volume, "The reasoning that equates built-in flexibility of tax yield with automatic stabilization does not seem to be fully applicable to the corporate income tax. The identification is justifiable for the individual income tax on the plausible assumption that consumer expenditures ordinarily respond promptly to changes in disposable income. An analogous assumption regarding business investment is not admissible." Therefore, before we accept Lusher's finding on the relative stabilizing effectiveness of the corporation income tax, we must be convinced that it is reasonable to apply the same c to changes in the effective rate of corporate taxation (tax revenue related to gross national income) that is applied to other components of the tax system.

Setting aside this difficulty about the appropriate c, another problem remains. In pursuing this I have experimented a little with some of the findings presented to this conference.

Pechman finds that the built-in flexibility of the individual income tax base in terms of total adjusted gross income is .65 and the marginal tax rate is about .27. If total adjusted gross income runs at about .7 of GNP (the figure suggested by Hart), then for every $10 billion decline in GNP, personal income tax revenue will fall by $1.23 billion.

A set of arbitrary but currently reasonable figures for the relevant variables would include GNP of $370 billion, personal tax collections of $30 billion, and corporate tax collections of $20 billion. With a $10 billion decline in GNP, Δr for the personal income tax will be

$$\frac{30}{370} - \frac{28.77}{360} = .001164$$

For the corporate income tax to have a ϕ twice as great as this, its Δr would have to be .002328. Therefore, corporate income tax collections will have to fall by $1.38 billion. (These figures conform fairly well with Lusher's model. With the corporate tax at 52 per cent, a decline in tax liability of $1.38 billion implies a fall of $2.65 billion in corporate profits. Lusher's model assumes that "Corporate profits plus inventory valuation adjustment . . . move with the private nonfarm gross national product, at a marginal rate of roughly one-fourth.")

When it comes to evaluating the meaning of ϕ, I am a little puzzled. Does it seem reasonable to conclude that a tax which "releases" $1.38 billion has twice the stabilizing effectiveness of a tax which "releases" $1.23 billions? How shall we, then, in concrete terms, evaluate the meaning of ϕ?

CHARLES L. SCHULTZE

In the last few paragraphs of his comment Holland presents a paradox apparently resulting from the relative ϕ's (flexibility coefficients) calculated by Lusher for the corporate and personal tax structure.

Assuming a $370 billion GNP, $30 billion in personal taxes, and $20 billion in corporate taxes, Holland then calculates the change in personal taxes attendant upon a $10 billion decline in GNP. This is found to be $1.23 billion and Lusher's Δr is then .001164;

$$\frac{30}{370} - \frac{28.77}{360} = .001164$$

Since Lusher calculates a corporate tax ϕ roughly twice as large as the personal tax ϕ, the corporate Δr would also have to be twice as great, i.e. .002328, and the decline in corporate taxes $1.38 billion;

$$\frac{20}{370} - \frac{18.62}{360} = .002328 \text{ (see footnote 1)}$$

Holland then asks how the stabilizing effectiveness of a tax which "releases" $1.38 billion can be twice as great as that of a tax which "releases" $1.23 billion.

This apparent paradox is easily resolved when it is remembered that Lusher's ϕ measures flexibility of the "actual" system *relative to a "zero flexibility" system in which all Δr's are zero as GNP*

---

[1] This checks out well with Lusher's model, which assumes a 52 per cent corporate tax rate and roughly a 25 per cent marginal rate of profits on GNP.

changes. Thus the relative ϕ's of two taxes are measures of the relative release of funds in the actual system (Lusher's Y_1 and Y_2) compared with the release which would have occurred in a zero flexibility system (Lusher's Y_{12}).

This can be shown from Holland's figures:

(1) Personal taxes, $\quad Y_1 = \dfrac{30}{370}$; $r = .08108$

Personal taxes, $\quad Y_{12} = \dfrac{29.19}{360}$; $r = .08108$, i.e. $\Delta r = 0$

Personal taxes, $\quad Y_2 = \dfrac{28.77}{360}$; $r = .079916$

Δ personal taxes, $\quad Y_{12} - Y_2 = \$.42$ billion

(2) Corporate taxes, $\quad Y_1 = \dfrac{20}{370}$; $r = .05405$

Corporate taxes, $\quad Y_{12} = \dfrac{19.46}{360}$; $r = .05405$, i.e. $\Delta r = 0$

Corporate taxes, $\quad Y_2 = \dfrac{18.62}{360}$; $r = .051722$

Δ corporate taxes, $Y_{12} - Y_2 = \$.84$ billion

Thus the release of corporate taxes in the "actual" system (Y_1, Y_2) is $\$.84$ billion greater than in the "zero flexibility" system (Y_{12}), while the release of personal taxes in the "actual" system is $\$.42$ billion greater than in the "zero flexibility" system. Hence, measured not in terms of their actual movements, but rather in terms of their difference from a hypothetical zero flexibility case, corporate taxes release twice as much in funds as personal taxes.

Earlier in his comment Holland questions the large ϕ for corporate taxes on the grounds that Lusher's model implies that corporate tax reductions have the same effect in stimulating expenditures as do personal tax reductions. He also quotes Goode on the same point.

Again remembering that Lusher's ϕ measures flexibility relative to a system in which all Δr's are zero as GNP changes, there is ample justification for his treatment of corporate tax reductions, given his model.

The corporate profit function in Lusher's model postulates a marginal rate of corporate profits on GNP greater than the average rate; i.e corporate profits $= CP = m + nY$, with m being a *negative* constant. In the "actual" system, corporate tax rates are constant and corporate taxes $= R(m + nY)$. However, the zero flexibility system is defined as one in which Δr (r being measured in this case against Y) equals zero with changes in Y. Hence corporate taxes in $Y_{12} = p + R(m + nY)$ and p must be a *positive* constant equal to Rm so that $p + Rm = 0$; corporate taxes equal RnY; and the average rate of corporate taxes on GNP is thus constant. With a positive constant in the corporate tax equation we get a regressive corporate tax structure. As GNP declines in the Y_{12} system the greater than average fall in corporate profits is offset by an increasing average effective corporate tax rate resulting in a constant corporate tax yield relative to GNP.

However, in Lusher's set of equations the function for business saving is the same for both the "actual" and the "zero flexibility" systems, i.e. $b + sY$. Hence a different corporate tax function in the two systems is added to a business savings function which is the same in both systems, indicating that corporate profits *before taxes* in the two systems are different,[2] i.e. the m and n of the Y_1, Y_2 system are different from the m and n of the Y_{12} system.

The difference in corporate taxes between the two systems is thus seen to turn up in personal income and has the same effect as a difference in personal taxes in terms of its effect on consumption. Lusher has measured the flexibility contribution of corporate taxes by assuming that the difference between the actual corporate tax rate and the one implicit in a zero flexibility system would be reflected in a difference in profits before taxes and not in business savings. The validity of this thesis rests, of course, on the incidence of corporate taxes, with Lusher's equations postulating that, as between the two systems, the different rates of change in corporate tax yields with respect to changes in GNP are reflected in different rates of change in personal income with respect to changes in GNP.

REPLY BY HOLLAND

I did not intend to imply that Lusher was incorrect within the context of his model. I hoped to elicit a more explicit and developed explanation of why this particular method of measuring stabilizing effectiveness was chosen in preference to and to the exclusion of others.

It still seems to me that in evaluating the stabilizing effectiveness

[2] We leave out the treatment of dividends for the sake of simplicity. Their inclusion would not alter the results.

of a tax the absolute amount by which it "buttresses" spending is a very relevant consideration, and one on which a set of relative rankings could be based. In these terms, with taxes ranked on the basis of their total stabilization effect rather than their stabilization effect relative to the proportional tax system bench-mark, the stabilizing effectiveness of the corporate and personal income taxes would not be as divergent as in Lusher's paper.

Something has been left out of ϕ, making it, in a sense, too refined. One salient piece of information—the relative importance of each tax in the revenue structure—is to some extent obscured, because ϕ deals only with offsets over and above those that a proportional tax system would provide. It is equally important to know how much of a given decline in GNP actually would be curtailed by each component of the tax system. The value for each tax would then be a function both of its flexibility of yield and its absolute size. In other words, is it not important to know that, given the contours of Lusher's model, in absolute terms the personal and corporate income taxes have just about the same strength in cushioning a potential decline in GNP? The greater revenue flexibility of the corporate tax is counterbalanced by the larger absolute amount of personal income tax.

Some special features of Lusher's model apparently help to account for the relatively high stabilizing effectiveness of the corporation income tax. For one thing, as Schultze points out, the "proportional" (with respect to GNP) tax system requires the unlikely (the adjective is mine) condition of a corporate tax structure regressive in relation to its own base. In the "actual" system, on the other hand, the corporate tax is proportional with respect to its own base. Therefore, is not the result in the "actual" system compared with an unreal base, and is not some of the strength of the ϕ of the corporation income tax explained by the fact that a proportional tax is contrasted with a regressive levy? The particular bench-mark chosen imparts unjustified vigor to the corporate tax's ϕ.

How is it that *"The difference in corporate taxes between the two systems is thus seen to turn up in personal income* and [have] the same effect as a difference in personal taxes in terms of its effect on consumption"? Schultze, in correspondence with me, has elaborated on the possibilities in this connection. As he explains it: "Undistributed corporate profits before tax (i.e. corporate profits before tax minus dividends) are different in his two systems precisely by the amount of corporate taxes. Personal income is statistically equal to GNP minus certain deductions, one of which, in Lusher's system, is corporate undistributed profits before tax. Since the decline in corporate undistributed profits *after* tax is the *same* in the actual as in the bench-mark system, and the corporate tax decline is *greater* in the actual than in the bench-mark system, the difference in tax declines shows up as a difference in the decline in corporate profits before tax (i.e. profits before tax decline *less* in the bench-mark system than in the actual system). This in turn means that personal income relative to GNP declines *more* in the bench-mark than in the actual system. This may be worked out in one or a combination of four ways (at least): (1) Wage rate changes may be different in the actual relative to the bench-mark system (rise more or fall less); (2) price changes may be different as between the two systems; (3) dividend changes may differ between the two systems; or (4) employers may be more willing to hold on to their labor force temporarily in the case of the actual system and its greater tax decline."

These various possibilities all imply something about corporate tax incidence. For example, (1) assumes the tax is shifted backward to the suppliers of services; (2) follows if the tax is shifted forward; and (4) implies, apparently, that the corporation income tax rests solely on distributed earnings. All these incidence assumptions are, of course, supportable. But what is probably the most valid assumption, particularly in the short run—that the incidence of the corporation income tax is primarily on profits—is not found in this list,[1] because it is ruled out by the postulated equality of after-tax corporate savings in the two systems. But if we take the incidence of the corporation tax to be (in whole or in part) on profits, then both dividends and retained earnings would be affected. In the case discussed by Schultze both would be higher in the "actual" then in the "proportional" system, so personal income in the "actual" system would not exceed personal income in the "proportional" bench-mark by as much as Lusher's model would have it.

It appears, then, that the failure to fit into the model what is probably the most widely accepted view of the incidence of the corporation income tax, is part of the explanation of its relatively high ϕ. Or to put it somewhat differently, as long as the incidence

[1] Richard B. Goode, who has devoted considerable time to this problem, recognizing that in view of all the complexities an unqualified answer is impossible, nonetheless concludes that "For both analytical and policy purposes, the most important conclusion is that the initial or short-run incidence is largely on corporate profits." Richard B. Goode, *The Corporation Income Tax*, Wiley, 1951, p. 72.

of the corporation income tax is to some degree on retained earnings, then the corporate tax's ϕ from Lusher's model is too high.

I would like to conclude on a note of agreement. A number of letters have passed between Schultze and myself, in the course of which some common ground has emerged. He has summarized the points on which we both agree as follows:

"1. The 'ϕ's' calculated by Mr. Lusher result from a comparison of income-generated tax yield changes in the 'actual' economic system with tax yield changes in a 'bench-mark' system where all taxes are proportional to GNP.

"2. The large 'ϕ' for corporate taxes results from two features of Mr. Lusher's model.

(a) He is comparing the actual corporate tax structure (taxes roughly proportional to profits) with a bench-mark system in which corporate taxes are regressive on profits (but proportional to GNP).

(b) An income-generated decline in corporate tax yields in the actual system is therefore relatively larger than a similarly generated decline in the bench-mark system. The difference between the two declines is reflected in a relative difference in personal income between the two systems.

"3. With respect to the incidence of corporate taxes this implies that differing marginal rates of corporate taxes lead to differing marginal rates of personal income relative to GNP, rather than to differing marginal rates of *after-tax* profits relative to GNP."

YIELD OF THE INDIVIDUAL INCOME TAX
DURING A RECESSION

Joseph A. Pechman, council of economic advisers

Although the individual income tax is of relatively recent origin in this country, it is now the most important single source of federal revenues. Despite its present importance, the full revenue potentialities of the individual income tax have been recognized only recently. For almost thirty years after its adoption, exemptions were high and relatively few people were subject even to the starting tax rate, let alone the higher graduated rates. In the early 1940's, as a result of the urgent need for revenues in World War II, personal exemptions were reduced and tax rates were increased, especially in the low and middle income brackets. At the same time, money incomes increased substantially. In combination, the lower exemptions, higher tax rates, and higher incomes increased the yield of the individual income tax from about $1 billion in 1939 to $17 billion in 1945. Since the end of the war, exemptions have been increased somewhat, but tax rates have remained high even by wartime standards. In addition, incomes have continued to increase. As a result, individual income tax liabilities have almost doubled in the past seven years—from a little over $16 billion in 1946 to an estimated $32 billion in 1953.

Almost as important as the change in the structure of the tax has been the change in the methods of tax payment. Prior to 1943, individuals had the option of paying their taxes in four equal installments in the year following the receipt of income. Now taxes are withheld currently from wages and salaries; individuals with other incomes are required to estimate their liabilities and to pay their taxes in four installments beginning on April 15th of the current year and ending on January 15th of the following year. Two important by-products of this current-payment system are that it synchronizes tax payments closely with receipt of income and that it permits tax rates to be raised or lowered at any time during the year, with assurance that the changes will affect disposable incomes of most taxpayers almost immediately. These features of the individual income tax make it admirably suited for economic stabilization purposes.

Both the revenue potential of the individual income tax and its adaptability to changing economic conditions were illustrated dramatically during the Korean emergency. In June 1950 the Congress was engaged in a revision of the tax system which had been promised since the end of World War II. An excise tax bill was then in process and the House of Representatives had already voted a $1 billion tax reduction. The greatly increased revenue needs of the emergency were imposed in the midst of this atmosphere of tax reduction. As an interim measure, the bill was quickly rewritten in the Senate and, within a few weeks, the excise tax reductions were eliminated, and corporation and individual income tax rates were raised by $4.6 billion in a full year. Of this total yield, the individual income tax contributed $2.9 billion.[1] The act was approved by the President on September 23, 1950, and the higher withholding rates became effective October 1, 1950.

Again, in 1951, the individual income tax was called upon to produce additional revenues. Under the 1951 act, effective November 1 of that year, tax rates in all the major categories of the federal tax system were increased to produce $5.4 billion in a full year.[2] The individual income tax contributed $2.5 billion of this additional yield.[3]

Even though the individual income tax remained unchanged between the fall of 1951 and the end of 1953, its yield increased as incomes rose. At 1951 income levels the yield of the 1953 rates and exemptions would have been approximately $27 billion, but they produced $32 billion in 1953. During the same period, total adjusted gross incomes in the United States increased from $227 billion to almost $252.5 billion. Thus the $25.5 billion increase in total incomes was associated with a rise in individual income tax liabilities of $5 billion; "built-in flexibility" therefore averaged $1.9 billion for every $10 billion increase in total incomes, or .19.[4]

[1] "The Revenue Act of 1950," Dept. of the Treasury, mimeographed, December 20, 1950.
[2] "The Revenue Act of 1951," Dept. of the Treasury, mimeographed, November 14, 1951.
[3] The combined $5.4 billion increase in individual income taxes between October 1950 and November 1951 may appear to be small in absolute terms, but it is actually a substantial fraction—one-fifth—of the rise in personal incomes in this thirteen-month period.
[4] The term "built-in flexibility" should be distinguished from "elasticity." Built-in flexibility equals $\Delta T/\Delta Y$, while elasticity equals

$$\Delta T/T \cdot Y/\Delta Y$$

where T is tax liability and Y is income. The figures cited above yield an elasticity of 1.6 (using the average 1951–1953 levels for T and Y).

The built-in flexibility of the individual income tax as economic activity drops cannot be estimated precisely, since we have had over a dozen years of almost sustained rise in incomes. However, a workable approximation can be obtained on the basis of the behavior of the individual income tax in the recent past. The basic data needed for the analysis are available in government publications. The problem is to select from the great mass of information the materials which are required to measure changes in the components of the individual income tax structure as incomes change. Part 1 will be devoted to this analysis.

In Part 2 we will attempt to show how the built-in flexibility of the individual income tax can be supplemented by discretionary changes in rates and exemptions. Our objective is to determine the direct revenue effects of these discretionary measures. An evaluation of their potential contribution to the maintenance of individual spending is beyond the scope of this paper.

The results of the analysis may be summarized briefly as follows:

1. Even though personal exemptions were somewhat higher than they were during World War II, the individual income tax base (i.e. total income after deductions and exemptions) reached an all-time high in 1953. It is estimated that the base in 1953 was about $117 billion, or 46 per cent of total adjusted gross income in the United States.

2. The $32 billion yield of the individual income tax in 1953 was also an all-time high. The tax reductions which became effective on January 1, 1954 reduced liabilities by $3 billion, or almost 10 per cent, assuming 1953 income levels.

3. Based on the record in the post-World War II period, the built-in flexibility of the individual income tax *base* is roughly .65. That is, a $10 billion change in total adjusted gross income produced a $6.5 billion change in the tax base. Our data indicate that the built-in flexibility of the tax base has not changed significantly since 1946, even though total incomes have risen by almost $100 billion.

4. Under 1953 tax rates the average effective rate applying to the tax base would have been roughly 27 per cent in each year since 1948. (While this result may be surprising, it can be explained by the fact that a large proportion of the additions to the tax base have been concentrated in the lowest tax brackets.) Since the *average* rate remained about the same during the period 1948–1953, the *marginal* rate applying to additions to the tax base was about equal to the average rate.

5. Since both the built-in flexibility of the *base* and the marginal

rate appear to have been constant, the built-in flexibility of the individual income *tax* was roughly constant. At 1953 rates it was between .17 and .18 (.65 × .27). Due to the 10 per cent tax reduction at the beginning of 1954, the built-in flexibility of the tax at 1954 rates will probably be 10 per cent lower, or between .15 and .16. Thus at 1954 rates the individual income tax will automatically offset $1.5 or 1.6 billion of a $10 billion decline in total adjusted gross income.

6. At 1953 income levels and 1954 rates, a reduction of one percentage point in the tax rates in all surtax brackets would reduce tax liabilities by $1.2 billion; an increase in exemptions from $600 to $700 per capita would reduce liabilities by $2.5 billion. In combination these changes in rates and exemptions would reduce tax liabilities by $3.6 billion. However, as incomes decline, built-in flexibility would reduce the size of the tax base and hence the tax reduction that might be obtained from rate and exemption changes. For example, if total adjusted gross incomes fall by $50 billion, the combined effect of a $100 increase in exemptions and a general rate reduction of one percentage point would be $2.8 billion.

7. Moderate rate and exemption changes combined with the effect of built-in flexibility can provide fairly substantial offsets to moderate declines in income. For example, if adjusted gross incomes drop by $25 billion, or 10 per cent below 1953 levels, built-in flexibility would reduce tax liabilities by $4 billion and a one percentage point rate reduction combined with an increase in exemptions to $700 would reduce them another $3.2 billion. In total, the offset would be $7.2 billion, or almost 30 per cent of the $25 billion drop in total income.

8. The larger the decline in individual incomes, the more difficult it becomes to offset the decline through the individual income tax alone. For example, to offset 30 per cent of a $50 billion drop in total income below 1953 levels, it would be necessary to raise exemptions to $700 per capita and to reduce the tax rates in all brackets by 7 percentage points. Much more drastic changes in rates and exemptions would be required to offset as much as one-quarter or one-third of a larger drop in income.

1. Built-in Flexibility of the Individual Income Tax

In order to trace the changes in the historical record of the individual income tax, the tax base since the end of World War II is converted to a comparable basis by adjusting for changes in exemptions and deductions. Yields of the adjusted base in each year since

1948 (when the present exemptions and income splitting were adopted) are then estimated on the basis of 1953 tax rates. In this way we measure not only the built-in flexibility for the individual income tax as a whole, but also the relative contributions of changes in the tax base and the graduated tax rates to this flexibility.

COVERAGE OF TAX RETURNS

Changes in the individual income tax base depend primarily on changes in the total amount of *adjusted gross income* received. This is the sum of all taxable sources of income in a given year before allowing for personal exemptions and deductions. It includes wages and salaries, interest (other than that paid by state and local governments), dividends, rents and royalties, business incomes, capital gains, and a number of other minor sources.[5] The principal items of personal income that are specifically exempt are nonmoney and imputed incomes and transfer payments.

A good estimate of the adjusted gross incomes reported by individuals filing returns can be obtained from the annual tabulations in *Statistics of Income,* but relatively little is known about the amounts not reported.[6] If the *Statistics of Income* total is compared with an income aggregate, such as the Department of Commerce estimate of personal income, a very large "gap" is found. For example, personal income exceeded total adjusted gross income reported on tax returns by an average of $46 billion or about 22 per cent in the period 1948–1950. Actually, a sizable portion of the gap can be accounted for by differences in definition. There is, of course, evidence of nonreporting and underreporting of income on tax returns, but the unadjusted gap overstates these amounts by a substantial margin.

To reconcile the Department of Commerce estimates of personal income with adjusted gross income, two sets of adjustments must be made: first, items included in personal income but not subject to tax must be deducted from personal income; second, several items included in taxable income but not in personal income must be added.[7]

[5] E.g. incomes from estates and trusts, annuities and pensions (other than old age and survivors' insurance and railroad retirement benefits), gambling winnings, competitive prizes, and awards.

[6] The *Statistics of Income* tabulations are based on a large sample of tax returns and the sampling error of the income aggregate is small. For a discussion of the sampling procedures see *Statistics of Income for 1947,* Bureau of Internal Revenue, Part 1, 1953, pp. 44–51.

[7] The laborious job of reconciling personal income and adjusted gross income was pioneered by Selma Goldsmith. See her article "Appraisal of Basic Data Available for Constructing Income Size Distributions," *Studies in Income and Wealth, Volume Thirteen,* National Bureau of Economic Research, 1951, pp. 266–373.

The most important items which are deducted are transfer payments, other labor income, income in kind, imputed interest, and nontaxable military pay and allowances. The most important additions are employee contributions to social insurance and net gains from the sale of assets. The adjustments are illustrated in detail in Appendix Table A-1 for one year (1948). Some of the adjustments may be estimated fairly accurately and others are little better than informed guesses. Fortunately, the largest adjustments can be obtained directly from the income accounts published by the Department of Commerce and from *Statistics of Income*.[8]

Total adjusted gross income and personal income are compared in Table 1 for the years 1939 through 1953.[9] In every year since 1939,

TABLE 1

Comparison of Total Personal and Adjusted Gross Income, 1939–1953

(*dollars in billions*)

	PERSONAL INCOME	ADJUSTED GROSS INCOME	DIFFERENCE	
			Amount	Per Cent of Personal Income
1939	$ 72.6	$ 63.4	$ 9.2	12.7%
1940	78.3	69.1	9.2	11.7
1941	95.3	84.0	11.3	11.9
1942	122.7	105.9	16.8	13.7
1943	150.3	127.7	22.6	15.0
1944	165.9	136.8	29.1	17.5
1945	171.9	139.9	32.0	18.6
1946	177.7	155.1	22.6	12.7
1947	191.0	170.9	20.1	10.5
1948	209.5	184.4	25.1	12.0
1949	205.9	181.9	24.0	12.1
1950	226.7	200.4	26.3	11.6
1951	254.3	226.9 a	27.4	10.8
1952	269.7	240.2 a	29.5	10.9
1953	284.0 a	252.4 a	31.6	11.1

a Estimates based on incomplete data.

personal income has exceeded adjusted gross income. Percentage-wise, the differences are largest in 1942–1945, when much of the pay of members of the armed forces was not subject to tax. For the other

[8] Except for employee contributions for social insurance, the estimate of taxable income not included in personal income covers only amounts reported by individuals filing returns. Since nonfilers also receive such incomes, the estimate somewhat understates total adjusted gross income.

[9] The 1953 estimate of adjusted gross income assumes total personal income of $284 billion.

years, adjusted gross income averaged 11 to 13 per cent less than personal income.[10]

Table 2, which compares the adjusted gross income reported by all individuals filing returns (including nontaxables) with the total adjusted gross income shown in Table 1, measures the changes in the coverage of federal tax returns since 1939. The striking feature of this

TABLE 2

Proportion of Total Adjusted Gross Income Reported on Individual
Income Tax Returns, 1939–1953

(*dollars in billions*)

	TOTAL ADJUSTED GROSS INCOME	ADJUSTED GROSS INCOME REPORTED ON TAX RETURNS	
		Amount	Per Cent of Total
1939	$ 63.4	$ 25.2	39.7%
1940	69.1	39.4	57.0
1941	84.0	62.5	74.4
1942	105.9	84.9	80.2
1943	127.7	105.7	82.8
1944	136.8	116.5	85.2
1945	139.9	120.1	85.8
1946	155.1	134.1	86.5
1947	170.9	149.7	87.6
1948	184.4	163.5	88.7
1949	181.9	160.6	88.3
1950	200.4	179.1	89.4
1951 [a]	226.9	205.9	90.7
1952 [a]	240.2	219.2	91.3
1953 [a]	252.4	231.4	91.7

[a] Estimates based on incomplete data.

table is the sharp rise in income covered by tax returns. In 1939 about 40 per cent of all adjusted income was reported on tax returns. The percentage rose sharply between 1939 and 1942 and then more gradually thereafter; in 1953, income tax returns probably covered about 92 per cent of total adjusted gross income. The trend was not reversed when exemptions were increased in 1946 and 1948, because millions of individuals continue to file, even though they are not taxable, in order to claim refunds on account of overwithholding or

[10] It should be noted that the concept of adjusted gross income dates back to 1944. For each of the prior years the estimates are derived from the definitions of taxable income then in effect.

overpayment of tax on estimated declarations.[11] Thus the upward sweep of income overwhelmed the effect of the increased exemptions, and the income coverage of tax returns continued to increase.[12]

DERIVATION OF THE TAX BASE

The derivation of the individual income tax base is shown in Appendix Table A-2, again using the year 1948 for illustrative purposes. This table duplicates the steps in the computation of taxable income on page 3 of the individual income tax Form 1040. From the adjusted gross income of taxable individuals we subtract personal deductions and personal exemptions and the amount of capital gains subject to the flat alternative tax rate.[13] The result is "surtax net income," which

---

[11] Actually, all persons with gross incomes of $600 or more are required to file returns, whether those incomes are taxable or not. However, the incentive provided by the prospective refund check is much more significant for most nontaxable individuals than the legal requirement to file. For the year 1950, 62 per cent of the 14.9 million nontaxable individuals who filed federal income tax returns received refunds.

[12] A discussion of the gap between personal and adjusted gross income which remains after adjustments are made for underreporting of income is beyond the scope of this paper. However, by pushing the above calculations a little further, a rough outside limit may be obtained.

Independent evidence on underreporting was made available for the first time by the Audit Control Program conducted by the Internal Revenue Service for the year 1948. (The preliminary results were summarized by Marius Farrioletti in the *National Tax Journal*, March 1952, pp. 65–78.) This study indicates that, if every return filed in 1948 were audited, the government would collect 9 per cent more tax than the total amount voluntarily reported, or 8 per cent of the correct tax liability. A substantial proportion of this tax deficiency is the result of errors in claiming exemptions and deductions and mathematical errors, all of which affect the tax liability without altering adjusted gross income. Accordingly, the underreporting of adjusted gross income is substantially less than 8 per cent —probably in the neighborhood of about 4 per cent.

Subtracting this 4 per cent from the 11 per cent of adjusted gross income not covered by tax returns in 1948 (see Table 2), the gap is reduced to about 7 per cent. Even this percentage is too high, because it does not take into account the incomes of persons not required to file. According to an estimate by Ulric Weil, these nonfilers received roughly 2 per cent of our estimated adjusted gross income in 1948 (*Journal of the American Statistical Association*, September 1950, p. 445). This leaves a discrepancy of no more than 5 per cent. The actual discrepancy may be less than 5 per cent because: (1) the sample of the Internal Revenue Service was confined to persons who filed returns, and therefore it failed to pick up the incomes of those who did not file; and (2) it is hardly likely that the field audits disclosed all the incomes not reported by taxpayers.

It should be noted that the 5 per cent estimate is an average which conceals significant variations for different income sources. Selma Goldsmith (*op. cit.*) found that income tax returns in 1946 covered 95 per cent of total wages, 76 per cent of dividends, 71 per cent of entrepreneurial incomes, and only 45 per cent of rents and 37 per cent of interest.

[13] As a final adjustment, the small amount of income of taxable fiduciaries which is subject to the individual income tax rates is added to the taxable income of individuals.

is equivalent to the individual income tax *base* for all practical purposes.[14]

The relationship between total adjusted gross income and surtax net income is shown in Table 3 for the years 1939–1953. The estimates of surtax net income were derived from *Statistics of Income* through 1950, the last year for which these tabulations are now available. To complete the series from 1951 through 1953, it was necessary to extrapolate the adjustments itemized in Appendix Table A-2.[15]

Table 3 shows the tremendous increase in the proportion of ad-

TABLE 3

Relationship between Total Adjusted Gross Income
and Surtax Net Income, 1939–1953

(*dollars in billions*)

	TOTAL ADJUSTED GROSS INCOME	SURTAX NET INCOME	
		Amount	Per Cent of Adjusted Gross Income
1939	$ 63.4	$ 7.5	11.8%
1940	69.1	11.0	15.9
1941	84.0	23.0	27.4
1942	105.9	36.3	34.3
1943	127.7	50.1	39.2
1944	136.8	55.3	40.4
1945	139.9	56.7	40.5
1946	155.1	64.8	41.8
1947	170.9	75.2	44.0
1948	184.4	74.6	40.5
1949	181.9	71.6	39.4
1950	200.5	83.9	41.8
1951 a	226.9	99.9	44.0
1952 a	240.2	109.0	45.4
1953 a	252.4	117.2	46.4

a Estimates based on incomplete data.

justed gross income subject to tax which resulted from the reductions in exemptions in the early 1940's and the persistent rise in income

[14] Although surtax net income differs from income subject to the normal tax rate, the difference is now very small. Beginning in 1946, all income subject to the surtax is also subject to the normal tax, except for "partially" tax-exempt interest and certain dividends of Federal Savings and Loan Associations. In aggregate, these items now amount to less than $100 million, or roughly .1 per cent of total surtax net income.

[15] For the year 1951, estimates by the Department of the Treasury were helpful as guides in the extrapolation. See the distribution given in the *Annual Report of the Secretary of the Treasury*, Fiscal Year 1952, Table VI, p. 483. For the years 1952 and 1953 the extrapolation is entirely my own.

since the beginning of World War II. In 1939 the tax base was $7.5 billion, or only 12 per cent of adjusted gross income; by 1947 it was $75 billion, or 44 per cent. The upward trend was interrupted by the increase in the per capita exemption from $500 to $600 in 1948 and by the slight fall in income in 1949. Beginning in 1950, however, the trend upward was reestablished as incomes rose. For 1953 it is estimated that the tax base was at an all-time peak of $117 billion, about 46 per cent of total adjusted gross income.

CORRECTION OF THE TAX BASE FOR CHANGES
IN EXEMPTIONS AND DEDUCTIONS

The important statutory changes that have affected the tax base in the post-World War II period are: an increase in the per capita exemption from $500 to $600, an allowance of an additional exemption of $600 for taxpayers who are sixty-five or over or blind, and an increase in the maximum standard deduction for single persons and married persons filing joint returns from $500 to $1,000. Since these provisions were enacted in 1948, it was necessary to adjust the 1946–1947 estimates of surtax net income to obtain a comparable series based on present exemptions and deductions.[16]

The corrected surtax net income series is compared with total adjusted gross income in Table 4. The effect of the adjustments in 1946 and 1947 is to give a series which rises continuously from 1946 through 1948, falls slightly in 1949 as a result of the small drop in incomes in that year, and then rises continuously from 1950 through 1953.

Over the entire period 1946–1953, total adjusted gross incomes rose from $155.1 to 252.4 billion, an increase of $97.3 billion. At 1953 exemptions and deductions, the tax base rose from $55.9 to 117.2 billion, an increase of $61.3 billion. Thus from 1946 to 1953 the tax base increased about $6.3 billion for every $10 billion increase in total adjusted gross income.

[16] The effect of the increase in the per capita exemption can be computed fairly accurately from the distribution of taxpayers by income classes and by exemption status published in *Statistics of Income*. See, for example, *Statistics of Income for 1947*, Part 1, Table 9. The increased standard deduction was taken into account by increasing the ratio of total deductions to adjusted gross income in 1946 and 1947 to the average ratio in the years 1948 and 1949. The effect of the additional exemption for the aged and the blind was more difficult to determine, since there are no statistics on the number of such taxpayers in 1946 and 1947. As a rough guide, it was assumed that the annual increase in the number of exemptions for the aged was the same in the two-year period 1946–1948 as it was between 1948 and 1949 and that there was no change in the number of exemptions for the blind between 1946 and 1948.

TABLE 4

Relationship between Total Adjusted Gross Income
and Surtax Net Income, Assuming 1953 Exemptions
and Deductions, 1946–1953

(*dollars in billions*)

	TOTAL ADJUSTED GROSS INCOME	SURTAX NET INCOME ASSUMING 1953 EXEMPTIONS AND DEDUCTIONS	
		Amount	Per Cent of Total Adjusted Gross Income
1946	$155.1	$ 55.9 [a]	36.0%
1947	170.9	65.7 [a]	38.4
1948	184.4	74.6	40.5
1949	181.9	71.6	39.4
1950	200.5	83.9	41.8
1951 [b]	226.9	99.9	44.0
1952 [b]	240.2	109.0	45.4
1953 [b]	252.4	117.2	46.4

[a] Adjusted for changes in exemptions and deductions under the Revenue Act of 1948.

[b] Estimates based on incomplete data.

These are average figures and therefore may cover up significant year-to-year variations. To determine whether such variations have in fact occurred, the ratios of the increase in the tax base to the increase in total adjusted gross income were computed for each year in the period 1946–1953 (see Table 5).[17]

As might be expected, this table shows some small, erratic changes from year to year, since the basic figures are not accurate enough to provide precise estimates. However, the ratios are remarkably stable, varying from a low of .61 for 1950–1951 to a high of .68 for 1951–1952. Equally important, the figures do not indicate any tendency to increase as incomes increased. We conclude that the built-in flexibility

[17] The change from 1948 to 1949 is not included in Table 5 because of the elimination of the tax exemption accorded to servicemen, effective January 1, 1949. As a result of this change, adjusted gross income was understated in 1948 relative to 1949. Surtax net income was probably not affected to the same extent, since much of the servicemen's salaries would have been absorbed by personal exemptions and deductions had they been taxable in 1948. Rough calculations indicate that the built-in flexibility of the tax base between the two years was probably in the neighborhood of .63, if this element of noncomparability is removed. This is within the range of the figures for the other years in the period 1946–1953, shown in the last column of Table 5.

of the tax base is roughly .6 to .7 for the income ranges covered by our data.

TABLE 5

Built-in Flexibility of the Individual Income Tax Base,
1946–1953

(*dollars in billions*)

	INCREASE Total Adjusted Gross Income [a]	Surtax Net Income [a]	RATIO OF INCREASE IN SURTAX NET INCOME TO INCREASE IN ADJUSTED GROSS INCOME
1946–1947	$15.8	$ 9.8	.62
1947–1948	13.5	8.9	.67
1949–1950	18.6	12.3	.66
1950–1951	26.4	16.0	.61
1951–1952	13.3	9.1	.68
1952–1953	12.2	8.2	.67

[a] Based on data in Table 4.

CORRECTION OF TAX LIABILITIES FOR CHANGES IN RATES

To measure the effect of the graduated rate structure on built-in flexibility, it is necessary to convert the individual income tax liabilities as given in *Statistics of Income* to a comparable series, assuming present rates, exemptions, and deductions. This conversion can be made on the basis of the estimated changes in tax liabilities prepared by the Department of the Treasury after the passage of the revenue bills enacted since 1948.[18] Appendix Table A-3 shows the steps in the procedure used to obtain the corrected series. This series extends back only to 1948, when income splitting and present exemptions and deductions were adopted.[19]

Table 6 compares the corrected tax liability figures with the tax base at present exemptions and deductions for the years 1948–1953. The average effective rates applying to the tax base in each year are shown in the last column of this table. Neglecting small variations, it appears that, at 1953 rates and exemptions, individual income tax

[18] See the summaries of the Revenue Acts of 1950 and 1951, cited in footnotes 1 and 2.

[19] It is possible, of course, to recompute the tax liability figures for 1946 and 1947, but this would require a long series of time-consuming computations to correct for the change in exemptions and for income splitting.

liabilities were roughly 27 per cent of the tax base, and this average rate apparently did not change significantly between 1948 and 1953.[20]

The fact that the *average* rate remained unchanged implies that the *marginal* rate on the additions to the tax base was about equal to this average rate. This may be surprising, because we are dealing with a graduated rate structure. Ordinarily, we would expect that the marginal rate would rise as incomes are pushed into higher surtax brackets. Actually, however, there is no basis for judging how the marginal rate will behave. It can go up or down, or remain constant, depending on the distribution of the increased income and the rate structure.

TABLE 6

Comparison of Total Tax Liabilities and Surtax Net Income, at 1953 Rates and Exemptions, 1948–1953

(*dollars in billions*)

	Tax Liability	Surtax Net Income	Effective Rate
1948	$20.2	$ 74.6	27.1%
1949	19.0	71.6	26.5
1950	22.9	83.9	27.3
1951	27.1	99.9	27.1
1952	29.5	109.0	27.1
1953	32.0	117.2	27.3

The constancy of the marginal rate under the present rate structure during the 1948–1953 period is, of course, a historical accident, and it may well be due to offsetting errors in the various approximations we were forced to make. However, it is not unreasonable in view of the following factors: (1) As incomes rise, practically all of the taxable incomes of those who become subject to tax for the first time are subject to the first bracket tax rate. (2) If it is assumed that adjusted gross incomes increase approximately proportionately throughout the income scale, the increase in *surtax* net income will be much larger for low- than for high-income taxpayers.[21] The changes in the relative distribution of income in the past few years were probably not large enough to overcome this tendency. (3) The surtax brackets

[20] An interesting by-product of this result is that the average effective rate exceeds the first bracket rate of 22.2 per cent by only 4.8 percentage points. This means that only about 18 per cent of the total tax yield (4.8 ÷ 27) is attributable to graduation above the first bracket.

[21] For example, assume two married taxpayers (each with two children) have adjusted gross incomes of $3,000 and $8,000 respectively. If their incomes in-

are so wide that few low-income taxpayers are likely to be pushed into higher brackets as their incomes increase.[22] Thus a large proportion of any increase in income is bound to fall in the two lowest brackets, where the rates are below the average rate.[23] Our finding that the average rate in 1953 was about the same as that in 1948 implies that the effect of graduation in the higher brackets was just enough to offset the effect of the additions to the tax base at the bottom of the scale.

Assuming that this conclusion is correct, the built-in flexibility of the individual income tax may be established within fairly narrow limits. Applying the 27 per cent marginal rate to the $6 to 7 billion increase in the tax base for every $10 billion increase in total adjusted gross incomes, we obtain an increase of $1.6 to 1.9 billion in *tax*. If, on the other hand, the marginal rate to be applied to the increase in the tax base differs from the effective rate, the range is increased. Since the first bracket rate is now 22.2 per cent, it is hardly likely that the marginal rate can be much lower than 25 per cent or much higher than 30 per cent. Applying the 25 per cent rate to the lower limit established for the built-in flexibility of the tax base ($6 billion) and the 30 per cent rate to the upper limit ($7 billion), we find that the individual income tax would have increased between $1.5 and 2.1 billion for every $10 billion increase in total adjusted gross incomes, if present tax rates had been applicable since 1948.

---

crease by 10 per cent, their surtax net incomes will increase by 90 per cent and 15 per cent respectively. This result was obtained as follows:

	Taxpayer A		Taxpayer B	
Adjusted gross income	$3,000	$3,300	$8,000	$8,800
Deductions (10 per cent)	300	330	800	880
Net income	$2,700	$2,970	$7,200	$7,920
Exemptions	2,400	2,400	2,400	2,400
Surtax net income	$ 300	$ 570	$4,800	$5,520
Per cent increase	–	90%	–	15%

[22] Since the enactment of income splitting in 1948, the brackets for married couples have been, in effect, doubled. Thus, whereas the statutory rate brackets cover $2,000 of taxable income at the bottom of the income scale, the actual rate brackets for married persons, after income splitting is taken into account, cover $4,000 of taxable income (see Appendix Table A-4). In terms of adjusted gross income, this means that a married man with no children remains taxable at the first bracket rate if his income varies from $1,333 to $5,778; if he has two children, he remains taxable at the first bracket if his income varies from $2,667 to $7,111. (These computations assume the taxpayer elects the optional standard deduction.)

[23] For 1953 the marginal rates in the first two brackets were 22.2 and 24.6 per cent (see Appendix Table A-4). As noted above, the average rate was 27 per cent.

In either case it seems clear that, at 1953 rates, built-in flexibility alone would offset no more than about 20 per cent of a change in total income. Our best guess is that the offset is more likely to be in the neighborhood of 17 or 18 per cent. Moreover, tax rates were reduced by almost 10 per cent beginning January 1, 1954. *It follows that, at 1954 tax rates, the offset due to built-in flexibility will probably be about 15 or 16 per cent.* This conclusion is based on data for a period of almost continuously rising incomes. I cannot predict whether it can be applied to a cyclical downswing. It seems clear, however, that only substantial changes in the relative distribution of income will alter the result significantly.

2. *Discretionary Changes in Rates and Exemptions*

As was demonstrated in the year following the outbreak of hostilities in Korea, rate changes can be employed to increase revenues substantially and quickly. They can be equally effective in reverse. If necessary, substantial additional reductions can be made by raising the personal exemptions. In combination, rate and exemption changes would greatly increase the offset to a drop in individual incomes which can be expected from built-in flexibility alone.

RATE REDUCTIONS

The effects of various types of rate reductions can be computed from a distribution of the tax base by rate brackets. The number of taxpayers and their surtax net incomes distributed by surtax net income classes are shown in columns 2 and 3 of Table 7, which is based on estimates for calendar year 1953.[24] The last five columns distribute the surtax net incomes by rate brackets.[25]

The shape of the distribution of surtax net incomes by rate brackets is very different from the distribution by size shown in column 3. Whereas taxpayers with surtax net incomes of less than $2,000 ac-

[24] In this table, married couples are counted as two taxpayers and their combined incomes are divided equally between the two spouses.

[25] For example, taxpayers with surtax net incomes between $2,000 and $4,000 received an estimated total of $27 billion. We know that they were taxed at the first bracket rate on their first $2,000, and at the second bracket rate on the remainder. Since there were 10 million taxpayers in the $2,000–4,000 bracket, $2,000 × 10 million, or $20 billion, was taxable at the first bracket rate and the remaining $7 billion was taxable at the second bracket rate. We proceed in this way for each bracket, multiplying the size of the bracket by the number of taxpayers; the entry for the last bracket is computed by subtracting the entries for all of the lower brackets from the total surtax net income in the class. The totals for the columns give the total amount of surtax net income which was taxable at the various bracket rates.

count for 45 per cent of total surtax net income, the first bracket accounts for 69 per cent of the total. By contrast, taxpayers with surtax net incomes of $8,000 or more account for 20 per cent of total surtax net income, but only 11 per cent is taxable at the rates applying to the brackets above $8,000.

TABLE 7

Estimated Distribution of Surtax Net Income by Size and by Rate Bracket, 1953

(*number of taxpayers in millions; surtax net income in billions*)

			DISTRIBUTION OF SURTAX NET INCOME BY RATE BRACKET				
SURTAX NET INCOME CLASS (1)	NUMBER OF TAXPAYERS a (2)	SURTAX NET INCOME (3)	$0–2,000 (22.2%) (4)	$2,000– 4,000 (24.6%) (5)	$4,000– 6,000 (29%) (6)	$6,000– 8,000 (34%) (7)	$8,000 & over (38–92%) (8)
$ 0–2,000	63.0	$ 53.0	$53.0				
2,000–4,000	10.0	27.0	20.0	$ 7.0			
4,000–6,000	2.0	9.0	4.0	4.0	$1.0		
6,000–8,000	.7	4.7	1.4	1.4	1.4	$ .5	
8,000 & over	1.3	23.5	2.6	2.6	2.6	2.6	$13.1
Total	77.0	$117.2	$81.0	$15.0	$5.0	$3.1	$13.1

a Married couples are counted as two taxpayers, each with half of the combined surtax net income.

Given the data in Table 7, it is simple to estimate the revenue effects of rate changes and their distribution by brackets. The following magnitudes may be helpful in judging the revenue potential of rate reductions:

1. Each percentage-point reduction in the rates in all brackets would reduce revenues at 1953 income levels by almost $1.2 billion.

2. A reduction of 1 percentage point in the first bracket rate would lose $810 million. By contrast, the same reduction in all tax rates above the first bracket would lose $360 million. Thus a reduction of 1 percentage point in the first bracket rate is equivalent to a reduction of about 2¼ percentage points in all other rates.

3. Reductions in the first bracket rate would be heavily concentrated in the lowest income classes. Of the $810 million loss resulting from a reduction of 1 percentage point in the first bracket rate, $530 million would go to taxpayers with surtax net incomes of less than $2,000 and $730 million to those with surtax net income of less than $4,000.

Since these figures are based on 1953 income levels they cannot be used directly to estimate the revenue loss from rate reductions if incomes decline. Under such circumstances built-in flexibility would reduce the size of the tax base and hence the tax reduction that might be expected from rate changes. For example, if total adjusted gross incomes fall from 1953 levels by $10 billion, the tax base will drop $6 to 7 billion. Using the midpoint of $6.5 billion, this means that the tax base would be reduced from $117.2 to 110.7 billion. Accordingly, the revenue loss from a reduction of 1 percentage point in all tax rates would be reduced from $1.17 to 1.1 billion. If adjusted gross incomes fall by as much as $50 billion, a 1-percentage-point rate reduction would reduce tax liabilities by only $850 million.

It is evident, however, that even small rate reductions could greatly enhance the effect of built-in flexibility in offsetting a drop in individual incomes. The combined effect under 1953 and 1954 tax rates is shown in Table 8.

TABLE 8

Revenue Effect of $10 Billion Decline in Adjusted Gross Incomes
Combined with a Rate Reduction of 1 Percentage Point

(*billions of dollars*)

	1953 Rates	1954 Rates
Reduction in taxes due to built-in flexibility	1.8	1.6
One-percentage-point reduction	1.2	1.1
Total reduction	3.0	2.7

Assuming a reduction of $10 billion in adjusted gross income, a general reduction of only 1 percentage point would increase the offset due to built-in flexibility by about two-thirds. Larger reductions in tax rates would, of course, provide correspondingly larger offsets.

INCREASES IN EXEMPTIONS

In 1953, taxable individuals probably claimed about 120 million exemptions on their returns. At $600 for each exemption, the total value of the allowance for exemptions is $72 billion. If exemptions were increased to $700 per capita, the value of these exemptions would rise by one-sixth, or $12 billion. However, not all of this increase would affect the tax base, because some taxpayers would "waste" part of it, i.e. they would not have sufficient taxable income to use all of the additional exemptions. Assuming the wastage is about 7 per cent,[26] the total reduction in the tax base due to a $100

[26] We do not know precisely how much this wastage would be. However, at 1948 income levels rough calculations based on *Statistics of Income* data indicate that it was in the neighborhood of 6 per cent, and it has probably increased somewhat because of the large number of entries into the lower tax brackets since then.

increase in the per capita exemption would be $11.2 billion (.93 × $12 billion) at 1953 income levels.

The marginal rate applying to this reduction in the tax base is probably roughly equal to the rate in the second surtax bracket. Thus the rate to be applied is approximately 25 per cent under the 1953 rate schedule and 22 per cent under the rate schedule for 1954 (see Appendix Table A-4). The revenue loss due to a $100 increase in the per capita exemption is, therefore, $2.8 billion at 1953 rates and $2.5 billion at 1954 rates.

The revenue effect of successive $100 increases in exemptions can be computed in a similar manner.[27] The reductions in the tax base and the revenue loss resulting from increases up to $1,000 per capita are summarized in Table 9 (assuming 1953 income levels).

TABLE 9

Revenue Effect of Successive Increases in Income Tax Exemptions

PER CAPITA EXEMPTION	CUMULATIVE REDUCTION IN TAX BASE	CUMULATIVE REVENUE LOSS	
		At 1953 Tax Rates	At 1945 Tax Rates
		(billions of dollars)	
$ 700	$11.2	$2.8	$2.5
800	20.8	5.3	4.6
900	29.1	7.4	6.4
1,000	36.4	9.2	8.0

COMBINED EFFECTS OF RATE AND EXEMPTION CHANGES
AND BUILT-IN FLEXIBILITY

The combined effects of rate and exemption changes and built-in flexibility, assuming reductions in total adjusted gross incomes ranging from 5 to 25 per cent below the 1953 level, are shown in Table 10. Since the tax rates were reduced at the end of 1953, the computations are based on 1954 rates. The top line of Table 10 shows the reductions in tax liabilities due to built-in flexibility. The remaining figures indicate the combined effect of rate and exemption changes, *including* the reductions due to built-in flexibility. For example, if incomes decline by $25 billion below 1953 levels, or 10 per cent, individual income tax liabilities would fall automatically by $4 billion. If exemptions were raised to $700 per capita and all rates were reduced by

[27] That is, adjust the total value of exemptions for wastage of about 7 per cent and then apply the second surtax rate to estimate the revenue loss. The percentage allowance for wastage and the marginal tax rate should fall somewhat with each successive increase in exemptions, but the effect would be small and our figures are too rough to warrant this refinement.

140

5 percentage points, tax liabilities would be reduced by an additional $6.8 billion; accordingly, the total reduction would be $10.8 billion.[28]

TABLE 10

Combined Effect of Built-in Flexibility and Rate and Exemption Changes on Individual Income Tax Liabilities [a]

(*dollars in billions*)

REDUCTION IN TAX RATES	REDUCTION IN TAX LIABILITIES ASSUMING TOTAL ADJUSTED GROSS INCOME FALLS BY:				
	$12.5 (5%)	$25 (10%)	$37.5 (15%)	$50 (20%)	$62.5 (25%)
No Change in Exemptions					
0 [b]	$ 2.0	$ 4.0	$ 6.0	$ 8.0	$10.0
1%	3.1	5.0	6.9	8.8	10.8
3	5.3	7.0	8.8	10.5	12.3
5	7.5	9.1	10.6	12.2	13.8
7	9.6	11.1	12.5	13.9	15.4
10	12.9	14.1	15.3	16.4	17.7
Increase in Exemptions to $700 per Capita					
0	$ 4.4	$ 6.3	$ 8.1	$10.0	$11.9
1%	5.4	7.2	9.0	10.8	12.6
3	7.3	9.0	10.6	12.3	13.9
5	9.3	10.8	12.3	13.8	15.3
7	11.3	12.6	14.0	15.3	16.7
10	14.2	15.4	16.5	17.6	18.7

[a] These computations are based on 1954 tax rates; the reductions in adjusted gross income are from the average 1953 level of $252 billion.
[b] This line shows the effect of built-in flexibility alone.

To summarize, if incomes decline moderately, the individual income tax can be used to hold the drop in disposable incomes to much smaller proportions. Although built-in flexibility alone would not necessarily be sufficient, it can easily be supplemented by moderate rate and exemption changes. However, if the income decline is substantial, the job becomes more difficult, because built-in flexibility cuts into the tax base and therefore reduces the effectiveness of both

[28] Although Table 10 indicates the potentialities of rate and exemption changes as incomes decline from 1953 levels, it can also be used to approximate revenue losses after incomes have already declined. Suppose incomes have already dropped by $12.5 billion and rates and exemptions have not been changed. Referring to the top line of Table 10, we find that tax liabilities have been reduced by $2 billion. Suppose that incomes decline another $25 billion, and that rates are reduced by 5 percentage points and exemptions are increased to $700 per capita. Then the total reduction in tax liabilities below the original level would be $12.3 billion. Subtracting $2 billion, we obtain a net tax reduction of $10.3 billion. Thus 41 per cent of the second decline of $25 billion (10.3 ÷ 25) would be offset by tax reduction.

rate and exemption changes.[29] Thus use of the individual income tax alone to offset as much as one-quarter or one-third of a large drop in incomes from 1953 levels would require substantial changes in rates and exemptions. For example, built-in flexibility combined with an increase in exemptions to $700 per capita and a reduction in tax rates by 7 percentage points would offset only $15.3 billion, or 30 per cent, of a $50 billion decline in total adjusted gross incomes. (This would reduce the yield of the individual income tax from $29 billion in 1954 to less than $14 billion.)

Although these results may be disappointing to those who expected more of a stabilizing effect from small changes in individual income tax rates and exemptions, it would be erroneous to conclude that individual income tax reduction should be discarded as an antirecession measure. It should be recognized that we have been dealing with only one of a number of measures which can be used to bolster individual incomes. Our results indicate that individual income tax reduction can be an important element in a well-rounded program to combat recession, but it will need to be supplemented by other measures in the event of a substantial decline in income.[30]

[29] The analysis in Part 1 provides no information regarding the effect of a higher level of exemptions on built-in flexibility. In the absence of such data, it was assumed that built-in flexibility at exemptions of $700 per capita would be about 10 per cent lower than built-in flexibility at present exemptions, i.e. that the reduction would be proportionate to the reduction in the tax base resulting from a $100 increase in exemptions at 1953 income levels.

[30] I should like to add a word of caution regarding the reliability of the conclusions in this paper and also to indicate the most important gaps in the data.

As the reader will have noted, rough approximations were necessary at crucial points in the analysis. Fortunately, even if the estimates are incorrect by a substantial margin, the conclusions will not necessarily be wrong. Table 10, for example, is probably accurate enough to support the inferences I have drawn from it.

It is clear, however, that further work is needed, especially at the points where I have been forced to substitute judgment for fact. In particular, the conclusion that the built-in flexibility of the individual income tax has been roughly the same since 1948 (assuming present rates and exemptions) needs further verification. This can be done on the basis of the data now available, but the computations would be too laborious and time-consuming for an individual research worker to undertake.

The most important missing link is a distribution of the tax base by rate brackets for past years. A fairly good approximation to this distribution can be obtained from the detailed tables now provided in the annual *Statistics of Income* volumes published by the Internal Revenue Service of the Department of the Treasury. This would require a substantial investment in clerical time, but it would add immeasurably to the value of the data we now have. For future years I would strongly suggest that the Department add such a table to its annual volumes. This table would be much more valuable for economic analysis (and also for the tax analysis needed by the Department) than any number of the tables now published.

Given a series of distributions by rate brackets for past years, it would be

Appendix

TABLE A-1

Adjustments of Department of Commerce Estimates of Personal Income Used in Arriving at Adjusted Gross Income, 1948

(*billions of dollars*)

1. Personal income	209.5
2. Portion of personal income not included in adjusted gross income	30.8
a. Transfer payments (except fees and military retirement pay)	11.3
b. Other labor income (except pay of military reservists)	2.5
c. Food and fuel produced and consumed on farms	2.9
d. Imputed gross rental value of tenant-occupied farmhouses	.4
e. Other personal income in kind except services of financial intermediaries	4.6
f. Noncorporate nonfarm inventory valuation adjustment	—.4
g. Value of change in farm inventories	1.3
h. Imputed interest	3.7
i. Nontaxable military pay and allowances	2.6
j. Accrued interest on U.S. government bonds	.6
k. Tax-exempt interest	.2
l. Fiduciary income (other than capital gains) not distributed to individuals	.7
m. Property income of nonprofit organizations	.4
n. Dividends received by mutual life insurance companies	.1
3. Portion of adjusted gross income not included in personal income	5.7
a. Employee contributions for social insurance	2.2
b. Net gains from sale of assets reported on indivdual income tax returns	2.2
c. Adjusted gross income of residents of Alaska and Hawaii reported on individual income tax returns	.7
d. Miscellaneous income (except other income on Form 1040A) reported on individual income tax returns	.7
e. Annuities and pensions reported on individual income tax returns	.3
f. Deductions for net operating loss carry-over and depletion	—.3
4. Total adjustment for conceptual differences (lines 2–3)	25.1
5. Estimated adjusted gross income of taxable and nontaxable individuals (lines 1–4)	184.4

Note: Figures are rounded and will not necessarily add to totals.

Source: Lines 2a, 2b, 2c, 2e, 2f, 2g, 2h, 2n, and 3a—Department of Commerce. Lines 2j and 2k—Estimates based on data in the *Annual Report of the Secretary of the Treasury*. Lines 2e, 3b, 3c, 3d, and 3e—*Statistics of Income for 1948*, Internal Revenue Service, Part 1, 1953. Lines 2d, 2i, 2m, and 3f—Based on estimates prepared by Selma Goldsmith.

---

possible to determine how the additions to the tax base since the end of the war have been distributed by brackets, and to test whether the marginal rate applying to these additions would have been constant if present rates had been in effect throughout the period. More generally, if such a series were available, it would be possible to establish the relationship between changes in the distribution of adjusted gross incomes and changes in the distribution of the tax base.

143

TABLE A-2

Derivation of the Individual Income Tax Base, 1948

(*billions of dollars*)

Total adjusted gross income	184.4
' Deduct: Nonreported adjusted gross income	—20.8
Equals: Adjusted gross income reported on individual returns	163.5
Deduct: Adjusted gross income of nontaxable individuals filing returns	—21.5
Equals: Adjusted gross income of taxable individuals	142.1
Deduct: Deductions of taxable individuals	—16.5
Equals: Net income of taxable individuals	125.6
Deduct: Personal exemptions	—50.9
Equals: Surtax net income of taxable individuals	74.7
Add: Taxable income of fiduciaries	+.5
Deduct: Income subject to alternative tax	—.6
Equals: Total surtax net income	74.6

Note: Figures are rounded and will not necessarily add to totals.
Source: Table A-1 and *Statistics of Income for 1948,* Internal Revenue Service, Part 1, 1953.

TABLE A-3

Method of Estimating Tax Liabilities at 1953 Tax Rates and Exemptions, 1948–1953

(*dollars in billions*)

Year (1)	Actual Tax Liability [a] (2)	Average Increase in Tax Rates over Prior Year (3)	Index of Tax Rates (1948 = 100) (4)	Correction Index (5)	Tax Liability at Present Rates and Exemptions (6)
1948	$15.6	. . .	100.0	1.295	$20.2
1949	14.7	. . .	100.0	1.295	19.0
1950	18.5	4.4%	104.4	1.240	22.9
1951	25.0	14.5	119.5	1.084	27.1
1952	29.5	8.3	129.5	1.00	29.5
1953	32.0	. . .	129.5	1.00	32.0

[a] Includes normal tax, surtax, and alternative tax.

Column	Source
2	1948–1950: *Statistics of Income,* Internal Revenue Service, Part 1. 1951–1953: Estimates based on individual income tax collections.
3	Based on estimates prepared by the Department of the Treasury (see "Revenue Act of 1950," mimeographed, December 20, 1950, and "Revenue Act of 1951," mimeographed, November 14, 1951).
4	Based on column 3.
5	Index for 1953 ÷ column 4.
6	Column 2 × column 5.

TABLE A-4

Federal Individual Income Tax Rate Schedules for 1953 and 1954

SURTAX NET INCOME		COMBINED NORMAL TAX AND SURTAX RATES	
Single Persons	Married Couples Filing Joint Returns	1953	1954
$ 0– 2,000	$ 0– 4,000	22.2%	20%
2,000– 4,000	4,000– 8,000	24.6	22
4,000– 6,000	8,000– 12,000	29	26
6,000– 8,000	12,000– 16,000	34	30
8,000– 10,000	16,000– 20,000	38	34
10,000– 12,000	20,000– 24,000	42	38
12,000– 14,000	24,000– 28,000	48	43
14,000– 16,000	28,000– 32,000	53	47
16,000– 18,000	32,000– 36,000	56	50
18,000– 20,000	36,000– 40,000	59	53
20,000– 22,000	40,000– 44,000	62	56
22,000– 26,000	44,000– 52,000	66	59
26,000– 32,000	52,000– 64,000	67	62
32,000– 38,000	64,000– 76,000	68	65
38,000– 44,000	76,000– 88,000	72	69
44,000– 50,000	88,000–100,000	75	72
50,000– 60,000	100,000–120,000	77	75
60,000– 70,000	120,000–140,000	80	78
70,000– 80,000	140,000–160,000	83	81
80,000– 90,000	160,000–180,000	85	84
90,000–100,000	180,000–200,000	88	87
100,000–150,000	200,000–300,000	90	89
150,000–200,000	300,000–400,000	91	90
200,000 and over	400,000 and over [a]	92	91

[a] Subject to a maximum effective rate limitation of 88 per cent in 1953 and 87 per cent in 1954.

COMMENT

Paul J. Strayer, Princeton University

Pechman has made a valuable contribution to our understanding of the effect of built-in flexibility and rate and exemption changes under the federal individual income tax during a recession. Because of the radical transformation of this tax during the war years, he has limited his statistical analysis to the period since World War II. As this period is one of boom, with the single exception of the slight readjustment in 1949, the factual record can show only the relationship between the important variables in a period of full employment, and the changes in yield that might be expected in a recession have to be inferred rather than measured. The primary question raised by Pechman is whether the relations found in a period of rapidly rising money and real incomes, inflation, and a general leveling of income distribution will be reversible in the event of a recession. He believes that such reversibility is a reasonable hypothesis, although he does not claim that there are sufficient data to prove his case or that his conclusions, at this stage, are more than tentative.

With regard to the built-in flexibility of the individual income tax he finds that there is a constant relationship between adjusted gross income and the tax base and that there is a constant average and marginal rate of tax. This leads him to the conclusion that the relation between tax yield and national income will be constant. Thus, if the postwar relations hold throughout a recession, we should expect that approximately $1.5 to 1.6 billion of a $10 billion decline in adjusted gross income would be offset by the built-in flexibility of the individual income tax rates which may be expected to prevail in 1954. This assumes that the relation of tax base to adjusted gross income and the marginal rates of tax which have been constant over the period since the end of World War II will hold in the event of a recession of some magnitude.

Although there is no direct evidence that can be brought to bear on this point, the following reasons may be cited to suggest that a more reasonable assumption is that the relations that will prevail in the event of a recession will be different from those which have held over the past few years. First, the inflation since the end of the war has lowered the real value of the exemptions and has tended to throw a disproportionate part of the rising total income within the tax base. Second, since the end of the war, changes in income distribution have occurred because of the leveling influence of full employment, private and governmental action taken to raise the level of those at the bottom of the income pyramid, and the long-range effects of progressive taxation which have reduced the number at the top. Third, the changes in the size and age composition of the population since the end of the war have been ignored by Pechman, as have their implications for the future.

Much more needs to be learned about the distribution of the expected cut in real and money incomes before it can be said that the tax base and marginal tax rate will decline in a constant pattern consistent with that followed in the period of rapid rise. A sense of proportion must also lead one to conclude that however much these

146

relationships may vary, the magnitudes will not be too different from those assumed by Pechman and that the need for discretionary action to supplement the gain from built-in flexibility cannot be controverted. It is this point that is of the greatest importance as a matter of public policy.

Pechman's findings about the effectiveness of rate and exemption variation as a means of sustaining individual incomes in the event of a recession are not subject to major qualification. They also reveal that there is less potency in this type of remedy than has been alleged by some. To put it another way, the type of action required to offset a sizable decline in income is much more drastic than has been assumed or suggested by many. This raises the question, only briefly touched upon by Pechman, of the practical political and administrative problems of gaining greater discretionary or legislative flexibility in our revenue measures. It is my belief that the cautious optimism he expresses about recent gains must be questioned. The lowering of exemption levels has transformed the income tax to a broad base tax and greatly increased its potential, as have the current-payment and deduction-at-the-source developments of recent years. The record following the outbreak of the Korean war at both executive and Congressional levels proved to be remarkably good. Two major tax increases were passed within a few months of the beginning of the war and their effectiveness in counteracting the inflation cannot be questioned. There still is, however, much evidence that the gap between executive and legislative thinking about tax policy and stabilization policy is substantial. There is also the problem of gaining the objective of coordinated economic policy within either branch of government. The recent record suggests that although there have been several instances when Congress followed a more intelligent policy than might have been expected, the reasons have been as often wrong as right. Current debates in Congress over tax revision and budget policy indicate that there is still a long way to go before we can give up the fear that too often the government will act in such a way that it aggravates the problem rather than corrects it. Memory of World War II debates over the need for additional taxes and the type of revenue measures required does not encourage one to believe that tax changes can be passed with dispatch whenever the economic situation requires them. The problem of those at or below the exemption level raises the question of the political practicality of tax reductions that do little for the group at the bottom of the income pyramid. Negative taxes or family allowances may prove to be the answer, but much more thought must be given to such measures before they can gain the sort of acceptability required to make them effective parts of an antidepression program.

In conclusion, it is well to emphasize that there still must be much more thought and attention directed to this issue. Experimentation, experience, and precedent must all be more extensive before the sort of countercyclical tax flexibility that is called for by most stabilization models can be thought of as a practical operating device. Let us hope that in the meantime the lessons of the past have been well enough learned so that we may at least avoid the worst sins of the past and may gradually move closer to the perfection and degree of rational behavior so ardently desired.

THE CORPORATE INCOME TAX
IN A DEPRESSION

RICHARD GOODE, INTERNATIONAL MONETARY FUND

This paper is addressed primarily to the effects of the present corporate income tax on the size and composition of aggregate demand in a depression and to the consequences of reducing or modifying the tax as an antidepression measure. No attempt is made to investigate the influence of the tax on the pattern of business organization or the possibilities of using corporate taxes to bring about desirable structural changes in the economy. Although considerations of tax equity and administration enter into the selection of possible modifications of the tax and their appraisal, the emphasis on these aspects of tax policy is secondary in the present discussion.

The paper is written on the assumption that raising revenue is a legitimate objective of taxation. The pure principles of functional finance do not recognize this objective. But, for both good and bad reasons, the size of the budget deficit is likely to be a matter of concern in the next depression although anxiety on this score will doubtless be less acute than it was in the 1930's. If this is so, an important subject of inquiry is the comparative efficiency of various tax reductions attributable either to cutting tax rates or to modification of the tax base. Efficiency in this sense would be measured by the multiplier effects of a tax reduction—that is, by the relation between the amount of the tax reduction and the resulting increase in aggregate demand. Even if one is unconcerned about the deficit, it is convenient to have some notion of the probable extent of reaction to tax changes in order to know where to begin and how large an application to prescribe.

The main questions to be discussed are: To what extent can the flexibility of the corporate tax be regarded as an automatic stabilizer? How do technical features influence built-in flexibility? What would be the consequences of reducing corporate tax rates in a depression period? Of reducing liabilities by modifying the tax base? Can corporate taxes be revised to make them more acceptable under depression conditions? [1]

[1] No account is taken in this paper of the general revision of federal tax law embodied in the Internal Revenue Code of 1954 (H.R. 8300, 83d Cong., 2d sess.), which was adopted after the paper was written. Among the most important fea-

Built-in Flexibility

Corporate tax liabilities are directly related to the usual measure of business success. Hence a firm automatically obtains a reduction of corporation income tax whenever its operating experience is unfavorable. Despite considerable diversity among firms, movements in aggregate profits coincide closely with the general business cycle.[2] For the Treasury this means that the yield of the corporate tax will automatically decline during a recession and rise during a recovery period. Nearly all taxes exhibit this built-in flexibility to some extent, but it is more pronounced for the corporate tax than for most other major taxes. Corporate profits, defined either as the algebraic sum of all profits and losses or as the total of profits reported by corporations realizing net income in any year, fluctuate more widely than national income as a whole or the other major distributive shares.

Built-in flexibility of tax yield is usually considered an automatic stabilizer of business conditions. In considering the extent to which this characterization holds for the corporation income tax, it is interesting to try to separate the influence of the fact that the tax is measured by net income from the timing of liabilities. This point may be clarified by two comparisons. First, a profits tax may be compared with taxes on sales, gross receipts, units of production, payrolls, or some other base that is more stable than profits. Second, profits taxes with different degrees of instability of yield may be compared. For example, a tax based on annual profits might be compared with one imposed on a moving average of profits covering a whole business cycle. An inquiry of this kind may help to determine whether it is feasible to approximate the effects of the automatic variability of yield of the corporate tax by adjustments of rates of other types of taxes and whether it is worthwhile to modify the corporation income tax to increase its built-in flexibility.

The larger automatic reduction in liabilities under the corporation income tax is certainly one reason for believing that, during a depression, this tax is less deflationary than sales, production, or cost-factor taxes that would yield the same amount of revenue over a com-

tures of this act are: (1) extension of the carryback of net operating loss from one year to two years, (2) liberalization of depreciation deductions by allowing taxpayers the option of using a modified declining-balance method or other methods which will concentrate a larger fraction of total allowances in the early years of life of depreciable property, and (3) exclusion from taxable income of individual stockholders of the first $50 of dividends received and allowance of a tax credit equal to 4 per cent of additional dividends.

2 Thor Hultgren, *Cyclical Diversities in the Fortunes of Industrial Corporations*, National Bureau of Economic Research, Occasional Paper 32, 1950.

plete business cycle. The income tax will leave firms more funds for working capital, fixed investment, and dividend distributions. But other differences between the two types of tax seem more important. The corporate income tax will not significantly alter the point at which short-run marginal costs and marginal revenues are equal and hence will be less likely to keep production below the capacity of existing plant and equipment. The income tax will interfere less with price reductions. Although this point is more debatable, it seems likely that the income tax will be less discouraging to new investment and to introduction of new products, because management will know that a tax liability will not be incurred unless and until profits are realized.

The conclusion that the corporate income tax is less harmful during a depression than other types of tax that happen to have less built-in flexibility does not necessarily imply that increased built-in flexibility of a profits tax is an important advantage. The only gain from a mere rescheduling of income tax liabilities over the cycle will be the increased availability of funds during the depression. The significance of this point will be further considered in a later section dealing with the effects of reducing corporate tax rates as an antidepression measure. A change in timing of liabilities but not in the total amount accruing over a cycle would not significantly affect the rate of return on investment in assets with useful lives as long as the duration of the cycle. Some technical features of the corporate tax that determine the degree of its built-in flexibility of yield affect only the timing of liabilities. Other features also influence the total amount of tax that a firm will pay over the cycle.

The foregoing paragraphs make no distinction between tax liabilities and tax yields. In practice, payments of corporate taxes are not synchronous with accrual, and changes in liabilities precede changes in collections. Liabilities were formerly paid in equal quarterly installments in the twelve months following the close of the tax year. In recent years, however, the date of payment has been advanced. Ninety per cent of 1953 taxes will be payable in two equal quarterly installments in the first half of 1954, leaving only 5 per cent to be paid in each of the last two installments. Liabilities of 1954 and later years will be payable in two equal installments in the first half of the following year.

Although the delay in payment may sometimes be important for the corporation's cash position, taxes begin to influence business decisions even before the final accrual of liability. In view of the comparatively short lag under present arrangements, in most instances it is not necessary to consider the difference in timing of liabilities and of payments in assessing the effects of built-in flexibility on business behavior.[3]

The reasoning that equates built-in flexibility of tax yield with automatic stabilization does not seem to be fully applicable to the corporate income tax. The identification is justifiable for the individual income tax on the plausible assumption that consumer expenditures ordinarily respond promptly to changes in disposable income. An analogous assumption regarding business investment is not admissable. The timing of liabilities may be of secondary importance in accounting for whatever advantages the corporate tax has under depression conditions. Nevertheless, it seems worthwhile to examine some of the technical features that influence the built-in flexibility of the tax. These features may also be important in other respects.

Technical Features Affecting Built-in Flexibility

The degree of built-in flexibility of the corporate tax depends on the exact definition of net income, particularly procedures for valuation of inventories and determination of depreciation allowances; the extent to which losses of one year can be offset against profits of other years; and the rate structure. All these features affect, to some extent, the total yield of the tax over the business cycle, but in this section they will be considered with particular reference to their influence on the timing of liabilities. In order to isolate the significance of built-in flexibility, it will be convenient to assume that tax rates are adjusted so that the yields of different versions of the corporate tax are approximately equal over a complete business cycle.

INVENTORY VALUATION

Historically, inventory profits and losses have been an important element in fluctuations of the reported total of profits. Changes in inventory profits or losses have accounted for the following percentages of the total change in reported corporate profits before taxes: from 1929 to 1932, 4 per cent of the decline; from 1932 to 1937, 12 per cent of the rise; from 1937 to 1938, 34 per cent of the decline; from 1948 to 1949, 68 per cent of the decline; from 1949 to 1950, 57 per cent of the rise.[4]

---

[3] As noted below, however, the timing of refunds attributable to loss carry-backs may be important.

[4] Inventory profits and losses are here taken to be equal to the inventory valuation adjustment (for corporations) included in the national income estimates prepared by the Department of Commerce (see *National Income Supplement, 1951, Survey of Current Business,* Dept. of Commerce, p. 150).

These fluctuations were partly attributable to the traditional accounting convention that when particular units cannot be identified goods should be assumed to be sold in the order of their acquisition. Under the first-in-first-out valuation method, the lag between assumed cost of goods sold and replacement cost becomes important in periods of rapidly changing prices. Reported profits are further reduced during business recessions by the accounting adjustments necessary to conform to the common practice of carrying inventories at the lower of cost or market value.

The last-in-first-out method of inventory valuation is intended to reduce variations in reported profits by shortening the lag in changes of cost of goods sold behind movements in replacement cost. This procedure is based on the assumption that the goods sold in any period are those most recently acquired. Under present law a taxpayer using Lifo forgoes the privilege of writing down the book value of inventories if market values fall below original cost. A further condition of use of Lifo for tax purposes is that the taxpayer's own books of accounts and reports be on the same basis.

Lifo did not become generally available for tax purposes until 1939, when it was made optional for all taxpayers. Experience with the method has, therefore, been dominated by war and postwar developments, rather than by ordinary cyclical movements. In fact, the procedure does not seem to have been widely adopted. In 1951 the Department of Commerce estimated that Lifo inventories of corporations represented about one-tenth of the total book value of nonfarm inventories or about one-eighth of all corporate inventories.[5] Later estimates place the book value of Lifo inventories for manufacturing at the end of 1951 at 15 per cent of the total for manufacturing industries.[6] Lifo accounting is concentrated among large manufacturing corporations in the fields of iron and steel, petroleum and coal products, nonferrous metals, paper and pulp, textiles, food processing, and leather and products, and among department stores.[7]

To the extent that it has been adopted, Lifo clearly reduces the built-in flexibility of corporate tax liabilities. During a recession, reported profits and tax liabilities of firms on Lifo will fall less rapidly than they would under Fifo. Inability to write down inventories when the market price of raw materials declines below cost may be especially significant for some of the manufacturing industries in

[5] Ibid., pp. 123–124.

[6] James P. Daly, "Lifo Inventories and National Income Accounting," *Survey of Current Business*, May 1953, pp. 16–18.

[7] Ibid., and J. Keith Butters, *Effects of Taxation: Inventory Accounting and Policies*, Harvard Graduate School of Business Administration, 1949, Chap. III.

which Lifo is most widely used. Downward revaluations of inventories were large for such firms in 1921, 1930–1932, 1934, and 1937.[8]

The effect of Lifo accounting on business activity is qualitatively uncertain, although it may be presumed that it will be quantitatively unimportant for the economy as a whole so long as Lifo is confined to the limited area that it now occupies. On the one hand, the cash position of firms on Lifo will be adversely affected during a recession. On the other hand, it is possible that the smaller decline in reported profits will help prevent the development of pessimism and thereby contribute to stabilization of business outlays.[9] I am inclined to believe that the adverse effect on cash resources will be more important than any beneficial influence on business sentiment, partly because I find it hard to believe that executives of firms with large stocks of raw materials will fail to make a mental adjustment for price changes. But I do not see how the question can be resolved.

Recent proposals to allow taxpayers using Lifo the option of valuing their inventories at the lower of cost or market prices would largely eliminate the disadvantage of the method during a recession. Such an amendment, however, seems objectionable on other grounds. It would allow taxpayers to minimize taxes on inventory profits when prices were rising and to take immediate advantage of inventory losses when prices fell below Lifo valuations. The result would be discrimination against taxpayers who have refrained from adopting Lifo partly because of fear that prices would fall, and against firms for which Lifo is not feasible.[10]

CURRENT-COST DEPRECIATION

Unlike Lifo, which was designed to reduce cyclical fluctuations in taxable profits, proposals for current-cost depreciation allowances for tax purposes have usually been intended to deal with a condition of secular inflation or a once-for-all increase in the price level. The more elaborate of these proposals would allow taxpayers to adjust depreciation deductions each year by reference to indexes of the cost of capital goods. Discussion of this subject has already abated in this country and probably will disappear in the quarters in which it

---

[8] Albert R. Koch, *The Financing of Large Corporations, 1920–39*, National Bureau of Economic Research, 1943, pp. 49–50.

[9] Professor Butters stresses the advantage of eliminating the "distorting effects of inventory profits and losses." *Op. cit.*, p. 11.

[10] For a good discussion see Douglas H. Eldridge, "Issues Raised by Proposal to Grant Cost or Market Option with Lifo," *National Tax Journal*, March 1953, pp. 52–68.

has been popular in the past few years if a significant decline in the price of capital assets occurs.

If consistently applied, current-cost depreciation resembles Lifo in that it would reduce cyclical variations in profits and tax liabilities, but the magnitude of the adjustment is harder to estimate. Although the book value of depreciable assets is much larger than that of inventories, the average useful life of depreciable property is much longer than the turnover period for inventories and annual depreciation charges are small in comparison with sales from inventories. The changes in costs of depreciable assets over the business cycle are probably greater than the fluctuations in prices of nonfarm inventory goods as a whole, but the fact that book values of depreciable property represent a wide range of price history means that, in intermediate phases of the cycle, adjustments necessary to convert original cost to replacement cost would involve both plus and minus items. To the extent that acquisition of depreciable property is concentrated in times of high prices, the present type of depreciation allowance is correspondingly large, and a shift to a current-cost basis would cut allowable deductions and increase taxable profits in depression periods more than it would if acquisitions were evenly distributed over the cycle. As compared with Lifo, current-cost depreciation would involve a greater departure from ordinary accounting methods, graver administrative difficulties, and a sharper clash with usual standards of equity. Lifo (without the proposed cost-or-market option) represents merely a change in the convention regarding the order in which goods are sold; it reduces, but does not eliminate, inventory profits or losses. Some versions of current-cost depreciation would completely destroy the link between historical costs and allowable deductions.[11]

Like Lifo, a consistent scheme for current-cost depreciation allowances would decrease liquidity during a depression but might have a beneficial influence on business psychology. Current-cost depreciation might be an additional deterrent to investment when prices are expected to decline, because future deductions would be smaller than under historical-cost depreciation. Inasmuch as the expectation of falling prices is always discouraging to investment, it would be undesirable to reinforce this influence with a tax consideration. It is true that the other side of this argument is that current-cost depreciation might offer an inducement to investment when prices

[11] E. Cary Brown, *Depreciation Adjustment for Price Changes*, Harvard Graduate School of Business Administration, 1952, and Richard Goode, *The Corporation Income Tax*, Wiley, 1951, pp. 172–178.

are expected to rise, but under these circumstances there is less need to encourage investment. Furthermore, it seems likely that business-men are enough subject to the so-called money illusion that, within fairly broad limits, they are more concerned about recovery of origi-nal cash outlays than about the purchasing power of allowable de-ductions for depreciation. Proposals for an upward adjustment of de-preciation allowances to reflect a price rise, but without provision for a downward adjustment when prices decrease, would, of course, avoid perverse effects during a depression. These schemes are not considered here, because they appear to constitute special pleading rather than suggestions for a fundamental reform in the definition of taxable income.

LOSS CARRYBACKS AND CARRYFORWARDS

Variability of corporate tax liabilities over the business cycle is greatly increased if corporations experiencing net operating losses are allowed to carry back these losses against profits of prior years and receive refunds of taxes already paid. The carryback produces nega-tive tax liabilities for many firms in depression years. A carryforward of net losses, on the other hand, decreases variability of tax liabilities. Losses suffered in bad years reduce liabilities in a later period of recovery or prosperity. The difference in variability of the govern-ment's tax revenues, however, may be smaller than the difference in variability of liabilities. The tax reduction attributable to a carry-back is in the form of a refund which will be paid only after a delay occasioned by auditing and other administrative steps, and by the time the refund is paid the recipient may already be earning taxable profits again. A carryforward, on the other hand, is taken into account by the corporation itself when it files its tax return and the tax pay-ment is adjusted accordingly. Carryback refunds may be greatly speeded by administrative arrangements for prompt payment on a tentative basis before a return is examined in detail. This was done immediately after World War II. It may be especially helpful to small businesses which often lack ready access to credit.

Like any other arrangement that increases built-in flexibility, the carryback has a desirable effect on liquidity during a recession or depression. But other aspects of the difference between carrybacks and carryforwards are probably more important.

The tax consequences of a carryback are more certain than those of a carryforward. The refund attributable to a carryback can be estimated as the year progresses and can be closely determined im-mediately after the end of the year. The value of the carryforward depends on future income and future tax rates. A further hazard is the possibility that the law will be revised before the carryforward can be used. In 1932, for example, Congress shortened the carryforward from two years to one year, and in 1933 it completely eliminated the carryforward.

With a carryback in effect, a firm with a record of prior earnings can be sure that if it suffers a loss the Treasury will absorb part of the cost of its current operating expenses, depreciation allowances, and interest payments. This consideration seems more likely to encourage a business to maintain operations and even to acquire new plant and equipment in a depressed year than the possibility that, at some time in the future, a carryforward will reduce tax liabilities.

At the present time, federal law allows only a one-year carryback of net operating losses but permits a five-year carryforward. This arrangement was adopted in 1950 to replace a two-year carryback and a two-year carryforward which had been in effect since 1942. It had been generally agreed that a liberalization of loss offsets was desirable. Two main reasons for preferring a carryforward were advanced: First, the carryforward is administratively simpler since it does not involve holding open or reopening old tax returns. Second, the carryforward is more advantageous to new and growing businesses, whereas the carryback favors established businesses that are either stable in size or declining. Both these arguments are valid, but the decision to concentrate on a carryforward seems to have been unquestionably disadvantageous from the countercyclical point of view.[12]

Extension of the carryback would help us prepare for combating a depression. Further investigation is needed to determine the ideal length of the period. Only a few statistical studies of loss offsets have been published, and most of these center attention on the carryforward.[13] If it is necessary to act before further factual information is available, a reasonable compromise might be to restore the

[12] *Business Loss Offsets*, a report prepared jointly by the technical staffs of the Treasury Department and the Joint Committee on Internal Revenue Taxation in 1947, strongly favored the carryforward. The report conceded that carrybacks might stimulate business expenditures during depression more than carryforwards but concluded that the difference was probably not very great and that neither was likely to have an important countercyclical effect (p. 7).

[13] For an exception see Morris Beck, "Carryover of Business Losses," *National Tax Journal*, March 1953, pp. 69–85. For a sample of sixty identical corporations, 1923–1939, Beck found that the following proportions of losses would have been offset by the indicated arrangements: two-year carryback, 58 per cent; two-year carryforward, 19 per cent; five-year carryback, 90 per cent; five-year carryforward, 76 per cent.

former balance between carryback and carryforward by allowing a three-year period for each. Provision for prompt refunds on a tentative basis would be a desirable feature. Perhaps it would be feasible to allow a longer carryforward for new firms as a partial answer to the criticism that a carryback discriminates against them.

RATE STRUCTURE

The existing degree of built-in flexibility of yield of the corporation income tax, as distinguished from the excess profits tax, is due almost entirely to fluctuations in the size of the base rather than to automatic changes in effective rates. Corporation income tax rates are graduated to only a limited extent, and the average effective rate paid by corporations realizing profits in any year does not vary appreciably with the size of profits. The average effective rate of excess profits tax does respond to changes in business conditions.

Further graduation of the corporation income tax according to the absolute size of net income or the rate of return on invested capital would increase built-in flexibility. Both possibilities, however, seem objectionable on other grounds. Graduation of a corporate tax on the basis of size of profits is inequitable because it takes no account of differences in optimum size of firms in various industries or the number of stockholders. Graduation according to rate of return overlooks differences in risk. Furthermore, experience with the excess profits tax has brought to light many practical difficulties in application of this principle. At the present time there seems to be little support for permanent adoption of rate-of-return graduation. This feature of the system will disappear with the expiration of the excess profits tax, now scheduled for December 31, 1953.

APPRAISAL

Lifo inventory valuation, current-cost depreciation, carryforwards of net operating losses, and a flat rate reduce the built-in flexibility of corporation income tax liabilities. The following favor built-in flexibility: Fifo, historical-cost depreciation, carrybacks, and graduated rates. The countercyclical advantages of appropriate timing of tax liabilities appear to be genuine, but their quantitative importance is uncertain. In the present state of knowledge, therefore, the other advantages and disadvantages of these procedures may appropriately be given primary consideration.

Reduction of Tax Rates

Perhaps we may assume that the "new economics" has gained enough acceptance to make it improbable that corporation income tax rates will be increased in time of depression in an attempt to maintain declining revenues. If this is so, the question arises whether the advantage of reducing corporate tax rates would be great enough to justify recommending this action as a means of lessening the severity or length of a depression.

The question of what action to take regarding tax rates in time of depression, like most other issues of tax policy, must be stated and answered in terms of a comparison of alternatives. This is awkward because it greatly complicates discussion, but there is no other fully satisfactory approach. Within the limits of the present paper it will not be possible to attempt a systematic comparison of alternatives, and the treatment must be recognized as incomplete. I shall, however, make explicit some judgments about other taxes without trying to support these opinions in detail.

It is advisable first to adopt some working hypotheses regarding the short-run incidence of the major taxes. For familiar reasons, it seems justifiable to assume that, for an interval of at least a few years, the direct effects of a reduction of the rate of the corporation income tax would be reflected almost exclusively in higher profits, rather than in lower prices or higher wage rates. The secondary repercussions, of course, might influence prices and wages, but these repercussions would be the consequence of the primary rise in profits after taxes. This hypothesis is much less subject to challenge than any judgment regarding the longer-run effects or ultimate incidence of the corporate tax. Fortunately, the latter judgment is not needed for present purposes.

There would probably be general agreement that the immediate consequences of a reduction of individual income tax rates would be mainly an increase in disposable income of taxpayers. Contrary to the impression that might be gained from most public finance textbooks, the primary beneficiaries of a reduction in excise tax rates are somewhat harder to identify. Nevertheless, the usual assumption that relative prices of taxed commodities would fall seems plausible, especially under depression conditions. There is, however, at least a reasonable possibility that part of the tax reduction would augment profits or diminish business losses. The same reasoning applies in the short run to the employer's share of payroll taxes. The employees' share is probably reflected in take-home pay. Whether a fall in the prices of taxed commodities would involve a decline in the average level of market prices or would be offset by increases in other prices would depend largely on what happened to total consumer expenditures and on the elasticity of supply of goods and services for which demand might increase.

It will hardly be possible to stimulate aggregate demand and business activity by cutting taxes unless the government maintains its own expenditures and finances them by expansionary borrowing. Under these conditions the effectiveness of the tax reduction will depend on its influence on private consumption and investment.

Only a minor fraction of a reduction in corporation income tax can be expected to be added to consumer expenditures. First, corporations will retain part of the additional funds. Corporate savings may well absorb the greater part of the total. Dobrovolsky found that in the period 1922–1943 all manufacturing corporations as a group distributed on the average only about 20 per cent of an increase in net income after taxes. (The change in profits was measured in relation to net worth rather than as absolute amount.) There was, however, a tendency to attempt to maintain dividends when profits fell in the early 1930's. Dividends were reduced only moderately in 1930 and sizable amounts were paid in 1931 and 1932, when manufacturing corporations as a group incurred net deficits.[14] If the desire to stabilize dividends holds in a future recession, some corporations may distribute in dividends a high proportion of the addition to available profits attributable to a reduction in corporate taxes at that time. But other corporations, which would otherwise maintain dividends by drawing on reserves, may in effect save the entire proceeds of the tax reduction. The net result of these two types of reaction is hard to predict.

Of additional dividend distributions, only a part, perhaps less than half, can be expected to be spent for consumption. Some of the dividends will go to nonresidents and nonprofit organizations. The amount received by resident stockholders will be subject to individual income tax at a fairly high marginal rate, and a considerable fraction of the net increment in disposable income of stockholders will be saved.[15] Up-to-date estimates of these magnitudes would be

[14] Sergei P. Dobrovolsky, *Corporate Income Retention, 1915–43*, National Bureau of Economic Research, 1951.

[15] On the basis of the 1941 distribution of dividends and individual income, 1948 individual income tax rates, and information on consumer budgets of 1941, I have estimated that a change in dividend distributions would be allocated approximately as follows: dividend income of nonresident foreigners and nonprofit organizations and retained income of taxable fiduciaries, 11 per

helpful in appraising the effects of a reduction of the corporation income tax.

Reduction of the corporation income tax will have a favorable influence on the two main determinants of the volume of corporate investment—the availability of funds and the anticipated return on a successful investment. The extent of the reaction is hard to guess. The tax cut will not transform an unprofitable investment into a profitable one. Hence it may be only a weak stimulus in time of severe depression, when pessimism is widespread and profound. Under these conditions measures to revive demand for final output are required to call forth a general increase in private investment. Under less extreme conditions the tax cut will move some projects over the line between acceptance and rejection.

If the tax reduction is announced to be temporary or is generally expected to be so, it may be much less effective than a permanent reduction. The returns on new investment of intermediate or long-term durability will be expected to be subject to the regular tax once business recovery is at hand and hence the outlook for these investments will be improved to only a minor extent if at all.

Some firms that would have been unable or unwilling to obtain outside financing will undoubtedly make greater investment outlays because the tax reduction makes more funds available to them from internal sources. Outside credit and equity capital may also become easier to get. But, on the average, lack of funds does not seem to be the main limitation on investment in a depression period. In years of severe business recession during the period 1919–1939, corporations partially liquidated their inventories, receivables, and fixed assets. They used a large fraction of the funds so obtained to reduce indebtedness and to distribute dividends in excess of current net income. Large corporations increased the ratio of cash to total assets and to total payments in the early 1930's.[16] A shortage of funds is most likely to interfere with investment when business enters a downswing with a large volume of short-term debt. Corporate short-term debt grew rapidly after the war, except for a minor decline in 1949, and at the end of 1952 was at a historically high level both in net amount and in relation to long-term debt.[17] However, it repre-

---

cent; individual income tax liabilities of stockholders, 32 per cent; individual savings, 19 per cent; consumption and gifts and contributions, 39 per cent. Goode, *op. cit.*, p. 108. Needless to say, these estimates are based on many assumptions, some of them rather shaky.

[16] Friedrich A. Lutz, *Corporate Cash Balances, 1914–43*, National Bureau of Economic Research, 1945.

[17] *Survey of Current Business*, October 1950, p. 10, and September 1953, p. 17.

sents a smaller fraction of income originating in corporate business than in 1929 or 1937.[18]

A drawback to cutting corporate taxes as a means of stimulating demand during a recession or depression is the possibility that a large fraction of the tax remission will be used to reduce short-term indebtedness or to increase idle reserves. When the business outlook is highly uncertain or when prices are expected to fall these uses may be the most prudent applications of funds for many firms. Although an increase in business liquidity and a reduction in fixed charges may be helpful, it seems unlikely that they will offer as much support to economic activity as an equal increase in spending power of individual consumers.

As compared with a reduction of corporate tax rates, a cut in the rates of the individual income tax, payroll taxes, or excises can be expected to offer a much greater stimulus to consumption. This judgment is based mainly on the hypothesis that the corporate tax has less direct effect on disposable income of consumers or its purchasing power. It does not depend on an assumption that the marginal propensity to consume of stockholders is lower than that of other groups. If, however, the marginal propensity to consume is inversely related to the size of family income, this factor will tend to widen the difference between the corporation income tax and the other taxes inasmuch as dividend receipts are highly concentrated in upper income groups.

Reduction of the individual income tax, excises, or payroll taxes will probably stimulate some additional private investment. But the direct effects on this component of demand are likely to be smaller than those attributable to a change in the corporate income tax.

In summary, it appears that a reduction of the corporate tax rate is always a relatively ineffective means of stimulating consumption. Its influence on investment is less certain but is likely to be weaker during a depression than in a period of recovery or prosperity. If the tax reduction is expected to be temporary, its force will be diminished because it will not significantly improve the anticipated return on long-lived investments. These considerations suggest that a reduction of corporate tax rates is a less promising antidepression measure than a cut in other major taxes.

Rapid Amortization

An alternative to a change in tax rates as a means of reducing the corporation income tax is to allow rapid amortization or accelerated

[18] *National Income Supplement, 1951, Survey of Current Business,* p. 156.

depreciation. Several countries have experimented with this method of removing obstacles to private investment. The United States adopted rapid amortization of emergency facilities during World War II and again during the Korean war in order to prevent high tax rates from interfering too much with selected types of investment. Could this technique be successfully employed for a similar purpose under depression conditions?

Rapid amortization of new depreciable property will result in an immediate reduction in reported profits and tax liabilities, by an amount depending on provisions of the particular scheme and the volume of eligible investment. If aggregate deductions are limited to original cost, the larger deductions allowed in the early years of useful life of an asset will be offset by smaller reductions in later years. With constant tax rates there will be a redistribution of tax liabilities over time rather than an outright reduction with respect to the income attributable to any one asset. So long as the plan remains in operation the Treasury will not recover its original loss of revenue, unless the rate of new investment in eligible assets declines. An individual firm can enjoy continued tax exemption by acquiring new assets as soon as the old ones are written off. If, however, rapid amortization is terminated once recovery has been attained, tax postponement will come to an end and the Treasury will begin to recoup the earlier loss of revenue.

The objective in granting a tax reduction in the form of accelerated depreciation rather than by a cut in tax rates would be to encourage investment in depreciable assets as distinguished from accumulation of idle reserves, debt retirement, additions to inventories, or other uses of funds. The first step in appraising this device is to consider its value as an investment incentive.

If tax rates are constant and all firms have enough operating income to absorb the extra deductions, the tax postponement due to rapid amortization would be equivalent to an interest-free advance of funds from the government. This would mean a small increase in the rate of return on the investment. It would also ease the financial position and working capital problems of a firm expanding its depreciable assets. But a more important aspect of accelerated depreciation would be the fact that it would reduce the risk that the income tax would interfere with recovery of the capital invested in a new asset.

Businessmen are accustomed to subject future earnings to a heavy discount because of their uncertainty. This attitude is reflected in repeated reports that most firms will undertake a new investment only if it promises to pay for itself within a rather short time. Commonly this "payoff period" is said to be about three to five years for machinery of a type that is usually considered to have a normal useful life of ten to twenty years. The insistence on the short payoff period implies that uncertainty is so great that the possibility of receiving earnings after the end of the period is not worth taking into account.

The corporate income tax makes it harder to recover the cost of an asset during its payoff period because depreciation allowances are based on the longer normal useful life. The greater the discrepancy between the payoff period and the depreciation period, the more repressive is the tax at any given rate. Since creditors are likely to adopt somewhat the same attitude toward the future as investors, the tax will also make it harder to borrow to finance acquisition of depreciable property when the depreciation period is longer than the payoff period (and the maturity of the loan).

By narrowing or eliminating the difference between the payoff period and the depreciation period for tax purposes, accelerated depreciation will lessen the tax obstacle to investment. It will not wholly eliminate tax deterrents, inasmuch as the net return above cost will still be subject to taxation.

It seems clear that, in a period of stable prosperity when tax rates are high and are not expected to change, introduction of rapid amortization will offer a significant stimulus to investment in depreciable property. Under depression conditions and with the possibility that profits will be larger and tax rates higher at some future time, the measure will probably be much less effective. First and most important, rapid amortization, like a cut in tax rates, does nothing to increase the gross yield of an investment. Rapid amortization will not induce investments which would be unattractive even in the absence of income taxes. Second, if tax rates are expected to be higher in the future, it may be disadvantageous to accelerate depreciation deductions. This suggests that a policy of countercyclical changes in tax rates will partially cancel the benefits of accelerated depreciation as an antidepression measure. Third, anticipated earnings may be too small to absorb deductions in excess of normal depreciation allowances over the shortened amortization period.

The significance of the third point depends on the availability of loss carrybacks or carryforwards and the form of the accelerated depreciation arrangement. Even when current profits are low or nonexistent, additional depreciation deductions may produce a tax benefit if they result in accounting losses that can be offset against profits of past or future years. For firms with a record of profits in the recent past, a carryback will assure a tax refund, whereas a carryforward offers only a contingent benefit. In the absence of provisions for averaging profits and losses, a compulsory plan for systematic accelerated depreciation might actually discourage investment in a period of low profits. This effect could be minimized by making rapid amortization optional with the taxpayer or by giving taxpayers freedom to write off depreciable property at any rate that is convenient.

Three forms of systematic accelerated depreciation may be distinguished: (1) an "initial allowance" equal to some fraction of the cost of new assets with the remaining cost written off according to normal depreciation practices; (2) amortization of new depreciable property over a fixed period without regard to normal useful life; (3) amortization allowances for the new assets equal to some multiple of normal depreciation. These plans could be combined in various ways. The initial allowance has been used, in combination with a normal declining-balance depreciation computation, in the United Kingdom, Canada, India, and some other countries. Amortization over a period of sixty months, with the possibility of a still shorter period under stated circumstances, has been the provision applied to emergency facilities in the United States. So far as I know, the third method has not been generally adopted by any large country.

A uniform initial allowance and a uniform amortization period for all assets, as well as complete flexibility for the taxpayer, favor investment in long-lived assets as compared with short-lived assets. The increase in deductions will be proportionately larger for the long-lived assets. This feature might cause some distortion in investment patterns, but in part it would only compensate for the greater risk associated with long-term investment. It is also true that the heavy capital goods industries and construction are likely to be most adversely affected by a depression. Hence, investment in these types of assets would stand in greatest need of a tax fillip. Application of a uniform multiplier to normal depreciation allowances will shorten the amortization period by the same fraction for all types of assets and in that sense can be considered neutral as regards long-lived assets.

Administrative and compliance problems associated with adoption and termination of rapid amortization probably would not be much greater than in connection with countercyclical changes of tax rates. In order to prevent tax avoidance, it would be advisable to tax gains from sales or exchanges of depreciable property (at least to the extent of the difference between book values under accelerated depreciation and under normal depreciation) at regular income tax rates rather than at capital gains rates. In the absence of such a rule, taxpayers could effect a tax saving merely by exchanging assets.

There is a strong presumption that, in proportion to the amount of revenue sacrificed, rapid amortization would stimulate more new investment than a reduction of corporate tax rates. The concession would be tied directly to the acquisition of depreciable assets, and the amount of tax revenue lost would depend on the volume of new investment. Nevertheless, part of the tax reduction would be "wasted" because some of the investment eligible for accelerated depreciation would have been made without that privilege. Some of the tax saving would go into idle reserves, but it seems likely that this fraction would be smaller than under a general reduction in the corporate tax rate. Rapid amortization would benefit most those industries in which depreciation constitutes a large part of total costs. In general, these are the industries that have suffered most in past depressions.

The stabilizing potentialities of adjustment of depreciation allowances as an alternative to countercyclical changes in tax rates deserve further study. Attention might well be given to the possibility of reducing or postponing normal allowances when inflation threatens as well as to accelerated depreciation in time of depression.

Taxation of Undistributed Profits or Uninvested Funds

An alternative to reduction of corporation income tax rates or liberalization of depreciation allowances would be basic revision of the method of taxing corporations. One approach would be to restrict the corporate tax to retained profits by transforming it into an undistributed profits tax or a withholding tax. Despite important differences in form, these two substitutes are fundamentally similar, and for present purposes attention can be confined to the undistributed profits tax. This measure has usually been advocated as a reform appropriate for all phases of the business cycle rather than as a means of alleviating depression. It raises a number of controversial issues that will not be examined here.[19] Brief attention will be given, however, to some of the economic implications of the undistributed profits tax during a depression. A tax on uninvested funds of corporations, either as an addition to the present corporate tax or as a partial substitute for it, will also be considered as an antidepression measure.

The United States experimented with an undistributed profits tax

[19] See *The Postwar Corporation Tax Structure,* Dept. of the Treasury, 1946, and Goode, *op. cit.,* Chap. 10.

in 1936–1937. The tax appears to have been an important stimulus to distribution of dividends in those years.[20] It is uncertain to what extent this reaction was peculiar to conditions of the times or to particular features of the statute, but it is clear that the tax would always exert pressure to distribute net profits.

Additional distributions of cash dividends would increase disposable income of stockholders and raise consumption expenditures. This effect would be desirable during a depression but undesirable under inflationary conditions. On the other hand, the liquidity of corporations would be reduced, and their ability to finance investment from internal sources would be impaired. This would partially or wholly offset the influence on consumption.

If the statute allowed a credit for stock dividends as well as cash dividends, as the 1936 act did, some corporations would be able to escape liability without jeopardizing their cash position. Other corporations, especially closely held ones, might arrange with their stockholders for reinvestment of part of the funds paid out in cash dividends. It is also possible that more generous dividend policies would improve the market for new equity securities. But this is doubtful, inasmuch as stock prices may be more closely related to earnings available for dividends than to dividends paid. In any event, if corporations succeeded in avoiding a reduction in the resources available for financing new investment and for building up reserves, the undistributed profits tax would fail as a stimulant to consumption.

The effect of the undistributed profits tax on the combined total of investment by corporations and consumption expenditures by stockholders seems too uncertain to justify recommending the measure as one especially suitable for depression conditions. Furthermore, if the tax is held to be desirable for depression use because it promotes consumption without greatly restricting investment, there is a presumption that it would be undesirable when the fiscal problem is to control inflation. In view of the complex and controversial nature of the undistributed profits tax there are strong objections to alternate imposition and suspension of the tax in different phases of the business cycle. This negative report on the value of the undistributed profits tax as an antidepression measure is not intended to suggest that it would be inappropriate to adopt the plan during a depression if it were considered a desirable permanent revision of the revenue system. Whether the tax qualifies as such is not considered in this paper.

[20] George E. Lent, *The Impact of the Undistributed Profits Tax, 1936–1937*, Columbia University Press, 1948, Chap. II, and Dobrovolsky, *op. cit.*, pp. 57–62.

In the late 1930's and in the discussion of postwar tax plans some attention was given to the possibility that a tax on "idle" funds of corporations would be more effective than the undistributed profits tax as a check on excessive savings and would not be subject to the same disadvantages as the latter. This tax was proposed as a levy on net profits plus current accruals to depreciation and depletion reserves but with deductions for dividend distributions and for new investment. The objective would be to apply a tax pressure against accumulation of inactive funds, whether from net profits or depreciation and depletion reserves, and in favor of dividend distribution and investment. If this pressure proved ineffective, the government would realize revenue from a tax that would not directly encroach on private investment or consumption.

A technical problem would be presented by the choice of a definition of "investment" and its application. A narrow definition would take in only depreciable or depletable property but would include outlays for replacement as well as expansion. A broader concept would include land, inventories, and accounts receivable. Securities would presumably not be an acceptable type of investment. Financial businesses would probably have to be exempted from the tax.

The most serious difficulty in devising a satisfactory tax on uninvested funds would be to make appropriate allowance for the difference in timing of fund accrual and investment outlays. Some businesses are accustomed to replace their assets at a fairly steady rate because the durability, age distribution, and size of individual property items allow this. These firms could also follow a policy of gradually expanding their physical assets. Other firms, however, necessarily have an irregular pattern of replacement or expansion, because their properties are long-lived and consist of a relatively small number of large units (hotels and real estate corporations are examples of this type of business). The first type of firm could adjust its investment outlays to the volume of retained profits and depreciation accruals and thereby avoid tax liability. The firm with an irregular investment pattern might become liable for the tax because it needed to accumulate funds over a period of years to finance a large outlay for replacement or expansion.

One way of dealing with the timing problem would be to allow a long period of averaging by means of carrybacks or carryforwards of investment outlays in excess of current accruals of funds. But this would introduce an important element of discrimination against firms that had made large investments just before the tax went into effect as compared with firms investing immediately thereafter. The former might be faced with a tax liability, while the latter would enjoy a carryforward sufficient to wipe out liability for many years. In fact, with a sufficient carryforward, the provision for inclusion of depreciation and depletion accruals in the tax base would become virtually meaningless because the original investment would result in a carryforward equal to all future accruals to depreciation and depletion reserves. While a carryforward or carryback would seem essential for equity reasons, it would greatly diminish the effectiveness of the tax in time of depression because accruals of funds in such a period could be offset by investment outlays made during prosperity.

It might be possible to solve the technical problems associated with a tax on uninvested funds if enough serious study were given to the subject. Even so, the tax would be appropriate only for a condition of secular stagnation and not as a means of helping counteract a brief depression. It would be much too cumbersome a machine to start and stop at frequent intervals.

Summary of Conclusions

The principal conclusions of this paper may be summarized as follows:

1. The marked built-in flexibility of corporation income tax liabilities does not mean that the tax is a powerful automatic stabilizer of business activity. The advantages of the corporate tax during a depression are probably due more to the fact that it is based on net income than to timing of liabilities as such. Nevertheless, built-in flexibility is a desirable feature.

2. Built-in flexibility could be increased by elimination of Lifo inventory valuation, by lengthening the carryback of net operating losses and shortening the carryforward, and by graduation of rates. In view of the uncertain importance of timing of corporate tax liabilities, however, it may be justifiable to evaluate these measures primarily in the light of their other advantages and disadvantages.

3. A temporary reduction of corporation income tax rates will probably increase private spending less during a depression than a temporary cut in the individual income tax, excises, or payroll taxes. It will be much less effective in stimulating consumption. A temporary reduction of corporate taxes will be less favorable to investment than a permanent reduction because it will not greatly improve the anticipated return on long-lived assets. In a severe depression,

lowering of corporate tax rates may have little influence because there are comparatively few investment opportunities that seem to promise any net profit.

4. In proportion to the amount of revenue sacrificed, rapid amortization of depreciable property can probably do more to improve investment incentives than a general reduction of corporate tax rates. Carrybacks or carryforwards of accounting losses or other elements of flexibility will be essential to allow realization of the full benefits of rapid amortization and to prevent it from actually discouraging some investment in time of depression.

5. Neither an undistributed profits tax nor a tax on uninvested funds of corporations appears to be a promising means of combating a short depression. The former would probably bring about some increase in consumption expenditures but would make internal financing of investment more difficult. The latter presents some unsolved technical difficulties. Both measures would be undesirable when fiscal restraints on private spending were appropriate, and they are too cumbersome to apply and remove in different phases of the business cycle.

COMMENT

RICHARD A. MUSGRAVE, University of Michigan

In commenting on this very interesting and constructive paper, I shall concentrate on a couple of points which leave me worried and which may stand further discussion. Most puzzling, perhaps, is the proposition that little can be expected, in terms of increased investment, from a reduction in the rate of the corporation tax. This, to be sure, is the prevailing opinion, and I am inclined to share it; but I don't quite know why, and feel uneasy about the matter.

To begin with, note an important distinction between possible inducements to investment by reducing the corporation tax and inducement to consumption by reducing the personal income tax. In the case of the personal income tax, the consequences of tax change take the form of income effects [1] and the same holds pretty much for conventional excises, the substitution effect of which is of minor importance insofar as consumption as a whole is concerned. Because we deal with the income effect, we know (1) that the resulting initial gain in consumption or "multiplicand" cannot exceed the reduction

[1] Substitution effects on work effort are a different matter and may be neglected in this connection.

in yield, and (2) that a decline in yield will have a favorable leverage effect, no matter whether this decline is due to a reduction in the tax rate or to a shrinkage in the tax base.

In the case of the corporation income tax, expenditures may be affected in two ways. As the tax is reduced, the corporation is left with more investable funds. If we assume that investment is a function of retained funds, the argument is quite analogous to the previously considered consumption effects of cuts in personal taxes. The only difference is that a propensity to invest is substituted for a propensity to consume. This propensity to invest or "liquidity" theory of investment behavior seems to underlie much of the recent tax discussion, especially the optimistic view of accelerated depreciation. The trouble with this theory is that it is more likely to work in the boom, when you don't need it, than in the depression, when you want it.

In any case, changes in available funds are only one aspect of the matter. Investment behavior, surely, also involves profit prospects as a determining factor. These prospects, of course, are prospects net of tax. It is necessary, therefore, to consider the substitution effect of tax changes on the profitability of investment. Profits, after all, are doubled if a tax of 50 per cent is repealed; or they are raised by 50 per cent if the tax rate is cut by one-half. What puzzles me is why we feel that investment might not be encouraged substantially by such a rather drastic change in profitability.

Here the principle involved is quite different from that of the income tax. Resulting changes in the level of investment need not bear any particular relation to the loss in yield; they may fall short of this loss or be a multiple thereof. Also, we know that a favorable substitution effect can result only from a reduction in the tax *rate*, not from a shrinkage in the profits base. Built-in flexibility, in other words, works only with regard to the income effect; it does not work (except where rates are progressive) with regard to the substitution effect.

Why is it that so little is expected of the substitution effect? Among a number of possible explanations, these might be offered: (1) To the extent that the corporation tax is shifted anyhow, reducing the tax rate will not affect investment, be it via income or via substitution effect. Pending an empirical study of the matter, I am still far from convinced by the usual view (adopted in Goode's paper) that the entire tax stays put in the short run. As I see it, there are many arguments, wholly compatible with conventional price theory, which permit the possibility of shifting. (2) Perhaps the fault lies in the very premise that a tax on profits reduces, and that removal of a tax increases, investment "yield." While this seems to be the case at first glance, the actual problem is much more complex. If perfect loss offset is assumed to exist, imposition of a tax may be shown to reduce the risk of loss as well as the prospect of yield.[2] Thus, the attractiveness of risk taking remains unaffected. But it does not follow necessarily that more cash will be held. In all, we must admit that we have little to go on when it comes to investment theory. The crude $L = f(M)$ and $I = f(I)$ functions usually employed tell us little. The whole problem is *how* they are affected by the imposition of a tax on investment income; and to answer this, a much more explicit theory is needed. (3) Finally, the explanation may be that the investment schedule is highly inelastic to yield. To the extent that this is true, the increase in investment induced by reduction in tax rate will not be able to offset such reduction in investment as results from a downward shift in the investment schedule during depression. If this is the case, the effectiveness of tax reduction falters at the same obstacle as does monetary expansion—although the latter may have the additional handicap of a highly elastic liquidity preference schedule.

Evidently, this is an area in which much work needs to be done. Until empirical results are obtained little can be said in an authoritative way. Nevertheless, I feel rather skeptical about the heavy emphasis on the liquidity approach to investment (with its stress on accelerated depreciation) and about the de-emphasis of the substitution effect part of the problem. What we are doing, perhaps, is to apply boom psychology to a depression problem.

Second, I have been much interested in Goode's treatment of price level change. On equity grounds, there would be an advantage to having income defined in real terms, provided that this could be done consistently.[3] But, as Goode shows, corrections in the tax base, working in this direction, will reduce built-in flexibility of tax yield. This consideration, to be sure, is disturbing only if we take the available funds approach to investment behavior; under a profitability approach, adjustment for price level change may contribute to stabilize investment. Also, there is the bothersome thought

[2] For an elaboration of the risk approach, see E. D. Domar and R. A. Musgrave, "Proportional Income Taxation and Risk Taking," *Quarterly Journal of Economics,* May 1944.

[3] Advocates of replacement cost depreciation usually overlook the facts that similar adjustments may be applied to other items on the balance sheet and that an analogous problem arises for personal taxpayers.

that built-in flexibility is a fine thing when you are at the top; but it is not so attractive after income has declined and you are trying for a recovery.

This, among other considerations, suggests the possibility of using different definitions of taxable income at different stages in the cycle. On the whole, I share Goode's skepticism toward such an approach. If we want a tax structure which is neutral as between investment in different firms, we need to work out an *income concept* which meets these requirements and then leave it alone, while using adjustments in tax *rates* as our major anticyclical device.

Perhaps Goode is correct in suggesting that anticyclical adjustment in depreciation rates is a proper exception to this rule, but I am not as optimistic regarding its effectiveness. Remember that recent years have been just the setting in which accelerated depreciation could be most effective. For one thing, investors looked forward to a subsequent decline in tax rates, a factor which more than anything else makes accelerated depreciation desirable to the investor. For another, investment was booming, thus emphasizing the gain-in-liquidity aspect of accelerated depreciation. Should a recession set in, neither of these factors would be present, and the effectiveness of accelerated depreciation would be greatly reduced. Certainly it is a policy which will be more helpful in maintaining than in restoring a high level of activity.

Nevertheless, Goode is probably correct when he concludes that per dollar of yield lost, the incentive to investment will be greater from accelerated depreciation than from a reduction in the tax rate. This, perhaps, is primarily due to the fact that accelerated depreciation will apply to new investment only, whereas the reduction in tax rate would apply, presumably, to earnings from old investment as well. Perhaps the main merit of accelerated depreciation is that it furnishes us with an administratively feasible way of giving preferential treatment to new investment.

STABILIZING STATE AND LOCAL FINANCE

CLARENCE HEER, UNIVERSITY OF NORTH CAROLINA

The initial effect of a marked business recession on state and local governments would be a decline or a prospective decline in the yields of state and local taxes. This in turn would necessitate budgetary adjustments affecting appropriations, tax rates, borrowing, the use of accumulated reserves, and other means of financing. The kind of adjustments made by each individual government would determine whether in the aggregate state and local governments made a net contribution toward recovery, whether their influence on the economy was neutral, or whether they added momentum to the downward movement.

Whatever the nature of state and local recession adjustments, their influence on the total economy is likely to be moderate. State and local purchases of goods and services currently constitute only about 7 per cent of the national aggregate of all purchases of goods and services. A 20 per cent variation in state and local expenditure, other factors remaining the same, would, accordingly, change the gross national product by less than 1½ per cent. This relatively low ratio, however, should not lead us to underrate the importance of stability in state and local finance. We are dependent upon state and local governments for vital services whose value cannot be measured solely by the effects of these services on aggregate demand. Fiscal programs which help to maintain the adequacy of state and local services in periods of recession are eminently worthwhile for their own sake.

Types of Recession Adjustments

Confronted by an actual or prospective decline in tax yields, state and local governing bodies may seek to adjust their budgets to the new fiscal situation by adopting at least one of the following general policies:

A. They may seek to reduce expenditure by the same amount that revenue has declined, keeping legal rates of taxation and utilization of reserves and borrowed funds at pre-recession levels.

B. They may endeavor to maintain their current rate of expenditure. This will require one or more of the following types of action:

175

(1) increasing legal rates of taxation or imposing new taxes, (2) securing additional grants-in-aid, (3) using up accumulated reserves more rapidly, and (4) expanding their volume of borrowing.

C. With a view to making a positive contribution toward recovery, state and local governing bodies may seek to expand expenditure during the recession. This policy will require more extensive resort to the types of action called for under policy B above. Taxes will have to be more steeply raised; additions to grants-in-aid will have to be more liberal; reserves will have to be drawn down more rapidly; a still greater expansion of indebtedness will be required.

D. As an alternative or as an additional stimulus to recovery, a policy of incentive tax reduction may be adopted. This would involve reducing the effective rates of selected taxes below their pre-recession levels. A policy of incentive tax reduction will require either drastic cuts in expenditure or types of action identical with those required to permit an expansion of expenditure, excepting, of course, tax increases.

It will be noted that all but the first of the four general policies which have just been outlined are not unique policies but families of policies. Thus the general policy of maintaining expenditure during a recession may be implemented in four different ways: through taxation, through grants-in-aid, through use of reserves, and through borrowing. If only one of these expedients is to be employed, four different choices are offered. If two of them are to be concurrently employed, there are six different choices; and if three of them are to be used, there are four different possibilities. A final possibility is that all four expedients may be used together. It should also be noted that in case more than one of the expedients are used, the relative degree of reliance placed on each may be varied.

Each of these policies or subpolicies involves one or more basic types of fiscal action. These are expenditure reduction, tax increases, increased reliance on reserves, expansion of borrowing, expansion of expenditure, incentive tax reduction, and additional grants-in-aid. In order to determine which policy or subpolicy will have the least favorable and which the most favorable influence on the general level of economic activity, it is necessary to ascertain the effect on aggregate demand of each of these basic types of fiscal action. The individual effects of the fiscal action associated with each subpolicy must then be added up.

A realistic appraisal of what state and local governments might do in the event of a recession cannot be limited to the effects of fiscal adjustments on aggregate demand. Depending on their financial and other circumstances, individual governments are subject to practical limitations with respect to the types of recession action they are in a position to take. What is more to the point, state and local governments exist primarily to promote the general welfare, and government actions which may be well adapted to raise the level of expenditure and employment are not necessarily actions which will conserve the long-term general welfare.

With the above considerations in mind, we can now proceed to examine the effects of specific types of fiscal action, each type being considered in conjunction with the other types of action with which it is necessarily linked as part of a particular policy.

Expenditure Reduction

Expenditures may be reduced in order to permit an equivalent amount of tax relief. In a recession, however, it is more likely that expenditure cuts will be made in order to offset a decline in revenue, in which event nominal rates of taxation may continue unchanged. Only this second case will be considered here.

Expenditure reductions which are not passed on to the public in the form of lower taxes obviously have an adverse effect on aggregate demand. They reduce government purchases of goods and services with no compensating increase in private purchases. The net result of such action is to give the economy a further push downward.

It does not follow from the above, however, that efforts to root out waste and inefficiency and to eliminate government activities which have lost their utility should be suspended during a recession. A business downturn generally brings new needs for public assistance. Savings resulting from improved efficiency may be used to meet these needs. They may also be used to remedy deficiencies in other facilities and services vital to the general welfare. Alternatively, the savings may be passed on to the public in lower taxes. In all of these cases the effect on aggregate demand will be neutral and the general welfare will be enhanced.

Aside from their unfavorable effect on aggregate demand, expenditure cuts which lower standards of public service or which result in a deterioration of public facilities have other untoward consequences. To the extent that the cuts are applied to services and facilities necessary to business operations, the task of recovery is rendered more difficult. To the extent that support of public education is reduced, irreparable damage may be done to the youth

177

who are unfortunate enough to be of school age at the time the recession occurs. A cut in health and welfare services is likely to aggravate the unrest and discontent which is the normal accompaniment of a recession. In short, as a method of adjusting to a business decline, expenditure reductions without offsetting tax reductions should be avoided, if at all possible.

Tax Increases

There are two distinct recession policies under which the expedient of increasing legal rates of taxation or of adding new taxes might be employed. Under the first policy an increase in tax revenue would be sought in order to finance an equivalent expansion of expenditure. Under the second and more likely policy, taxes would be raised in order to offset a recession-induced decline in revenue and to maintain rates of expenditure at their former levels.

Under the first policy the effect of a tax increase on aggregate demand is apparently neutral. The tax increase will probably reduce private purchases of goods and services by at least as much as government expenditures are increased. Certain other aspects of this policy will be considered below.

The effect of the second policy on aggregate demand is definitely adverse. When a government increases its collections from the public merely to maintain its preexisting level of expenditure, it reduces aggregate demand. It diminishes the amount of purchasing power available for personal consumption and private investment with no compensating increase in its own purchases of goods and services. This result does not, of course, follow where the new revenue collections represent private funds that would not otherwise be used. This exceptional case may be dismissed as far as most state and local governments are concerned. The limited tax sources at their disposal bear down heavily on the income and expenditure of the lower and middle income groups, who are not likely to have idle funds.

Under recession conditions an upward adjustment of taxes not only tends further to reduce the gross national product, but it has an unfavorable impact on business incentives, creating uncertainties which slow up the process of recovery. Tax increases during a business downturn are unquestionably badly timed, but unless state and local governments have previously followed long-run budget policies which have taken into consideration the contingency of a recession, such increases may represent the only way of financing high-priority services.

Stabilization Reserves

Governments can accumulate reserves only by spending less than they receive. The size of their reserves, if any, at the beginning of a recession will therefore depend upon their past budgetary policies. To the extent that they have any reserves when a recession hits them, such reserves may, under the appropriate conditions, be used to implement three different objectives: to maintain expenditures at current levels without increasing taxes, to permit a temporary expansion of expenditures without a tax rise, and to permit a temporary reduction of taxes without cutting expenditures.

When reserves are used to fill in the gap resulting from a revenue decline and to maintain expenditures at current levels without increasing tax rates, the effect on aggregate demand is neutral. Government purchases of goods and services remain as they were before and, since tax rates continue the same, private purchases of goods and services are likewise unaffected. In this case the reserves perform a protective function. They make it unnecessary to give the economy an additional downward thrust through expenditure cuts or tax increases.

When reserves are used to finance a temporary expansion of expenditure, the economy is given an upward boost. Government purchases of goods and services are increased with no offsetting reductions in private purchases. There are, however, certain limitations on the use of reserves to finance an expenditure increase.

Expansion of Borrowing

Private demand for loanable funds usually shrinks during a recession, and in this situation an expansion of public borrowing is not likely to reduce the volume of private purchases financed on a credit basis. In the recession programs of state and local governments, increased borrowing may therefore have the same effect on aggregate demand as the use of reserves. When a government increases its borrowings in order to maintain its current rate of expenditure without raising its taxes, the effect on aggregate demand is neutral. When it borrows to finance an expansion of expenditure, it makes a positive contribution to aggregate demand.

For practical reasons, borrowing is likely to have a more important role in state and local recession adjustments than that of reserves. Many governments with no reserves have unused borrowing capacity. Even in the case of the most thrifty governments, reserves are relatively small compared with borrowing potential. But borrowing involves a future cost in interest and amortization charges. Moreover, there are restrictions of various kinds on the purposes and amounts of government borrowing.

Although government spending of borrowed funds during a recession is conducive to employment stability, this does not justify borrowing for any and all purposes. Borrowing to defray current operating expenses and current charges is undesirable under any circumstances, since it means that future taxpayers will be saddled with debt service charges for which they will receive no compensating benefits. Borrowing should as far as possible be restricted to the financing of durable capital facilities which will yield worthwhile services to the public during the period in which the applicable debt charges are being met. Even in this case, however, the fact that a project would be useful and that its construction would provide employment does not constitute sufficient justification for borrowing.

Bond-financed projects must meet the same budgetary tests as tax-supported activities, since bond projects will ultimately have to be paid for through taxation or some other form of revenue. The significant questions are: Is the need for the project as urgent as the need for other projects? Will the benefits which the project yields to the public be worth their cost in debt service charges? and Has the public the ability and the willingness to pay the applicable charges over the indicated span of years? Projects which meet the above tests cannot be dreamed up overnight. It is only through the advance preparation of a long-term capital budget that a sound selection can be made.

It goes without saying that bond issues should never exceed the reasonable life expectancy of the improvements they are intended to finance. Otherwise taxpayers may find themselves paying debt service charges on dead horses. To save interest cost, moreover, governments should in normal years finance at least the annually recurring part of their capital expenditure from current revenue. Borrowing should in general be used to finance the peaks in the long-term capital budget and to maintain capital expenditures at their programed amount during a period of recession and revenue decline.

Stepping Up Expenditure

The case for increasing government expenditure during a recession centers around the premise that, as private demand recedes, governments must expand their purchases of goods and services to help fill in the gap. Ruling out the possibility of federal aid, the funds for a stepped-up program of expenditure can be obtained in only two ways: by heavier taxation or by recourse to reserves and borrowing. As has already been pointed out, higher taxes are likely to curtail private demand still further and will in addition have unfavorable effects on business incentives.

If the stepped-up expenditure program is financed by means of reserves and borrowing, its wisdom would appear to depend on the purpose for which the new funds are spent. To supply a more costly program of current services during recession years than taxpayers have the ability and willingness to pay for in normal years is obviously to invite future trouble. Under any circumstances borrowing to finance current expenditure is unwise.

A good case may be made for a stepped-up, bond-financed program of expenditure for capital outlays, provided all of the projects included meet the budgetary tests previously set forth. A government which has a master plan of development based on adequate surveys, which has a shelf or reserve of needed public works conforming to the master plan, and which follows the procedures of long-range budgeting should be in a safe position to advance the construction dates of certain projects, if a decline in construction costs or other developments during a recession should make such a change worthwhile. Under these circumstances a stepped-up construction program not only would contribute toward employment stability but would save the taxpayers money.

Incentive Tax Reduction

Proposals to reduce taxes during a recession are commonly based on the assumption that tax reduction will increase personal consumption and private investment expenditure, thus expanding employment. This result can hardly be expected to occur when tax reduction is accomplished by cuts in government appropriations. In that event it would seem highly probable that the ensuing decline in government purchases of goods and services would fully cancel the increase in private expenditure. Indeed, to the extent that any part of the tax relief given is not used for consumption or investment but is retained by its recipients in the form of idle cash, the net result of tax reduction based on budget cuts would be a net decline in aggregate employment.

When funds needed for tax reduction are obtained by borrowing or through the use of accumulated surplus, it is still a moot question whether larger and prompter effects on employment might not be obtained by government expenditure of these funds on a stepped-up program of public works. There is, of course, the possibility that tax reduction would so encourage taxpayers as to lead them to increase private expenditure by more than the amount of their tax relief. The odds for and against this eventuality are, however, not determinable.

Assuming that a government has adopted the proper rates of taxation for a normal or average year, any reduction from this level financed by mean of surpluses or by borrowing must necessarily be temporary. As soon as the emergency is over, rates will have to be restored to their normal level. Where tax relief has been based on borrowing, the new normal level of rates will, in fact, have to be somewhat higher than the original normal rates in order to take care of debt service charges on an unproductive addition to the public debt. It is more difficult to raise taxes than it is to reduce them; and at least so far as state and local governments are concerned, temporary tax reduction for the sole purpose of stimulating employment would not seem to be worth the risks and costs involved.

Additional Federal Aid

The effect on aggregate demand of extending additional federal aid to state and local governments during a recession depends almost entirely on how the federal government obtains the funds required for this purpose and on the disposition which state and local governments make of them. If the federal government obtains the requisite funds by reducing its own expenditures, and if the states and localities use their additional aid merely to offset their recession-induced revenue losses, maintaining their purchases of goods and services at former levels, the net result is to reduce aggregate demand. If states and localities use the federal aid to expand their expenditure, the net effect on aggregate demand is neutral. The only change is the replacement of a given amount of federal expenditure by a like amount of state and local expenditure. The effects are substantially the same when the federal govern-

182

ment obtains its funds through new or higher taxes. In this event, private purchases of goods and services are reduced and, if state and local governments employ the new aid solely to maintain their current levels of expenditure, aggregate demand will be reduced. If the tax-financed aid is used to expand state and local expenditure, the effect on aggregate demand will be neutral, but a certain amount of state and local expenditure will now have been substituted for a like amount of private expenditure.

It is only when the federal government obtains its funds through deficit financing that federal aid is capable of exercising a sustaining influence on the economy. When funds so obtained are employed by the states and localities to maintain pre-recession levels of expenditure, the effect on aggregate demand is neutral, but state and local tax increases and expenditure cuts which would have reduced aggregate demand may thereby have been averted. When aid based on borrowed funds is used to expand state and local expenditure, aggregate demand receives a net addition.

If consideration is limited to the effect on aggregate demand, it would appear to be a matter of indifference whether borrowing for state and local purposes is performed by the federal government or by the governments most directly concerned. From the standpoint of political philosophy, however, the difference is important. Those who believe that state and local governments should preserve a maximum degree of independence in matters not directly affecting the national interest will prefer state and local borrowing. This raises a practical question which is reserved for later consideration. Under the conditions which now govern the marketing of state and local securities, will state and local governments be able to expand their borrowings during a recession to the degree needed to enable them to maintain and perhaps to expand their total expenditure?

Requisites for Stability

The preceding analysis indicates that the two most common ways of adjusting state and local budgets to a recession—expenditure cuts and tax increases—are likely to exert a depressing influence on the economy. In the face of declining tax yields, the only way in which state and local governments can maintain or expand their expenditures without adverse effects on aggregate demand is by more extensive reliance on reserves and borrowing. Since it is probable that reserves will be small, reliance must rest mainly on an expansion of borrowing. Incentive tax reduction and additional federal aid must also be based on borrowing, if they are to accomplish their intended purpose.

But borrowing is subject to limitations. In the case of state and local governments, it is not desirable to borrow to defray current expenses, current charges, and current obligations. With a few possible exceptions, borrowing should be restricted to the financing of durable capital facilities. This additional restriction complicates the problem of budgetary adjustment. During a recession, state and local governments must avoid expenditure cuts and tax increases; they must maintain or expand their total expenditure by increased borrowing; but they must not increase their long-term indebtedness for purely current purposes.

To satisfy all of the above conditions simultaneously, a government must either possess unusually ample reserves or approach a recession with revenue receipts substantially in excess of current expenditure needs. A partial pay-as-you-go plan for financing capital projects offers a rational method of providing both the required revenue excess and an expansion of borrowing for capital outlays during a recession.

A partial pay-as-you-go plan means that revenue in a normal nonrecession year must be large enough to cover not only all expenditure on current account but a sizable proportion of capital expenditure as well. Where a plan of this kind has been followed, revenue normally used to finance capital outlays may be shifted to the support of current activities when a recession occurs. Current expenditures may thus be maintained at pre-recession levels without necessitating a rise in taxes. If the proper advance preparations have been made, a stepped-up program of capital construction may be financed on the basis of expanded borrowing.

The Present Situation

The main defenses of state and local governments against a recession would appear to be: a substantial margin of revenue which is presently being utilized for capital outlays but which might be shifted to the support of current services should the necessity arise; accumulated reserves; and the capacity to expand borrowing as needed to maintain or to increase the pre-recession volume of capital construction. These defenses must, for the most part, be built up in times of high prosperity. To attempt to provide a revenue surplus and to accumulate reserves after a recession has arrived would obviously be self-defeating.

This leads us to inquire into the present state of our defenses. To what extent are state and local governments now financing their capital outlays on a pay-as-you-go basis? How much of the revenue so used could be shifted to the support of current services should the need arise? What is the present size of state and local reserves and what restrictions, if any, would apply to their spending? Are there any impediments which would limit or slow up an expansion of state and local borrowing during a recession? Finally, what can state and local governments do in the period immediately ahead to strengthen their recession defenses?

For answers to these questions we must rely mainly on the annual compilations of the Governments Division of the Bureau of the Census, which cover only state governments and governments of cities with populations of 25,000 or more. These units of government originally receive about 70 per cent of all state and local revenue. The latest period for which published data are at hand is the fiscal year which ended in 1952. Unsatisfactory as these data are, they yield important information.

Revenue

At first glance, the revenue situation of state governments appears fairly bright. Excluding the receipts of insurance trust funds, aggregate state revenue from all sources reached a total of $14.4 billion in 1952. Expenditures for current purposes—including current operation, assistance and subsidies, payments to other governments, interest, debt redemption, and contributions to employee retirement funds—came to a total of $12.5 billion. This left a margin of $1.8 billion, or 13 per cent of total revenue, available for capital outlays and increase of reserves. The relative size of the revenue margin varied, of course, from state to state. Thus it was over 20 per cent of total revenue in Minnesota and Texas but less than 6 per cent in New York and Pennsylvania.

When these revenue margins are further analyzed, however, it becomes apparent that they are attributable almost entirely to the operations of state highway funds. For all of the states combined, highway revenues exceeded highway expenditures exclusive of capital outlays by nearly $1.6 billion in 1952. This indicates an average revenue margin of only 2 per cent for all other state funds. In not a few states general fund revenue in 1952 was barely sufficient to cover current expenditure needs. Unless these states find it possible to shift some of their highway revenue to the support of other functions, they will be obliged to make expenditure cuts or to raise taxes in the event of a recession.

In only four states—Delaware, Georgia, New York and Rhode Island—are gasoline tax revenues covered into the general fund. In all other states they are dedicated to specific purposes or segregated in special funds. The Hayden-Cartwright Act of 1934, moreover, imposes a penalty with respect to the allocation of federal highway aid on states that divert highway-user imposts to nonhighway uses.

In the 481 cities with populations of 25,000 or over, the revenue situation in 1952 was as follows: Total revenue, excluding the receipts of insurance trust funds, amounted to $6.4 billion. Total expenditures, excluding capital outlays, totaled $5.8 billion. The revenue margin available for capital outlays or increase of reserves was therefore $600 million, or about 9 per cent of total revenue.

The ratios for individual cities, however, showed a wide range of divergence. On the basis of the method of calculation used for the present purpose, which does not take into account amounts drawn from reserves, Philadelphia had an indicated revenue deficit. New York City had a revenue margin of less than 3 per cent. Los Angeles and Charlotte, North Carolina, on the other hand, had revenue margins in excess of 20 per cent. We are thus obliged to conclude that unless some of the cities increase their present revenue margins, they will be forced either to reduce their expenditure or to impose additional taxes in the event of a recession.

Reserves

The total cash and security holdings of all state governments, excluding offsets to long-term debt and the holdings of insurance trust funds, amounted to approximately $7.7 billion at the end of the fiscal year 1952. This was equivalent to about 53 per cent of the aggregate of all state revenue for that year. A quick look at individual states shows Minnesota with cash and security holdings equivalent to 125 per cent of its revenue; California with the equivalent of 76 per cent; and Pennsylvania and New York with holdings representing about 30 per cent of total revenue.

The available statistics give no clue of the extent to which these liquid assets would be available for the support of current services in the event of a revenue decline. There is evidence, however, that at least a fifth of the assets in question belong to highway funds. Another substantial fraction probably represents the proceeds of

186

bond issues pledged for specific nonhighway construction projects. Still another fraction presumably represents past revenue surpluses which have already been appropriated and against which commitments for construction have already been made.

The 481 cities with populations of 25,000 or over had cash and security holdings to the amount of $2.5 billion at the end of the fiscal year 1952. This amount does not, of course, include offsets to long-term debt and the assets of insurance trust funds. For all cities combined, the average ratio of liquid assets to revenue was 39 per cent. In the case of Philadelphia, however, such assets represented 67 per cent of revenue, whereas in the case of New York City they represented only 17 per cent. As in the case of similar liquid reserves held by the states, there is no way of ascertaining from the census statistics the extent to which these reserves are already subject to commitments, or the extent to which they represent minimum requirements for working capital.

Borrowing Power

The capacity of state and local governments to expand their borrowing is undoubtedly greater at the present time than it was in the 1920's and early 1930's. Striking evidence of this is furnished by the lower ratio of interest costs to total revenue. In 1929 the aggregate interest payments of all state and local governments represented about 10 per cent of their total revenue. In 1952, despite an 80 per cent increase in state and local indebtedness, interest payments represented less than 3 per cent of total revenue.[1]

But serious obstacles to the prompt expansion of state and local indebtedness in the event of a recession still exist. In most of the states the incurring of debt by state and local governments is subject to both constitutional and statutory restrictions. The constitutions of a few states forbid their state governments to contract any debt for any purpose whatsoever. In other states an affirmative referendum vote is required to legalize a bond issue. A common form of statutory restriction limits local indebtedness to a specified percentage of the total assessed value of the taxable property within the local jurisdiction.

The above obstacles are not necessarily insurmountable. Bond elections may be held to authorize bonds which are not to be issued immediately. Given time, statutory debt limits may be liber-

[1] *Survey of Current Business,* Dept. of Commerce, National Income and Product Series, Tables 8 and 9.

alized through legislative enactments. If this is not considered desirable, assessment ratios and assessed valuations may be raised. Debt limitations commonly apply only to so-called "full faith and credit debt," i.e. obligations for which the credit of the issuing government is unconditionally pledged. Nonguaranteed securities which do not carry the full faith and credit pledge are generally exempt from legal debt limitations. The most common type of nonguaranteed obligation is the so-called revenue bond. The volume of revenue bonds outstanding has been growing rapidly. Last year they accounted for approximately a third of all new state and local long-term issues.

The so-called "government authority," which usually issues only revenue bonds, represents a convenient device for circumventing both exhausted debt limits and constitutional restrictions on borrowing. The New York–New Jersey Port Authority is an institution of long standing. There are now scores of toll highway and bridge authorities. School building authorities are now functioning in Pennsylvania, Georgia, and Maine. School buildings are leased to local jurisdictions and the bond issues of the authorities are secured by leasehold rental payments financed from local appropriations.

Another obstacle which might prevent state and local governments from expanding their borrowing to the required degree during a recession is the fact that small units of government issuing securities in small volume and at rare intervals are at a disadvantage in selling their bonds. The states and larger cities ordinarily find a ready market for their securities, but smaller units of government are frequently forced to rely exclusively on their local banks and local capitalists. When they attempt to tap the national capital market, they are penalized by higher interest rates which may or may not accord with their actual financial condition.

One way of improving the credit position of the small government unit is the marketing of all local securities through a central state agency. This method has been successfully employed in North Carolina for the last two decades. All local governments in the state must secure the approval of the North Carolina Local Government Commission in order to borrow for any purpose whatever. As a prior condition to its approval, the Commission requires the submission of financial and economic data bearing on the ability of the petitioning government to service the proposed new debt. Centralized marketing permits the Commission to consolidate small bond issues into blocks large enough to interest the more important national underwriting groups. The Commission's knowledge of the sources of investment funds, both within and without the state, has resulted in a marked reduction in interest costs for the smaller units of government.

State loans to counties and school districts, from funds secured through the sale of state bonds, represent another way of solving the credit problem of the small political unit. The state of California recently put into effect a $435 million program of state capital outlay loans to local school districts. This program was financed by bonds secured by the full faith and credit of the state government. A similar program financed through the sale of state bonds was adopted by the state of Washington. Under the Washington plan, state loans to local school districts for capital outlays are repayable within a period of ten years, circumstances permitting. Instead of loans, a number of states, including Delaware, Maryland, North Carolina, and South Carolina, are making grants-in-aid to local jurisdictions for school construction, the funds for this purpose being obtained through the sale of state bonds.

A final doubt concerning the capacity of state and local governments to expand their borrowing during a recession relates to the ability and willingness of investors to purchase an expanded volume of security issues on reasonable terms. However, state and local governments are in a better position than they have ever been before to purchase a large share of their own issues. State and local governments now hold $12.5 billion worth of federal securities in their various trust funds and reserves. Assuming that the Federal Reserve System will support the market for federal securities, state and local governments should be able to substitute their own new issues for a portion of their federal holdings if necessary.

State and local employee retirement funds now have assets in excess of $6 billion and their reserves are growing at the rate of $700 million per year. These funds furnish a market for state and local bonds which, if need be, could be extended. The Controller of New York State recently purchased, at yields below the current market rate, ten bond issues of rural school districts, amounting to $20 million, as investments for public employee pension funds. Similarly, in Pennsylvania, the state School Building Authority placed over $16 million of 3 per cent school revenue bonds directly with state pension funds.

For Action Now

The best time to prepare for a recession is a period of rising prosperity, but there are certain steps which state and local governments can take at any time to strengthen their recession defenses. These steps may be summarized as follows:

PARTIAL PAY-AS-YOU-GO

1. As a means of stabilizing their current services and of avoiding expenditure cuts and tax increases during a recession, state and local governments should seek to place themselves on a partial pay-as-you-go basis with respect to the financing of capital outlays during nonrecession years.

2. In a period of economic uncertainty, governments should strive to secure the revenue margin necessary for the above purpose through the elimination of waste and inefficiency. The resulting savings should not be allowed to reduce total expenditure but should be used to finance new and needed additions to the capital construction program.

3. State governments should consider ways and means of temporarily shifting to the support of current government services a portion of the highway revenue now used for construction purposes as a means of averting expenditure cuts and tax increases during a recession. An expanded bond-financed program of highway construction and the assumption by state general funds of amounts of highway indebtedness equal to the amounts of highway revenue diverted should meet the requirements of the Hayden-Cartwright Act.

RESERVES

4. State and local governments with accumulated revenue surpluses appropriated but not as yet spent for construction projects should consider the advisability of financing a portion of such projects through bond issues in order to create reserves which could support current services during a recession.

BORROWING

5. The states and localities should prepare shelves or reservoirs of needed public works scheduled in order of urgency with a sufficient number of projects in the blueprint stage to permit a prompt expansion of construction work should that become desirable.

6. State and local governments should ascertain now what ob-

stacles, if any, would prevent or slow down an expansion of their borrowing during a recession and should make appropriate advance preparations to remove or to circumvent them. Whether such preparations call for the advance approval of bond issues, the liberalization of obsolete debt limitations, the creation of authorities, or other measures, will depend on the circumstances of each case.

7. State governments should develop plans to assist local governments in maintaining or expanding their construction programs during a recession. In this connection they should consider such devices as the marketing of local bonds through central state agencies, the purchase of local securities by public employee retirement funds, state guarantees of local bond issues, and state loans or grants for local construction financed on the basis of state bond issues.

COMMENT

C. HARRY KAHN, National Bureau of Economic Research

I cannot entirely agree with Heer's appraisal of the importance of the state-local sector in a prospective downturn of economic activity. It is true that state-local expenditures for goods and services constitute at present only 7 per cent of the gross national product. However, their importance may also be measured in relation to such strategic variables as gross private domestic investment and federal government expenditures for other than national security purposes. State-local expenditures, measured in GNP terms, are one-half as large as gross private investment and three times as large as federal civil expenditures. They may thus be significant in offsetting a decline in private investment, and they certainly constitute a larger base for possible government action to combat depression than do comparable federal expenditures (obviously, civil rather than defense expenditures best lend themselves to this purpose).[1] I do not intend to suggest that state-local governments are well suited and likely to engage in such countercyclical action. But if the answer is in the negative it is likely to be for reasons other than their aggregative importance relative to the rest of the economy.

In his discussion of various types of budgetary adjustment to a decline in economic activity, Heer states that an expenditure cut

[1] The President's Economic Report indeed indicates as much in stating that "if it should become necessary, outlays for federal public works could be stepped up by one-half or more within a year. State and local outlays, which are now the highest on record, might be expanded to a similar extent if financial arrangements were adequate." *Economic Report of the President,* January 1954, p. 103.

balanced by an equivalent tax cut "will be neutral" in its effect on aggregate demand, and he similarly concludes that when coupled with an expenditure increase "the effect of a tax increase on aggregate demand is apparently neutral." He then goes on to discuss the case in which tax rates would be raised in order to "offset a recession-induced decline in revenue and to maintain rates of expenditure at their former levels." For this third—and I think very relevant—case Heer believes the effect on aggregate demand "is definitely adverse." If, as Heer says, a balanced tax and expenditure cut has a neutral effect, why should the maintenance of a given level of tax collections and expenditures have an adverse effect? My reaction to these three cases is that, from a purely analytical point of view, only situations in which expenditures for current output and taxes are maintained can be considered neutral. The balanced increase may be considered expansionary, the balanced decrease contradictory.

Part of the difficulty of Heer's position appears to be due to his failure to distinguish clearly between tax rates and tax collections. This becomes particularly noticeable in his discussion of stabilization reserves. Here it is stated that "When reserves are used to fill in the gap resulting from a revenue decline and to maintain expenditures at current levels without increasing tax rates, the effect on aggregate demand is neutral." It is true that tax rates in this model remain the same, but tax collections obviously do not. Hence filling the gap by means of a stabilization reserve fund leads to the same approximate result as an automatically induced deficit and should be considered as expansionary in its effect on aggregate demand. However, in his discussion of expansion of borrowing Heer again concludes that "When a government increases its borrowings in order to maintain its current rate of expenditure without raising its taxes, the effect on aggregate demand is neutral." In the discussion on additional federal aid the interpretation of the effects on aggregate demand is in several similar cases at variance with that indicated above.

Heer also deals with the question of the extent to which borrowing may be used as a means of state-local recession adjustment. He says that in times of tight budgets it is advisable to channel current revenues into operating funds and to restrict borrowing to durable capital facilities. As a general, long-run maxim this may be a good rule to guide policy. But when the kinds of recession situations that may develop in the state-local area are considered it seems to me unnecessarily stringent. It is entirely possible that because of the rise in recession-type expenditures to be made out of state-local general funds, outlays for current needs will largely replace expenditures for capital improvements. Capital outlays may, and probably will, continue to be made by user-financed special purpose funds and authorities whose revenues usually are cyclically stable and whose reserves often are large. It is the expenditures dependent on general fund revenues, such as sales, excise, income, and property taxes, that are exposed to the greatest amount of instability. Usually these expenditures are for administrative, welfare, and school purposes. Heer states that "Borrowing to defray current operating expenses and current charges is undesirable under any circumstances, since it means that future taxpayers will be saddled with debt service charges for which they will receive no compensating benefits." It is my impression that he is here emphasizing a general principle of private and governmental finance under ordinary circumstances. I would prefer to ask: How much of state-local expenditures can, if necessary, be temporarily financed through borrowing and paid off in later years of prosperity? This is in effect a stabilization reserve plan in reverse. The objection that future taxpayers would be saddled with charges for which they receive no compensating benefits may also be made against a reserve fund, only again in reverse.

On the factual level, I fully share Heer's skepticism as to the size of available reserve funds and the probable need to rely heavily on borrowing to close revenue-expenditure gaps. As he indicated, the census statistics on cash and security holdings of state-local governments are difficult to evaluate without information as to what type of funds hold them and how much of the holdings constitute unspent proceeds of recent bond issues and minimum working balances. My own scant information suggests that bona fide reserves, which are available for stabilization purposes, are considerably smaller in amount than the census figure of $15.5 billion of cash and security holdings (excluding offsets to long-term debt and trust funds). For instance, reserves currently available for New York City's executive budget amount to a mere $32 million.[2] The census reports New York City's liquid assets as $288 million. It seems doubtful that the difference can be accounted for by semi-autonomous bodies and special purpose units whose budgets are outside the Mayor's. A quick glance at the figures for some state

[2] Strictly speaking, New York City, like many other cities, is at present not permitted by state law to build up any general fund reserves against depression contingencies.

executive budgets, such as those of New York, New Jersey, and Wisconsin, also indicates that reserve funds are considerably lower than what might be inferred from liquid assets figures. These budgets indicate that reserve funds, on the average, amount to 12 per cent of general fund revenues. This admittedly crude evidence leads me to suggest that an estimate of about $3 billion for all state-local reserve funds would be more accurate than the liquid assets figure of $15.5 billion.

This would indeed still constitute a sizable amount of reserves, and its significance is marred only by the fact that an aggregate for state-local governments cannot be interpreted in the same fashion as if it stood for a single governmental unit such as the federal government. The probability that these reserves are unevenly distributed means that some governmental units will have more than the amount of reserves required to fill a prospective expenditure-revenue gap whereas others may have practically none. In consequence these reserves are not strictly additive.

I agree with Heer's analysis of the states' and localities' aggregate borrowing power, and conclude from it that the outlook here is much more sanguine than in the case of reserves. It is generally held that states and localities could sell several billion dollars' worth of additional bonds without appreciably affecting the yield rates on such issues. This expectation is based on the following facts: (1) present interest costs are still low, on the basis of historical comparison, relative to revenues of state-local governments and relative to national income; (2) state and local governments hold billions of dollars' worth of federal securities in various trust accounts which could be exchanged for their own securities; and (3) the bonds of most states are rated Aaa or Aa by *Moody's Manual of Investments*. Serious obstacles to a prompt expansion of debt on a large scale, as has been pointed out, exist primarily on the supply rather than the demand side. Constitutional prohibitions and limitations as well as requirements for time-consuming referenda may force some projects to be postponed by time periods ranging from several months to a few years.

This delay in the issuance of new debt is not as serious as it appears at first sight. The major tax revenue of local governments, the property tax,[3] is relatively stable over cycles and experience has

---

[3] Comprehensive data on the tax revenues of state and local governments in eleven eastern and middle western states show that of the total of such revenue the amount derived from property taxes varies from 43 per cent in Michigan (fiscal 1952) to 67 per cent in New Jersey (fiscal 1949).

shown that collections from this source decline with a time lag of one and sometimes even two years, so that tax revenues may hold up fairly well until proceeds from new debt issues become available. The problem is a little more serious for the general funds of state governments, whose major revenue sources are frequently sales and income taxes, which are relatively sensitive to cycles. Much of the difficulty that state budgets face in recession is caused by the segregation of major operating funds and the earmarking of revenues. Some state activities are thereby well insulated against economic adversity whereas others bear the full brunt of it. The fact that the total of state and local tax revenues is not very cycle-sensitive loses thereby much of its value, if it has any.

As Heer points out, highway revenues, the most important stable element among state taxes, are almost universally segregated. He suggests that consideration be given to shifting temporarily a portion of highway revenues to the support of current government services (as was indeed the practice in the thirties before earmarking became a common device). Heer seems to hold that the federal Hayden-Cartwright Act of 1934 against the diversion of highway revenues might be an obstacle here. Yet the Hayden-Cartwright Act has not been a significant cause of the present state of affairs. The main difficulty lies at the state level, where there has been a lack of budgetary comprehensiveness. The chopping up of budgets prevents flexibility in budget making and tends to destabilize what might otherwise be a stable budget.[4] The states have revenues which are relatively insensitive to business fluctuations when viewed in the aggregate. There will of course still be some falling off of revenues with a decline in income, but an equally troublesome source of budgetary instability is the effort, primarily self-imposed, to circumscribe the free use of available funds and borrowing power by various legal prohibitions.[5]

The usual justification for stable revenues at the state-local level is the stabilization of expenditures which might otherwise have to

[4] This should not be construed as an argument against highway construction and maintenance in times of depression. On the contrary, little would be gained if by filling in one gap we merely created a new one. The great need for additional modern roads which is at present perceived throughout the nation constitutes a convenient antidepression weapon. The above argument does not concern highways as such but rather is aimed at budgetary rigidity.

[5] Replies to a questionnaire circulated by the Council of State Governments in 1948 showed that of the twenty-six state governments which stated their answer in quantitative form, sixteen, or almost two-thirds, found that over one-half of their revenue was earmarked. However, the two most important states—New York and California—are not included in this sample.

be reduced. If the stabilization of expenditures is prevented by devices such as the segregation of revenues into earmarked funds, one more justification for the type of revenue structure that states and localities now have becomes greatly weakened.

MELVIN I. WHITE, Brooklyn College

Federal expenditure and revenue reactions automatically induced by a decline in aggregate income are usually considered a first line of defense against economic recession. The task of quantitative analysis, then, is to evaluate the stabilizing contributions of these reactions—applying the concept of built-in flexibility. It can be assumed that the federal government would hardly dare cut its autonomous expenditures—at least not in *deliberate* response to the forces of deflation. And since it would likewise not raise tax rates, built-in flexibility can be counted on as a minimal contribution to stability.

Why not a similar approach to state and local finance—that is, initial concentration on built-in flexibility before use of other policies? If all state and local governments followed a coordinated policy—with direction as well as assistance from the federal government—it might be possible for them to assume a share of the responsibility for controlling fluctuations. But most state or local governments are obliged to act more or less autonomously with limited financial resources and in the economic interest of the area they serve. Under these circumstances it is impossible for them to contribute much to the control of economic fluctuations. Rather it is their responsibility to seek an optimal *adaptation* to the fluctuations that occur. Any contribution they may make to economic stabilization must emerge more or less as a by-product of policies adopted to minimize the disturbing effects of fluctuations and to leave the governmental units as free as possible to pursue their appropriate welfare objectives.

Fluctuations ordinarily cause state and local governments to modify or cut back programs that it would be desirable to carry out. As Heer suggests, these changes must be assessed on the basis of what they mean for the standard of services rendered to the communities. The criterion for a successful adaptation of expenditures to economic fluctuations should be expressed in terms of maintaining some designated (quite possibly secularly rising) standard of

I wish to acknowledge the participation of Anne White in the preparation of these comments.

"real" per capita services. The actual dollar outlays involved in maintaining such standards would then automatically vary at least with population and prices. Further, as I construe maintaining standards, outlays would also vary inversely with the level of unemployment through the impact of the latter on public assistance; for it is part of the job of maintaining standards to carry through on a commitment to provide a given "real" amount of general relief to all persons who qualify on the basis of eligibility rules unchanged from those prevailing in a prosperity period.

On the revenue side a successful adaptation would make it unnecessary for the governmental unit to tinker with the rate structure as a reaction to fluctuations—permitting constant tax rates during depression and a minimum of rate increases during inflation. If initially rates are high enough and the tax structure sufficiently sensitive to income changes, expenditures for maintaining standards can be balanced over a whole cycle through a system of multiyear carryback or carryforward of revenue surpluses from the prosperity period. This mode of adjustment meets and goes beyond Heer's stricture that expenditure reduction without offsetting tax reduction should be avoided if possible.

A maintenance-of-standards policy, then, would produce an automatic decline in revenues at constant tax rates and a semiautomatic expansion of expenditures as the minimal response to depression. A degree of built-in flexibility would thus be provided at the state and local level.

A maintenance-of-standards policy also can serve a more fundamental diagnostic purpose. To get some idea of the magnitude of the problem to which adjustment must be made—that is, to isolate the effects of fluctuations themselves from the effects of any short-run policy adjustments to them—it is necessary to work with an expenditure and revenue policy that can remain invariant with respect to economic fluctuations and that can be readily translated into quantitative terms. The obvious solution on the revenue side is an unchanged tax rate. A maintenance-of-standards budget is a possible solution on the expenditure side—with the budget assumed here calling for a constant rather than a rising standard of services. The two devices together would make it possible to estimate an expenditure-revenue gap associated with any assumed decline in employment and corresponding fall in gross national product. They thus provide a useful tool for measuring both the problem that confronts the state and local governments and their possible minimal contribution to economic stability.

A rough indication of the over-all expenditure-revenue gap that a maintenance-of-standards policy would produce in a forthcoming period of economic depression can be obtained by means of projections based on state and local expenditure and revenue data for recent years. As a supplement to Heer's paper, I want to present some figures using this type of analysis. The purpose of these estimates is twofold, as already suggested: to obtain some measure of the magnitude of the problem of adjustment that state and local governments may have to face, and to develop a measure of a possible minimum automatic contribution to economic stabilization.

The size of the expenditure-revenue gap will depend, of course, on the severity of the depression; and the financial problem the gap presents to state and local governments will be influenced by the amount of federal aid that becomes available. Recurrence of a gap with anything like the catastrophic proportions of 1929–1933 can probably be ruled out of consideration. Or, to put it another way, any such eventuality may be clearly regarded as a failure of federal policy, justifying emergency measures, and need not be taken into account by state and local government in planning their finances. On the other hand, even a successful federal policy for controlling fluctuations cannot be taken to imply continously full employment at stable prices, and hence state and local governments must count on a significant degree of fluctuation both upward and downward. The current concern about state and local autonomy or independence implies interest in the extent to which state and local governments can make their way in a moderately fluctuating economy with no expansion of federal aid beyond that already built into the structure of federal-state-local fiscal relations.

Needless to say, no great refinement of estimation underlies the derivation of these expenditure-revenue figures; they represent a quick adjustment to extend figures worked out in detail for large cities to cover all state and local governments.[1] The procedure was this: A simplified cycle model indicating hypothetical fluctuations in gross national product in terms of annual figures was constructed. The model allows for three years of less than full employment with unemployment in the lowest year averaging 8 million, or 12 per cent of the labor force. This results from an assumed man-hour loss equal to 15 per cent of available man-hours—that is, 15 per cent of the product of the civilian labor force and the standard workweek—accounted for in part by an assumed shift to shorter

---

[1] Cf. Melvin and Anne White, "Impact of Economic Fluctuations on Municipal Finance," *National Tax Journal,* March 1954, p. 17.

hours for those remaining employed. This probably represents about the limit of severity which state and local governments can be expected to plan for. In a depression more serious than this, the state and local problem and its contribution to economic stabilization would probably be swamped in the national emergency. Fairly stable prices were assumed, with a maximum decline of 5 per cent. Combined with other assumptions, this implied a peak-year-to-trough-year decline of about 10 per cent in gross national product.

In this model, increase on the expenditure side reflects changes in the cost of continuing a standard of services established during the last pre-depression year, which is taken to be 1953. Calculations were made on the basis of the per capita standard of service provided in 1953 at an estimated cost of $29 billion. On this basis, expenditures for maintenance of standards rise through the depression period, reaching $30.5 billion at the trough—about two years after the onset of the depression—or $1½ billion above the initial year expenditures. Expenditures then maintain a fairly even level for the subsequent recovery year, when the reduction in public assistance outlays due to rising employment is just about offset by the increase in requirements due to rising prices and growing population.[2]

[2] Estimates of expenditures—and revenues—for 1953 were obtained by adjusting available 1952 data given in the Bureau of the Census's *Summary of Governmental Finances in 1952* according to the government-purchase-of-goods-and-services component of the national income accounts. The 1953 expenditure total excludes expenditures out of unemployment compensation and other trust funds but includes contributions of state and local governments to their employee retirement funds, which constitute a charge on the budget. Also excluded is a portion of the actual capital outlay figure. This exclusion is implied by the decision to measure the impact of depression on the cost of maintaining standards of per capita services at the pre-depression (1953) level, rather than on the cost of a secularly rising standard. Insofar as services derived from capital assets are concerned, constant standards are assumed to require a constant ratio of real assets to population. On the basis of the only data readily available on capital assets of state and local governments, a reasonable allowance for depreciation and population growth during 1953 yields a capital outlay requirement of $4.5 billion. The estimated excess of outlays in 1953 over this figure—which comes to almost $3½ billion—is taken to indicate net expansion of capital in relation to population; if projected throughout the depression it would imply a continuously rising ratio of assets to population, and therefore for purposes of estimating constant standards it is subtracted from the base figure for capital outlays.

The rise in general relief case loads is the most important factor contributing to the increase in expenditures. There are no data available to measure how many cases would be added to welfare budgets in a future depression as severe as that assumed here, since welfare standards have changed greatly. The rise in case loads underlying the rise in welfare expenditure is derived by linear projection of a correlation between case loads and unemployment for recent years, allowing in one-half the cases for a six months' time lag between the increases in

In 1953, revenues from state and local governments' own sources (excluding revenues of insurance trust funds) are estimated to have been enough to cover the expenditures of $29 billion included in the maintenance-of-standards budget. The decline in tax revenues induced by the drop in gross national product hypothesized in the model is calculated on the basis of an estimated income elasticity for the state and local revenue structure of .5. Between the peak year and the trough year the decline amounts to about $1.3 billion. It is slightly offset by an increase in federal aid to state and local governments. On the assumption that legislation governing these programs in 1952 is continued unchanged throughout the cycle, the increase in federal aid is about $.2 billion and thus the net decline in revenue is about $1 billion.[3]

unemployment and the associated increase in case loads. The public welfare case loads in the categories of old age assistance and assistance to the blind and disabled are assumed to rise with population growth during the depression years, but the rise in aid to dependent children is assumed to be predominantly a cyclical reaction. The increase in the final public welfare figure reflects the above factors offset to some extent by the hypothesized decline in prices, which reduces the dollar requirement per case load grant.

Expenditure categories in which payrolls absorb a high proportion of outlays, such as education and police and fire protection, also rise. This rise reflects the increase in personnel required to maintain standards for a growing population, and the assumption that state and local governments will maintain constant wage rates during the depression—neither cutting them nor providing usual "productivity" increases. Categories in which materials purchased are important—such as health, sanitation, and highway maintenance—as well as capital outlays, do decline somewhat as a result of the assumed general decline in prices. The behavior of interest charges depends on the financial policies pursued. But even if the entire expenditure-revenue gap is financed by borrowing, the impact on interest charges is still slight.

[3] The elasticity coefficient of .5 is an average of individual elasticities weighted by the amounts collected under the respective taxes in the base year. It is assumed for these calculations that this elasticity remains stable over the whole period. Actually the coefficient would vary somewhat with changes in the level of income as taxes with high individual elasticities shifted in relative importance compared with taxes of low elasticity. However, for the present model the variation in the over-all coefficient would not be great.

It may be noted that for a period as long as that covered by the model, there may be some distinction between the cyclical and secular responsiveness of tax yields to income changes. Such a distinction is probably of significance only in estimating the elasticity of the property tax. Measurement of elasticity is also complicated by the problem of time lags. No attempt has been made here to deal with these complexities, and the elasticities for the individual revenue sources are based on the findings of H. M. Groves and C. H. Kahn as given in "The Stability of State and Local Tax Yields" (American Economic Review, March 1952), and on certain theoretical considerations.

Federal aid for nonwelfare purposes is simply assumed to rise proportionately with population. On the basis of existing legislation, federal aid for welfare assistance could be expected to rise proportionately with the number of recipients, assuming the dollar grant per case remained constant. The fact that the dollar

For the trough year, then, expenditures are about $1½ billion higher and revenues $1 billion lower than they were in the pre-depression year, when revenues just balanced the maintenance-of-standards budget. The total gap, excluding the operations of trust funds, is $2½ billion for the trough year. The model allows for three years of less than full employment, and the total depression period gap comes to just about $5 billion.

It should be noted that not all of this $5 billion depression gap is the result of reactions that can be properly included in the concept of built-in flexibility. Built-in flexibility refers to changes in revenues and outlays contingent on changes in gross national product and other income aggregates; specifically it does not refer to expansion in expenditures as a result of population growth. Consequently the built-in flexibility gap would be somewhat less than $5 billion. It would reflect only the cyclical expansion in welfare case loads and the net decline of revenues, offset by the price level decline affecting all categories of expenditures.

Two questions can be raised about this gap: One, are the state and local governments able to finance a $5 billion gap either out of reserves or by borrowing? Second, assuming that all states and localities pursue such policies, will their outlays help to stabilize aggregate demand?

To turn first to the financing of the gap. According to the Bureau of the Census's *Summary of Government Finances,* state and local governments in 1952 held $15 billion in cash and securities, for which no specific allocation is indicated. Unfortunately I have nothing to add to Heer's information on the extent to which these liquid holdings are subject to commitments or minimum working balances and thereby are restricted from use as a free reserve fund. But even if something of the order of $5 billion could be made available to finance the expenditure-revenue gap, there is no reason to suppose that the distribution among states and localities of this total would parallel the distribution of the total expenditure-revenue gap.

If reserves are not available, the alternative is borrowing. Heer has made it clear that state and local governments have a large

grant per case is assumed to decline, reflecting the fall in consumer prices, might imply that federal aid would rise slightly more than in proportion to state and local expenditures (due to the provision for reducing the proportion paid by the federal government when the payment per case rises above a certain sum). However, the price factor in this instance is very small and has been ignored, and federal aid for assistance is assumed to maintain a constant ratio to state and local expenditures for welfare assistance programs.

and unused borrowing capacity and that the numerous institutional difficulties in the way of expanding debt in depression are probably not insurmountable. I differ with him, however, on his apparent restriction of borrowing to capital outlays. It seems to me that financing current expenses by a program of short-term borrowing repaid in a subsequent period of prosperity amounts to essentially the same thing as financing out of reserves accumulated in previous prosperity periods—one is a carryback of surplus, the other a carryforward, and neither requires any permanent increase in debt. As a matter of fact, the practical difficulties in the way of administering and maintaining the integrity of a reserve fund program seem to me more impressive than those raised by a program of depression short-term borrowing. And insofar as ultimate cost to the taxpayer is concerned, borrowing is no more expensive than reserve fund accumulation.

The question of depression financing makes clear the importance of considering what comes after the depression is over. Financial difficulties do not necessarily terminate with the return of full employment. Assuming that the hypothesized three-year depression were followed by a steady business expansion at stable prices, figures based on my illustrative model indicate that revenues from a tax structure with an elasticity of .5 (plus federal aid) would not quite keep pace with expenditures for maintaining standards. Thus tax rates would have to be raised to produce the surplus necessary to replace the drain on reserves or to repay the depression period addition to debt. If a price inflation were assumed, the costs of maintaining standards would rise even more rapidly, and the cumulative deficit over the whole cycle might become very large. Thus the present financial structure, with constant tax rates, would not raise adequate funds over the cycle as a whole. The problem would be more acute for localities—as indeed it was during the postwar inflation—than for the states, which tend to have more elastic tax structures.

It is probably worth giving special notice at this point to the cyclical pattern of expenditures that is implied here, particularly when depression is followed by some price inflation. After adjustment for the long-term upward trend, expenditures vary essentially with prices and unemployment. Wages and prices tend to be more sensitive to upward than to downward pressures; thus price level declines are not much of an offset to the effects of rising unemployment. On the other hand, price rises as unemployment tapers off help to produce further expansion of expenditures—especially if an inflationary upswing develops. Thus expenditures tend to rise during both depression and full employment, reaching a minimum point somewhere in the period of recovery.

I have some reservations about Heer's analysis of the demand effects of expenditure and revenue movements generally—particularly his discussion of stabilization reserves and incentive tax reduction. Apparently he considers that if state and local expenditures remain constant and the structure of tax *rates* is unchanged, state and local finance will be neutral in its effects on aggregate demand. One aspect of this problem is covered in the discussion of David Lusher's paper in this volume: the need to specify a bench-mark by which to measure the impact of automatically induced changes in revenues (or expenditures) on aggregate income, and the correlative problem of what constitutes a good bench-mark. I do not believe that Heer's bench-mark, if I have interpreted it correctly, of constant *rates* and constant dollar expenditures is the most useful one. It tends to conceal the significance of induced movements on the tax side, which implies an asymmetric treatment compared with the expenditures side.

I would suggest a bench-mark policy of constant expenditures and constant tax collections. Such a bench-mark is oriented to the question: How much more or less are state and local governments contributing (in absolute terms) to aggregate demand than they were in the last pre-recession year? Then, however the contribution in the pre-recession year is itself evaluated, a depression-induced expenditure-revenue gap becomes an incremental contribution.

Quantitative assessment of the impact of the expenditure-revenue gap as developed here requires the usual assumptions about the spending functions involved in national income models with perhaps specific attention to the spending propensities of the recipients of welfare payments and the beneficiaries of tax reduction, taking into account the offsetting effect of state and local tax reduction on the federal income tax base. Liquidity implications and non-induced investment effects can certainly be ignored. A thoroughgoing analysis would take into account the time lags involved in the income-spending-income sequence.

The results of such an analysis can be expressed following Lusher and Musgrave-Miller in terms of the decline in gross national product (assuming a given decline in autonomous expenditures) that would be forestalled by state and local outlays to cover the expenditure-revenue gap. But a budgetary policy that would eliminate the expenditure-revenue gap also implies a somewhat different functional relation between changes in national product and changes in consumption; thus it becomes quite difficult to estimate how much decline in gross national product would be forestalled by a policy which permits, as compared with one which does not permit, the gap to develop.

Therefore I prefer to express what a maintenance-of-standards policy would contribute in somewhat different terms—in terms of the incremental decline it would permit in autonomous expenditures, give a pattern of decline in gross national product of a maximum of, say, 10 per cent. That is, an incremental expenditure-revenue gap of $5 billion by states and localities would permit autonomous expenditures to drop $4 billion farther than otherwise (this decline might be about 10 per cent of a depression period level of gross private domestic investment) without producing a decline in gross national product of more than the original 10 per cent. In general, in appraising potential contribution to stabilization it seems to me better to relate changes in state and local expenditures and revenues to gross private domestic investment rather than, as Heer does, to gross national product. In any event, if the relationship is to be to gross national product, the multiplier cannot be left out.

SOCIAL SECURITY PROGRAMS AND
ECONOMIC STABILITY

IDA C. MERRIAM

ASSISTANT DIRECTOR, DIVISION OF RESEARCH AND STATISTICS
SOCIAL SECURITY ADMINISTRATION
DEPARTMENT OF HEALTH, EDUCATION, AND WELFARE

The social security program in this country came into existence as a result of the most serious depression in our history. There had been earlier social security measures—most notably workmen's compensation. And the full employment and the semicontrolled economy of the war years have left their impress on the program, both in the rapid growth of supplementary private plans and in attitudes toward the basic national system of old age and survivors' insurance and its place in our economy. The social security programs are now generally regarded as a continuing mechanism for providing income to individuals and groups who—whether in time of full employment or depression—are for short or long periods without income from employment.

The existence of such programs, however, cannot but have an effect on the course of any future depression, recession, or lesser adjustment in economic activity. As this paper will attempt to demonstrate, the social security programs should be counted among the significant built-in stabilizers. But considerably more analysis is needed of the nature and the strength of the stabilizing effect which is exerted by existing programs or which might be exerted by somewhat modified and expanded programs. Such an analysis must be concerned with (1) the direct compensatory action of unemployment insurance and, to some extent, of all the social security programs; (2) the steady base of demand provided by the programs; (3) the effect of methods of financing; and (4) the psychological, political, and administrative importance of the programs as going institutions.

In the absence of social security programs, individuals who have no current income from employment and earnings, and their dependents, draw their support from families or relatives, from

The views expressed herein are those of the author and are not necessarily those of the Department of Health, Education, and Welfare.

205

private charity, or from use of personal savings and assets. The family or clan system that, largely through a widespread sharing of income in kind, was the major guarantee of security in earlier societies has shown itself unable to survive in industrial and highly organized economies. In our society, support by relatives and friends is still important in meeting the needs of persons who lack sufficient independent sources of income, but it has largely a supplementary role. In this respect we are in a transitional stage. There are, for example, still a considerable number of older persons who do not qualify for benefits under the old age insurance program, but this number is rapidly decreasing. At present, about 45 per cent of all persons aged 65 and over are eligible for benefits; by 1960 about 75 per cent and by 1980 nearly 95 per cent will be eligible as a result of the maturing of the system and the broad coverage extensions effected by the 1954 amendments of the Social Security Act. Unemployment insurance—in spite of limitations of coverage and of benefit adequacy—has become the primary method of channeling current income to persons who are temporarily unemployed. For those who are sick or disabled, our social security provisions are much more limited. Railroad workers and most government employees—as well as veterans—have disability insurance protection. Otherwise, the major organized arrangements are paid sick leave or private employee benefit plans, which ordinarily stop for an individual when he leaves the particular employment, and public assistance for the permanently and totally disabled.

In assessing the economic effects of the existing or of an expanded social security system, we are concerned with the amount of the transfer payments involved in relation to other aggregates, such as wages and salaries or personal consumption expenditures. We are concerned with the net effect on consumption and, indirectly, on productivity of this organized method of providing for the non-earning groups. And we are concerned with the way in which these programs adjust automatically to changing economic conditions, and the kind of stabilizing influence which they thus exert.

1. Unemployment Insurance

Certain easily stated relationships give one kind of quantitative measure of the possible compensatory action of unemployment insurance. In 1954 the state and railroad unemployment insurance programs together covered about two-thirds of all civilian employees and about 77 per cent of civilian wages and salaries or just under 60 per cent of total earnings (including earnings of the self-employed). Since average weekly benefits for total unemployment are only about one-third of average weekly wages, under existing civilian programs the maximum replacement of aggregate wage loss due to unemployment would be about 25 per cent even in the initial stage of a downturn if the incidence of unemployment were proportionately the same in the covered and noncovered sectors of the economy.[1] This figure must be further reduced to take account of compensation for partial unemployment at a rate of less than one-third of the wage loss, and the substantial amount of uncompensated earnings loss resulting from disqualifications for benefits, initial waiting periods before benefits are payable, and the exhaustion of benefit rights before the individual is re-employed.

In most states the initial waiting period after a claim is filed and before benefits become payable is now one week or less. The extent of uncompensated wage loss resulting from this factor can be measured by comparing the figures on average weekly insured unemployment with the average weekly number of beneficiaries. In 1949, for instance, almost 13 million weeks of unemployment were uncompensated because they were waiting-period weeks under the state, railroad, or veterans' programs (as compared with 115.7 million weeks compensated). Had these weeks been compensated at the average rate, the total unemployment benefits paid in that year would have been increased by about 11 per cent.

It is more difficult to measure the effect of ineligibility for benefits resulting either from insufficient wage credits or from disqualifications. At the outset of an employment decline, those who fail to meet the wage credit requirements will be primarily marginal workers and also new entrants to the labor force. The longer a depression continues, the more significant will be this factor of new entrants who cannot qualify for benefits. The disqualification provisions of most state unemployment insurance laws have become increasingly restrictive. In almost all states, workers who are fired for misconduct (a term subject to wide variations of interpretation) are disqualified for benefits for specified periods or for the duration of a spell of unemployment. So also are workers who leave a job without "good cause." This means that workers who leave one job with the expectation of finding a better one which then does not

---

[1] Special provisions for veterans' unemployment benefits may also be a significant factor in some periods. This point is discussed below in connection with the analysis of the 1949–1950 experience. Coverage was extended somewhat by the 1945 amendments to the Social Security Act (see below).

materialize, secondary workers who move to another locality when the primary earner moves, workers who are forced to give up particular jobs for reasons of health, and many others who are not voluntarily unemployed in the ordinary meaning of that term, fail to qualify for benefits. There is no basis for judging whether the administration of the disqualification provisions is likely to result in proportionately more uncompensated wage loss in good times, at the beginning of a depression, or after a depression has continued for some time.

At the beginning of a decline in economic activity, a large part of the wage loss may result from partial unemployment—three- or four-day workweeks, a drop in overtime hours, etc. All the state unemployment insurance laws and the railroad unemployment insurance program provide some coverage for partial unemployment, but most states limit the payment to an amount equal to the difference between weekly earnings (from a short workweek or odd jobs) and the maximum weekly benefit amount plus a variable allowance (in most states, $3). Thus, on the average, workers may suffer a wage loss of two-thirds of their previous earnings and still not be entitled to any compensation, and may be compensated at a rate of only 15 or 20 per cent of an even larger wage loss. How important an effect this factor will have on the proportion of aggregate wage loss compensated in a particular recession may depend on which industries are most seriously affected by unemployment and their customary or depression-induced employment practices.

The maximum potential duration of unemployment insurance benefits was originally limited to 16 weeks or less in most states, largely as a result of what proved to be gross overestimates of the costs of the program. The maximum duration of benefits has gradually been increased in all states until it now ranges from 16 to 26 weeks. In only 14 states, however, is the potential duration uniform for all eligible claimants. In the others potential duration varies depending on the individual worker's past employment and earnings, being as low as 5 weeks for some workers. In 1948 a million workers exhausted their benefit rights under state unemployment insurance laws before becoming re-employed; in 1949 the number jumped to 1.9 million, and in 1950 it was 1.8 million. Both the total number of persons exhausting benefit rights and the length of time they remain unemployed thereafter tend to increase as a depression becomes more severe.

The compensatory effect of unemployment insurance would be

increased by a number of proposed modifications of the program. As a result of the 1954 amendments, coverage will be extended beginning in 1955 to about 2.5 million federal employees and about 1.3 million workers in firms employing 4 to 7 people. It could easily (in terms of administrative feasibility) be extended to the 2.1 million employees of firms in industry and commerce that employ less than 4 and to some 5.0 million government and borderline agricultural workers who will still be excluded. It would be more difficult but entirely possible to cover all farm and domestic workers as well.

The original legislative intention was to cover about 50 per cent of the wage loss by insurance benefits. The present situation results not so much from an explicit change in what is regarded as the appropriate proportion of wage loss to be compensated as it does from what might be called the fallacy of absolute numbers. Benefits today are only one-third of average wages primarily because the fixed dollar maximums have not been raised proportionately with rising wage levels. It is probable that many persons have not fully adjusted their thinking to what today's dollar wage levels should call for in the way of maximum weekly benefits. It can also be argued that unemployment insurance would better serve its purpose if benefits compensated for something like two-thirds rather than one-half of the wage loss, particularly in the case of workers with families.

The uniform provision of benefits for 26 weeks to all workers who remain unemployed that length of time would further greatly increase the effectiveness of the program. Even if the amount of wages required to qualify for benefits were as a result increased somewhat in some states, thus disqualifying additional marginal and seasonal workers, the net effect of such uniform duration provisions would be to increase the proportion of wage loss compensated in a period of moderate decline and still more in a deeper depression.

In summary, a practicable scheme of expanded unemployment insurance might have the following maximum compensatory result: Assuming 90 per cent of civilian wages and salaries to be covered, the effective rate of compensation to be two-thirds of gross weekly wages (at all levels of earnings), and disqualification provisions to be less restrictive than they are today, unemployment benefits could at the maximum compensate for something less than 60 per cent of the aggregate loss of civilian wages and salaries resulting from declining economic activity at the beginning of a decline. Whether unemployment insurance should be relied upon to provide the major source of income to unemployed workers throughout a long depression is debatable. Some would argue that benefit duration should be extended to 39 or even 52 weeks. Depending on circumstances, however, a vigorous public works and public service program might be a more desirable alternative for unemployed persons and for society as a whole.

All of the figures presented thus far as to the possible portion of wage loss that might be compensated have been based on the tacit assumption that the rate of decline in employment and earnings would be about the same in the covered as in the noncovered sectors of the economy. Were as much as 90 per cent of civilian wages and salaries covered, it would make little difference whether or not this was the case. With more limited coverage, there may be significant differences in the extent of wage loss in the covered industries and the net loss in the economy as a whole. If unemployment were concentrated in covered industries and among lower-paid workers, even the present limited program could compensate for a larger portion of aggregate wage loss than the figures cited above suggest. The opposite situation might also occur. Timing may be important. The period of time over which the program plays a significant sustaining role will ordinarily be greater if employment declines come at different times in different industries or areas than if the same total decline is concentrated in time and widespread.[2]

[2] These observations and the detailed analysis of the 1949–1950 experience which follows assume that what we are concerned with are (1) the net aggregate wage loss for the economy as a whole resulting from fairly general declines in economic activity and (2) the extent to which unemployment benefits replace this wage loss. That is to say, for purposes of this analysis the (individual) wage loss—and benefit payments—resulting from seasonal fluctuations in employment are ruled out. Wage loss is computed on the basis of seasonally adjusted data. For benefit payments a similar result is achieved for the 1949–1950 period by taking into account only the amounts above the payments in the same month of the preceding year (of full employment). This procedure rules out also benefits paid to compensate for wage losses to the individual resulting from normal job mobility. Such wage losses are automatically excluded from any aggregate wage figure.

The wage loss concept used here is a net concept in that any increases in employment are offset against declines in other sectors. To illustrate some of the factors operative in the 1949–1950 period, the net aggregate wage loss is computed separately for total civilian wages and salaries, private wages and salaries, and covered payrolls. Even within the latter, more restricted sector, however, there will be divergent movements, with some firms or industries expanding even during a general decline. Such divergent movements would occur in the absence of unemployment insurance, or of any stabilization policy. The most general measure of the stabilization potential of unemployment insurance would thus appear to be that used here—that is, the ratio of the additional or depression-

UNEMPLOYMENT INSURANCE IN THE 1949–1950 DECLINE

An analysis of the operation of unemployment insurance during 1949 and 1950 illustrates some of the factors that determine the program's effectiveness as a stabilizing device.

The 1949–1950 decline in economic activity was relatively moderate—whatever specific term be used to describe it. Between the fourth quarter of 1948 and the first quarter of 1949, gross national product (seasonally adjusted) dropped 2.4 per cent, and it continued to drop, but by less than 1 per cent, in each of the remaining three quarters of 1949. In the first quarter of 1950 it turned upward, almost reaching the level of the fourth quarter of 1948, and it increased steadily thereafter.

Personal consumption expenditures (seasonally adjusted) dropped less than 1 per cent (.6) from the fourth quarter of 1948 to the first quarter of 1949 and increased slightly thereafter through the middle of 1950, when the outbreak of war resulted first in a spurt and then in a relative falling off in consumer buying.

The initial drop in total wages and salaries on a seasonally adjusted basis was 2.6 per cent, only fractionally higher than the drop in gross national product. The first upturn in wages and salaries came in the fourth quarter of 1949, but it was not until the second quarter of 1950 that this figure reached and surpassed the fourth-quarter 1948 level.

Unemployment did not reach its peak until February 1950, when it stood at 4.7 million, or 7.6 per cent of the labor force. In July of 1949 it had reached a peak for that year of 6.4 per cent of the labor force (see Table 1). Persons receiving unemployment benefits from the state, railroad, and veterans' programs constituted a larger proportion of the total number unemployed in March 1949, however, when they were 84 per cent of the total, than in any subse-

induced benefits to the net (nonseasonal) wage loss of the economy as a whole. In terms of this ratio the effectiveness of unemployment insurance will be less in a general and major decline than in a minor depression (assuming the same relative replacement of individual weekly wage loss), even without taking account of the factor of the limited duration of benefit payments. This accords with common sense, and it points up one reason why such an automatic stabilizing measure is relatively more effective at the outset of a decline and in minor than in major depressions. On the other hand, in situations where employment declines are concentrated in particular areas or regions, and what is important is the maintenance of consumer income in those regions (i.e. where the effect of a regional decline has not yet spread to the economy as a whole), this method of measurement and analysis may overstate the effectiveness of unemployment insurance as a stabilization measure.

211

TABLE 1

Unemployment and Unemployment Insurance Beneficiaries, October 1948–December 1950

(*numbers in thousands*)

Year and Month	Number Unemployed	Average Weekly Number of Beneficiaries— State, Railroad and Veterans' Programs	Unemployed as a Per Cent of Civilian Labor Force	Beneficiaries as a Per Cent of Total Unemployed	Number Exhausting State Unemployment Insurance Benefit (Quarterly)
1948					
October	1,642	973	2.7%	59.3%	...
November	1,831	1,047	3.0	57.2	...
December	1,941	1,351	3.2	69.6	241
1949					
January	2,664	1,809	4.4	67.9	...
February	3,221	2,234	5.3	69.4	...
March	3,167	2,651	5.2	83.7	371
April	3,016	2,425	5.0	80.4	...
May	3,289	2,419	5.3	73.5	...
June	3,778	2,504	6.0	66.3	439
July	4,095	2,464	6.4	60.2	...
August	3,689	2,346	5.8	63.6	...
September	3,351	1,972	5.3	58.8	534
October	3,576	1,776	5.7	49.7	...
November	3,409	1,973	5.4	57.9	...
December	3,489	2,121	5.6	60.8	591
1950					
January	4,480	2,315	7.3	51.7	...
February	4,684	2,254	7.6	48.1	...
March	4,123	2,326	6.7	56.4	730
April	3,515	1,701	5.7	48.4	...
May	3,057	1,672	4.9	54.7	...
June	3,384	1,466	5.2	43.3	528
July	3,213	1,233	5.0	38.4	...
August	2,500	1,050	3.9	42.0	...
September	2,341	852	3.7	36.4	342
October	1,940	692	3.0	35.7	...
November	2,240	771	3.5	34.4	...
December	2,229	873	3.6	39.2	253

Source: *Monthly Report on the Labor Force*, Bureau of the Census; Social Security Administration, Dept. of Health, Education, and Welfare; Bureau of Employment Security, Dept. Labor.

quent period. The absolute number of weekly beneficiaries under the three programs combined was also higher in March 1949 than at any other time during this period. By February 1950, beneficiaries represented only 48 per cent of the total unemployment figure. The decreasing proportion of persons receiving benefits was probably related in part to changes in the previous labor force experience of the unemployed group. More important, however, was the increasing number of persons exhausting their benefit rights before becoming re-employed. Almost three-quarters of a million persons exhausted their benefit rights under the state unemployment insurance programs in the first quarter of 1950. The number of exhaustions in this quarter was almost twice as great as in the first quarter of 1949, when unemployment insurance was having its maximum effect.

Per Cent of Wage Loss Compensated. Wage and salary receipts on a seasonally adjusted annual basis reached a peak in October 1948 which they did not again touch until May 1950. The aggregate total wage loss over this period, measured from the October 1948 level, was $6.3 billion, and the aggregate civilian wage loss $5.8 billion. Government civilian wages and salaries on a seasonally adjusted basis increased throughout the period, however, and the wage loss that occurred was concentrated in the private sector. For private wages and salaries the total wage loss from October 1948 to May 1950 was $7.2 billion. Unemployment benefit payments (state, railroad, and veterans combined) in the same period totaled $3.2 billion. Some of these benefits would have been paid, however, even had aggregate wages and salaries not decreased. Normal labor turnover and seasonal unemployment give rise to some unemployment benefit payments even in periods of full employment. To measure the extent to which unemployment benefits compensated for wage losses resulting from the decline in the level of employment, one has to use some figure representing "additional" benefits.

For state and railroad unemployment benefits, the amount by which benefits in each month exceeded the payments in the same month of 1948 (or 1947 if the measurement is on a monthly rather than a quarterly basis) may be taken as an approximate measure of such additional or depression-induced benefit payments. Veterans' unemployment benefit payments, however, had been high in 1947 and 1948 for reasons other than general employment conditions and fell off rapidly in the last five months of 1949 because the period of eligibility expired for most veterans on July 25, 1949 (two years after the official end of the war). Since many veterans would have been receiving state or railroad unemployment benefits in the absence of the special program for veterans, and considerable numbers did file claims and receive payments under the regular programs after July 1949, the veterans' benefits cannot

213

TABLE 2

Wage Loss Compensated by Unemployment Benefits, 1949 and First Quarter of 1950

YEAR AND QUARTER	QUARTERLY WAGE LOSS FROM LEVEL OF FOURTH QUARTER, 1948 (billions of dollars)			ADDITIONAL UNEMPLOYMENT BENEFITS [a] (millions of dollars)			PER CENT OF WAGE LOSS COMPENSATED			
	Civilian Wages and Salaries	Private Wages and Salaries	Payrolls Covered by State Unemployment Insurance	State, Railroad, and Veterans'	State and Railroad	State	Civilian Wages and Salaries, All Benefits	Private Wages and Salaries — All Benefits	Private Wages and Salaries — State and Railroad	Payrolls Covered by State Unemployment Insurance — State Benefits
1949										
I	$ .9	$ .9	$1.2	$ 261.3	$ 181.1	$ 174.0	29.0%	29.0%	20.1%	14.5%
II	1.2	1.3	1.3	316.8	237.0	226.0	26.4	24.4	18.2	17.4
III	1.3	1.5	1.2	347.1	300.6	281.5	26.7	23.1	20.0	23.5
IV	1.4	1.6	1.6	306.9	298.4	260.9	21.9	19.2	18.6	16.3
1950										
I	.9	1.1	1.1	377.2	368.7	344.3	41.9	34.3	33.5	31.3
Entire period	$5.7	$6.4	$6.4	$1,609.3	$1,385.8	$1,286.7	28.2%	25.1%	21.7%	20.1%

a Amount of state and railroad benefits above amounts in same months of 1948 and one-half of total veterans' benefits paid in indicated quarter.

Source: Computed from data from National Income Division, Dept of Commerce and Social Security Administration, Dept. of Health, Education, and Welfare.

be disregarded in an analysis of the 1949–1950 experience. As an expedient it was assumed that half of the veterans' benefits paid in 1949 and 1950 were additional to those that would have been paid had employment remained at 1948 levels. This is probably an understatement, but there is no ready basis for a more refined estimate.

The quarterly wage loss during 1949 and the first quarter of 1950 as measured from the fourth-quarter 1948 level is shown in Table 2 for civilian wages and salaries, private wages and salaries, and payrolls covered by state unemployment insurance programs.[3] The total wage loss over the entire period is, of course, less when measured from the fourth quarter of 1948 than from the peak month of October.

The additional unemployment benefits paid under the state unemployment insurance laws would appear to have compensated for about one-fifth of the aggregate loss in covered payrolls during 1949 and the first quarter of 1950. Additional state and railroad benefits combined represented about 22 per cent of the private wage and salary loss, and these plus half of the veterans' benefits paid, about 25 per cent. Because all civilian wages and salaries, including government, declined less than those in the private sector alone, the depression-induced state, railroad, and veterans' benefits together amounted to a little more than 28 per cent of the aggregate civilian wage loss.[4]

[3] The seasonal factors applied to payrolls covered by state unemployment insurance programs to obtain this measure were developed by Mr. Hyman Kaitz of the Bureau of Employment Security, Department of Labor.

[4] Beginning with data for January 1950, the National Income Division of the Department of Commerce has computed a seasonally adjusted unemployment benefit payments figure. An alternative method of calculating the increase in benefits as a result of employment declines—that is, comparison with the level of seasonally adjusted payments in the base period—is therefore readily available for periods after 1950. To test the results of the two methods, the increase in seasonally adjusted benefit payments in the fourth quarter of 1953 and the first quarter of 1954 above the third quarter of 1953 was computed. The additional benefit payments in the two quarters were also computed by the method used for the 1949–1950 analysis—that is, the excess of payments in the given quarter over payments in the same quarter of the previous year. For state and railroad benefits combined, the "additional benefit" figures derived by the two methods were identical for the fourth quarter of 1953; for the first quarter of 1954 the figure based on the seasonally adjusted data was 92 per cent of the figure based on the previous year comparison. Using the same method as in the 1949–1950 analysis, state and railroad unemployment benefits compensated for 15.8 per cent of the wage loss in private wages and salaries in the fourth quarter of 1953 and 25.6 per cent in the first quarter of 1954, or 22.1 per cent over the two quarters. Using seasonally adjusted benefit payments data, the extent of wage loss compensated over the two quarters is 20.9 per cent.

It is possible to derive a rough measure of the effect of the limited duration provisions of the state unemployment insurance laws on the total benefits paid. From the fourth quarter of 1948 through the second quarter of 1950, some 3.4 million persons exhausted their benefit rights under the state unemployment insurance programs before they were re-employed. They had received benefits for an average of about 19.5 weeks. Had all of them received benefits for a full 26 weeks at the average benefit rate, the aggregate benefits paid during the period would have been some $467 million higher than they actually were. Here again, however, account must be taken of the fact that some workers (particularly those with limited potential duration) will exhaust benefits even in periods of high employment. If only exhaustions in excess of those occurring in the same quarters of 1948 and only through the first quarter of 1950 are considered, the additional benefit payments resulting from a uniform potential duration of 26 weeks would have been about $177 million and state unemployment insurance benefits would have compensated for 23 instead of 20 per cent of the loss in covered payrolls.

This entire analysis neglects the fact that under conditions of full employment, wages and salaries would have been rising throughout 1949 and early 1950 and not merely holding the fourth-quarter 1948 level. It is perhaps sufficient for present purposes to recognize this factor without attempting a quantitative measure.

There might be some interest in a comparison of the extent of wage loss compensated in different states. Such comparisons would reflect not only differing economic conditions but also differences in the benefit provisions of the several states. Time did not permit any such elaborate analysis in connection with the preparation of this paper. Nor was there any state in which unemployment was of such magnitude and duration as to illustrate the operation of unemployment insurance in a really serious depression. The wage loss compensated was calculated for one state, Connecticut. This state was selected because it had a substantial increase in unemployment from 1948 to 1949, although the absolute level was not unusually high, and a relatively large wage loss continuing into the second quarter of 1950. Its benefit provisions were perhaps a little above average, primarily because of the provision for dependents' benefits. The additional benefits paid in 1949 and the first two quarters of 1950 in the state compensated for 20.6 per cent of the wage loss in covered payrolls (on a seasonally adjusted basis) during that period. Had all of the additional persons who exhausted benefits (those above the number exhausting in the same quarter of 1948) received payments for 26 weeks, the proportion of covered wage loss compensated would have been 25.7 per cent.

Benefits Related to Consumption Expenditures. Another measure of the impact of unemployment benefit payments on the economy is the relation between aggregate benefits and personal consumption expenditures. In the fourth quarter of 1948, unemployment benefit payments (state, railroad, and veterans') represented .6 per cent of personal consumption expenditures. This ratio more than doubled in the first quarter of 1949 and stood as follows in subsequent quarters:

1949

First quarter	1.3
Second quarter	1.4
Third quarter	1.3
Fourth quarter	1.0

1950

First quarter	1.4
Second quarter	.9
Third quarter	.5
Fourth quarter	.4

In a period when consumption expenditures dropped significantly (it will be remembered that on a seasonally adjusted basis they were below the fourth-quarter 1948 level only in the first quarter of 1949), there could be a much larger increase in the ratio.

Payments and Contributions. In the initial phase of a downturn in economic activity, the stimulating or, more properly, the sustaining effect of an increase in unemployment benefit payments is presumably little if at all affected by what happens on the contribution side of the program. Indeed, throughout even a fairly long depression the economic effects of the benefit payments are probably quite separate and distinct from the effects of contribution collections. By and large, benefit payments are spent promptly and in their entirety. Whatever the ultimate incidence of the employer payroll tax, it seems unlikely that the continued payment of the tax, at an established rate, during a period of declining economic activity would have a significant effect on wages or prices or, therefore, on consumption expenditures. Under existing laws, however, rates are not fixed.

Declining covered payrolls would automatically result in lower aggregate contributions throughout a depression were it not for the effect of rate changes under the experience-rating provisions of the state unemployment insurance laws. Since there is some time lag in rate changes, there is likely to be a falling off of contributions in the early stages of a decline. To what extent contribution rates will subsequently be increased depends on the severity of the depression. Rate increases are very likely to come just at the wrong time from the economic point of view—that is, just when employment and production are beginning to pick up and increased tax rates may most discourage employers and deter the needed expansion in economic activity.

The 1949–1950 recession was too brief to show the potential effect of experience rating. The amounts of contributions collected and their relation to aggregate benefit payments, by quarter, in 1949 and 1950 are shown in Table 3. Contributions as a per cent of covered payrolls—which, it will be noted, were higher in 1950 than in 1949—continued to increase in 1951, amounting to 1.5, 1.6, and 1.5 per cent in the first, second, and third quarters, respectively, and not dropping to 1.1 per cent until the fourth quarter of that year.

Because of the operation of the experience-rating provisions, contribution rates would have increased in 1951 in a number of states even had employment continued to decline. The precise timing of rate changes varies from state to state, depending on the nature of the experience-rating formula used. Thirty-five states have some requirement of a minimum fund balance before rates may be reduced below the standard 2.7 per cent, and others have different rate schedules depending on the status of the reserve fund. The requirements are too detailed and too varied to lend themselves to brief summary. The net effect of the provisions is to require rate increases—some quite substantial—following any serious drain on the state's reserve fund. The economic consequences could be unfortunate. One may question whether the existing provisions would be permitted to stand in a serious depression.

In addition, the separate financing of unemployment insurance on a state-by-state basis makes it highly probable that in a depression of any size one or more state funds would be exhausted. Such exhaustion would be in states that always have a higher than average rate of unemployment and that can provide benefits comparable to those in other states and accumulate adequate reserves only by collecting much higher than average contributions from the employers in the state. Federal loans to states threatened with bankruptcy of their unemployment insurance funds would help tide them over an immediate crisis but would do nothing to meet

TABLE 3

Unemployment Insurance Contributions and Benefit Payments, Fourth Quarter of 1948 to Fourth Quarter of 1950

(dollars in millions)

YEAR AND QUARTER	UNEMPLOYMENT INSURANCE CONTRIBUTIONS		UNEMPLOYMENT BENEFIT PAYMENTS			BENEFIT PAYMENTS MORE (+) OR LESS (−) THAN CONTRIBUTIONS			TOTAL CONTRIBUTIONS AS A PER CENT OF COVERED PAYROLLS
	Total— State, Federal, Railroad	*State Laws*	*Total— State, Railroad, Veterans'*	*State and Railroad*	*State*	*Total Benefits; Total Contributions*	*State and Railroad Benefits; Total Contributions*	*State Benefits; State Contributions*	
1948									
I	$297.9	$280.0	$282.3	$203.4	$197.6	$ −15.6	$ −94.5	$ −82.4	1.1%
1949									
I	362.8	181.4	547.6	387.2	370.5	+184.8	+24.4	+189.1	1.5
II	270.8	252.3	617.4	457.8	438.0	+346.6	+187.0	+185.7	1.1
III	301.8	280.0	590.2	497.1	473.5	+288.4	+195.3	+193.5	1.2
IV	292.1	273.3	519.0	501.8	458.5	+226.9	+209.7	+185.2	1.1
1950									
I	391.6	218.7	591.8	574.9	540.8	+200.2	+183.3	+322.1	1.6
II	344.3	322.5	418.1	408.0	395.2	+73.8	+63.7	+72.7	1.3
III	351.3	332.4	266.8	261.1	253.9	−84.5	−90.2	−78.5	1.3
IV	337.4	317.9	194.7	193.0	186.9	−142.7	−144.4	−131.0	1.1

Source: Social Security Administration, Dept. of Health, Education, and Welfare and Bureau of Employment Security, Dept. of Labor.

the fundamental problem of risk sharing across state boundaries. This problem, of course, involves other issues than those specifically related to economic stabilization.

THE INSTITUTIONAL ASPECTS OF UNEMPLOYMENT INSURANCE

So many factors contribute to the turn of economic events that it is difficult to evaluate the significance of a 20 per cent—or indeed a 50 per cent—replacement of wage loss in any particular recession or depression. As was said earlier, both the timing and the localization of employment declines may make a considerable difference.

It would seem probable, however, that the availability of unemployment insurance would have a significant effect on the attitudes and on the expenditures of those who are still at work as well as of those who are unemployed and drawing benefits. Unemployment insurance may thus contribute more to sustaining consumer spending than the ratio of aggregate payments to aggregate wage loss would suggest.

These secondary effects of unemployment insurance will presumably be weak and could even become nonexistent when benefits are very low in relation to previous earnings and when the potential duration of payments is very limited. One may hazard a guess that an increase in maximum benefit amounts and benefit duration beyond what they now are in most states would result in a larger increase in the sustaining force of unemployment insurance than the actual dollar increases in aggregate benefit payments.

While the compensatory effect of unemployment insurance is more important at the beginning of a downturn than it would be in a long depression, the program has a stand-by value that might be of considerable importance in the event of a serious decline. The existence of the unemployment insurance machinery would in such circumstances greatly facilitate both the payment of extended benefits—if this were regarded as desirable—and the orderly referral of workers to public works and service programs. While one may hope that the unemployment insurance system will not be called upon for extensive operations of either type, its availability may properly be regarded as an institutional safeguard over and above its automatic stabilizing effect.

2. Old Age and Survivors' Insurance and Related Programs

The importance of the long-term benefits—old age, survivor, and disability benefits—for economic stability derive primarily from the assured base of demand which they provide for increasingly large segments of the population. In terms of individual benefit amounts the base may be somewhat meager. Nevertheless, the programs probably support larger aggregate consumption expenditures than would be made were these same persons entirely dependent on children or other relatives, on their own savings, or on relief. The assured nature of the benefits is particularly important in a period of declining employment, not only to the beneficiaries but also to the children whose earnings might otherwise have to be shared, or more largely shared, with the beneficiary group.

Furthermore, even these long-term benefit payments do expand or contract in the aggregate with changing economic conditions. The tight labor market and increased employment opportunities for the aged held down the old age and survivors' insurance benefit rolls during World War II. A serious depression might force many older persons out of employment and thus substantially increase the number of beneficiaries and amount of benefit payments beyond what they would otherwise be.

PRESENT MAGNITUDE OF LONG-TERM BENEFIT PROGRAMS

During 1953 just under $7 billion was paid in monthly benefits under old age and survivors' insurance, the railroad retirement system, retirement systems for federal, state, and local government employees, and the veterans' pension program. Benefit payments and beneficiaries under the several programs were as follows:

	Beneficiaries as of December 1953 (thousands)	Benefits Paid in 1953 (millions)
Old age and survivors' insurance	5,981.4	$2,918.8
Railroad retirement	543.1	457.4
Government employees	740.0 a	1,099.2 a
Veterans' pensions	3,647.3	2,435.9
		$6,929.4

a Partly estimated.

There are no good estimates of the number of persons receiving benefits under workmen's compensation. The amounts paid to persons with long-continued disabilities and to survivors under this program may be in the neighborhood of a quarter of a billion dollars a year.

Private pension plans, it may be estimated, paid benefits to something like 650,000 persons in 1953 at an annual rate of something under $.4 billion. Most but not all of the persons receiving private pensions were also receiving benefits under one (or more) of the public programs.

The approximately $7.5 billion a year being paid under these long-term benefit programs at the end of 1953 represented 3.3 per cent of total consumption expenditures in 1953, 2.7 per cent of personal income, 4.1 per cent of civilian wages and salaries.

POTENTIAL EXPANSION OF OLD AGE AND SURVIVORS' INSURANCE IN THE NEAR FUTURE

The old age and survivors' insurance program is still in a period of fairly rapid expansion benefitwise. Even with no further increase in the system's coverage (or benefit provisions) beyond that in effect in 1953, the number of beneficiaries and the aggregate benefit payments would have been substantially larger in the future than today. The major factors involved in the maturing of the system are: the increasing proportion of persons reaching the age of sixty-five who will have had an opportunity to acquire insured status, the increasing number and proportion of aged persons in the population, and the increasing proportion of beneficiaries who will be receiving the higher benefit amounts based on earnings after 1950.[5]

The upward trend in old age and survivors' insurance beneficiaries and benefit payments (present price levels) under the program in effect in 1953 would—according to actuarial projections—have continued throughout this century. The expansion of coverage under the 1954 amendments will result in a more rapid maturing of the system but, primarily because of the increasing number of aged persons in the population, will not change this trend.

For present purposes, however, we are concerned not with the year 2000 but with the 1950's. The analysis which follows makes use of estimates of benefit payments in the fiscal years 1956, 1957, and 1958 on two alternative assumptions as to the economic conditions in those years which were developed in connection with the preparation of the Fourteenth Annual Report of the Board of Trustees of the Old-Age and Survivors Insurance Trust Fund.[6]

[5] The 1950 amendments brought in a substantial number of persons under the "new start" relaxed eligibility provisions, at minimum benefit levels; furthermore, the increase effectuated by the 1950 and 1952 amendments in the benefits of those already on the rolls in 1950 were smaller than the benefit formula increases (including the effect of the new start in the computation of average wages) for persons with earnings after 1950. The 1954 amendments do not include another "new start" provision, but they will result in somewhat higher benefits for persons qualifying on the basis of earnings after 1954 than on the basis of comparable earnings in earlier periods.

[6] I am indebted to my colleagues in the Bureau of Old-Age and Survivors Insurance, particularly Mr. Lawrence Alpern and Miss Roslyn Arnold, for help in converting these estimates to a calendar year basis and in preparing comparable estimates for an expanded program.

The estimates were developed early in 1954 and relate to (1) the program then in effect and (2) the expanded program proposed by the Administration for Congressional consideration. The amendments adopted by Congress in August 1954 differ somewhat from these proposals. Coverage was extended to most but not all of the groups for whom it had been recommended (the most important of the groups left out are self-employed doctors, dentists, lawyers, and members of a few other professions). On the other hand, overall benefit liberalizations were slightly greater than those proposed. It has not been possible in the time available to prepare comparable estimates based specifically on the 1954 amendments. Such estimates would differ very little from those shown for an expanded program. Certainly the general conclusions to be drawn from the figures for the purposes of this analysis would be the same. The estimates based on the act prior to the amendments have been retained for purposes of comparison. In any use of either set of figures it should be remembered that the specific amounts derive from a stated set of economic assumptions and will differ somewhat from estimates based on other economic assumptions.

The economic assumptions underlying the estimates are intended not as predictions of what is likely to happen in the next three years, but as illustrations of the way the program would operate under conditions of relatively high employment or, alternatively, with moderately heavy unemployment. A mild contraction in 1954 and early 1955 is assumed to preface both these alternatives. Specifically, the assumptions as to civilian employment and unemployment are as follows:

		ALTERNATIVE I RELATIVELY HIGH EMPLOYMENT			ALTERNATIVE II LOWER EMPLOYMENT LEVELS			
		Labor Force (m i	Em- ployment l l i	Unem- ployment o n s)	Unemployed as Per Cent of Labor Force	Labor Force (m i	Em- ployment l l i	Unem- ployment o n s)	Unemployed as Per Cent of Labor Force
Dec.	1954	63.4	61.1	2.3	3.6%	63.4	61.1	2.3	3.6%
June	1955	66.1	62.9	3.2	4.8	66.1	62.9	3.2	4.8
Dec.	1955	64.0	61.9	2.1	3.3	64.0	60.1	3.9	6.1
June	1956	66.3	63.7	2.6	3.9	66.3	60.8	5.5	8.3
Dec.	1956	64.5	62.9	1.6	2.5	64.4	58.8	5.6	8.7
June	1957	66.9	64.2	2.7	4.0	66.6	60.2	6.4	9.6
Dec.	1957	65.1	63.5	1.6	2.5	64.9	59.1	5.8	8.9

With continuing moderately high employment, benefit payments in 1957 under the old age and survivors' insurance program in effect in 1953 amount to about $4.5 billion (present price levels).

Should economic activity decline to a point where unemployment was as high as 9 or 10 per cent of the civilian labor force, a considerable number of older persons would probably be forced out of jobs and onto the old age and survivors' insurance benefit rolls. The additional benefit payments under the assumed conditions might be in the neighborhood of $300 million a year (Table 4).

TABLE 4

Benefits and Beneficiaries under Existing Old Age and Survivors' Insurance Program, 1953, and Same Program, Alternative Employment Conditions, 1955–1957

Calendar Year	Relatively High Employment	Lower Employment Levels	If All Eligible Aged Retired
	Total Benefit Payments (*billions of dollars*)		
1953		$3.0	$4.3
1955	$3.8	$3.9	5.1
1956	4.2	4.4	5.5
1957	4.5	4.8	5.8
	Number of Beneficiaries (Midpoint of Year) (*millions*)		
1953		5.6	7.3
1955	7.0	7.0	8.7
1956	7.5	7.8	9.2
1957	8.0	8.4	9.7

At the present time, almost 1.4 million persons between sixty-five and seventy-five years of age and with insured status—that is, persons who could receive benefits if they retired—are still at work. An indication of the maximum expansion of benefit payments (without changes in legislation) in the event of a major depression can be obtained by assuming that all of this group retire and they and their eligible dependents receive benefits. While this limit would never actually be reached, the figure is nevertheless of some interest. Because the persons in this group are in general among the higher-paid workers, their benefits would also be higher than average. As Table 4 indicates, according to the old age and survivors' insurance program in effect in 1953, 1957 aggregate benefit payments would amount to about $5.8 billion if conditions were such as to induce all persons with insured status to retire.[7]

[7] No account has been taken in these estimates of the fact that some additional children and younger widows could receive benefits if they stopped working; the

The total old age and survivors' insurance benefits paid in 1957 as shown in Table 4 represent about 1.3 per cent of aggregate personal income under the high-employment assumptions used and 1.7 per cent under the low-.

EFFECT OF EXPANDED COVERAGE AND BENEFIT PROVISIONS

The old age and survivors' insurance program in effect in 1953 covered almost four-fifths of the civilian labor force. The 1954 amendments extended coverage to almost all paid employment effective as of January 1, 1955. The major groups still not covered are: railroad workers (who have a separate system partially integrated with old age and survivors' insurance); federal government workers covered by the Civil Service Retirement system and military retirement systems (for whom old age and survivors' insurance coverage also has now been recommended); self-employed doctors, dentists, lawyers, and members of a few other professions; and irregularly employed agricultural workers. The immediate effect of coverage extension alone is to increase contributions more than aggregate benefit payments, since it takes a little time for individuals in newly covered jobs to acquire insured status. There will, however, be an increase in the number of beneficiaries on the rolls in 1957 as compared with the number who would have qualified under the law in effect earlier. And in the long run, of course, the effectiveness of the program will be substantially increased.

In spite of the increases in benefits as a result of the 1950 and 1952 amendments of the Social Security Act, the benefits payable to workers retiring in 1953 and early 1954 were lower, when adjusted for price changes, than the dollar amount of benefits that would by this time have been payable under the 1939 act to workers with the same average earnings. The deterioration in the value of the benefits is most striking in terms of the proportion of wage loss compensated. Under the 1939 act the taxable wage base, which sets a limit on both the amount of the individual earnings on which contributions are payable and the amount credited for benefit purposes, was $3,000. At the time, 97 per cent of the workers covered by the program (and 95 per cent of those in covered employment in each of the four quarters of the year) had total covered earnings of less than $3,000 a year. Benefits, in other words, were related to the total earnings (in covered employment) of all but the very

---

amounts involved would be small and would be partially counterbalanced by the smaller number of valid claims for survivor benefits at low than at high employment levels.

highest-paid group. To achieve a similar result in early 1954, the taxable wage base would have had to be $7,500 rather than the $3,600 set by the then-existing law or the $4,200 adopted under the 1954 amendments.

Because the 1950 amendments changed the benefit formula, the benefits paid in 1953 and early 1954 covered a larger proportion of the worker's previous average earnings, and those payable under the 1954 amendments will also cover a larger proportion, than the above comparison alone would suggest. The benefit formula has from the beginning provided compensation at a higher rate for the lower-paid workers. Under the 1939 act the maximum old age benefit (worker alone) would have been about 23 per cent of his previous average earnings for a worker with the maximum creditable earnings when the program reached maturity (the 1939 act provided a small increment in the benefit for each year of coverage and contributions; this was eliminated in 1950 and there is now no such differential). Under the law in effect in 1953, a worker with maximum earnings credits ($3,600 a year) could receive a benefit equal to 28 per cent of his earnings. But 44 per cent of all four-quarter workers (about 40 per cent of all workers) now earn considerably more than $3,600. For the $7,500-a-year worker, the proportion of previous earnings compensated was 13.6 per cent. Where a beneficiary has a wife who is aged sixty-five or over, the family situation and the total wage loss compensated are somewhat better, since the wife will receive a benefit half that of her husband's.

The 1954 amendments both increased the taxable wage base to $4,200 and modified the benefit formula. The new maximum individual old age benefit of $108.50 a month represents 31 per cent of the previous earnings for a worker with the maximum wage credits ($4,200) and 17 per cent for a person with earnings of $7,500 a year.[8]

Had the original Administration proposals been adopted to go

[8] One qualification must be noted with regard to all of the figures on percentage of earnings loss compensated. The figures given are strictly the percentage of computed average monthly wage. Since the average monthly wage is computed by dividing total wage credits by total elapsed time since 1951 (or 1937 for most of those now on the rolls), it is likely to be lower than actual average earnings when the worker was engaged in covered employment or than such earnings in the five or ten years prior to retirement. This would be particularly true in periods when earnings levels were rising. The 1954 amendments improve the correspondence between actual and computed earnings for all except the newly covered group (and for those in this group who are regularly employed after 1954), by dropping out of the computation up to five years in which the individual's earnings were lowest (or non-existent).

into effect by January 1, 1955, aggregate benefit payments in 1955, 1956, and 1957, under the same employment conditions as were assumed above, would amount to:

AGGREGATE BENEFIT PAYMENTS

(*billions of dollars*)

	Relatively High Employment	Lower Employment Levels	If All Eligible Aged Retired
1955	4.5	4.5	5.9
1956	5.0	5.2	6.5
1957	5.6	5.9	7.2

As was indicated earlier, the 1954 amendments enacted by Congress liberalized benefits a little more but extended coverage to somewhat fewer persons than the original Administration proposals. The retirement test, under the amendments, does not apply beginning with age seventy-two rather than age seventy-five, and the test itself is somewhat easier to meet. Aggregate benefit payments in 1955, 1956, and 1957 under the act as now amended and under the assumed economic conditions would be slightly but not significantly larger than the estimated amounts shown above.

Other proposals for the modification of old age and survivors' insurance which have been advanced by various groups would result in larger increases in benefit payments than those effectuated by the 1954 amendments. It has not been possible, nor would it be particularly useful, to attempt similar estimates for all the proposals that might be reviewed in an analysis of the program aspects of old age and survivors' insurance.

Some mention should perhaps be made, however, of the magnitude of the benefit payments that would result if the old age and survivors' insurance program were expanded to provide monthly long-term disability benefits, similar to the benefits now provided under the railroad retirement program and most retirement systems for government employees. Such benefits are generally more sensitive than old age retirement benefits to fluctuations in economic conditions and employment levels. Depending on the precise specifications, long-term disability benefit payments under old age and survivors' insurance might, on the average, amount to as little as .01 per cent of taxable payrolls (as estimated for the proposals of the 1949 Advisory Council on Social Security to the Senate Committee on Finance) or up to 1 per cent with more liberal provisions, after the program had been in effect long enough so that most disabled persons had had time to acquire insured status before becoming disabled. In terms of present payroll levels and the coverage and taxable earnings base provided in the 1954 amendments, this would mean payments in an average year of up to about $2 billion. At the outset of any such program expansion, the aggregate disability benefits paid would be considerably smaller, since many persons already disabled would presumably not be able to qualify for benefits.

CONTRIBUTIONS AND BENEFIT PAYMENTS

The contribution income of the old age and survivors' insurance fund is at present larger than the benefit outlays, at least at high levels of employment (Table 5).

TABLE 5

Old Age and Survivors' Insurance Contributions and Benefit Payments under Alternative Assumptions as to Employment Conditions and Provisions of the Program, 1953 and 1955–1957

(billions of dollars)

CALENDAR YEAR	CONTRIBUTIONS COLLECTED a		BENEFIT PAYMENTS LESS (−) OR MORE (+) THAN CONTRIBUTIONS	
	Relatively High Employment	Lower Employment Levels	Relatively High Employment	Lower Employment Levels
		Program in Effect in 1953		
1953	3.9		−.9	
1955	5.7	5.5	−1.9	−1.6
1956	6.1	5.5	−1.9	−1.1
1957	6.3	5.3	−1.9	−.5
	Expanded Coverage, Somewhat Liberalized Benefits			
1955	6.3	6.0	−1.8	−1.5
1956	7.2	6.5	−2.2	−1.3
1957	7.6	6.4	−2.0	−.5

a The contribution rate in 1953 was 1.5 per cent each for employers and employees and 2.25 per cent on earnings from self-employment; in 1955, 1956, and 1957 the rate in the 1953 law and under the 1954 amendments is 2 per cent each for employers and employees and 3 per cent on earnings from self-employment.

Under the program in effect in 1953, total contributions in 1957 would have been about $1.9 billion more than aggregate benefit payments if economic conditions were good, but only about $.5 billion more under conditions in which 10 per cent of the labor force were unemployed.

Under an expanded program with coverage and benefit provisions such as those proposed by the Administration or embodied in

228

the 1954 amendments, the net excess of total contributions would be somewhat smaller in 1955 and larger in 1956 than under the law in effect in 1953, because the benefit increases would take effect in 1955 while the increased contribution income from expansion of coverage to self-employed groups would not show up in collections until 1956. With unemployment of about 10 per cent of the civilian labor force, the total benefit payments under the Administration's program in 1957 would amount to about $5.9 billion, and contributions collected to about $6.4 billion, resulting in the same net difference as under the program in effect in 1953. Because of the more limited coverage provisions actually adopted in 1954, contributions under the assumed economic condition would be slightly less than shown in Table 5.

OTHER RETIREMENT PROGRAMS, 1955–1957

Neither the railroad retirement program nor the government employee retirement programs as a group are growing at the same rate as old age and survivors' insurance. Many of the larger government retirement systems were established thirty or more years ago and have thus had time to reach relative maturity. The railroad system began by taking over the pensioners on the rolls of the private railroad pension plans and crediting past railroad employment and thus covered a large proportion of the current aged railroad workers immediately.

By 1957, with present statutory provisions and present price levels, aggregate benefit payments under these programs might be in the neighborhood of $1.6 billion if employment conditions were relatively good, or $1.7 billion if something like 10 per cent of the civilian labor force were unemployed. The Railroad Retirement Board estimates that at the end of 1951 there were more than 150,000 persons working in railroad employment who could have retired and drawn benefits. Had all eligible persons retired, benefit payments under the railroad act in 1953 might have been about $.2 billion higher than they actually were. There are probably relatively fewer persons in government employment who could retire on a full age annuity if they so wished than persons eligible for old age and survivors' insurance but still at work. On the other hand, most retirement systems for government employees as well as the railroad retirement system pay monthly disability benefits. Because persons with disabling conditions have difficulty holding jobs when employment conditions are bad, aggregate disability benefit payments are likely to increase as unemployment becomes more serious.

If old age and survivors' insurance coverage were extended to all employments and the railroad and government systems made supplementary, payments under these special programs would eventually be less than they would be under present law. Since present annuitants would not be affected, however, any such change would make very little difference in the amounts paid under the special systems in 1957, and for present purposes this kind of program change can be disregarded.

Veterans' benefits will probably be considerably larger in 1957 than they were in 1953, with no changes in existing veterans' legislation and assuming no wartime service between now and then. The largest increases to be anticipated are in the non-service-connected pensions, as more and more World War I veterans reach the age of sixty-five. (On June 30, 1953, the average age of the 3.3 million World War I veterans was fifty-nine.) By 1957, total compensation and pension benefits for veterans will probably be somewhat over $3 billion if employment is at a high level and still larger if employment declines.[9] Since the non-service-connected pensions are subject to an income test (at present $1,400 a year for a single veteran, a widow without children, or for the child of a veteran; $2,700 for a veteran who is married or has minor children or for a widow with a child), the aggregate benefits paid are likely to increase rather substantially if there is a serious drop in employment.

The number of persons receiving private pensions is also increasing. By and large, however, private pensions are paid only to persons who have remained with a single employer for a considerable period of time, and in many plans, particularly the large collectively bargained plans, these persons must be in that employer's pay at the time of retirement. As a result, many of the persons who at one time or another are covered by private plans will never qualify for pensions. Many plans, furthermore, do not give credits for service prior to the time the plan was initiated and will therefore pay no benefits or very small benefits to workers now approaching retirement age. A very rough estimate might place the aggregate amount of private pensions in 1957 at between $.5 and .6 billion.

The rate of fund accumulation is much greater under private pension plans than under old age and survivors' insurance. At present, employer contributions to pension plans are about $2.3 billion a

[9] See statement of Phillip S. Hughes, Bureau of the Budget, on "Veterans Benefits in Relation to Old-Age and Survivors Insurance," in *Hearings* before the Subcommittee on Social Security of the Committee on Ways and Means, House of Representatives, 83d Cong. 1st sess., November 12 and 13, 1953, Part 2, 1953.

year and employee contributions about $.5 billion. Thus at present, aggregate private pension payments (under $.4 billion) are still less even than employee contributions and, of course, very much less than total contributions. Total private pension fund reserves have been estimated to be about $17 billion (the old age and survivors' insurance reserve at the end of 1953 was $18.7 billion).

Total contributions under the railroad retirement program in 1953 amounted to $.6 billion. Benefit payments in that year were $150 million less than total contributions. The most recent estimates of contributions under all government employee retirement programs are for 1952. In that year, when aggregate benefit payments were $1.0 billion, employee contributions to federal, state, and local retirement programs amounted to $.9 billion, and earmarked government (employer) contributions to these retirement systems were $.9 billion; in addition, the general revenues were drawn on to provide the $.35 billion of benefits paid by the federal noncontributory retirement systems. Veterans' benefits are, of course, financed directly from general revenues.

3. Public Assistance

It is perhaps debatable whether the public assistance programs should be included among the built-in stabilizers, since the size of the payments is not specified in law and the amounts appropriated are subject to budget and debt limitations just when there is most need for their expansion. Nevertheless, the institutional weight of public assistance is such that it would seem to deserve some consideration in a discussion of this kind.

At the end of 1953 there were about 5.4 million persons receiving public assistance—2.6 million aged persons, 1.5 million children and .5 million parents or adult relatives of such children, .1 million blind and .2 million permanently and totally disabled, and about .6 million persons receiving general assistance. The total amount of public assistance paid in 1953 was $2.5 billion. The number of persons sixty-five and over in need of assistance should decrease fairly steadily as old age and survivors' insurance expands over the next decade—assuming that old age and survivors' insurance benefit levels keep up with any increases in prices. It is more difficult to predict what will happen in the other programs.

The size of the public assistance rolls is influenced by economic conditions. Not only can some older persons, some disabled persons, some widows and other women in families in which the normal breadwinner is absent or incapacitated, and some children get jobs when conditions are good who would not otherwise be able to do so. In addition, contributions from relatives are more frequent when earnings are high, and less assistance is needed to maintain the same level of living for the recipients. Indeed, one way in which families adjust to wage loss when economic conditions are bad is to shift part of the support of parents or other relatives to public assistance.

The compensatory effect of public assistance is sharply limited, however, by the unavailability or inadequacy of general assistance in many states. In a number of states general assistance is not given to persons regarded as employable. This limitation might be swept away under the pressures of a severe depression. It is also somewhat modified by the existence of general assistance programs in practically all large cities where industrial unemployment tends to concentrate. These programs tend in most instances to be adjusted to urgent local needs. But in the continued absence of federal grants-in-aid, it is unlikely that the necessary changes would come quickly enough to have any significant effect in a moderate recession. In the 1949–1950 recession, general assistance payments increased from about $16 million a month in October 1948 to a high of $33 million in March of 1950 and then dropped slowly until by the end of 1950 they were again near the 1948 levels. Over the entire two-year period, aggregate general assistance payments were only $180 million larger than they would have been had each month's payment been the same as the amount paid in the same month of 1948.

Federal grants-in-aid now provide about 55 per cent of the old age assistance payments, 57 per cent of the aid to dependent children, and 49 and 51 per cent respectively of the payments under the programs of aid to the blind and aid to the permanently and totally disabled. On a nationwide basis, but with great variation from state to state, about 39 per cent of the old age assistance payments and more than a third of the payments under the other federally aided programs are financed from state funds, with only 6 per cent coming from local funds in the case of old age assistance and 11 per cent or less in the case of the other three. For general assistance, however, almost half the funds come from local revenues, with local funds carrying the entire burden in fifteen states and 80 or 90 per cent in several more. The heavy reliance on local financing of general assistance seriously limits the potential importance of that program in a depression. It is partly in recognition of this problem that a number of states have taken over all or a large share of the financing of general assistance. One state, New York, increases the proportion of state funds available for general assistance when unemployment is heavy.

While the existing federal grants for public assistance are not related directly either to the relative economic capacity of the states or to the level of employment, they do nevertheless provide a broader basis of financial support than would be available in many states from state and local funds alone. The flexibility of the federally aided assistance programs would be greater if—as has frequently been proposed—the extent of federal matching were directly related to the states' fiscal and economic capacity, with proportionately more federal funds going to the states with lower than average per capita incomes.

It is probable that in any serious depression the federal government would be forced to provide financial aid for general assistance and on condition that such assistance be available to employable as well as unemployable persons. Such emergency extension of aid would be much more easily accomplished today than was possible in the early 1930's, when very few states had state welfare departments and the whole machinery for federal grants and for the distribution of assistance had to be improvised. The administrative mechanism is now available; the fiscal arrangements that would make public assistance a more reliable built-in stabilizer are still to be adopted.

4. Conclusion

An established social security system is a stabilizing factor in the economy because of the assured income provided to large segments of the nonworking population, the compensatory expansion of aggregate benefits when employment falls off, the probably wider effect on consumer spending of the knowledge that unemployment benefits or old age benefits will be available, and the institutional mechanism the system provides for any desired emergency measures. The quantitative importance of these several factors will depend not only on the scope of the program actually in existence at any time, but also on the circumstances and timing of economic change. Social security programs are particularly vulnerable to the erosion of inflation. The extent of their contribution in a period of economic decline may be greatly affected by the degree to which benefits have been kept in line with rising prices and with rising wage levels. This is a problem which has received too little attention.

The quantitative analysis of the operation of unemployment insurance in the 1949–1950 recession and of potential old age and survivors' insurance and related benefit payments in 1955–1957 presented in this paper is intended to do no more than illustrate the general magnitude of the direct economic effects of our existing social security programs. It may finally be useful—again only for illustrative purposes—to summarize the magnitudes involved by relating them to the wage loss that is implied in the second alternative set of economic assumptions used above in projecting old age and survivors' insurance benefit payments and contributions. The pattern of economic change illustrated is one of a decline from only moderately high levels of employment in 1954 and early 1955 to fairly substantial unemployment in 1956 and 1957.

The loss in total earnings in employments covered by old age and survivors' insurance over the three-year period when measured from 1954 levels is about $20 billion. The difference between total covered earnings under the relatively high employment of alternative I and those under the lower levels of alternative II over the three-year period is $93 billion.[10]

Against these earnings-loss figures one may set certain program data. If the additional depression-induced unemployment benefit payments compensated for 20 per cent of the wage loss measured from 1954 levels, such additional unemployment insurance benefits during the three years would aggregate $3.1 billion. This is perhaps too high a proportion to assume unless one also assumes some liberalization of the duration provisions of existing state laws. On the other hand, both wage loss and hence the computed additional unemployment benefits would be higher if measured on a monthly or quarterly basis. If legislative changes were extensive enough and rapid enough to result in compensation of as much as one-third of wage loss in covered industries in 1956 and 1957, the aggregate additional unemployment insurance benefits over the three-year period could be closer to $5.2 billion.

One dilemma that arises in short-run projections of payments under any social security program is how much weight to give to existing program provisions and how much to proposed or possible

[10] Gross national product is asumed to be $380 billion in 1955 and $420 billion in 1957 under alternative I; $357 billion in 1955 and $346 billion in 1957 under alternative II.

modifications. On the one hand, it should be recognized that the built-in stabilizing effects of the program are only those which are already in existence and that changes in legislation take time. However, the stimulus of an emergency situation may result in much faster action than would otherwise occur.

Total old age and survivors' insurance benefit payments during the three years with the assumed lower levels of employment would amount to $13 billion under the program in effect in 1953 and to about $16 billion under an expanded and liberalized program such as that brought into effect by the 1954 amendments. While old age and survivors' insurance contributions would exceed benefit payments over the three years by perhaps $3 billion, the excess would be at least $2.5 billion smaller than would have occurred at relatively high levels of employment.

Payments during the three years under the railroad and federal, state, and local government employee retirement systems might be close to $5 billion, private pensions about $1.5 billion, and veterans' pensions about $9 billion. Total long-term benefits plus additional unemployment insurance benefits might thus aggregate close to $35 billion under existing programs or $37 billion were the unemployment insurance program further expanded and liberalized.

It may be noted that the two alternative estimates on which these figures are based do not carry through to an upturn and renewed high levels of employment. The story is left incomplete. It is perhaps sufficient to suggest, however, the great actual and the greater potential importance of social security programs not only to the millions of individuals and families for whom they are the main source of income but to the functioning of the economy.

THE ROLE OF MONETARY POLICY
IN COMBATING DEPRESSION

ROBERT V. ROOSA, FEDERAL RESERVE BANK OF NEW YORK

Summary

The paper on monetary policy presented by Robert V. Roosa is not available for inclusion in this volume. The main contents of the paper are presented here in a summary prepared by the editor.

The effectiveness of monetary policy in promoting stability, and the means by which it can be most effective, depend upon the phase of the business cycle and upon the nature of the monetary influence at work in the particular cyclical situation.

Five different roles of monetary influence in cyclical fluctuations may be distinguished:

1. Causal, in terms of the aggregate supply of money and credit
2. Causal, in terms of the selective influence of shifts within the distribution of the available volume of credit that create serious distortions in the pattern of demand
3. Accelerating, in the aggregative sense
4. Accelerating, in the selective sense
5. Expediting, or passive, in the sense of "servicing" without either initiating causally or accelerating the effects of other causes

Even in this fifth case, where monetary factors neither cause nor accelerate expansion or contraction, there will be an opportunity to use monetary policy to offset or control the underlying causal influences.

The first case, in which the aggregate supply of bank reserves and money exert a causal influence upon business, is unlikely to be important in the United States any more. Control directed to the volume of bank reserves alone (along with control over the reserve ratio) should be adequate to check any monetary and credit expansion that could threaten to become so large, in the aggregate, as to be an initiating cause of inflation. Conversely, since the only circumstances in which a general shortage of money and credit would precipitate an economic contraction appear to be those in which reserve funds suddenly become inadequate or secondary re-

237

serves become frozen, a policy of increasing the volume of reserves could, if pushed far enough soon enough, prevent that potential cause of contraction.

Restraining Excesses during the Boom

Monetary policy can make its main contribution to economic stability by removing or reducing the financial causes of "over-exhilaration" during periods of prosperity or boom.

A "narrow" policy of restraining the growth of total bank reserves by Federal Reserve operations confined to the Treasury bill market would probably be sufficient to limit any tendency for the credit mechanism to accelerate the forces of inflation. However, if the forces of expansion are very strong, the central bank may become instrumental in causing an actual collapse in using reserve requirements to check the inflationary forces. Moreover, so limited a policy will not be able to cope with distortions that may have serious general consequences. And it will be unable to cope with nonmonetary causes of instability in the boom.

A more pervasive and more selective monetary policy will be needed, a policy that will enable the central bank, by direct contact, to maintain varying degrees of pressure in all parts of the capital market. The central bank should be able to exert a restraining influence on the markets for longer-term funds without having to tighten the short-term market so severely as to cause a financial stalemate of some sort. Also it should be possible to direct the influence of monetary policy in such a way as to restrain a tendency for credit factors to accentuate distortion among sectors of the economy—such as, for example, a relative flooding of funds into the mortgage market.

In order to meet these requirements of a restraining policy in booms, the monetary authority should be free to conduct open-market transactions in government securities of various maturities and should not be confined to dealing in bills. Even this broader use of open-market policy may not be enough. The central bank should have stand-by authority to use selective controls in parts of the market where impersonal regulations can be devised and administered.

Cushioning the Upper Turning Point

As the forces of expansion weaken, and the economy enters a plateau, with signs or danger of a decline, there are two things that monetary policy can do.

First, it should prevent financial panic. This is now generally regarded as assured.

Second, it should minimize any financial pressures that might accentuate a tendency toward decline. The most effective way to do this will be to remove from the minds of lenders any expectation of further increase in interest rates and create the expectation of a decline. This change in expectations should extend throughout the maturity structure. It will be most important in the longer maturities, where the fact and expectation of lower interest rates can create the fact and expectation of large appreciation in capital values.

A monetary policy that operates in all parts of the maturity range will be able to achieve the desired results more quickly than operations confined to Treasury bills and without action so extreme as to suggest that the central bank regards the situation as critical.

Resisting a Downswing

If monetary policy has prevented the development of serious credit distortions or excesses on the upswing and at the upper turning point, the causes of a downswing would center in the physical processes in the economy. In this case, monetary policy would have two functions:

1. It should aim to prevent the development within the financial mechanism of cumulative factors that would aggravate the downturn. Concentration on expanding bank reserves by open-market operations in Treasury bills would be relatively ineffective for this purpose; it would be unable to bring about the kind of change in expectations that would help to halt a cumulative acceleration.

2. It should try to work through the monetary and credit mechanism to counter disruptive downward developments in the physical sectors. A state of credit ease, brought about by expansion of bank reserves, may well have important stimulative influence, particularly in the case of borrowers for whom current economic fluctuations are less important than long-range prospects. To assure a wide diffusion of credit ease, without so sharp a reduction of interest rates as

to create havoc among institutional investors, the central bank should be able to inject funds directly into the various segments of the market.

Combating a Cumulative Downswing and Deep Depression

In a cumulative downswing or deep depression the appropriate monetary policy would be one of outright ease, which would have a valuable ameliorative effect. The main responsibility for combating the depression would, however, lie with other measures, notably fiscal policy.

In addition to creating a general condition of credit ease, financial policy can take other steps to limit the enforced, or distress, liquidation of assets and debt. These steps include:

1. Checking the tendency for bank examination standards to become tighter during a depression.

2. Avoiding bank closings and their consequences. Protection against bank closings is already substantially assured by the establishment of Federal Deposit Insurance and the authorization for the Federal Reserve banks to lend on any assets of any bank.

3. Avoiding pressure for banks to liquidate private credits to meet loss of deposits in depression. This is probably taken care of by the large amounts of government securities held by banks and by the widened lending authority of the Federal Reserve banks.

4. Direct lending to nonbank enterprises by the central bank. The amount of such lending is likely to be small. However, the authority and machinery should be kept available to permit some testing of the possibilities of special need during the stages of a downswing.

HOUSING POLICIES TO COMBAT DEPRESSION

LEO GREBLER, INSTITUTE FOR URBAN LAND USE AND HOUSING STUDIES,
COLUMBIA UNIVERSITY

With helpful suggestions by David M. Blank and Louis Winnick

The objective of this paper is to outline various possible housing policies to combat depression and to raise questions for further exploration, rather than to recommend specific actions.

The mere fact that housing policies are included in this symposium on policies to combat depression illustrates a significant development. The establishment of the Federal Home Loan Bank System, the mortgage insurance program of the Federal Housing Administration and mortgage guarantee program of the Veterans' Administration, a government-owned secondary mortgage lending facility (the Federal National Mortgage Association), and federally supported public housing and urban redevelopment programs created instrumentalities which it is widely believed can be used for purposes of economic stabilization.

All of these instrumentalities are products of the past twenty years or so. Their potentials in economic stabilization programs are uncertain and untested, but there is fairly general agreement that they can influence and modify the market forces operating on the volume of residential construction and, indirectly, of nonresidential construction usually associated with house building. There is much less certainty about the extent and implications of their influence.

The principle of meshing housing policies with general economic stabilization policies has slowly gained recognition. It was embodied in several provisions of the Housing Act of 1949.[1] It was put into

This paper was originally drafted in the fall of 1953 and was revised in June 1954. Legislative and other changes since that time have not been taken into account. The opinions expressed in this paper are exclusively those of the author and do not in any way necessarily represent the views of any organization with which he has been or is now associated.

[1] Section 102(e) of the act stipulates that the annual amount of the federal notes and obligations authorized for loans to local public agencies for urban redevelopment may be increased by specified amounts "upon a determination by the President, after receiving advice from the Council of Economic Advisers as to the general effect of such increase upon the conditions in the building industry and upon the national economy, that such action is in the public interest." Section 304(a) of the act contains identical language in regard to the maximum amount of annual contributions which the Public Housing Authority is authorized to contract for with local housing authorities. Public Law 171, 81st Cong.

practice after the outbreak of the Korean hostilities when mortgage credit was restricted by the institution of Regulation X and accompanying limitations on FHA- and VA-insured loans. It was expressed in the Housing Amendments of 1953 which gave the President stand-by authority to liberalize FHA maximum terms. A further extension of the principle is found in the President's Housing Message and Economic Report of January 1954, which propose executive authority to vary, within certain limitations, the maximum terms for both VA and FHA mortgage loans.

Some quantitative relationships may help define the potential role of housing policies in economic stabilization programs:

1. Expenditures for new housekeeping residential construction (inclusive of additions and alterations) in the postwar period 1946–1953 equaled 36.2 per cent of total new construction expenditures and 20.5 per cent of gross private domestic investment.

2. The ratio of residential construction expenditures to total gross capital formation (Kuznets' definition) has shown a secular decline at least since 1890. In five-year moving averages in 1929 prices, the ratio fell from about 30 per cent in the nineties to about 25 per cent in the twenties and about 13 per cent in 1950.

3. The residential mortgage debt in 1952 was 45 per cent of the total net private long-term debt and exceeded net corporate long-term debt. This percentage was only 16 in 1900 and roughly 30 in both 1929 and 1939.

4. From 1946 to 1953, about 43 per cent of all privately financed new dwelling units were acquired with loans insured by the Federal Housing Administration or guaranteed by the Veterans' Administration.

5. The estimated balance outstanding of FHA and VA loans at the end of 1952 approximated 40 per cent of the aggregate residential mortgage debt.

6. Under the low rent public housing programs of the federal government, about 400,000 dwelling units were completed from 1937 to 1953 or were under construction at the end of 1953 (exclusive of war housing). The largest annual volume during the postwar period (in 1951) was roughly 7 per cent of all new nonfarm dwelling units started.[2]

Housing policies to combat depression include federal aids in-

[2] For data on the quantitative importance of government housing programs see Leo Grebler, *The Role of Federal Credit Aids in Residential Construction,* National Bureau of Economic Research, Occasional Paper 39, 1953. Other data in this section are from a forthcoming monograph by Leo Grebler, David M. Blank, and Louis Winnick, *Capital Formation in Residential Real Estate: Trends and*

volving primarily transfer payments as well as expenditures operating directly on income and employment. Federal aid in this field is not limited to measures having an income-producing effect. Transfer payments may be necessary to relieve financial distress and are required by legal obligations in FHA insurance and VA guarantee of mortgages. Consequently, these five types of policies are considered in this paper:

1. Financial "holding operations"
2. Financial "rescue operations"
3. Stimulation of *new* residential construction
4. Stimulation of repairs and modernization
5. Aids to slum clearance and redevelopment

Transfer payments are involved in 1 and 2 and partly in 5. Income-producing expenditures are involved in 3 and 4 and partly in 5.

The applicability and effectiveness of each of the above policies and of various combinations of them will depend upon, among other things, the specific characteristics of a depression. For the purpose of this essay, four situations are envisaged:

1. A decline in rents, house prices, and residential construction without appreciable decline in general business activity for some considerable period of time. The 1926–1929 period is perhaps the closest historical example of this situation.
2. A short but possibly sharp business recession, of the 1920–1921 or the 1949 variety.
3. A long, moderate depression of general character involving widespread (rather than localized) unemployment.
4. A long, severe depression of general character, as above.

Any such classification raises, of course, questions of definition and diagnosis, which cannot be discussed in this paper. In addition, specific conditions in housing and mortgage markets would have a bearing on the desirability and timing of various courses of action. Some of the additional information needed to diagnose conditions in housing and mortgage markets is outlined in the Appendix.

Policies to combat a sector depression of type 1 would be important primarily because of cumulative effects on the economy, although these may be delayed, particularly if other types of building construction hold up well.

The following questions would have to be raised in connection with a type 1 depression:

Prospects, Princeton University Press for National Bureau of Economic Research, in press.

Is this situation worth considering? And if so, would intensified government aids to housing be warranted? Or would such aids serve only to delay the reduction of specific maladjustments in the housing market? Declining occupancy, rents, and house prices will produce financial difficulties. Is it reasonable to expect that the difficulties will not be of sufficient magnitude to call for financial "holding" operations other than those involved in existing FHA insurance and VA guarantee of mortgages?

As to depression type 2, many of the housing policies of an income-producing character would be ineffective in a short business decline or, for that matter, in the first stage of a longer decline. The time lag between legislation or regulation and execution is long, particularly when new programs (rather than modifications of existing programs) are involved. For example, Congressional adoption of the first major public housing program in 1937 was induced partly by the recession of that year. But the recession was over before the first foundation of any housing project under the United States Housing Act of 1937 was dug. Stimulation of repairs and modernization, which could operate fairly rapidly, is likely to be more immediately effective than any measure to raise the level of *new* construction. The main problem of public policy in this situation will be to resist pressures for new or intensified programs which must be judged on other merits, rather than on their effectiveness in dealing with a short recession or the first stage of any recession.

For the purpose of this paper it is assumed that housing programs will be used primarily as means to combat depressions of type 3 (long but mild) as well as type 4 (long and severe). The difference would lie solely in the admixture of policies and in the scope and intensity of programs. All of these policies might be appropriate ingredients for both types of long depression—except for financial "rescue operations," which would be required only in the case of a severe depression, if at all. To clarify this point, the next few paragraphs discuss the need for, and content of, "financial holding" vs. "financial rescue" operations.

Financial Holding and Rescue Operations

Any substantial and fairly general decline in economic activity will create financial difficulties in the housing field. Home owners and owners of rental housing will default on mortgages. The federal government will be involved directly through its potential contingent liabilities in FHA insurance and VA guarantee. The following considerations are relevant to an appraisal of the need for financial holding or rescue operations:

1. Because of the massive volume of new mortgage lending associated with the postwar building and real estate boom, a large proportion of residential mortgages now outstanding are unseasoned loans. More than four-fifths of the residential mortgages outstanding in 1950 were originated or assumed after the beginning of 1946, and roughly one of every eight home mortgages in 1950 was 80 per cent or more of the estimated property value. The present ratio of unseasoned loans is probably not lower and may be higher.

2. Many recent home purchasers having high-percentage home loans probably also have large debt obligations on consumer durables.

3. Like earlier housing booms, the postwar boom has been associated with overcommitments by certain numbers of home purchasers in relation to their current and prospective incomes.

4. Measures to stimulate business activity may not operate with sufficient rapidity or effectiveness to relieve financial distress.

These points emphasize the need for financial "holding operations" in a long depression even of moderate dimensions. For perspective, it is important to add that in 1950 less than half the owner-occupied homes were mortgaged, and that the median ratio of debt to value of the mortgaged homes was only 42 per cent. Also, since most residential mortgage loans are on a regular amortization schedule, the difficulties arising from inability to renew straight loans will be avoided or minimized. Nevertheless, there will be a large enough number of borrowers unable to meet payments on unseasoned high-percentage loans to produce trouble. The debt-to-value ratio deteriorates rapidly when real estate prices fall and unpaid debt charges accumulate.

Financial holding operations may include:

1. Temporary waiver of amortization (complete or partial) or rewriting of loans for longer maturities, depending on borrowers' circumstances. In the case of FHA and VA loans these steps would require sanction by the agencies through regulation without new legislation. In the case of conventional loans the approach would be to encourage financial institutions to waive amortization or rewrite loans and to assure sanction of these measures by federal and state supervisory authorities.[3] Waiver of amortization will, of course, reduce the flow of funds into financial institutions, but so would

---

[3] This is important. There have been cases in the past in which federal agencies encouraged a given policy, but institutions found themselves criticized by federal as well as state examiners for adopting it.

foreclosures. Looking back over the thirties, one wonders whether mortgagees as well as mortgagors would not have been better off if lenders had "played along" with many of the borrowers who went through foreclosure. The case for "playing along" is strengthened by the difficulties of mass foreclosures against veterans. Waiver of amortization will also minimize the tendency of borrowers to "walk out" on the mortgagee and rent or buy more cheaply somewhere else. Consideration must be given to consistent criteria for waiver, at least for FHA and VA loans. Because of the absence of home-ownership motivation and the possibilities of "milking" properties, great discrimination will be required in the case of rental housing.

2. Expansion of advances of Home Loan Banks to member institutions to improve their liquidity position. If the banks have difficulty in selling their debentures in the capital market, the Secretary of the Treasury's authority to buy the banks' obligations would be used and perhaps expanded. This measure will be operative primarily for savings and loan associations. Few institutions of other types are members of the Home Loan Bank System.

3. Expansion of the purchase program of the Federal National Mortgage Association for FHA and VA loans in good standing, to improve the liquidity position of institutional leaders. In such action, purchase at discount would be carefully considered to prevent wholesale dumping of loans by financial institutions. As an alternative to purchase, and one that is preferable in many respects, the FNMA may be authorized to make loans to financial institutions on the security of FHA and VA mortgages.[4]

4. Use of existing emergency authority of the Federal Reserve banks for discounting of or loaning on mortgages, particularly conventional mortgages.

This outline of financial holding operations assumes that in view of the insurance of bank deposits and savings and loan shares, no general runs on financial institutions will develop. The absence of general runs on financial institutions should make it possible for mortgagees to minimize resort to foreclosure and should act as a brake on any tendency of institutions to exchange VA and FHA loans in default for cash (in the case of VA) or for debentures convertible into cash (in the case of FHA).

[4] There is a great deal of discussion on the establishment of a truly comprehensive secondary mortgage bank system, in lieu of or in addition to the FNMA and possibly incorporating the Home Loan Bank System. If such a system existed at the time of action, it could perform the above function with special government aid.

Even in the case of a severe, long depression (type 4), it is this writer's hope that financial *rescue* operations can be avoided and that a combination of "holding operations" and of positive measures to sustain general income and employment, if taken in time, will make major rescue operations unnecessary. Mass financial difficulties in the mortgage market are typically delayed, and preventive medicine has a good chance to be effective in time. Also, difficulties of this kind are symptoms of the disease rather than the disease itself.

The need for another Home Owners' Loan Corporation is reduced by the insurance and the guarantee program of the FHA and the VA, respectively, which practically involve HOLC's of their own. The problem here is to devise consistent and noncompetitive policies as to resale, renting, and pricing of properties taken over by the two agencies, so as to avoid further deterioration of the real estate market.

In an emergency, consideration may be given to authorizing the FHA to take over directly home mortgages with specified defaults, without the mortgagee being required to foreclose. This procedure is now used for VA loans at the option of the Administrator of Veterans' Affairs and has the advantage of permitting a government agency capable of setting uniform policies to make decisions affecting the borrower.

As to conventional mortgages in default, the measures outlined earlier—viz. the temporary waiver of amortization, expansion of Home Loan Bank advances, and mortgage loan discounts by the Federal Reserve banks—combined with general policies to sustain income and employment, should minimize the need for another HOLC.

Stimulation of New Residential Construction

Turning to income-producing aids to housing, there is a general problem of choosing criteria for determining the place of housing programs as against the place of general monetary and fiscal measures and of public works. From a housing point of view, any significant decline in general business and construction activity appears to liberate resources that can be used for the advancement of worthwhile housing objectives. From the point of view of the best strategy in combating a depression, the effectiveness of government aids for housing, relative to that of other policies, is less clear. Clarification is perhaps more important for decisions in connection with a long but mild depression than for those in connection with a long and severe depression, on the ground that measures to combat the former can and should be more selective.

QUERIES

Do we know enough about criteria such as effectiveness in obtaining any results, speed of results, multiplier effects? Even if some housing programs, such as slum clearance, should rank low on economic criteria, they might rank high in terms of community benefits. How can these benefits be equated with strictly economic criteria of effectiveness?

Stimulation of new residential construction may be approached in various ways, of which the following are here considered:
1. Within the framework of FHA and VA programs (more liberal terms and/or more liberal insurance and guarantees)
2. Direct federal loans on new owner-occupied houses and new privately sponsored rental housing
3. Tax incentives
4. A new or intensified public housing program

Any attempt to stimulate new residential construction through modification of FHA and VA programs will start with a severe handicap: The ammunition of liberal terms has been largely shot away during the postwar boom, and there is comparatively little left. The possibilities of stimulating construction through more liberal financing terms under the FHA and VA would be far greater if we entered a depression with a more conservative pattern of maximum terms. But this statement is almost theoretical today.

Assuming that interest rates must fall into a pattern making FHA and VA loans attractive to financial institutions, the three "handles" for stimulation of demand are higher mortgage ceilings, lower minimum downpayments, and longer maximum contract terms. Higher ceilings for FHA mortgage loans and VA guarantees, which make larger loans and higher-priced houses eligible for government aid, would probably have small effects on the demand for residential construction in a period of declining employment and growing uncertainty. As to lower minimum downpayments, there is some leeway under the FHA program but none under the VA program with its 100 per cent maximum loans. The present maximum maturities, 25 to 30 years for FHA and VA home loans and 30 to 40 years for FHA rental housing and cooperative housing loans, can theoretically be extended. But the effect on borrowers' monthly payments and therefore on demand would be relatively small unless extreme maturities, probably unacceptable to financial institutions, were contemplated. Moreover, the percentage reduction of periodic ownership outlays (or rent) is roughly but half the percentage reduction of debt payments associated with more liberal terms. More liberal terms do not affect real estate taxes, maintenance and repair, and similar operating costs.

Some leeway may exist even within the present framework of maximum terms. In the past few years the FHA and VA, as well as lending institutions, in many cases did not apply maximum terms. As a result, average terms have been substantially less liberal than maximum terms. In a buyers' market, maximum terms might be applied to a larger percentage of cases without seriously lowering underwriting standards.

New legislation could permit loans to be written on the basis of partial rather than full amortization, that is, the amortization schedule would provide for repayment of, say, 50 per cent of the mortgage principal within a given maturity of the loan. This step, however, would be a radical departure from the principle of full amortization and would dilute one of the few lasting reforms of our mortgage debt structure.

The effectiveness of the mild doses of credit liberalization still left under the FHA and VA programs must be considered quite uncertain. The price elasticity of housing demand (including mortgage loan terms) probably is quite low. Reluctance of consumers to enter into long-term commitments even at more favorable terms will be great when incomes decline or are uncertain. Under such conditions many bargains in existing housing will compete with new construction. These uncertainties must be taken into account in weighing the effectiveness of more liberal FHA and VA terms against the effectiveness of other policies (such as business or personal income tax policies, public works, or public housing).

In addition to stimulating borrowing, there may be need for stimulating lending under the FHA and VA programs. "Apart from higher interest rates there is little leeway left for making investments in insured or guaranteed mortgages more attractive under unfavorable business conditions. Further inducements might be covering more or all of the risks still left with the mortgagee (such as the excess of foreclosure costs over the maximum covered by FHA and liberalization of the "waste provisions" under which the mortgagee bears the risk of unusual damage to property after institution of foreclosure proceedings), or in making the interest rate and terms of FHA debentures exchanged for foreclosed properties more attractive. In the case of VA loans, the maximum amounts and percentages of the guaranty could again be raised. The effectiveness of these inducements must be weighed against the conditions that would create caution and reluctance in lending on new construction." [5]

In summary, liberalization of loan terms and loan insurance provisions under the FHA and VA programs would stimulate new construction only mildly. To give a crude and blunt illustration, these methods would probably be insufficient to raise the level of housing starts more than 10 to 15 per cent over the volume that would obtain without them.

Under conditions of declining employment, public demands will unquestionably develop for "stronger medicine" in the way of federal credit aids. While many "schemes" will be proposed, demands for direct use of public credit for privately owned new housing are probably the most realistic ones to contemplate. The precedents of the HOLC, of direct VA loans for home purchase, of the use of the FNMA as a primary source of funds, of the Connecticut and other state programs for veterans' housing, and of New York City's non-cash-subsidy public housing program point in this direction. Quite apart from interest rates, the downpayments, borrowers' credit ratings, and maturities in public lending programs could be adjusted to a degree of liberality not acceptable to portfolio lenders even with FHA or VA protection.

The use of public credit could be compatible with *pro forma* maintenance of the institutional framework of private building and mortgage servicing operations, as under a program using the FNMA as a primary source of funds. Or it could be executed as a direct federal agency operation similar to that of the HOLC. Credit terms, and therefore much of the effectiveness of a program, would depend on whether or not the operation were designed to be self-liquidating. If it were, assuming a going federal long-term interest rate of 2½ to 3 per cent, the contract interest rate might be 3 to 4 per cent. Even though such a rate might not be much lower than the rate for FHA and VA loans, the case for public credit would rest on an "insufficient" volume of credit for new construction at the going terms for FHA and VA loans or conventional loans. If designed as a non-self-liquidating operation, the interest rate could, of course, be lower.

[5] Grebler, *op. cit.*, p. 61.

In spite of the precedents mentioned earlier, the substantial use of public credit would be a radical departure from past institutional arrangements. If a public lending program should be instituted as a countercyclical device, it would be most difficult to withdraw it when it was no longer needed for countercyclical purposes. Such a program has long-run implications exemplified by the paralysis in the flow of private capital into residential real estate in some of the European countries, where there is a real question whether the total flow of funds into this field in the long run has been augmented or diminished by injection of public credit. These observations do not necessarily argue against the use of public credit for specific long-term programs of social betterment. They do argue against sliding into permanent public financing through the back door of temporary countercyclical measures.

Among the many problems associated with public credit is the establishment of standards for its use. Upper limits on appraised values and mortgage loans (and on rents in the case of rental housing) would be one approach. More direct "need tests" or demonstration of the unavailability of private credit would be another. But it is easy to foresee the pressures for more liberal standards no matter how the standards are designed originally.

QUERIES

In view of these difficulties, should the use of public credit be reserved for a long depression of great severity? What should be the objective of standards? Maximizing the volume of housing construction? Limiting public credit to housing for certain income groups, defined in what fashion?

In view of the limited possibilities of stimulating new construction through the FHA and VA programs and of the problems involved in the use of public credit, it is perhaps appropriate to consider stimulation of new housing construction through means other than debt financing, which has been ridden so hard during the past twenty years.

QUERIES

How can equity financing supplemented by conservative mortgage financing be encouraged (1) for rental builders and (2) for owner occupants? Low income tax rates for rental housing corporations conforming to certain operational standards? Accelerated depreciation and/or permission to carry loss deductions for rental projects over longer periods? Deduction from current taxable income of a portion of equity investment in new houses by owner occupants? Are these devices possible legally, tolerable from a fiscal point of view, and promising as to effectiveness? [6]

Interrelationships between the markets for new and existing housing must be considered in any program of easier credit for new construction. These interrelationships limit the extent to which mortgage loan terms on new and existing construction can be differentiated. If new construction is pushed too hard, it will be more difficult to maintain an orderly market in existing residential real estate, in which the federal government has a great stake, and the need for financial holding or rescue operations in existing construction may be increased. Thus a balance must be maintained between federal measures to stimulate new construction and federal measures to prevent a collapse of the market for old housing.

Finally, a period of declining or low employment would be appropriate for reinstituting or expanding a public housing program involving periodic subsidies as well as public financing of capital expenditures. It is impossible here to deal with the controversial aspects of the present program, which evolved from the United States Housing Act of 1937. There is urgent need for an impartial study that would lead to such modifications of the program as would assure more general public support in a period of business decline.

If public housing with federal support is adopted or continued as a matter of long-run policy, public housing should be an important element of housing policies to combat a depression (and should be substantially reduced in scope during periods of high income and employment). In terms of effectiveness of antidepression measures, a public housing program would offer several advantages. It would be unhampered by the uncertainties of consumer and lender reaction to programs involving private credit. It could be so designed as to minimize competition with markets for other housing construction or with market segments in need of financial holding or rescue operations. Consequently there would be minimum "leakages" for a given amount of public capital expenditures.

[6] Since this paper focuses on federal policies, local real estate tax exemption on new construction is not considered.

252

Stimulation of Repairs and Modernization

Stimulation of expenditures for maintenance, repair, and modernization should have high priority in programs to combat a depression. Potentials in this field are large. Decade totals of expenditures for maintenance, repairs, additions, and alterations in residential real estate relative to expenditures for new residential construction run as follows:

1920–1929	33%
1930–1939	107
1940–1949	64

These percentages are underestimates reflecting substantial understatements of repair and modernization expenditures in official statistics. In a period of declining and uncertain incomes, expenditures of this type probably respond more readily to easy credit than does new construction. The fact that many houses built during the postwar period are without garages, porches, and similar facilities and have structural provisions for additions (such as unfinished attics) adds to the opportunities.

The principal vehicle here is the FHA Title I program for the insurance of loans for repair and modernization. This program was perhaps more effective in encouraging construction expenditures during the middle and late thirties than was the FHA mortgage insurance program. Its relative importance during recent years has diminished, but it could be stepped up if the need for such action should arise. The President's Housing Message of January 1954 recommends larger maximum amounts and longer maturities for loans under this program. There may be an opportunity also for reducing the maximum interest charges, which are equivalent to an effective interest rate of 9 to 10 per cent including the insurance premium.

In the conventional loan field, lenders could be encouraged, where circumstances justify, to make additions to existing mortgages at costs much below those of personal loans and other credit sources for the financing of modernization and repair. Because of the many other demands on their funds, financial institutions during the past few years have given little attention to these possibilities.

Slum Clearance and Urban Redevelopment

Federal aids for slum clearance and urban redevelopment, already on the statute books, could be stepped up during a period of declining business activity and combined with more vigorous local enforcement of safety and sanitary codes. The immediate income-producing effects of this program would probably be small, for land acquisition involves transfer payments only and, so far as re-building is concerned, it would be difficult in a depression to find private sponsors willing or able to proceed with redevelopment. But the clearance operations themselves would provide employ-ment; tenant relocation—a great obstacle during periods of full em-ployment and low vacancies—would be much easier; the costs of acquiring land and old structures would be lower than during a boom; and the community benefits of slum clearance are large. Local law enforcement would be an important factor in reducing costs of land acquisition, for landlords in many instances would rather board up their properties than invest the funds necessary to remove violations.

Because an expansion of this program in a period of uncertainty will probably be handicapped by the difficulties of finding spon-sors for private redevelopment of cleared areas, means should be examined of enabling cities to acquire, clear, and hold land even if actual redevelopment may be delayed for several years.

This difficulty, of course, does not apply to slum clearance for public improvements such as parks, highways, bridges, tunnels, public buildings, etc. But such improvements are in a different category—public works.

Appendix. Additional Information Needs

Although data have greatly improved in this field, there are few if any comprehensive series designed to give early warning of trou-bles and their dimensions. The following items seem vital:

1. Mortgage loan collections. Foreclosure statistics (which do exist) come too late because foreclosure is the last step in a long series of events.

2. Continuous local and national vacancy statistics providing data classified by characteristics of vacant dwelling units.

3. Number and per cent of new houses completed by operative builders which are left unsold after specified periods—probably a highly sensitive indicator.

4. Because of the importance of multiple debt obligations of consumers, Consumer Finance Surveys and similar surveys should be designed to yield better data on concentration of home mortgage

indebtedness and other indebtedness among certain consumer groups.

C O M M E N T

DAVID M. BLANK, Institute for Urban Land Use and Housing Studies, Columbia University

Grebler mentions the problems created by the close relationship between the markets for new and existing homes and by the fact that the stock of homes plays a dominant role in short-term market fluctuations. Existing homes are, of course, close substitutes for new homes. Further, the number of new homes built in any year is always small compared with the size of the existing housing stock. Over the last half century the ratio of new nonfarm dwelling units built in each year to the stock of such dwelling units in that year has averaged between 2 and 3 per cent. Housing construction is currently running at about 1 million units a year, the highest annual rate in our history with the exception of 1950; however, the stock of existing nonfarm dwelling units is well over 40 million.

Visualize, then, the effect on the demand for new construction if the market for existing structures weakened perceptibly. Thus if incomes declined merely enough to reduce demand for existing shelter by as little as 2 per cent, the development of vacancies and the consequent pressure on real estate prices would probably be sufficient to offset almost completely current rates of household formation and to reduce substantially the volume of new construction. Although the decline in new construction would probably be somewhat smaller if more favorable credit terms were available on new homes than on existing homes, it would still be of major proportions. The importance, therefore, of supporting the price and mortgage structure on existing homes through "financial holding operations" can be clearly seen.

The relationship between the two markets is, of course, reciprocal. If new construction is stimulated (e.g. through differential mortgage terms) when income and the prices of existing homes are dropping, the additional dwelling units thrown onto the market will increase the pressure on the market for existing homes. Such a result not only would go counter to holding operations that the federal government would probably be putting into effect at the same time, but would also have direct repercussions on the government's financial position, since it insures or guarantees about 40 per cent of the outstanding residential mortgage debt.

The development of housing policies to combat depressions thus is not a simple problem, and great care will be required to insure consistency among the housing programs selected to help alleviate a decline in income and business activity.

Grebler also has pointed out that, despite the fact that the great bulk of mortgage loans now outstanding are of recent origin and that federally insured or guaranteed mortgages have provided for high loan-to-value ratios, more than half of the owner-occupied homes in the United States were debt-free in 1950 and the median ratio of debt to value for mortgaged owner-occupied homes was only 42 per cent. A glance at the distribution of debt-to-value ratios of mortgaged owner-occupied homes further supports the view that there is surprising strength in the mortgage debt structure and that it would take a major decline in real estate prices to place a significant portion of the debt on the housing stock in jeopardy. In 1950, 19 out of 20 owners of mortgaged homes had more than 10 per cent equity in their homes; 9 out of 10 had more than 20 per cent; 4 out of 5 had more than 30 per cent.

SELF-LIQUIDATING PUBLIC WORKS
TO COMBAT DEPRESSION

WILFRED OWEN, THE BROOKINGS INSTITUTION

This report deals with the volume of certain types of self-liquidating public works that might be undertaken as part of a program to combat depression, the obstacles that stand in the way of undertaking such a program, and the actions that need to be initiated now to minimize these obstacles.

In the strictest sense the term "self-liquidating" might be interpreted as meaning those facilities that are financed through revenue bonds secured by the earnings of the project. But departures from this strict interpretation will develop as certain variations of the revenue bond and toll-financing approach enter into the discussion; and consideration of earmarked tax revenues for highway purposes will add to the scope of projects that may be considered self-supporting.

The discussion will be focused on the toll road as an example of self-liquidating public works, both because of the magnitude of recent developments in this area and because of the experience in self-liquidating public works that such undertakings have provided. Consideration will also be given to certain nontoll highway projects, and to a growing area of self-supporting facilities that includes truck and bus terminals, parking facilities, airports, and urban transit. The report omits many other possible self-liquidating projects, such as water and sewer facilities, river valley development, power, and irrigation.

In general this report discusses the following:

1. The scope of certain public works activities and self-liquidating projects that appear desirable in and adaptable to a program designed to combat depression.

2. Specific features peculiar to self-liquidating projects that might prove to be obstacles in a program designed to combat depression.

3. Steps that might be taken now to improve the potential contribution of self-liquidating public works to an antidepression program.

The paper does not presume to resolve questions of countercyclical

Prepared with the assistance of Priscilla St. Denis, research assistant, the Brookings Institution.

effects that might be expected to follow from this particular anti-depression tool, or to judge what timing and magnitude of public works activities would be desirable under the peculiar circumstances that might accompany various types and degrees of economic depression.

1. Possibilities of Self-Liquidating Public Works

To provide some perspective, it may be noted that during 1953 the total value of new construction in the United States, including public and private activities, was $35.3 billion (Table 1). Public

TABLE 1

Value of New Public and Private Construction, 1953

	1953 (millions of dollars)	Per Cent Distribution
Total new construction	$35,256	100.0%
Private construction	23,877	67.7
Residential	11,930	33.8
Nonresidential	5,680	16.1
Industrial	2,229	6.3
Commercial	1,791	5.1
Other	1,660	4.7
Farm	1,731	4.9
Public utility	4,416	12.5
All other private	120	.3
Public construction	11,379	32.3
Residential	556	1.6
Nonresidential	4,352	12.3
Industrial	1,771	5.0
Educational	1,728	5.0
Hospital and institutional	353	1.0
Other	500	1.4
Military and naval	1,307	3.7
Highway	3,165	9.0
Sewer and water	861	2.4
Miscellaneous public service enterprises	201	.6
Conservation and development	830	2.4
All other public	107	.3

Source: *Construction and Building Materials,* Dept. of Commerce, June 1954, p. 17.

works were over $11 billion, or about one-third of the total. Self-liquidating public works, under any reasonable definition, were a fairly small part of the public construction total. There were, of course, substantial volumes of private construction that might in depression periods provide opportunities for self-liquidating public works or for publicly aided private undertakings.

Relating public works to the gross national product (and omitting military expenditures), expenditures have been approximately 2.5 to 3.5 per cent of the total national product in most years since 1930. A high of 4 per cent was reached in 1936, 1938, and 1939; during the war the figure was naturally below the long-run average (see Table 2).

A number of recent estimates have been made of the magnitude of the state and local public works backlog. A figure frequently cited is $100 billion. Although the accuracy of this figure will not be defended, its magnitude does reflect both the inability to provide needed facilities during the war and the rapid expansion of requirements after the war. Population growth and shifts and expanding industrial plant have created vast new community requirements; and an extended period of prosperity has made the ability to pay for such facilities an added factor in the size of the backlog.

Table 3 presents a conservative estimate of state and local construction projects in need of immediate attention. The fact that the estimate either is conservative or is intended to cover only high-priority or immediate needs is evident from the fact that highway construction requirements alone over the next decade and a half have been estimated by highway agencies at $40 to 55 billion. Here they total only $10.4 billion. The tabulation does indicate, however, that public works projects could provide a large volume of needed construction activity as a means of counteracting a decline in economic activity.

The question, then, is what part of the public works requirements of the United States can be considered self-liquidating, either in whole or to any substantial degree; and what specifically are these projects that might serve as a means of stimulating the construction industry in time of depression.

Although the most prominent example of self-liquidating public works is the toll road, there are a number of other kinds of public construction that have self-supporting potentials. Some of these are relatively new postwar developments: union truck terminals, bus depots, parking garages, airports, and other terminal facilities. An example of longer standing is the highway financed through limited-obligation bonds secured by anticipated gasoline tax reve-

TABLE 2

Public Construction as Related to Gross National Product, 1921–1954

	Public Construction a (millions of current dollars)	Highway and Street Construction as Per Cent of Total Public Construction	Public Construction as Per Cent of GNP
1921	$1,515	56.3%	2.2%
1922	1,659	52.8	2.4
1923	1,606	50.1	2.0
1924	1,892	52.2	2.3
1925	2,130	50.8	2.4
1926	2,133	50.0	2.3
1927	2,397	51.0	2.6
1928	2,470	52.2	2.7
1929	2,467	49.7	2.4
1930	2,829	53.6	3.1
1931	2,619	51.7	3.4
1932	1,828	52.4	3.1
1933	1,612	52.5	2.9
1934	2,264	44.2	3.5
1935	2,196	38.5	3.0
1936	3,487	39.1	4.2
1937	3,059	40.1	3.4
1938	3,358	42.3	4.0
1939	3,684	37.5	4.1
1940	3,243	40.1	3.2
1941	4,131	25.8	3.2
1942	5,644	13.0	3.5
1943	3,772	11.8	2.0
1944	2,236	16.2	1.0
1945	1,708	23.3	.8
1946	2,174	41.2	1.0
1947	3,229	44.9	1.4
1948	4,667	38.0	1.8
1949	6,268	34.0	2.4
1950	6,823	33.3	2.4
1951	8,444	29.8	2.6
1952	9,438	30.3	2.7
1953	10,072	31.4	2.7
1954	10,779	34.8	3.0

a Includes residential and nonresidential building, sewer and water, highway, miscellaneous public service enterprises, conservation and development, and other (parks and playgrounds, memorials, etc.). Excludes military construction.
Source: *Construction and Building Materials*, Dept. of Commerce, Statistical Summary, May 1953; June 1954; June 1955.

nues allocated to that specific purpose. Still other examples of self-liquidating public works are found in water supply systems, sewage facilities, and irrigation plants. A few of the newer developments in self-liquidating public works will be discussed and the needs and possibilities described before turning to the problems that a self-liquidating construction program might be expected to encounter in any large-scale compensatory spending effort.

TABLE 3

Immediate Construction Backlog, State and Local
Government, May 31, 1954

Class of Work	Backlog (millions of dollars)	Per Cent
Waterworks	$ 1,571	2%
Sewerage	2,881	4
Bridges	2,401	3
Earthworks-drainage	8,758	12
Streets and roads	8,026	11
Public buildings	14,801	19
Industrial buildings	10,868	14
Commercial buildings	11,745	16
Unclassified	14,661	19
All classes	$75,712	100%

Source: *Construction and Building Materials*, Dept. of Commerce, July 1954.

HIGHWAYS

Unfortunately for policies to combat depression, the urgency of programs to reduce postwar congestion have made it impossible to postpone traffic relief, and as a result the extraordinary highway construction work of recent years has coincided with the highest levels of economic activity.

Highway expenditures in 1954 reached a total of approximately $6 billion, of which about $3.7 billion was new construction. Table 2 shows the trend in highway construction outlays in relation to total civil public works expenditures, in current dollars. About 31 per cent of the total civil public works outlays in 1953 were for highways, but in the depression period the proportion was as high as 50 to 54 per cent.

Highways are financed largely by road-user payments, which now amount to about $3.2 billion per year (Table 4). Although user payments cover somewhat less than 60 per cent of the total sum spent for highway (maintenance and new construction) in the United States each year, they constitute the only important source

261

TABLE 4

Revenues Collected for Highway and Street Purposes, 1945–1954

	1945	1946	1947	1948	1949	1950	1951	1952	1953 [a]	1954 [b]
					Millions of Dollars					
Federal funds	$ 78	$ 168	$ 323	$ 402	$ 486	$ 465	$ 459	$ 526	$ 613	$ 648
State highway-user imposts	1,086	1,450	1,594	1,808	2,075	2,270	2,483	2,724	2,998	3,196
Toll receipts	59	81	87	97	108	115	140	181	200	211
Property tax and miscellaneous	640	783	805	972	1,049	1,108	1,179	1,208	1,237	1,273
Total	$1,863	$2,482	$2,809	$3,279	$3,718	$3,958	$4,261	$4,639	$5,048	$5,328
					Per Cent Distribution					
Federal funds	4.2%	6.8%	11.5%	12.2%	13.1%	11.7%	10.8%	11.3%	12.1%	12.2%
State highway-user imposts	58.3	58.4	56.7	55.1	55.8	57.4	58.2	58.7	59.4	59.9
Toll receipts	3.1	3.3	3.1	3.0	2.9	2.9	3.3	3.9	4.0	4.0
Property tax and miscellaneous	34.4	31.5	28.7	29.7	28.2	28.0	27.7	26.1	24.5	23.9
Total	100.0%	100.0%	100.0%	100.0%	100.0%	100.0%	100.0%	100.0%	100.0%	100.0%

[a] Preliminary estimate.
[b] Forecast.
Source: Bureau of Public Roads, Tables HF-1.

of current revenue outside of federal aid for main state highway work.[1]

Although most of the borrowing for nontoll highway construction has in the past been through general-obligation bonds, any program of self-liquidating public works could take advantage of the peculiar nature of highway revenues and their ability to finance revenue bonds or limited-obligation bonds. In most states motor vehicle registration fees and gasoline taxes are considered user charges rather than general taxes and are allocated specifically to highway purposes. In half the states the application of such funds for highway purposes is guaranteed by amendments to state constitutions prohibiting any other use. These revenues proved to be highly stable even during the last depression, when, for example, a reduction in automobile production to 25 per cent of the 1929 level was accompanied by a slight increase in automobile use and therefore in the productivity of gasoline taxes and other user charges. In a future depression this source of revenue for highways could be expected to remain at fairly high levels, but total funds available for road work would be reduced by property tax delinquencies.

Borrowing for highways by the states and by toll road authorities has in recent years been primarily in the form of limited-obligation bonds, secured by highway-user taxes, and in the form of toll-secured revenue bonds. Bonds outstanding at the end of 1951 totaled $2.4 billion, which compares with $1.6 billion in 1945 (see Table 5). The general-obligation bonds will also, for the most part, be paid out of highway "earnings" in the form of user tax revenues.

TABLE 5

State Highway Obligations Outstanding,
December 31, 1951

General-obligation bonds	$1,202,743
Limited-obligation bonds	319,696
Toll revenue bonds	871,885
Reimbursement obligations	51,939
Total	$2,446,263

Source: Hugo C. Duzan, William R. McCallum, and Thomas R. Todd, "Highway Bond Financing," *Public Roads*, October 1952, p. 73.

An example of the type of bond financing on recent expressway projects, combining methods of self-support with general tax sup-

[1] Local roads and streets, on the other hand, derive principal support from property taxes and general tax revenues.

port, is provided by a recent Michigan financing plan. Detroit's $180 million Edsel Ford and John Lodge expressway program is being financed jointly by the state, county, city, and federal governments. A law passed by the 1950 special session of the state legislature permitted financing through revenue bonds which will be retired by the weight and gasoline tax collections. A state-county-city agreement was signed for sharing the cost of the debt and to take advantage of the amendment to the Federal Aid Highway Act which provides that federal aid appropriations can be used to help retire bonds for toll-free urban highway projects on the primary system. The agreement pledges $1,125,000 annually from both the city and county, and $2,500,000 from the state highway department. A total of $80 million in twenty-five-year bonds were sold at an average of 2.12 per cent interest rate.

In Florida a $224 million Miami expressway program will make use of a variety of financial devices, including a combination of tolls and taxes. The financing plan includes a 10 cent bridge toll, a special downtown district benefit tax, the county's share of the state 7 cent gasoline tax, a special 1 cent county gasoline tax, and a special motor vehicle license fee for the county.

A relatively new example of a self-supporting road and bridge program which makes use of the limited obligation bond is to be found in Pennsylvania. In 1949 the General Assembly passed the State Highway and Bridge Authority Act, which provides for the issuance of revenue bonds secured by highway-user revenues. Under the terms of this law, the Authority may issue thirty-year bonds at interest rates not exceeding 4 per cent and use the proceeds to build highways which when completed are leased to the state. The bonds are paid with the proceeds of the rental. This arrangement is based on cooperation between the State Highway Department and the Authority. All plans and specifications must be approved by the Department of Highways, and the Authority is empowered to lease property to the State Highway Department for a ninety-nine-year period. Interchangeability of employees, equipment, and services is provided for. The borrowing power of the Pennsylvania Authority, however, is limited to $40 million.

Although this special authority affords a means of circumventing constitutional debt limits, it is limited as a means of overcoming restrictions on large-scale borrowing, because it does not remove the problem of obtaining sufficient current revenues to service the debt. As demonstrated by the experience in New Jersey, Maine, and other states that have adopted toll-road financing, available funds from current taxes are not sufficient to pay the service charges on any substantial amounts of new debt because tax rates have not kept pace with construction costs and existing laws governing the distribution of user revenues do not permit concentration of available revenues on major arteries. Consequently the type of special public works authority operating in Pennsylvania does not appear to offer a real alternative to the toll road.

TOLL HIGHWAYS

Increasing acceptance is now indicated for toll finance as a means of raising the necessary capital for high-cost highways and avoiding the obstacles of debt limits, inadequate current revenues, and other legal obstacles to highway modernization. The facts, as of late 1953, were as follows:

1. A total of 734 miles of toll roads had been constructed in 9 states at a cost of approximately $651 million.

2. Another 1,102 miles of toll roads were under construction in 8 states involving an estimated cost of $1.4 billion.

3. A further 1,716 miles had been authorized involving an estimated expenditure of $2.2 billion.

4. Some 706 miles involving an estimated cost of $674 million were in the planning stage (Table 6).

TABLE 6

Mileage and Cost of Toll Roads Completed, under Construction,
Authorized, or Proposed, as of September 1, 1953

	Miles	Cost [a] (thousands of dollars)
Completed and in operation		
Colorado: Denver Boulder Turnpike	17.3	$ 6,366
Connecticut: Merritt and Wilbur Cross Parkways [b]	67.0	38,092
Florida: Buccaneer Trail	15.0	4,600
Maine: Turnpike	47.2	20,600
New Hampshire: Turnpike	14.7	6,770
New Jersey: Turnpike	117.6	280,000
New York: Hutchinson River and Saw Mill River Parkways [b]	39.5	14,000
Oklahoma: Turnpike	88.0	38,793
Pennsylvania: Turnpike System	327.2	241,664
Total	733.5	$650,885

(continued on next page)

265

TABLE 6 (continued)

	Miles	Cost [a] (thousands of dollars)
Under construction		
Florida: Jacksonville, expressway system [c]	41.0	$ 69,000
Maine: Turnpike extensions	60.0	55,000
New Hampshire: Turnpike extensions	40.0	36,500
New Jersey: Garden State Parkway [d]	165.0	285,000
New York: Thruway	427.0	500,000
Captree Parkway	7.0	7,300
Ohio: Turnpike	241.4	326,000
Pennsylvania: Turnpike extensions	33.0	65,000
West Virginia: Turnpike	87.6	96,000
Total	1,102.0	$1,439,800
Projects authorized but not financed		
Connecticut: New York line to Rhode Island line	125.0	$ 213,000
Florida: Stuart to Miami Turnpike	110.0	96,000
Indiana: Turnpike	150.0	193,000
Massachusetts: Cross-State Turnpike	130.0	200,000
New Jersey: Turnpike extensions	92.0	483,000
New York: Thruway extensions	108.0	150,000
North Carolina: Gastonia–Mt. Airy Turnpike	125.0	200,000
Pennsylvania: Turnpike extensions	280.0	240,000
Texas: Dallas to Fort Worth	33.0	31,000
Dallas–Fort Worth area to San Antonio	276.0	150,000
Wisconsin: Cross-state toll road	287.0	200,000
Total	1,716.0	$2,156,000
Proposed [e]		
Georgia: Florida line to St. Marys and beyond	50.0	$ 20,000
Kansas: Kansas City to Wichita via Topeka	210.0	105,000
Kentucky: Louisville to Elizabethtown	40.0	22,000
Ohio: Cincinnati to N.E. border of state	300.0	400,000
Virginia: Richmond to Petersburg	36.0	57,000
Washington: Tacoma to Everett	70.0	70,000
Total	706.0	$ 674,000
Grand Total	4,257.5	$4,920,685

[a] Where actual costs are not yet available, bond sales or estimated costs are shown.

[b] Built as free roads.

[c] Although tolls will be collected only on two bridges, the project is classified as a toll road because of the co-mingling of toll and other revenues for debt service, operation, and maintenance of the entire system.

[d] Total parkway length is 180 miles; 15 miles of free-road links built by Highway Department.

[e] Includes only projects currently under consideration for which mileage and costs have been estimated by state officials or in published releases. Projects for which mileage and costs are not known have been authorized or are being studied in Illinois, Michigan, Nebraska, North Carolina, and Pennsylvania, among others.

Source: Bureau of Public Roads.

There is the possibility, therefore, that 4,258 miles of toll roads at a cost of $4,920.7 million may be operating in the United States on principal intercity routes within the next few years. Additional toll-road construction might be undertaken in states which have general authorization to provide toll roads but have taken no steps to designate specific routes. Altogether, 34 states have given consideration to toll-road legislation and 23 have enacted legislation of some type.

At the present time, therefore, about 2,500 miles of toll highways involving close to $3 billion of construction are in the stage of being authorized or proposed. How many more miles of these self-liquidating facilities might be built in the United States as part of a self-liquidating public works program? Some indication of an answer can be obtained from a report made by the federal government some fifteen years ago and submitted to Congress in 1939 by the President.[2] This report was prepared by the Bureau of Public Roads under provisions of the Federal-Aid Highway Act of 1938. The purpose of this investigation was to determine the possibility of financing such a system of transcontinental routes through tolls.

Even at that early date the report provided substantial evidence of the feasibility of financing highways through tolls. Conditions since then have provided much greater support for toll finance, because motor vehicle registrations have doubled and the problem of traffic congestion has made the motorist much more willing to pay the high cost of the roads that are needed.

The conclusions reached by this report must be modified by the events which have occurred since the study was made. Estimates of the volume of traffic that would be willing to pay the toll, for example, were based on conditions existing in the middle 1930's, when neither consumer incomes, nor volume of traffic, nor the cost of express highways were as high as they are today. Fifteen years ago the degree of traffic congestion and highway inadequacy had not reached the point where the possibility of paying a toll to avoid the inadequacies of the "free road" system offered any widespread appeal. Thus the estimates of possible toll-road patronage presented in the report were low. Average daily traffic estimated for the Pennsylvania Turnpike route was 715 vehicles per day compared with 11,000 vehicles per day actually using the Turnpike by 1952; toll-paying traffic between Portland, Maine and the New Hampshire border was estimated at 1,348 per day, while traffic now using the Maine Turnpike averages in excess of 5,300 vehicles per day.

[2] *Toll Roads and Free Roads*, H. Doc. 272, 76th Cong., 1st sess.

Table 7 shows that many sections of road that in 1939 seemed to offer only a moderate possibility of self-support are now accommodating successful toll facilities. Much of the mileage indicated as being unable to pay its way could do so now. Although costs have risen far above the 1939 estimates as a result of both postwar in-

TABLE 7

Self-Liquidation Possibilities for Toll Roads, 1945–1960
(as Estimated in 1939)

| DESCRIPTION | | LENGTH | CUMULATED LENGTH | REVENUE AS PER CENT |
From:	To:	(miles)	(miles)	OF COST
Jersey City, N.J.	New Haven, Conn.	65.6	65.6	93.8%
Junction Route 4, Pa.	Jersey City, N.J.	106.8	172.4	91.1
Route 5, Calif.	Whitewater, Calif.	91.0	263.4	89.2
Washington, D.C.	Baltimore, Md.	39.3	302.7	88.1
Route 2 Mass.	Portland, Maine	133.9	436.6	85.1
Miami, Fla.	Jacksonville, Fla.	326.5	763.1	83.2
Baltimore, Md.	Route 4, Pa.	76.2	839.3	81.8
Richmond, Va.	Washington, D.C.	108.3	947.6	80.5
San Ysidro, Calif.	Route 6, Calif.	124.4	1,072.0	78.9
Whitewater, Calif.	Indio, Calif.	32.7	1,104.7	78.7
Route 3, Ill.	Route 3, Mich., Ind.	156.9	1,261.6	76.8
Brigham, Utah	Salt Lake City, Utah	52.3	1,313.9	76.5
Odessa, Texas	Route 3, Texas	337.9	1,651.8	74.6
Route 6, Calif.	San Fernando, Calif.	44.8	1,696.6	73.5
Buffalo, N.Y.	Albany, N.Y.	287.6	1,984.2	70.2
Route 6, Calif.	Ludlow, Calif.	69.1	2,053.3	70.0
San Fernando, Calif.	Tracy, Calif.	291.7	2,345.0	68.5
Minneapolis, Minn.	Route 3, Ill.	392.6	2,737.6	66.5
Route 4, Calif.	Redding, Calif.	153.7	2,891.3	66.1
San Antonio, Texas	Route 6, Texas	250.7	2,142.0	65.1
Portland, Maine	Bangor, Maine	121.3	3,263.3	74.6
St. Joseph, Mo.	Route 3, Ill.	275.7	3,539.0	63.6
Route 3, Ill.	Indianapolis, Ind.	203.7	3,742.7	62.9
Carlisle, Pa.	Route 1, Pa.	94.8	3,837.5	62.3
Route 2, Ind.	Detroit, Mich.	102.2	3,939.7	61.6
Tracy, Calif.	Route 4, Calif.	69.1	4,008.8	61.3
Route 3, Texas	Shreveport, La.	190.4	4,199.2	60.4
Ludlow, Calif.	Las Vegas, Nev.	117.0	4,316.2	60.2
Fargo, N.D.	Minneapolis, Minn.	219.1	4,535.3	59.7
New Haven, Conn.	Route 2, Mass.	99.8	4,635.1	59.0
Greeley, Colo.	St. Joseph, Mo.	529.7	5,164.8	58.0
Indianapolis, Ind.	Columbus, Ohio	156.6	5,321.4	57.4
Phoenix, Ariz.	El Paso, Texas	391.1	5,712.5	56.9
Cleveland, Ohio	Buffalo, N.Y.	220.7	5,933.2	55.8
Oakland, Calif.	Auburn, Calif.	110.0	6,043.2	55.3
Boise, Idaho	Rupert, Idaho	182.2	6,225.4	55.0
Shreveport, La.	Vicksburg, Miss.	168.8	6,394.2	54.7

(continued on next page)

flation and expanding highway design requirements, the tremendous expansion of postwar traffic, the mounting congestion on existing free roads, and the ability and willingness of consumers to pay the bill for good roads more than offset the higher cost. It is quite possible that those routes indicated in 1939 to be 50 per cent self-

TABLE 7 (continued)

| DESCRIPTION | | LENGTH | CUMULATED LENGTH | REVENUE AS PER CENT |
From:	To:	(miles)	(miles)	OF COST
Salem, Ore.	Portland, Ore.	56.9	6,451.1	54.3%
Route 4, Ill.	Route 2, Ill.	155.5	6,606.6	53.9
Perrysburg, Ohio	Cleveland, Ohio	79.3	6,685.9	53.5
Route 6, S.C.	Richmond, Va.	362.6	7,048.5	52.9
St. Louis, Mo.	Route 4, Ill.	88.8	7,137.3	52.7
Albany, N.Y.	Route 1, Mass.	147.2	7,284.5	52.0
Pittsburgh, Pa.	Carlisle, Pa.	166.6	7,451.1	51.4
Tulsa, Okla.	Springfield, Mo.	171.3	7,622.4	51.1
Route 3, Mich., Ind.	Perrysburg, Ohio	69.9	7,692.3	51.0
Jacksonville, Fla.	Route 6, S.C.	219.3	7,911.6	50.6
Detroit, Mich.	Port Huron, Mich.	72.5	7,984.1	50.4
Springfield, Mo.	St. Louis, Mo.	165.2	8,149.3	50.1
Route 4, Pa.	Route 1, Mo.	88.5	9,237.8	50.0
Roseburg, Ore.	Salem, Ore.	133.3	8,371.1	49.7
El Paso, Texas	Odessa, Texas	245.2	8,616.3	49.3
Indio, Calif.	Phoenix, Ariz.	254.0	8,870.3	49.0
Columbus, Ohio	Pittsburgh, Pa.	195.0	9,065.3	48.5
Portland, Ore.	Route 2, Wash.	146.7	9,212.0	47.8
Route 2, Wash.	Canadian boundary	124.7	9,336.7	47.3
Route 6, Texas	Tulsa, Okla.	270.5	9,607.2	46.9
Auburn, Calif.	Reno, Nev.	106.5	9,713.7	46.6
Ashland, Ore.	Roseburg, Ore.	122.9	9,836.6	46.3
Las Vegas, Nev.	Salt Lake City, Utah	407.5	10,244.1	45.7
Birmingham, Ala.	Atlanta, Ga.	141.2	10,385.3	45.5
Boardman, Ore.	Boise, Idaho	253.1	10,638.4	45.0
Salt Lake City, Utah	Greeley, Colo.	463.3	11,101.7	44.2
Rupert, Idaho	Brigham, Utah	119.7	11,221.4	44.1
Redding, Calif.	Ashland, Ore.	138.2	11,359.6	43.7
Seattle, Wash.	Ellensburg, Wash.	90.0	11,449.6	43.4
Vicksburg, Miss.	Birmingham, Ala.	270.5	11,720.1	42.9
Bangor, Maine	Canadian boundary	196.6	11,916.7	42.6
Portland, Ore.	Boardman, Ore.	163.4	12,080.1	42.2
Mexican boundary	San Antonio, Texas	156.2	12,236.3	42.0
Augusta, Ga.	Charleston, S.C.	116.3	12,352.6	41.8
Reno, Nev.	Salt Lake City, Utah	514.9	12,867.5	41.3
Spokane, Wash.	Fargo, N.D.	1,169.6	14,037.1	39.8
Ellensburg, Wash.	Spokane, Wash.	145.9	14,183.0	39.5
Atlanta, Ga.	Augusta, Ga.	153.2	14,336.2	39.2

Source: *Toll Roads and Free Roads*, H. Doc. 272, 76th Cong., 1st sess.

liquidating might now prove fully self-supporting. This would mean a potential toll-road system of 9,238 miles.[3]

Intercity routes, however, do not provide the only potential for the toll highway. To the extent that roads financed by tolls can be adapted to the local short-haul requirements of urban areas there is a substantial additional mileage of routes that might be financed with revenue bonds and tolls. In recent years there have been a number of demonstrations of how controlled access roads in urban areas have been able to afford relief for downtown commuter traffic. Thus far most of these expressways have been nontoll facilities, although several have introduced toll collection at key points such as bridges or tunnels. With the possible exception of Los Angeles, however, there has been little in the way of a system approach to urban expressway development.

Thus far the high cost of achieving solutions to urban transport problems on a broad scale has postponed many highly desirable undertakings. Costs ranging from $5 million to $10 million a mile are common for urban expressways, and financing methods to achieve anything worthwhile in the way of expressway systems have not been devised. The feasibility of the toll-secured revenue bond for urban projects has been questioned on the grounds that toll collection from large volumes of short-run rush hour traffic would impede rather than facilitate traffic movement.

It is now apparent that one stop to pay the toll on an urban expressway interferes far less with traffic than a dozen or more stops at traffic lights and other traffic interferences. Hollywood Boulevard, for example, by eliminating traffic lights and cross streets is reputedly saving Los Angeles motorists 120 million stops a year. In any event, there are mechanics other than cash toll collection that can eliminate this objection to the toll road in urban areas. One is the commuter ticket which can be purchased and displayed by regular users of a toll system to gain entrance and exit without stopping to pay toll. Variations of this method have been used for some time both by the Port of New York Authority at its bridge and tunnel entrances and on the Merritt Parkway.

A second possibility might be to issue revenue bonds for both expressway and adjacent downtown parking areas, with facilities so designed that all traffic destined for the downtown area would terminate in the parking areas and pay a fee at the parking lot or

---

[3] Note that Pittsburgh to Carlisle, now the successful western extension of the Pennsylvania Turnpike, is indicated in the table to be able to cover only 51 per cent of costs.

270

garage that would include both the cost of parking and the cost of using the expressway. The revenue bonds could also include funds for the modernization of mass transportation. Rapid transit, for example could be provided on the same rights of way used by motor vehicle traffic.

Along with toll highways there continue to be a large number of expensive bridge and tunnel projects that can be self-supporting through the charging of tolls. Some of the problems associated with toll projects as a possible means of combating depression will be discussed in a later section.

PARKING FACILITIES

Multi-million-dollar parking structures being constructed or planned in most cities throughout the country provide a new category of private and public construction that could be promoted on a large-scale in depression periods. Parking accommodations are being financed by both government and private enterprise, separately and cooperatively. In most states a municipality may participate in providing parking garages either by providing facilities itself, by delegating the work to an authority or agency of the government, by furnishing financial aid to private construction, or by leasing to private operators. This whole area of public interest and participation has developed since the war, when previous indifference to the problem of automobile parking became intolerable in the face of automobile ownership trends that have doubled the number of cars since 1935.

There are at least 33 states that permit cities or other units of local government to borrow to finance parking. In some states the county, metropolitan district, or a state agency is authorized to issue the bonds. These must be revenue bonds in 13 states and general-obligation bonds in 4 states, and may be either type in 16 states.

Legislative provisions with respect to the ownership or operation of parking facilities by local units of government sometimes stipulate the maximum amount that may be borrowed, fix the maximum interest rate and maturity period, and designate the kinds of revenues that may be used. Life of the bonds varies from 20 to 50 years, amounts specified may be as high as $100 million, and revenues to be used may include general taxes, fees charged against users of the facility, parking meter revenues, and special assessments.

Although most government action in this field is provided through the regular channels of municipal government, there are at least

54 parking authorities, commissions, or boards in the United States with varying degrees of power to provide off-street parking accommodations. As yet only a few have specific authority to plan comprehensive systems of parking facilities, as is the case, for example, in Wisconsin. About half the parking authorities have the power of condemnation to permit the necessary land to be assembled, and half the authorities may issue revenue bonds, which are, however, frequently contingent on approval of the electorate.[4]

In addition to parking agencies, there are approximately 16 public authorities that are authorized to provide for parking among other responsibilities for public works. For example, in Massachusetts the Metropolitan Transit Authority may provide parking accommodations in conjunction with transit operations. Market authorities in Maryland and Virginia are in a similar category; and the Triborough Bridge and Tunnel Authority in New York City may provide parking and other terminal accommodations in connection with other transportation facilities.

TERMINALS

In recent years the problems of interchange in the terminal area, and the large number of transportation companies involved in terminal operations, have given impetus to the provision of self-liquidating union bus and truck terminals and terminals that combine rail, highway, and water facilities. This in turn has led to a wider participation in financing arrangements, and to mixed public and private undertakings often administered by a quasi-governmental body such as a port authority. This type of construction activity is rapidly growing in importance both in the category of public works and as private undertakings that might be aided by government.

An illustration of the magnitude of truck terminal needs is provided by measures being taken in Chicago. Seven or eight large truck terminal areas adjacent to the expressway system have been planned to house all trucking companies in the city. Necessary ordinances were passed by the city and a new zoning classification was created known as Truck Terminal Districts. It is anticipated that the present program will require a total investment of $100 million.

The $24 million Port of New York Authority Bus Terminal, joined with the Lincoln Tunnel, is a good example of a self-supporting

---

[4] Data on parking from David R. Levin, *The Effectiveness of Parking Agencies,* Highway Research Board, 1952.

project that is needed in many urban areas of the United States. About 90 per cent of intercity buses and bus passengers traveling to and from mid-Manhattan use the Terminal. Financing was through terminal bonds secured by the earnings of the structure and by the Port Authority general reserve fund. The project was designed to be fully self-supporting over the long run. The Terminal includes a shopping center of over seventy consumer services. Concession rentals provide about 60 per cent of the Bus Terminal's total income, and the percentage is expected to increase to 70 per cent in the near future.

In some cities bus terminals are being constructed by individual bus companies or jointly by several companies, while in other locations municipal revenue bonds are providing the capital for such facilities. In all cases the support for such undertakings is largely in ancillary revenue producers that shift the financial burden from direct users of the terminal to related business activity.

The number of extensive terminal plans, many of them being undertaken with private capital, with or without public assistance, indicates the potential for government stimulation of such works if business conditions make it necessary for private industry to postpone such undertakings.

In many cities the relocation of railroad terminals and yards has provided valuable properties for the development of more appropriate land uses. In Philadelphia the new Penn Center made possible by abandonment of the Pennsylvania Railroad's Broad Street Station will provide hotel and office accommodations, parking, and civic buildings. In Cleveland the Pennsylvania Railroad has sold an 11-acre terminal site in the heart of the city to make way for a $200 million development that may ultimately cover 60 acres. The land will be used to provide a hotel, office buildings, government buildings, underground parking for 25,000 cars, freight sidings, and a 3-story warehouse beneath hotel and apartment buildings. In Boston, removal from the Back Bay of yards occupied by the Boston & Albany Railroad has paved the way for comparable development of a Boston Civic Center.

A new deep-water terminal is under construction in Boston as part of the Boston Port Authority's master plan of port terminal development, and in Houston the Port Commission is preparing a master plan for port development to be carried out during the next twenty years. In San Francisco the first financing of harbor bonds entirely on a revenue bond basis has been accomplished by issuance of $6 million of thirty-year obligations to construct a world trade center and to finance pier improvements at the California-owned port of San Francisco. Bonds will be serviced from the port's operating income.

These developments, involving very heavy capital requirements, could be undertaken in nearly every large city. The possibilities of government incentives to help finance such undertakings in times of business depression may be a significant part of a so-called public works program. Urban redevelopment planning indicates not only that extensive self-liquidating facilities are feasible but that any plans for public works to combat depression will need to promote private and municipal undertakings already conceived if there is to be not merely a shift from private to public investment and from local to federal financing. The need appears to be one of encouraging similar large-scale plans in other cities now, and of assuring the desired stimulation of these activities later through appropriate financial aid and incentive.

TRANSIT

Most cities are coming to the realization that large-scale investment in new plant and equipment may be necessary to provide additional mass transportation capacity and improved service. This is an area that is for the most part under private management, although a growing number of cities have municipal transit systems or public authorities. Whatever the present management arrangement, however, the need for bold plans is obvious in the inadequacy of commutation facilities in large cities. Cooperation between private industry and government is needed now to begin the difficult task of outlining what needs to be done, and what could be done if the means of providing the necessary capital were made available.

Recent transit plans and modernization projects in several cities indicate the nature and magnitude of the task in this area. The New York Transit Authority approved a $1 billion improvement program and a six-year plan that would provide for construction of a new subway line, rehabilitation of existing facilities, extensions to the system, and new equipment and power plants. A charter amendment in Cleveland cleared the way for a $22.5 million Reconstruction Finance Corporation loan for modernization of the Cleveland Transit System, to be financed from fares over a period of twenty years. A rapid transit plan for metropolitan Boston in 1947 proposed improvements which at that time called for an estimated investment of $73 million. Expansion of the Metropolitan Transit Authority facilities will be financed by bonds of the Boston Metropolitan District.

AIRPORTS

The dimensions of airport capital requirements and the extent to which airports provide an opportunity for self-liquidating projects are questions that need to be answered in present-day planning for public works. The financing of airports has undergone substantial change in the course of the past two decades. Prior to 1933, airport capital expenditures were supplied 50 per cent from commercial and private sources and nearly 48 per cent by municipal governments. Federal financing was less than 1 per cent of the total.

The rapid development of aviation in the thirties, however, combined with the financial difficulties of local governments during the depression, changed this picture. Federal participation in airport development increased rapidly as part of the work-relief program, and from 1933 through 1940 over 70 per cent of all airport capital outlays were federal grants.[5]

After the war the Federal Airport Act of 1946 authorized expenditures of $500 million over a seven-year period, but actual appropriations have been less than half this sum. When it came to filling the gap, city voters were reluctant to approve general-obligation bond issues for the financing of airports. As airport costs rise with increasing length of runways and greater capacity of terminal buildings, the limits to which cities are willing to go in financing airports are being rapidly approached. This reluctance has been fortified by mounting air transport business and increasingly profitable air operations.

A picture of the possibilities of airport self-support under these circumstances is provided by the Port of New York Authority's experience. City, state, and federal agencies had invested $121 million in New York International, La Guardia, and Newark Airports before the Port Authority assumed responsibility for them in 1947. By the end of 1953 the Port Authority had spent or committed an additional $98 million, including expenditures at Teterboro Airport, which it purchased in 1949. Except for federal grants of $4.1 million, financing has been accomplished by the Authority through air terminal bonds.

Gross operating revenues for the four Port Authority airports in 1953 reached a high of $9.5 million, and net operating revenues before debt service totaled $1.5 million. After deducting interest

---

[5] Through the Civil Works Administration, the Federal Emergency Relief Administration, and the Work Projects Administration.

275

charges of $2.0 million on air terminal bonds, the net deficit in 1953 was $500,562, which was paid out of the general reserve fund.[6] This degree of airport self-support was achieved in the heaviest air traffic center in the United States, and has been made possible by a comprehensive regional development of public works which taken as a whole is self-supporting. The problems of achieving self-supporting air terminals in other cities with less traffic and no regional plan of financing are obviously great.

There are now about 6,000 airports in the United States. Most of them are small airports for private flying, which do not offer opportunities for large-scale construction projects. But they can be made largely self-supporting through agricultural pursuits on unused airport acreage. At the other end of the scale are some 734 major civil airports designed for commercial flights that could use considerable large-scale construction but have doubtful possibilities for self-support. However, with the development of concession revenues at major airports, a very significant trend toward self-support is indicated, and with airline gross revenues already exceeding $1.5 billion annually the outlook both for expanding facility requirements and for increasing self-support is promising.

Total expenditures for airports in recent postwar years, including capital and maintenance outlays, have averaged only about $80 million. This sum includes private facilities, municipal airports, and airports operated by state governments and authorities. Municipal airports in the 41 largest cities of the United States accounted for $37 million of expenditures in 1952, of which $29.3 million was for capital outlay. Of 1,819 airports under direct control of municipal or county governments, only 614 were showing a surplus of revenues over operating expenditures (Table 8).

TABLE 8

Airports under Municipal or County Governments, 1952

Financial Status	Number of Airports
Income exceeds expenditure	614
Deficit financing required	850
Unknown	341
Break even	14
Total	1,819

Source: Civil Aeronautics Administration. Review includes Regions 1 to 7.

[6] *Annual Report,* Port of New York Authority, 1953.

With mounting air cargo carriage and continued expansion of passenger traffic, the demand for major terminals continues to mount, but rapidly changing technology makes it difficult to foresee at this time what the location, size, and design of future airports should be. The helicopter and the convertiplane, along with the advent of jet power, have the airport planners in a difficult position. In any event the future capital requirements for United States airports as estimated by the Civil Aeronautics Administration in its 1952 National Airport Plan include 2,232 new airports and improvements at 2,583 existing airports. Cost of the program was estimated at $650 million.

Much more needs to be learned about the prospects for self-liquidating or partially self-liquidating public works in this area, looking to the probable growth of air passenger and cargo operations and changes in technology that can be anticipated in the years immediately ahead.

2. Obstacles to Self-Liquidating Public Works Program

From the standpoint of potential construction and employment, it is helpful that the principal opportunities for a program to combat depression are in the cities and their suburbs, where 100 million people live and where much of our economic activity is concentrated. These metropolitan areas present the most urgent need for public works as a result of the past two decades of their growth, and they therefore offer the greatest opportunities for new investment in community facilities.

But along with the advantages of public works activity in urbanized areas, the task of actually planning and agreeing on what is to be done is particularly formidable. The difficulties of undertaking large-scale public works arise from the inflexibility of the established urban pattern, the absence of space in which to provide new facilities of adequate capacity, and the absence of governmental machinery to plan and carry out needed solutions.

Thus far only superficial efforts have been made to solve the problems of urban blight. Much of the activity now under way treats the symptoms of urban congestion rather than its causes. Generally this activity represents far too small an effort in relation to the magnitude of the problem. A basic question, therefore, is how a public works program to combat depression should be designed so that at the same time it can combat the problems of our urban society, and not multiply them. In using the device of large-scale public works as a tool for economic stabilization we could be creating long-run economic problems of even greater consequence by making erroneous decisions with respect to location, type, and conception of the public works we undertake. Conversely, the opportunity for real accomplishment is equally clear.

One example of the problem of determining a desirable program of public improvements is provided by the arguments now being carried on in almost every large city over whether construction activities should be permitted to encourage more densely populated urban areas or whether they should promote a more rapid decentralization or dispersal of urban concentrations to other locations. These arguments need to be resolved in every community, and whatever agreement can be reached must take the form of an acceptable regional plan to provide the framework into which a public works program could be fitted.

Public works programs for anticyclical purposes may be vitiated by such obstacles as the absence of detailed plans and failure to acquire the necessary land in advance. In the case of self-liquidating public works these obstacles are magnified by the fact that such undertakings are generally of considerable magnitude and cost and as such involve difficult problems of land acquisition, planning, and financing. Moreover, conflicting views among city planners as to what the city of the future should be like create substantial barriers to agreement.

The additional problems of self-liquidating public works are especially striking in the case of toll highways. Among them are the absence of agreement concerning self-liquidation as an objective, the absence of techniques for achieving self-support, the problem that arises from the threat of competition from parallel "free" roads, the absence in many states of adequate enabling legislation, and the absence of federal policy that recognizes and helps to overcome some of the problems of using public works as a tool to combat depression.

DESIRABILITY OF SELF-SUPPORT

Attitudes about the question of self-liquidation vs. general-fund financing are in many respects of key importance to the development and acceptance of a program of self-liquidating public works. There is a basic conflict in the transportation field, for example, with respect to the question of how facilities should be paid for. One point of view holds that since nearly everybody uses the streets and

278

highways and everyone benefits from a good transit system, the total bill should be paid through general taxes. A contrary view is that the provision of transportation services is more in the nature of a public business enterprise and as such should be considered apart from the general functions of government and paid for directly by those who use the services. Between these extremes are numerous positions that combine self-support and general tax support, and these are reflected in the situation today.

The case of the New York subway deficit provides a current illustration that the conflict at the community level between those who favor self-support and those who argue for general tax support is not academic.[7] According to one view of the recent $50 million annual subway operating deficit (which was in addition to general tax support of the existing subway debt structure) the desirable course would have been to maintain the fare at 10 cents, and to make up the deficit through a tax on the profits of business "which prospers because buses and subways feed commerce right to their doors." Such a plan would assure that "all who benefit from the transit system contribute to its upkeep." [8] The opposite view, that mounting subway deficits had become an intolerable threat to the entire fiscal position of the city government, won a partial victory in that users now are required to pay more in accordance with the rising cost of providing service. But the decision to move toward a higher degree of self-support for New York's subways was not made overnight, and other communities in which self-liquidating public works might be undertaken may be equally reluctant to accept the view that self-liquidation is a desirable characteristic for a program of public works. Especially is this likely to be the case in periods of depression.

METHODS OF PAYING THE BILL

Even where the attempt is made to provide self-supporting transportation facilities, there are sharp differences of opinion as to desirable financing methods. In New York, for example, the Port of New York Authority confines its activities to those which are self-liquidating or which have a reasonable chance of ultimate self-support. But the Port Authority concept is that transportation facilities in the New York region should be financed not as separate projects but as parts of the whole port development system, which

[7] Another illustration may be found in the battle that still goes on between toll-road and anti-toll-road philosophers.

[8] New York Times, March 27, 1953, p. 18.

279

taken together must be self-supporting. Thus the Authority's six bridges and tunnels provided much of the revenue needed to support eleven other enterprises operating at a loss in 1953, including airports, grain terminals, and bus and truck terminals.

There has been widespread objection, however, to this system type of development on the grounds that it is unfair, for example, to require motor vehicle users to defray the deficit incurred at the Authority's airports. Supporters of this view argue that toll-supported facilities should be accomplished on an individual project basis rather than in accordance with a regional system of development. The same issues have arisen with respect to toll roads and are implicit in questions of extending transit operations to unprofitable suburban areas.

Perhaps one reason why self-supporting public facilities are in the minority lies in the absence of any rational plan for establishing charges to be paid by consumers. Existing charges often have little relation to the cost of providing needed services and often have no relation to possibilities of influencing the volume and character of the demand for services.

To illustrate, on most transit lines the passenger who boards at the beginning of the line and sits pays the same fare as the rider in the downtown area who travels only a few blocks and stands. And passengers in rush hours pay no more than those who ride in off-peak hours. In many cases they pay less. The gasoline tax is also a poor pricing mechanism since it is collected at a uniform rate throughout the state, regardless of the cost of providing the specific facility being used. Thus a vehicle may be traveling on an urban expressway costing 1 cent per vehicle-mile to provide, or on a less costly highway at .1 cent per vehicle-mile.

The inadequacies of transportation pricing policies raise the question whether sufficient emphasis has been given to cost considerations and the pricing mechanism as a means of accomplishing transportation objectives. Fares, tolls, fees, and other charges for public services frequently lack any rational scientific basis, unlike, for example, electric power or telephone rates, which involve many similar problems. It is likely that more attention directed to pricing in the field of potentially self-liquidating public works will reveal important possibilities for self-support.

FREE ROAD COMPETITION

The closest we have come to experiencing what might happen to toll-road patronage under depression conditions was under the restrictions on motor vehicle use imposed by the war. During World War II, traffic on our only important toll highway, the Pennsylvania Turnpike, dropped to 3,000 vehicles per day. Revenues during the three fiscal years 1943 to 1945 failed by $1.4 million to cover the combined requirements for interest and maintenance. The Pennsylvania General Assembly in 1945 prepared to meet the situation by authorizing the Turnpike to issue revenue bonds for war emergency financing of interest and sinking fund requirements. However, with the end of the war, the end of gasoline rationing, and the resumption of automobile production, a rapid increase in Turnpike traffic removed any necessity for emergency measures.

The problem of building new toll roads during depression is closely related to this experience. First, it is possible that existing toll roads might suffer considerable loss of traffic during a prolonged depression wherever the use of alternate "free" roads would seem to be worth the saving of the toll. This problem, it will be noted, does not apply to most toll bridges, which generally exercise a monopoly either because there is no other nearby way across or because all local crossings are under the same management. But in the case of the New Jersey Turnpike, for example, a considerable volume of traffic might shift to toll-free U.S. Route 1 in order to avoid the extra out-of-pocket costs of as much as $1.75 per passenger car on the toll road, despite the fact that hidden costs on the old road, in time lost and higher operating costs, might more than offset saving the toll.

The point is simply that public reaction to the building of new toll roads might be unfavorable at a time when objection to existing toll facilities was mounting. This possibility, however, depends on a number of factors, including the extent to which motorists by that time have accepted the toll as part of the cost of highway transportation. But there is the additional possibility that toll authorities in a depression might adjust rates to reduce the competitive pull of alternative "free" routes. In any event, if the depression of the 1930's is any guide, no conceivable magnitude of economic adversity will reduce motor traffic in populous areas to the point where it could be accommodated by the free road system alone (see Table 9).

STATE ENABLING LEGISLATION

To finance a highway with revenue bonds and collect tolls requires legislation. In most of the twenty-three states with this power the legislative battle has been lengthy and the resulting

TABLE 9

Effect of Economic Conditions on Motor Vehicle Registrations, Production, and Traffic, 1929–1940

(*index numbers; 1929 = 100*)

	Motor Vehicle Registrations	*Production of Motor Vehicles*	*Vehicle-Miles of Travel*	*Total Highway User Revenues*
1929	100.0	100.0	100.0	100.0
1930	100.0	64.2	104.3	124.0
1931	97.4	45.3	109.3	113.1
1932	90.9	24.5	101.4	101.6
1933	90.2	35.8	101.5	103.7
1934	94.3	50.9	109.0	102.0
1935	98.9	75.5	115.6	103.8
1936	106.4	88.7	127.5	116.7
1937	112.1	90.6	136.6	211.5
1938	110.9	47.2	137.2	208.0
1939	115.5	67.9	144.3	217.0
1940	120.8	84.9	152.8	233.7

Source: Based on *Highway Statistics Summary,* Bureau of Public Roads, to 1945, and *Automobile Facts and Figures,* 1953.

legislation has often been restricted to specific roads rather than providing broad authority (Table 10). If a program of toll highway construction were considered necessary in the near future as part of a program to combat depression, it would be found that half the states are without authority to build such roads and many of those that do have authority either have already used it to build the roads specified in the legislation or need new legislation to specify additional routes. Those that do not have authority would not be able to get it very quickly, if past experience is any guide.

Such past experience illustrates the time problem and the need for obtaining necessary enabling acts now (Table 11). The initial toll-road undertaking was inspired by the possibilities of creating employment in Pennsylvania during the depression. A resolution requesting investigation of the feasibility of such a project was introduced in the Pennsylvania Assembly in 1935, and a commission comprising members of the House and Senate was created for this purpose. Through the efforts of the Highway Department a grant was obtained from the Works Progress Administration to make a preliminary survey of the route, and on the basis of this survey the commission reported favorably on the toll-road project. Legislation was passed in 1937 establishing the Pennsylvania Turnpike Commission.[9] Construction started in November 1938, and on October

[9] Public Law 774, 1937.

TABLE 10

(X) States Having Authority to Construct Toll Roads

	Alabama	X	Nebraska
	Arizona		Nevada
	Arkansas	X	New Hampshire
	California	X	New Jersey
X	Colorado		New Mexico
X	Connecticut	X	New York
	Delaware	X	North Carolina
X	Florida		North Dakota
X	Georgia	X	Ohio
	Idaho	X	Oklahoma
X	Illinois		Oregon
X	Indiana	X	Pennsylvania
	Iowa		Rhode Island
	Kansas		South Carolina
X	Kentucky		South Dakota
	Louisiana		Tennessee
X	Maine	X	Texas
X	Maryland		Utah
X	Massachusetts		Vermont
X	Michigan	X	Virginia
	Minnesota		Washington
	Mississippi	X	West Virginia
	Missouri	X	Wisconsin
	Montana		Wyoming

TABLE 11

Comparative Time Schedules for Toll Roads

Toll Road [a]	Authority Established	Construction Authorized	Construction Started	Road Opened	Construction Period (months)
Colorado	April 1949	April 1949	Fall 1950	Jan. 1952	15
Maine	April 1941	April 1941	May 1946	Dec. 1947	19
New Hampshire	July 1947	July 1947	Oct. 1948	June 1950	20
New Jersey	Oct. 1948	April 1949	Feb. 1950	Nov. 1951	23
Pennsylvania	May 1937				
Original sect.		May 1937	Oct. 1938	Oct. 1940	23
Eastern ext.		May 1940	Sept. 1948	Nov. 1950	26
Western ext.		June 1941	Oct. 1949	Dec. 1951	26
33-mile ext.	Jan. 1952	Jan. 1952	Dec. 1952		
Oklahoma	July 1947	July 1947	Dec. 1950	April 1953	28
West Virginia	1947	March 1952	Aug. 1952		
Ohio	June 1949	Sept. 1949	Oct. 1952		
New York Thruway	March 1950	March 1950	Dec. 1950		
New Jersey Garden State					
Parkway	April 1945		Nov. 1946	(22 miles in 6 years)	
	April 1952	April 1952	Aug. 1952		

[a] Turnpike or turnpike system unless otherwise designated.

283

1, 1940 the original Turnpike, 160 miles in length, was opened to traffic.

Legislation that mentions specific routes or points that the authorized turnpike shall connect limits the authority of toll-road commissions in many states. In Maine, for example, the road was to be built "at such location as shall be approved by the State Highway Commission from a point at or near Kittery in York County to a point at or near Fort Kent in Aroostock County." In some states general authority to construct toll roads has to be implemented by further legislation designating specific routes. This is true, for example, of New Jersey, Massachusetts, and Pennsylvania.

In other legislation full authorization to designate turnpike routes is granted the turnpike or highway agency. The Indiana Toll Road Commission may construct toll projects at the locations it selects provided the routes are approved by the governor. The Colorado Highway Department, which is responsible for toll-road work, is authorized to adopt "a master plan for the development and improvement of the State Highway System by the construction of turnpikes. . . ." In Ohio the Turnpike Commission is empowered "to designate the locations" of the turnpike projects, but with the stipulation that the locations selected be considered necessary or desirable by the director of highways.

Financing provisions contained in toll-highway laws generally specify that revenue bonds shall be issued and secured by tolls and other revenues collected specifically from the projects constructed, without pledging the faith and credit of the state. In some states, such as New Hampshire and New York, however, the credit of the state is pledged.

In some cases toll-road legislation specifies the maximum amount that may be borrowed. Specific sums may be appropriated for advance planning, but generally it is provided that the turnpike commission may borrow from the highway department for planning and engineering services in advance of the sale of bonds. Other stipulations in toll-road legislation include permission to accept gifts of land and money, and in particular to accept aid from the federal government.

POSITION OF THE FEDERAL GOVERNMENT

The current position and past attitudes of the federal government on the question of toll roads are important in any consideration of plans for an extensive system of self-liquidating highway facilities financed with revenue bonds.

In the Federal-Aid Road Act of 1916, the secretary of agriculture was authorized to cooperate with the states in the construction of rural post roads, provided "that all roads constructed under the provisions of this act shall be free from tolls of all kinds." [10] This prohibition against the imposition of tolls on roads constructed with federal aid was restated in the Federal Highway Act of 1921, and the prohibition still stands.[11]

Departure from this policy in the case of bridges, however, occurred in legislation passed in 1927. This law provided that the secretary of agriculture might extend federal aid to any state or its political subdivisions for the construction of any toll bridge and approaches, provided that such bridge was owned and operated by a state or its subdivision.

The works financing bill of 1939, designed to provide employment through self-liquidating improvement programs, set the stage for a program of self-liquidating public works, but it failed to pass. The self-liquidating projects proposed by this legislation were to be carried out through the Reconstruction Finance Corporation and were to include projects undertaken by the Department of Agriculture, the Bureau of Public Roads, the Public Works Administration, and the Rural Electrification Administration.[12] The bill provided that the Bureau of Public Roads should have the power, with the approval of the RFC, to fix, maintain, and collect tolls and other charges for the use of highway improvements. Revenues derived from such collections in excess of what was needed to operate and maintain the improvement could be used for further highway projects.

In addition, the works financing bill provided for the acquisition of land to be held as an investment by the government to permit the recoupment of values resulting from highway improvements. The Bureau of Public Roads was to have the power ". . . to acquire by purchase, but not by condemnation, for investment purposes, any real property in the vicinity of any highway improvements or Federal-aid construction. . . ."

In testifying in favor of this legislation, the commissioner of public roads pointed out that the bill provided for improvement in four categories: ". . . First. Bridges and tunnels and similar individual projects on direct toll basis. Second. Very limited mileage of toll roads, including excess taking of land. Third. Land acquisition for rights-of-way, particularly, at the outset in metropolitan

[10] 39 Stat. 355, sec. 1.   [11] 42 Stat. 212, sec. 9.
[12] S. 2759, 76th Cong., 1st sess.

285

areas and connecting such areas. Fourth. Express highways in metropolitan areas. These are all essential parts of an adequate and truly national master plan for highway development." [13] The commissioner pointed out that aside from the limited possibilities of providing fully self-liquidating toll projects, financing on other routes might be accomplished through a combination of tolls, excess land takings and resale of some of those lands, and income from the gas tax and motor vehicle license fees.

In 1948 a bill was introduced in the House which would have extended provisions of the 1927 legislation to federal grants for highways.[14] This bill proposed also that the federal aid apportionment to a state might be expended not only by the state or any political subdivision, but by any agency or instrumentality of the state, or any instrumentality created by an agreement between two or more states. Thus the bill would have permitted toll roads to be constructed which might not otherwise be capable of self-support, with federal aid furnishing the type of assistance rendered through the Public Works Administration for the Pennsylvania Turnpike.

For a number of years prior to the war, interest in the possibility of constructing transcontinental toll highways was indicated by the introduction of bills for this purpose in Congress. These proposals culminated in a meeting in Atlantic City during 1941, to discuss transcontinental toll superhighways, costing between $50 and 100 billion. The chairman of the Pennsylvania Turnpike Commission was among those sponsoring the plan which was offered primarily with the idea of providing useful public works in the postwar period. It was stated that the proposed highway system could be paid for out of revenue bonds, with the federal government guaranteeing the interest.

Since the war a number of similar proposals have been submitted to Congress. In 1946 a bill was introduced to authorize a $12 billion system of highways financed through tolls.[15] In 1950 a bill was introduced for establishing the Crozet Transcontinental Superhighway Commission to construct and operate a coast-to-coast highway, using wherever practicable such free roads and toll roads as were already built or under construction.[16] This bill provided that the Bureau of Public Roads should supervise the construction and

[13] Statement of Thomas H. MacDonald, commissioner of public roads, *Works Financing Act of 1939*, Hearings before the Senate Committee on Banking and Currency, 76th Cong., 1st sess., 1939, p. 51.
[14] H.R. 6527, 80th Cong., 2nd sess.   [15] H.R. 50, 79th Cong., 2nd sess.
[16] H.R. 7578, 81st Cong., 2nd sess.

operation of any section of the highway "where the State . . . does not have proper toll-road laws or will not construct, maintain, and operate such a through super-highway within its borders." Wherever the Commission found it necessary to build sections of the road, it could issue revenue bonds secured by anticipated toll collections, "Without recourse against the Federal Government." No federal funds would be spent on the project "except in the form of direct grants to offset the benefit to the national defense."

3. Concluding Views

The foregoing discussion has indicated that, with the expansion of the American economy, a large backlog of needed public works has accumulated and that a considerable proportion of it is made up of either fully or partially self-liquidating projects. To the extent that public works are a useful tool to combat depression, a great volume of important needs could be met through a large-scale construction effort. In addition, many activities now under way or planned by private enterprise which might otherwise be postponed in a depression could be aided by government as part of the over-all program to stimulate construction.

Many of the most urgent needs and most promising possibilities for self-liquidating facilities are in urban areas, where most of our population and economic activity are located. This advantage may be outweighed, however, by the intricacies of urban planning with which any public works program must cope. In the city, decisions as to location and type of facilities may have important impacts on the whole urban structure, and they must be carefully considered if public works are to contribute to the ultimate goals of the community. In many metropolitan areas the administrative machinery required to arrive at intergovernmental decisions does not exist, and communities continue to be hampered in their efforts to plan a program of public works because the problem they face goes far beyond the outmoded political boundaries of government control and taxing power. The importance of developing adequate administration, in port authorities, regional commissions, or other forms, is accordingly great; and the coordinating functions of the federal government should be recognized and developed.

When large self-liquidating public undertakings are under consideration, many of the problems associated with public works in general are compounded: the tasks of advance planning, of planning on a comprehensive scale, of developing the necessary administrative machinery, and of acquiring the necessary land. Further obstacles are imposed by opposition to self-liquidation as a principle and to toll collection as a method; the absence of accepted pricing policies for public service introduces added difficulty. To wait until the need for an accelerated program of public works is upon us would, under these circumstances, result in confusion and frustration and certainly find us without the plans and procedures that would make possible the kind of facilities we really need.

To avoid such a situation, intelligent mobilization of efforts is required now. Otherwise our efforts in time of need not only might fall short of combating depression but might fail at the same time to take advantage of the opportunities afforded by a full-scale public works program.

A number of public works have been singled out as offering the dual possibility of providing worthwhile construction activity and effective attack on long-range urban development problems. Some 10,000 miles of toll highways might be feasible, together with extensive systems of urban toll highways. Substantial needs are emerging for truck, bus, and rail terminals; airports; transit facilities; parking garages; and related facilities. The additional needs of water, sewerage, and other community facilities not examined in this report would provide a large reservoir of necessary undertakings. Many now being carried on or planned by private enterprise, and by private and public enterprise combined, offer a significant area of activity to be promoted by public action. What can be done now to prepare for such a program? Can we match the efforts we would make to combat a depression with preparations now to assure the accomplishment of a worthwhile public works strategy?

Legislative obstacles to a program of self-liquidating public works at federal, state, and local levels include the following: absence of state and local enabling legislation for tax anticipation or revenue bond financing, limitations in existing toll-road laws, public opposition to tolls and self-supporting facilities, absence of detailed plans, failure to acquire land in advance, inadequacy of administrative tools, and the like.

The greatest obstacles, however, are financial, and in this area, while the limited-obligation bond, the revenue bond, and the expansion of toll facilities and self-supporting terminals provide a large potential volume of projects, there would still be a need for the federal government to assure that the capital required would be forthcoming under adverse economic conditions. This would have to be accomplished either through grants of federal aid to assure the financial success of partially self-liquidating facilities, or through guarantees that would induce investors to provide the necessary capital at a time when the returns from self-supporting projects would be less than usual.

Both government and private industry are spending billions of dollars annually for scientific research, but little is being directed to research to develop the administrative, legal, and financial tools that have lagged so far behind. The federal government could take the lead in supporting research of this kind. Although American universities have been called upon by the federal government to carry on scientific study in the interest of developing military power, there has been no comparable program for mobilization on the economic front.

It may be anticipated that highway construction will not fall off during a depression as rapidly as many other construction activities because of the relative stability of highway-user revenues, which provide the major part of highway support. Moreover, highway and other transportation construction has been at peak levels during the height of prosperity, so that further expansion to provide an anti-cyclical effect will be the more difficult. Since the major declines may occur in such construction activities as housing, an outlet for housing materials and labor might be found in the construction of terminals, garages, and urban redevelopment projects rather than highways.

But the most effective program to compensate for declining home construction might be found in the kinds of public works that are not self-liquidating—libraries, schools, recreation facilities, and similar public facilities—as well as in private undertakings of a comparable nature. The latter are important to the total program if an increase in government construction is not merely to provide an offset for declines in private construction.

In conclusion, if the problem of promoting a self-liquidating public works program on a large scale should arise, it is unlikely that present efforts at public works planning would find us ready with the comprehensive projects that are needed, or with the financial tools that would make them possible. If, on the other hand, it were possible to prepare now in bold terms for the kinds of facilities and financial aids that are needed, a public works program of tremendous significance could be in readiness that might have important antidepression effects as well as extraordinary long-run economic benefits.

289

COMMENT

SIDNEY G. TICKTON, The Seventh Company, Inc., New York City

Owen's paper has outlined the kinds of public works that might be undertaken to provide employment during a depression. His concentration on the construction of public roads and urban redevelopment permits me to eliminate from this discussion some types of public works that involve problems that are even more controversial in their philosophical and political background—such projects, for example, as the St. Lawrence Waterway and the Missouri River Basin Development program.

A point of considerable importance with respect to the construction of public works by state and local governments during a sharp depression concerns financing. Owen touches on this lightly. I should like to comment on the matter at a little greater length because the financing problem can make all the difference between getting a program started quickly—and thus allowing it to become useful for consideration as an antidepression project—and not getting it started at all, or doing it too slowly to be effective.

The long lapse of time since 1930–1933 and the high volume of economic activity in this country have obscured the facts with respect to the financial position of state and local governments during a sharp depression, particularly the fact that under adverse economic circumstances state and local governments are in no position to finance large-scale public works projects. Many of them, including some of the largest cities and states, were in default on their current obligations for the salaries of teachers, policemen, firemen, and other municipal employees. They were far behind in paying the bills of their trade suppliers. Some were postponing their liability on their short-term notes; others were defaulting on long-term bonds. A large proportion were running substantial deficits and were borrowing heavily in anticipation of the following year's taxes. As a result, the credit of many state and local government units was impaired and their ability to borrow for new programs of public works greatly curtailed.

This unfavorable financial position in the case of many cities and towns came about more as a result of delinquent tax collections than as a result of increased expenditures for relief. Cities and towns depended heavily then—as they do now—on the tax on real property for their current revenues. During the last depression—and the situation is not likely to change very much if there should be another—millions of property owners throughout the country failed to pay their real estate taxes on time. In many cases, collections of the real property tax at the end of the fiscal year amounted to only 50 or 60 per cent of the levy—as against a normal rate of 95 per cent. The tax sale laws in many states allow a relatively long waiting period before a city or town can offer for tax sale those properties on which taxes have not been paid. Accordingly, in the first or second year after tax default, cities and towns experiencing large delinquencies can do very little about collecting the amounts due from taxpayers.

To complicate the situation even further, the tax collection laws on the statute books are frequently relaxed in times of economic stress. The pressure comes from two sides: First, there are the small taxpayers in distress who are unemployed or only partly employed. They are politically powerful and are apt to put considerable pressure on the local administrations to prevent an aggressive tax collection policy. Second, there are the large taxpayers who own hotels, apartment houses, office buildings, etc., who frequently are the leading citizens of the state, are influential in policy determination, and account for a large part of the dollar volume of delinquent taxes outstanding. This was the case in Detroit in 1932 when I prepared a study of the subject for the Detroit Bureau of Governmental Research.[1] Forty or fifty leading taxpayers together were responsible for about 25 per cent of the aggregate tax delinquency because of the high assessed valuation, in proportion to the total, carried by the multi-story office buildings, the big hotels, and the large apartment developments, most of which were partly vacant and many of which were in receivership during this period.

In such a situation the existing units of state and local government are in no position to undertake large-scale public works. It is not a question of how desirable such works might be from an economic point of view, or how necessary to the well-being and economical future operation of the unit of government. It makes no difference either that construction costs would be relatively low. The existing units of state and local government just cannot, themselves, undertake the job financially, and their banking advisers are likely to suggest a delay in capital expenditures until the current stringency passes.

It is in such circumstances that new public bodies such as authorities which have no past history of financial difficulty and no

[1] *An Analysis of Tax Delinquency,* Detroit Bureau of Governmental Research, Report 128, June 30, 1932.

portfolio of defaulted real estate taxes can fit into the picture. They would make it possible to finance the type of public works that Owen has in mind. It would not have been enough for a city or county, for example, to plan to build a toll road in 1932, financed from revenues gained from users of that road. The city's or county's credit might well have been too badly impaired. A brand new road authority, however, having exclusive jurisdiction over the road and complete control of its revenues would have been in a somewhat better position to undertake the project.

This was the case in 1932 in New York. Robert Moses wanted to build a toll road to Jones Beach; the project would provide employment and would be self-liquidating. But he needed a device that would make it a certainty that the tolls would not be diverted to other purposes. To meet the situation his lawyers drafted legislation for the Jones Beach State Parkway Authority, and this became the first of what was to be a series of authorities for road construction throughout the country. The Parkway Authority was patterned after the Port of New York Authority, which had been in existence as an interstate operation for ten years. But the Parkway Authority was much more restricted in its powers.

The self-financing authorities that have been set up charge fees, rentals, service charges, etc., for the use of their facilities in order to provide funds sufficient to pay for the cost of acquiring and operating properties over a period of years without levying a general assessment on the taxpayers in the vicinity of the project. In the postwar period the operation and financing of self-liquidating projects on a pay-as-you-go basis by self-financing authorities outside of the regular state and local government budgets are becoming one of the new cornerstones of state and local finance.

Few people recognize the extent and scope of self-financing authorities at the present time and the flexibility of their use under a wide variety of circumstances. Their flexibility and adaptability is what makes them useful during a depression period. They can be tied in to the federal government through contracts and guarantees, as in the case of the local public housing authorities now operating under the jurisdiction of the Federal Public Housing Authority Act. They can construct office buildings and lease them to governmental units under a wide variety of circumstances; a recent case in Detroit involving the construction of a building for the use of the city and county jointly is a good illustration. They can be used to construct school buildings, as is being done extensively in Pennsylvania and Georgia at the present time. They can be used to construct office buildings, parking lots, airports, markets, sewer and water systems, and other public works under circumstances in which the governmental unit itself may be relatively impotent.

I bring these matters to your attention primarily because the mechanics of "how you go about doing it" in a depression are even more important than "being a goood idea." State and local public works can bog down indefinitely on the question of financing. The mechanics I have described could well be used to surmount what might otherwise become an impossible situation.

WESLEY LINDOW, Irving Trust Company

I would like to comment briefly on the problems of financing an expanded program of public works by state and local governments, particularly in view of the wide variation in the financial status of these governments. There are of course a large number of different units issuing securities, and the market ratings vary considerably. Some small issuers have trouble finding a market even though their basic financial position is satisfactory. It may be that an expanded volume of public works would require an improved method of approach to the marketing of these securities. Some pooling arrangement by which a number of small issues of a similar quality could be combined into one large offering to improve marketability might help considerably. It is hard to say exactly how this could be done but municipal bond men might be able to offer some suggestions. The pooling of local public housing issues recently into various grades may provide some ideas. Although these securities have a virtual guarantee by the federal government, the issues have been grouped into several classifications to improve marketability. It is obvious that the difficulties of pooling other types of issues would be great, but the problem of financing an expanded program of state and local public works may well be so serious that new marketing methods will be needed.

THE CONTRIBUTION OF
FARM PRICE SUPPORT PROGRAMS TO
GENERAL ECONOMIC STABILITY

KARL A. FOX, COUNCIL OF ECONOMIC ADVISERS

Ever since 1929, price support activities have been a central element in the farm program. From decade to decade, research, technology, and education may be more fundamental to the improvement of agriculture and rural life. But from year to year, price support has been the major, and at times the most controversial, expression of public policy in the field of agriculture.

In framing price support legislation, Congress probably has been most influenced by considerations of prospective benefits to farmers relative to prospective costs to the federal Treasury. The interests of processors, distributors, and consumers have, of course, been given some weight, as have problems of reconciling farm policy with policy in other fields such as labor, social security, and international trade. The central issues in legislative debate are the *level* of price support, the *commodities* for which price support is to be mandatory rather than permissive, and the *methods* by which the farm price level objectives are to be attained.

From a practical standpoint, then, price support programs are chosen largely on the basis of their effects on the level and stability of particular *farm prices*. Effects on *farm income* are less clearly recognized. However, as the domestic demand for most farm products is less than unit elastic, a program which increases farm prices will generally increase farm income during at least the first few years of its operation. The effects of farm price supports on *general economic stability* have not been spelled out clearly even in the technical literature, and considerations of these effects have not thus far entered in a major way into the selection of alternative farm programs.[1]

The views expressed in this paper are the author's. They are not official findings of the agency by which he is employed.

[1] It is probably true that many legislators have been influenced by an intuitive feeling that stabilizing prices of farm products must somehow contribute to stability in the economy as a whole. Allegations that depressions are farm-fed and farm-led, or that an increase of one dollar in farm income causes an increase of seven dollars in national income, are frequently made in connection with price

This paper attempts to analyze the effects of a farm price support program as one of a number of built-in safeguards against depression. The paper includes, first, a discussion of the place of agriculture in the general economy; second, a detailed examination of the workings of the existing price support program during a hypothetical recession; and third, a brief consideration of the behavior of alternative price support programs in a similar recession and the differences, if any, in their contributions to general economic stability.

1. The Place of Agriculture in the General Economy

The relative importance of agriculture in the general economy determines, of course, how far any farm price support program can affect economic stability. Agriculture is important not only for its sheer economic size but also for its dynamic interrelationships with other parts of the economy.

ECONOMIC SIZE

In 1952 the gross national product for the United States economy as a whole was estimated at $348 billion. A comparable measure for the farm economy itself—the so-called "gross farm product"— in the same year was $23.5 billion, or slightly less than 7 per cent of total GNP. In the same year, employment in agriculture averaged about 6.8 million workers, equivalent to 11 per cent of the employed labor force. However, average income per worker was lower in agriculture than in other sectors of the economy.

Several alternative measures of the economic size of agriculture could be used, but they would give results somewhere between the two just mentioned. Of these possible measures, the series on cash receipts from farm marketings will frequently be used in this paper as a convenient but rough measure of the size of agriculture. In 1952, cash receipts from farm marketings were $32.4 billion, equivalent to 9 per cent of GNP. This concept is, however, "grosser" than that of GNP.

CROSS-SECTION INTERRELATIONSHIPS

Major sources of cash farm income in the United States in 1947 are shown in Table 1. Each *source* of cash receipts is the *destination* of a flow of goods moving off the farm. Impacts resulting from changes in demand for farm products and their derivatives are

support arguments, but it is not clear that they carry much weight in the final legislative decisions.

transmitted to the farm economy in the form of changes in the volume of these money flows and the prices and volumes of sales associated with them. Because of the existence of some special data for the year 1947, a number of these interrelationships will be discussed in terms of that year.[2] The general picture would be much the same in 1952 and other recent years.

TABLE 1

Sources of Cash Farm Income, United States, 1947

	CASH FARM INCOME [a]	
	Amount	
	(billions of	*Percentage*
SOURCE	*dollars)*	*of Total*
Total cash receipts from farm marketings	$29.75	100.0%
Sales for food use by domestic civilians	18.23	61.3
Food use by armed forces	.50	1.7
Nonfood products and by-products for domestic use	5.22	17.6
Interfarm sales	2.66	8.9
Exports and shipments	2.87	9.6
Balancing item [b]	.27	.9

[a] Equivalent farm values of commodity flows.
[b] Includes changes in nonfarm stocks, statistical discrepancies, and rounding errors.

In 1947, nearly 10 per cent of total farm cash receipts represented commodities exported to foreign countries, plus a more limited movement to United States territories. Another sizable flow, nearly 9 per cent, was derived from sales to other farmers. Most of these sales were mediated by the marketing system. Available data report only such sales of *livestock* as moved across state lines. About half of the value of "interfarm sales" represents the receipts of original producers from *feed grains and hay* purchased, directly or ultimately, by other farmers. Much of this feed was processed by the mixed feed and milling industries, and the price paid for end products by purchasing farmers averaged roughly twice that received for the raw products by original producers.

Over 60 per cent of the cash receipts in 1947 were derived from sales for food use by the domestic civilian population. About 1.7

[2] The 1947 data cited were prepared in the former Bureau of Agricultural Economics in connection with the Interindustry Relations Study of the Bureau of Labor Statistics. In the following tables these data have been rearranged to conform with certain regularly published series of the Agricultural Marketing Service (see Karl A. Fox and Harry C. Norcross, "Some Relationships between Agriculture and the General Economy," *Agricultural Economics Research*, January 1952, pp. 13–21).

per cent represented food use by the armed forces. Another 17.6 per cent were derived from sales of nonfood products and by-products for domestic use, including cotton, tobacco, and portions of various other commodities.

Table 2 shows a breakdown of these major sources of cash farm income among nine major commodity groups. It will be noted that the great bulk of cash receipts from meat animals, dairy products, poultry and eggs, and fruits and vegetables is derived from sales for food use by the domestic population. Exports and shipments are small for these commodities. Interfarm sales of meat animals, primarily feeder and stocker cattle, are fairly large ($1.2 billion), but prices and values of feeder cattle move up and down with the demand for meat animals for food use. A sizable proportion of the cash income from food grains (mainly wheat), cotton, and tobacco comes from the export market. Hence, in the absence of price supports, prices of these products are subject to impacts from all parts of the world economy.

Farm price support programs contribute to economic stability mainly by offsetting or diverting the impacts upon farm income of changes in the demand for farm products. Table 3 reflects the fact that changes in domestic consumer demand for food products must be transmitted through the distributing, processing, and transportation industries before being translated into impacts upon farm income. In 1947, a year of extreme inflation, the farmer's share of the consumer's food dollar (valued at retail store prices) was at a near-record level of 53 per cent. Marketing charges, in the broadest sense, absorbed less than 40 per cent of the consumer's dollar spent for meat, poultry, and eggs, and about 45 per cent of the consumer's dollar spent for dairy products. The marketing system absorbed almost 60 per cent of the consumer expenditures for fruits and vegetables and more than two-thirds of the consumer expenditures for cereal and bakery products. The farm value of the *grain* used in bakery and cereal products was little more than 20 per cent as large as the amount spent for such products by consumers.

While similar breakdowns are not available for cotton, wool, and tobacco products, the farmer's share of the retail dollar spent for these items ranged from 12 to 17 per cent. The marketing margin concept is hardly appropriate for cotton used in industrial fabrics, such as tire cord, bagging, and conveyor belts.

Marketing margins are notoriously rigid. Freight rates are changed only at considerable intervals. Processing costs include many utilities and materials whose prices are quite rigid. More

TABLE 2

Sources of Cash Farm Income by Commodity Groups, United States, 1947 [a]

(billions of dollars)

	Meat Animals	Dairy Products	Poultry and Eggs	Fruits and Vegetables	Food Grains	Feed Grains and Hay	Cotton and Cotton- seed	Tobacco	Miscel- laneous	All Commodi- ties
Sales for food use by domestic civilians	7.18	3.80	2.64	2.56	1.00	.22	.19	—	.64	18.23
Plus:										
Food use by armed forces	.24	.06	.05	.11	.04	—	—	—	—	.50
Nonfood products and by- products for domestic use	.40	.01	.09	—	.39	.80	1.60	.68	1.27	5.22
Exports and shipments	.13	.18	.14	.23	1.07	.34	.43	.24	.11	2.87
Interfarm sales	1.20	—	—	—	.15	1.07	—	—	.24	2.66
Balancing item	.19	—	.01	-.10	.12	-.10	.02	.11	—	.27
Equals: Cash receipts from farm marketings	9.34	4.05	2.93	2.80	2.77	2.33	2.24	1.03	2.26	29.75

[a] Figures are equivalent farm values of the respective commodity flows.

TABLE 3

Retail Value, Marketing Charges, and Equivalent Farm Value of Food Products, by Commodity Groups, United States, 1947 [a]

(billions of dollars)

	Meat Animals	Dairy Products	Poultry and Eggs	Fruits and Vegetables	Food Grains	Feed Grains and Hay	Cotton and Cottonseed	Tobacco	Miscellaneous	Commodities
Retail value of farm food products	11.14	6.30	3.75	6.15	4.52 [b]				2.32 [c,d]	34.18 [a]
Less: Food marketing changes	4.02	2.59	1.19	3.63	3.04		Nonfoods: "Farmer's share" on retail cotton, wool, and tobacco products averaged 12 to 17 per cent. Margin concept inappropriate for industrial fabrics and feed crops.		1.46	15.93
Trade	2.28	1.73	.93	2.19	1.12				.59	8.84
Transportation (intercity)	.40	.10	.10	.90	.20				.13	1.83
Processing	1.34	.76	.16	.54	1.72				.74	5.26
Equals: Equivalent farm value	7.12	3.70	2.56	2.52	1.49				.84 [e]	18.23

[a] Figures in this table apply to products sold from United States farms and purchased for food use by United States consumers. The equivalent farm value of this commodity flow in 1947 accounted for 61.3 per cent of total cash receipts from farm marketings.

[b] Bakery and cereal products. Farm value includes value of other bakery-product ingredients as well as value of flour, corn meal, etc.

[c] Food only. Includes some cottonseed oil products and corn products (wet process) in addition to products classified as "miscellaneous" in Table 2.

[d] Includes $.02 billion of marketing taxes, mainly on oleomargarine and sugar.

than 50 per cent of the total food marketing bill is required to cover costs of labor directly involved in transportation, distribution, and processing activities. The wage rates of these workers are largely determined in a labor market which extends over the whole range of industrial and service occupations. Thus food marketing charges are only slightly affected by changes in either the retail or the farm price of food products. If prices and wage rates in other parts of the economy are rigid, any sudden drop in retail prices of food is transmitted (in the absence of price supports) almost dollar for dollar to the farm level.[3]

Farmers buy from as well as sell to the rest of the economy. Table 4 shows a breakdown of cash production expenditures, plus depreciation allowances, for the year 1947. Production expenditures in that year totaled $17.2 billion. Of this, $1.4 billion went for livestock moving across state lines and involving only transportation and related services in addition to the prices received by other farmers in the state of origin. Farmers spent $3.7 billion for feed, of which roughly $2.0 billion was reflected back to other farmers and $1.7 billion distributed among marketing agencies. Over $2.8 billion was spent on hired labor. Operation of motor vehicles cost $1.6 billion and miscellaneous goods and services used in farm production $2.5 billion. Taxes, interest, and net rent claimed another $2.6 billion, and the allowance for depreciation on farm buildings and equipment was also $2.6 billion. Actual cash outlays for building and equipment may, of course, differ substantially from the depreciation allowance in any one year.

As in the case of marketing margins, production expenditures are relatively inflexible. The *quantities* purchased of many of these items are dictated by technological requirements—so many units of gasoline or hours of machine use are necessary to handle an acre of a given crop, and the individual farmer has nothing to gain

---

[3] The moderate degree of correlation which exists between changes in retail food prices and in food marketing margins is due primarily to the common effect of general economic activity upon wage rates, upon costs and prices of manufactured items, and upon consumer demand for food as expressed in terms of retail prices and consumption. If consumer income and employment were held constant at a stable general price level, a decline in retail food prices, presumably caused by an increase in food supplies, would likely be transmitted almost dollar for dollar to the farm level. This implies percentage changes in farm prices from 1½ to 2 or more times as large as changes at retail, varying by commodity. If the quantity of a farm product available or its rate of production remains fixed, the net effect of a change in consumer demand is a change in its farm price with no immediate change in consumption. However, if the commodity is backed by an effective price support program, much of the impact of a decline in consumer demand is transmitted into stock accumulations by the price support agency.

TABLE 4

Gross and Net Farm Income and Production Expenditures, by Commodity Groups, United States, 1947

(billions of dollars)

	Meat Animals	Dairy Products	Poultry and Eggs	Fruits and Vegetables	Food Grains	Feed Grains and Hay	Cotton and Cottonseed	Tobacco	Miscellaneous	All Commodities
Cash receipts from farm marketings [a]	9.34	4.05	2.93	2.80	2.77	2.33	2.24	1.03	2.26	29.75
Plus:										
Farm-home consumption	.72	.79	.48	.85	.01	.03	—	—	.22	3.10
Rental value of farm dwellings	.20	.24	.09	.11	.11	.10	.17	.08	.08	1.18
Equals: Gross farm income [b]	10.26	5.08	3.50	3.76	2.89	2.46	2.41	1.11	2.56	34.03
Less: Production expenditures [c]	4.19	3.05	2.48	1.91	1.23	.81	1.09	.39	2.08	17.23
Purchased livestock	1.20	—	.22	—	—	—	—	—	—	1.42
Purchased feed	.92	1.00	1.47	—	—	—	—	—	.30	3.69
Hired labor	.40	.49	.08	.85	.13	.14	.37	.09	.30	2.85
Operation of motor vehicles	.28	.24	.11	.16	.23	.15	.11	.02	.27	1.57
Misc. goods and services	.29	.35	.18	.54	.19	.15	.21	.07	.53	2.51
Taxes, interest, net rent	.68	.40	.24	.16	.34	.20	.21	.07	.28	2.58
Depreciation	.42	.57	.18	.20	.34	.17	.19	.14	.40	2.61
Equals: Realized net income of farm operators [b, d]	6.07	2.03	1.02	1.85	1.66	1.63	1.32	.72	.48	16.80

[a] Same as bottom line of Table 2.
[b] Excluding government payments.
[c] Cash expenditures for current operations, plus allowance for depreciation.
[d] Calculated as gross farm income minus production expenditures. Implicitly, realized net income includes all returns for the labor of farm operators and unpaid family workers, as well as for management and investment.

by curtailing his total acreage. Quantities of fertilizer may be cut back, but this will jeopardize output. The individual's taxes, interest, and rental payments are beyond his control and are relatively rigid over a period of two or three years. Prices of petroleum products, steel-using items, and other industrial products used by farmers are determined in a nationwide market so far as demand factors are concerned, and the individual prices are often administered by manufacturers. Due to locational factors, wage rates of hired farm labor are sympathetic to changes in farm prices, but only partly so. In many areas, nonfarm work is readily available, and the farmer-employer must compete with industrial wage rates.

Over a period of years the index of prices paid by farmers (including interest, taxes, and farm wage rates) has fluctuated from year to year only half as much percentagewise as has the index of prices received for commodities sold by farmers. A significant fraction of the movement shown by the prices-paid index is due to variations in the prices of livestock and feed purchased by farmers.

Farmers also buy consumers' goods from other sectors of the economy. Data on expenditures for farm family living on a nationally representative basis are limited. However, in most essential respects farmers' demands for nonfarm consumers' goods are similar to those of other consumers. A notable exception is the smaller proportion of net farm income going for purchased food; another is the relatively low imputed rental value of farm dwellings (cash rents for the farm dwelling as such are rare). Incidentally, the evaluation of food produced for farm-home use and imputed rents of farm dwellings is a major area of controversy in comparing the real incomes of farm and nonfarm people, or defining "parity income." The official evaluations of these items for the year 1947 are given in Table 4.

Parenthetically, it should be noted that farm price supports operate at the cash receipts or gross income level. As net farm income averages less than half as large as gross, a 10 per cent drop in the price of a farm product may mean a 20 per cent drop in the *net* income received from a given volume of output. Net farm income, as defined in Table 4, includes all returns for the labor of farm operators and unpaid family workers as well as for the operator's investment and his management function. Hence, in terms of income available for family living, a 10 per cent change in farm prices may be as serious for many farm families as a 15 or 20 per cent change in wage rates would be for industrial workers.

Farm income and employment vary widely in the various regions

303

of the country. Table 5 shows that in 1952, in the New England and Middle East group of states, agricultural income payments accounted for less than 2 per cent of total income payments. The Southeast is a major farming region, but agriculture accounted for only 11.5 per cent of its total income payments. The percentage was almost the same in the Southwest, including the important agricultural states of Texas and Oklahoma.

TABLE 5

Agricultural and Total Income Payments, by Regions, United States, 1952

(*dollars in millions*)

	Total Income Payments	Agricultural Income Payments a	Agricultural Income Payments as Per Cent of Total
New England	$ 16,635	$ 266	1.6%
Middle East	68,873	1,033	1.5
Southeast	36,160	4,158	11.5
Southwest	17,049	1,944	11.4
Central	72,997	5,183	7.1
Northwest	12,873	2,613	20.3
Far West	30,780	1,970	6.4
United States	$255,367	$17,167	6.7%

a Computed from columns 1 and 3.
Source: Compiled from *Survey of Current Business*, Dept. of Commerce, August 1953, pp. 9 and 12.

The Central region, including most of the Corn Belt and the Lake States, is an important and relatively prosperous farming area. However, in view of the great manufacturing and trading centers in the region, agriculture accounted for only 7.1 per cent of its total income payments. The Northwest region, including the Northern Great Plains and some of the Mountain States, shows the highest proportion of agricultural to total income payments among the regions listed—20.3 per cent. This region contains only a few large cities and industrial centers. The Far West shows about the same relation between agricultural and total income payments (6.4 per cent in 1952) as does the nation as a whole (6.7 per cent in 1952).

Except for the Northwest region, these figures suggest that the immediate impact of changes in farm income upon other sectors of the economy would be rather small. However, there are individual states for which the farm income percentages run much higher: Arkansas 22, Mississippi 24, Arizona 18, Iowa 28, Idaho and Kansas each 22, Montana 21, Nebraska 27, North Dakota 26, South Dakota 31. The last six states mentioned are all in the Northwest region. Table 6 compares farm and nonfarm labor forces for the year 1950 by major regions. Because per worker incomes are lower in agriculture than for the average of nonfarm occupations, the percentage of the total labor force engaged in agriculture is higher in each region than the corresponding percentage of income payments going to agriculture. The greatest disparity is in the South,

TABLE 6

Experienced Civilian Labor Force, Total and Agricultural, by Regions, United States, 1950

	Experienced Civilian Labor Force	Farmers and Farm Workers	Farm Labor Force as Per Cent of Total
Northeast	15,446,331	481,467	3%
North Central	17,220,229	2,330,518	14
South	16,494,500	3,184,278	19
West	17,064,280	709,784	10
United States	56,225,330	6,706,047	11%

Source: Compiled from *Census of Population, 1950*, Bureau of the Census.

which in 1950 included nearly 50 per cent of the farm labor force of the nation but received about 40 per cent of the nation's agricultural income payments.

A drop in farm income in an area directly affects the townspeople in that area who sell goods and services to farm people. The impact of reduced purchasing power in the area is then diffused among the larger distributing and manufacturing centers from which the various goods used in the area are supplied. The effects of a highly localized drought or flood upon farm incomes might cause scarcely a ripple in the big wholesaling and manufacturing centers. A substantial drop in the price of wheat, on the other hand, could reduce the incomes of farmers in a few neighboring states by $200 or 300 million. Such a drop would cause an appreciable reduction (as much as 5 per cent) in *total* income payments in a several-state area. While additional income effects would radiate into other regions, their percentage impacts would be small.

DYNAMIC INTERRELATIONSHIPS

In the preceding section we have described some major cross-section relations between agriculture and the rest of the economy.

305

CHART 1

Basic Economic Relationships Affecting Agriculture
(billions of dollars)

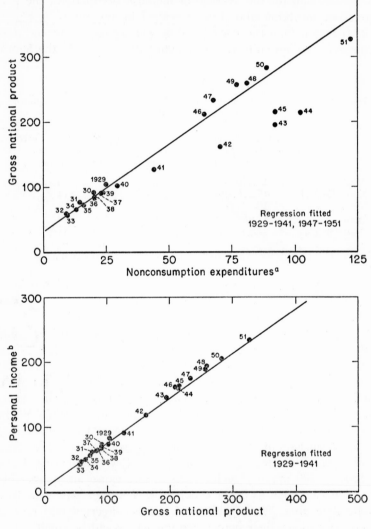

a Nonconsumption expenditures equals gross national product less personal consumption expenditures.

b Personal income adjusted equals personal income less government and business transfer payments and government interest payments.

CHART 1, continued
(billions of dollars)

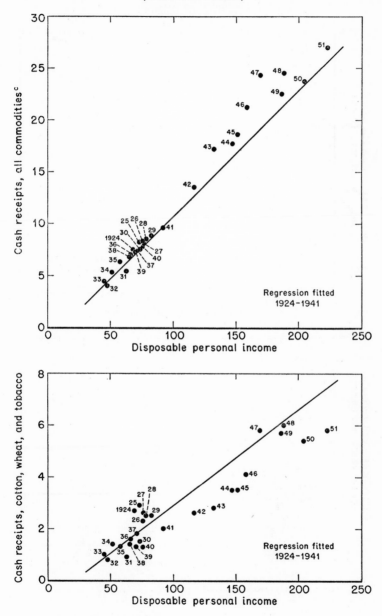

c Excluding cotton, wheat, and tobacco.
Source: U. S. Department of Agriculture.

307

CHART 2

Farm Receipts in Relation to Selected Variables
(billions of dollars)

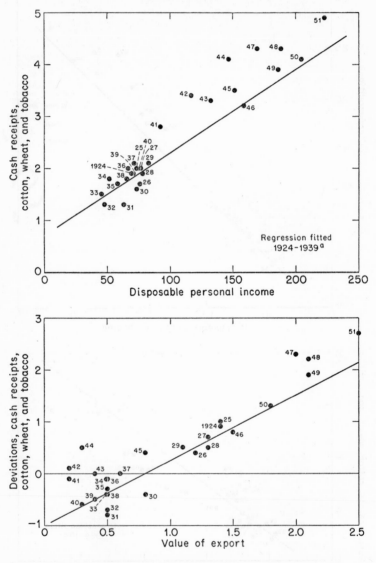

a Net regression of cash receipts on disposable income.

CHART 2, continued
(billions of dollars)

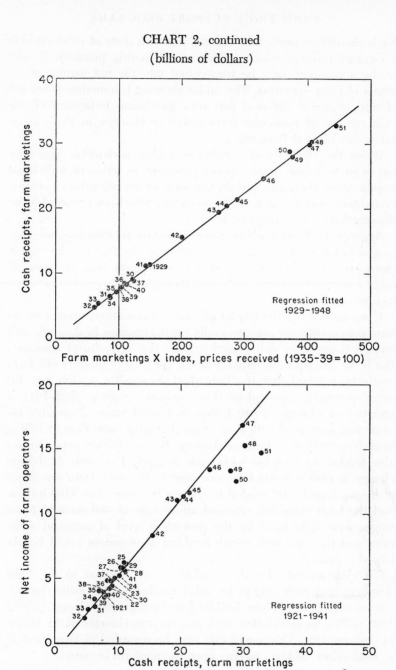

Source: U. S. Department of Agriculture.

Each element of marketing charges and cash costs of production is a channel through which influences originating primarily in the nonfarm economy may be transmitted into the net income statements of farm operators. The tables showing commodity flows out of agriculture to different end uses give some indication of the vulnerability of particular farm prices to changes in the various categories of final demand.

While the diversity of conditions within agriculture generally forces us to frame price support programs in terms of individual commodities, there are certain dynamic interrelationships between agriculture and the rest of the economy which can profitably be discussed on an aggregative level.

Aggregative Relationships. Some important relationships are suggested in Charts 1 and 2.[4] If we disregard the three major export crops—cotton, wheat, and tobacco—cash farm income from all other commodities bears a close relationship to disposable personal income.

If we are tracing the impact of changed conditions upon a single farm commodity, we may generally regard changes in domestic and foreign demand as determined outside the agricultural economy. But if we add up such impacts for all (or a large number of) farm products, we find that the individual commodity models are, for some purposes, incomplete. For example, during 1922–1941 a year-to-year change of $10 billion in United States disposable income was associated with an average change of more than $1 billion in cash receipts from farm marketings. But production expenditures also tended to increase with cash receipts. For each $1 billion change in cash receipts from one year to the next, farm purchases of livestock and feed tended to change by more than $100 million and the farm wage bill changed an average of $80 million. Farm wages were influenced by the prevailing level of nonfarm wage rates and the ease with which nonfarm employment could be obtained.

To some extent, the above relations are internal to the farm economy. But cash outlays for other production requisites, including net investment in farm buildings and equipment, changed about $300 million in association with year-to-year changes of $1 billion in cash receipts. This association may be regarded in large part as a "back effect" of farm income upon the nonfarm economy.

[4] These charts are reproduced from James P. Cavin, "Forecasting the Demand for Agricultural Products," *Agricultural Economics Research*, July 1952, pp. 65–76.

As an average during 1922–1941, the realized net income of farm operators rose nearly $700 million in response to a year-to-year increase of $1 billion in cash receipts from marketings.[5] Of this, over $100 million represented net new investment in farm buildings and equipment, an item mentioned in the preceding paragraph. The remainder also had a back effect on the nonfarm economy through increased expenditures on goods and services for family living.

Hence if we try to trace the ultimate effects of an initial decrease in consumer income, we are led through a series of approximations. The "first round" decrease in farm cash receipts leads to a secondary decrease in nonfarm income (perhaps no more than 10 per cent of the initial one). This leads to a secondary decrease in farm income, which produces a third-order effect on nonfarm income (perhaps no more than 1 per cent of the initial decrease).

But we must also consider another stream of influences. The bulk of the initial contraction in consumer income means reduced outlays for nonfarm goods and services. This curtailment leads to a decrease in nonfarm employment and income, which reinforces the original one and leads to a further (but smaller) contraction in expenditures. If, for example, a cut in defense spending and private investment reduced the rate of income payments *directly* by $10 billion, the final decrease in the level of consumer income might be around $20 billion.[6] If so, farm cash receipts would tend to decrease by twice the amount suggested by the initial impact, rather than by 1.11 times that amount as suggested by considering back effects through farm income only.

If the "multiplier" at a given time were about 2, one might expect that the effect of a price support program in maintaining total national income would be about twice as large as the government outlay for price support. Of the total income-supporting effect, a little more than half would accrue to farmers (at the cash receipts level) and a little less than half would accrue to nonfarmers. If

[5] The sum of net income and production expenditures (including depreciation allowances) is equal to gross farm income. Gross income is larger than cash receipts by the imputed rental value of farm dwellings and the value of home-grown products consumed by the farm family. The latter value changes directly with cash receipts, because the price components of the two series are quite similar. As a result, gross farm income during 1922–1941 changed about $1.1 billion per $1 billion change in cash receipts. Production expenditures (including depreciation allowances) accounted for a little more than $400 million and net income for a little less than $700 million of the change in gross farm income.

[6] Magnitude based on Arthur Smithies, "The Multiplier," *American Economic Review*, May 1948, pp. 299–305.

the multiplier were 2.5, the total effect would be 2.5 times the price support outlay, divided about equally between farm and non-farm people.

Demand and Supply Relationships for Individual Commodities. An aggregative relationship which has been useful in the outlook work of the Department of Agriculture is as follows:

log (prices received by farmers) = 2.812

    −1.658 log (physical volume of farm marketings)
    (.273)

    +1.241 log (disposable income)
    (.102)

    +.142 log (value of agricultural exports).
    (.035)

The figures in parentheses are standard errors. During the period 1924–1947, 97 per cent of the variation in the index of prices received by farmers was associated with the three explanatory variables shown. The relevance of this relationship to a discussion of farm price supports may be suggested as follows:

1. A 10 per cent drop in disposable income leads to a 12.4 per cent drop in farm prices, other factors remaining constant.

This price drop could be offset by a reduction of 7.5 per cent (equal to 12.4/1.66) in the volume of farm marketings. Or, if all prices were rigidly supported at their initial levels, the price support agency would acquire 7.5 per cent of the total quantity of farm products marketed.

2. An increase of 10 per cent in the physical volume of farm marketings would tend to reduce farm prices about 16.6 per cent. Or, if prices were rigidly maintained, the entire increase in farm marketings would be acquired by the price support agency.

3. A decline of 10 per cent in the value of agricultural exports would tend to reduce the average level of farm prices by 1.4 per cent. Or, if prices were rigidly maintained, about .9 per cent (1.4/1.66) of total farm marketings would be acquired by the price support agency.

Relationships of this sort also figure prominently in the analysis of price support programs for individual commodities. Chart 3 shows a simple demand and supply structure roughly applicable to certain crops, including potatoes. In this structure, it is assumed that the crop has already been planted and production is either fully determined and ready for market or is subject to further influence only by noneconomic factors such as weather. With minor qualifications, the entire production of the crop is moved through the marketing system to the retail store (and restaurant) level. The main determinants of retail price for such a commodity, based on statistical and economic evidence, are the supply available for consumption and the disposable income of consumers. Marketing mar-

CHART 3

Demand and Supply Structure for Perishable Crops
(supply predetermined; single market)

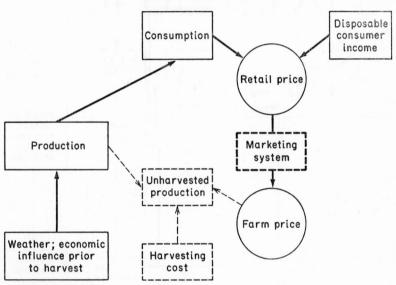

Arrows show direction of influence. Heavy arrows indicate major paths of influence which account for the bulk of the variation in current prices. Light dashed arrows indicate paths of negligible, doubtful, or occasional importance.

Source: U. S. Department of Agriculture.

gins are assumed to be established by competition between marketing agencies, and the farm price is equal to the retail price minus marketing charges. The impact of changes in other parts of the economy would come primarily through the disposable consumer income variable, and to a lesser extent through such changes in wage rates and material costs as might occur within the marketing system. The acreage planted to the crop in the subsequent year would be influenced somewhat by the price received by farmers for the current crop; variations in weather would have an important bearing upon the actual production in the next year.

Chart 4 shows a simplified demand and supply structure for export crops such as wheat, cotton, and tobacco. If we consider a point in time at which the current production of cotton in the United States and in foreign countries has been determined, the farm

CHART 4

Demand and Supply Structure for Export Crops

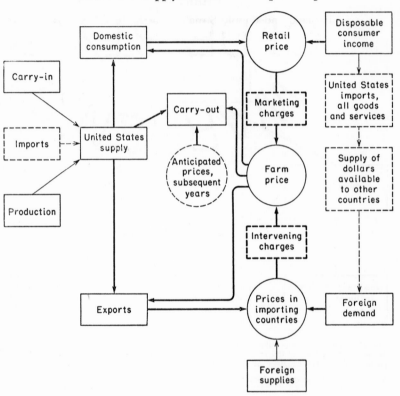

Arrows show direction of influence. Heavy arrows indicate major paths of influence which account for the bulk of the variation in current prices. Light solid arrows indicate definite but less important paths; dashed arrows indicate paths involving more remote variables.

Source: U. S. Department of Agriculture.

price of United States cotton (in the absence of price supports) will be determined by the level of demand in the United States and also in other countries. As indicated by the column of boxes on the right-hand side of this chart, foreign demand for United States cotton is not entirely independent of the major domestic demand factors. There are, of course, other factors affecting foreign demand which are wholly independent of income changes in the United States.

While the demand and supply structures for export crops would be complicated enough under a system of international free trade, for many years export demand has also been subject to disturbances

CHART 5

Demand and Supply Structure for Feed Grains

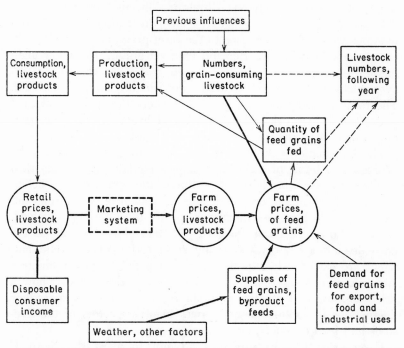

Arrows show direction of influence. Heavy arrows indicate major paths of influence which account for the bulk of the variation in current prices. Light solid arrows indicate definite but less important paths; dashed arrows indicate paths of negligible importance in the determination of current price.

Source: U. S. Department of Agriculture.

because of government actions. It is worth noting that producers of the major United States export crops—cotton, wheat, and tobacco—have been among the strongest advocates of government price support programs. The combination of major uncertainties and arbitrary elements in export demand, coupled with highly inelastic demands for domestic consumption, made prices of these commodities inherently less stable and predictable than those of many other farm products after 1933.

Chart 5 shows a simplified demand and supply structure for another commodity group which has figured prominently in our price support program—corn and other feed grains. Normally only 3 or 4 per cent of our feed grains is exported, and more than 90 per cent of our production is consumed by domestic livestock. In turn, our livestock products are almost wholly consumed in this country, neither exports nor imports being of great quantitative importance.

The impacts of changes in economic activity are transmitted into the feed grain economy via disposable income, retail prices of livestock products, and changes (if any) in marketing charges on livestock products, and thence to the farm prices of livestock products, which influence the demand for feed grains. The other main factors influencing farm prices of feed grains are weather, carry-over stocks, and the numbers of grain-consuming livestock on hand. The resulting price of feed grains influences the quantity of feed grains fed to livestock and the number of livestock which are produced or carried over into the following season.

The information contained in the above diagram could also be expressed in terms of a set of structural equations.[7] For practical applications, we would have to estimate the numerical coefficient related to each of the arrows or lines of influence; where relevant, we would also have to estimate or specify the time lags involved. Chart 6 shows a diagram for corn with the relevant numerical coefficients added, but without any specification of the time lags which are particularly important in the area of livestock production and prices. The right-hand side of this chart also suggests how a price support and storage program for corn operates to reduce fluctuations in production and prices in other sectors of the livestock and feed economy.

Farm price support programs attempt to avert the "normal" consequences of free market demand and supply structures such as those illustrated above. They act to maintain farm prices and cash farm income in the face of adverse changes in either supply or demand conditions. How they affect the nonfarm economy through the maintenance of farm income has been discussed earlier. Other effects, and perhaps important ones, radiate from the stabilization of farm prices themselves, which creates some pressure to maintain retail food prices and wage rates. Analysis of these effects would require a model of the economy more complex that any I have had

[7] Such a set is given in Richard J. Foote, "A Four-Equation Model of the Livestock-Feed Economy and Its Endogenous Mechanism," *Journal of Farm Economics*, February 1953, pp. 44–61.

an opportunity to work with. Some first steps toward such a model are presented later in this paper.

CHART 6

Demand and Supply Structure for Corn

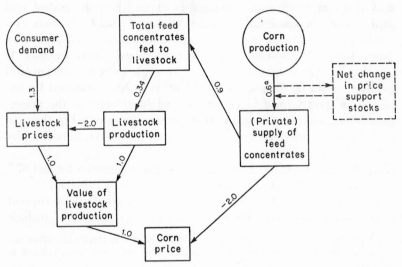

a In absence of price support. May be reduced considerably by price support and storage.

Arrows show direction of influence. Figures represent percent change in the "influenced" variable typically associated with 1 percent change in the "influencing" variable.

Source: U. S. Department of Agriculture.

2. Farm Price and Income Supports as Defenses against Depression

In the preceding section we have described the relative economic size of agriculture and some of its major interrelationships with the rest of the economy. The farm price support program in 1953 directly involved commodities accounting for less than half of total cash receipts from farm marketings.

DIRECT PRICE SUPPORTS

The price support program now in effect [8] and applicable to crops produced in 1954 may be summarized as follows: The six so-called basic commodities—cotton, wheat, corn, tobacco, rice, and peanuts— are required to be supported by means of nonrecourse loans at 90 per cent of parity through the 1954 crop year. Parity prices for wheat, corn, cotton, and peanuts are equal to their average prices during

[8] As of May 1954.

317

1909–1914 multiplied by the current level of an index of prices paid by farmers (including interest and taxes) on a 1910–1914 base. For rice and tobacco and for nearly all "nonbasic" commodities, the parity price is calculated by dividing the most recent ten-year-average price of the commodity by the index of prices received by farmers for all commodities during the same period, and multiplying the result by the index of prices paid by farmers (including interest, taxes, and farm wage rates), again on a 1910–1914 base. This is the so-called new or modernized parity formula. If applied to every commodity, the average level of modernized parities would be identical with the average level obtained by use of the old parity formula (except for slight changes in the prices-paid index, such as the inclusion of farm wage rates); but the new and old parity prices for individual commodities differ, sometimes by substantial percentages.[9]

In 1953, cash receipts from the six basic commodities totaled $7.7 billion, or 25 per cent of total farm cash receipts (Table 7).

There is a second group of commodities for which price support is also mandatory. The "designated nonbasic commodities" include

[9] A specimen calculation for wheat as of April 1954 may clarify the difference between "old" and modernized parity prices. The *old* parity is calculated as follows:

Item	Unit	Amount
1. Average price of wheat, August 1909–July 1914	Dol. per bu.	.884
2. Prices paid, interest, and taxes, April 1954	1910–1914 = 100	283
3. Old parity (equals item 1 times item 2)	Dol. per bu.	2.50

In contrast, *modernized* parity is calculated as follows:

Item	Unit	Amount
1. Average price of wheat, 1944–1953	Dol. per bu.	1.93
2. Prices received by farmers, all commodities, 1944–1953	1910–1914 = 100	256
3. Adjusted base price (equals item 1 divided by item 2)	Dol. per bu.	.754
4. Prices paid, interest, taxes, and farm wage rates, April 1954	1910–1914 = 100	283
5. Modernized parity (equals item 3 times item 4)	Dol. per bu.	2.13

As the index of prices received is essentially a weighted average of price relatives (1944–1953 as a per cent of 1910–1914) for individual commodities, an appropriately weighted average of all the "adjusted base prices" should be precisely 1/2.56 of the 1944–1953 prices-received index. But this is identical with the index number base, formed of actual 1910–1914 prices.

Hence the average level of modernized parities differs from the average level of old parities only when, and to the extent that, the inclusion of farm wage rates changes the parity index used. As of April 1954 the two parity indexes happened to be identical at 283. In July 1954 the parity index including wage rates was again at 283, but the index excluding wage rates had declined to 280.

TABLE 7

Commodities for Which Direct Price Support Programs Were
in Effect in 1953, and Their Relative Importance in Terms of
Cash Receipts from Farm Marketings

| | CASH RECEIPTS, 1953 | |
| | Millions | Per Cent |
COMMODITY	of Dollars	of Total
Basic commodities	$ 7,714	24.9%
Cotton lint	2,766	8.9
Wheat	2,156	7.0
Corn	1,283	4.2
Tobacco	1,094	3.5
Rice	253	.8
Peanuts	162	.5
Designated nonbasic commodities	4,419	14.3
Dairy products [a]	4,269	13.8
Wool	129	.4
Mohair	11	b
Tung nuts	10	b
Honey	c	c
Other nonbasic commodities	1,804	5.8
Soybeans	672	2.2
Cottonseed	308	1.0
Oats	216	.7
Barley	172	.5
Dry edible beans	156	.5
Flaxseed	143	.5
Sorghum grain	103	.3
Rye	21	.1
Hairy vetch seed	4	b
Common rye grass seed	5	b
Crimson clover seed	3	b
Wild winter peas	1	b
Naval stores	c	c
Total price-supported commodities	$13,937	45.0%
Cash receipts from all farm marketings	$30,975	100.0%

[a] Support extended directly to milk for manufacturing only.
[b] Less than .5 per cent.
[c] While the price of this commodity is supported, no data are available on cash receipts.

dairy products, wool, mohair, tung nuts, and honey. Dairy products are required to be supported at such levels between 75 and 90 per cent of parity as will insure an adequate supply. Wool is to be supported at 90 per cent of parity until United States production of shorn wool reaches a level of 360 million pounds. It seems unlikely that this level will be reached for many years. The other three commodities are minor in terms of the cash farm income involved. In 1953, cash receipts for this group of commodities amounted to $4.4 billion, or about 14 per cent of total farm cash receipts. Dairy products alone accounted for almost $4.3 billion of the total for this group.

During 1953 a number of other nonbasic commodities were accorded price support. Under the law the Secretary of Agriculture may elect to support these and other nondesignated nonbasic commodities at any level from 0 to 90 per cent of parity. The most important price-supported commodities in this category during 1953 were the oilseeds (soybeans, cottonseed, and flaxseed) and the minor feed grains (oats, barley, and sorghum grains). In 1953, cash receipts from the three oilseeds totaled $1.1 billion; cash receipts from the three minor feed grains totaled $.5 billion. Rye, dry edible beans, naval stores, and a number of grass and cover crop seeds also received price support in 1953. The nonbasic commodities (other than "designated") which were supported in 1953 accounted for $1.8 billion, or 6 per cent of total cash farm income.

Altogether, commodities which received direct price support in 1953 accounted for $13.9 billion, or 45 per cent of total cash receipts from farm marketings. The remaining commodities, accounting for 55 per cent of cash receipts ($17 billion), were not directly supported. It could be argued that fluid milk should be added to the list of commodities not directly supported, as dairy price support operations were confined to manufactured products.

EXTENT AND EFFECTS OF OTHER FARM PROGRAMS

Marketing Agreements and Orders. During 1953 some twenty-four federal marketing agreements and orders were in effect for commodities other than fluid milk. Federal marketing orders were applied to a number of tree fruits and nuts grown in the Pacific Coast states and to a few other commodities produced in small geographical areas. In general, such orders provide for regulation of the grades or qualities of the products which can be sold in primary commercial channels. Remaining portions of the crops are directed into processing outlets or surplus pools which typically yield lower returns than do the primary markets. No comprehensive study of the effects of these programs on farm income is available. However, commodities other than fluid milk subject to marketing orders in 1953 accounted for approximately $.8 billion of (1952) cash receipts from farm marketings.

In addition, some forty-nine federal milk marketing orders were in effect during 1953. The volume of milk subject to these orders amounted to 25.9 billion pounds in 1953 and returned milk producers a cash income of approximately $1.2 billion. The fluid milk prices maintained under federal orders are frequently linked to prices of manufactured dairy products; in some markets various other supply, cost, and demand factors are also considered. In addition to the federal marketing orders, some states have milk control laws of their own. The bargaining strength of milk producers' associations also influences local prices of fluid milk. No estimates of the income effects of federal milk marketing orders are available.

Section 32 Activities. During 1952 the Department of Agriculture spent $74.7 million to purchase surplus commodities for use in school lunch and other domestic programs or to cover export payments (subsidies) and other incentives to divert products from normal domestic markets. These so-called Section 32 (of the Agriculture Adjustment Act of 1938) activities are financed each year out of 30 per cent of the general tariff revenues of the United States. During the past five years new funds accruing under Section 32 have averaged $150 million a year. An average of $95.8 million a year has been actually used and about $300 million remained in a special carry-over fund as of July 1, 1953.

Agricultural Conservation Program Payments. For several years these payments, ranging roughly from $200 to 300 million annually, have been used for soil building and soil conservation in a fairly strict sense. However, there has been some discussion of using these payments to secure more effective control of production under price support programs. In this connection the ACP payments would serve in part as compensation for income which is forgone by withdrawing certain acreages from currently productive use.

During 1938–1941 an average of $319 million a year was paid to producers of wheat, cotton, corn, rice, peanuts, tobacco, potatoes, and a few other commodities, equivalent to some fraction of the gap between the parity price value of those commodities and the market price value actually received by farmers. The ACP payments began as rewards for keeping land out of production, but as economic pressures eased they were gradually focused upon, and largely confined to, rewards for soil conservation and soil building. There is always the possibility, however, that the amount of such payments will again be increased as an aid to production control in case of large supplies or a recession in demand.

Sugar Act. Growers of sugar beets and sugar cane, products accounting for $139 and 53 million of cash farm income respectively in

1953, benefit from a special program operated under the Sugar Act of 1948. The price objective under the Sugar Act is not related to parity. In the event of a recession it seems likely that the Sugar Act would continue to operate to restrict imports and maintain prices to domestic growers at a higher level than would otherwise be the case.

RELATED FACTS

The preceding paragraphs give only a broad outline of the price support and related programs. There are a number of real or potential qualifications and hazards which are a part of the over-all price support picture. Among them are those described below.

Limitations on the Borrowing Authority of the Commodity Credit Corporation. From 1945 through 1949 the CCC was authorized to own, or extend credit on, a maximum of $4,750 million worth of commodities at any given time. Any *losses realized* in one year, however, were supposed to be made up by appropriation from the Treasury during the following year.

In June 1950 the CCC's borrowing authority was raised to $6,750 million. Actual commitments of the CCC totaled $4.3 billion in February 1950, and there appeared to be a distinct hazard that favorable yields on the 1950 crops would force the CCC either to exceed its mandatory borrowing authority or to default on its mandatory price support program. This same problem arose again in January 1954, and the President was obliged to request an increase in the CCC's borrowing authority to $8.5 billion.[10]

[10] This increase was approved on March 20, 1954. On August 18, Congress authorized a further increase, to $10 billion. CCC borrowing authority has been raised several times since 1938, as follows:

Date of Change	CCC Borrowing Authority (millions of dollars)
March 8, 1938	$ 500
March 4, 1939	900
August 9, 1940	1,400
July 1, 1941	2,650
July 16, 1943	3,000
April 12, 1945	4,750
June 28, 1950	6,750
March 20, 1954	8,500
August 18, 1954	10,000

Factors necessitating these increases have included (1) increases in the parity index (of prices paid by farmers), (2) increases in the percentage of parity at which loans were required to be set, and (3) expansions in the number of commodities supported. The physical volume of the CCC's price support investment in March 1954 was only moderately higher than in (say) 1941–1942, but the dollar-and-cents loan rates at which current stocks were acquired were two to three times as high as those prevailing during the 1939–1942 stock build-up.

322

So far Congress has raised the CCC's borrowing authority whenever price support commitments threatened to exceed it. But there is always a chance that the request for an increase, by dramatizing the size of commodity investments and potential losses, may lead to retrenchment in price support and marketing quota levels in subsequent years.

Storage Charges Borne by Growers. Market prices of grains and some other storable commodities often fall considerably below the announced loan rate early in the marketing year. This reflects the fact that growers receive the full loan rate only if they turn their crops over to the CCC at a specified time late in the marketing year. Growers must bear the cost of storing and handling their grain up to this point. On this count alone, growers would be just as well off selling their wheat or corn 10 cents below the loan rate at harvest time rather than holding it for the full loan rate several months later. Certain other cost and convenience factors may lead grain producers to accept still further discounts below the loan rate during the height of the harvest season.

Price Limitations on Release of CCC Stocks. However, in some years or parts of years, the effect of the price support program is to raise market prices several per cent above the announced loan rates. This is because the CCC is prohibited from releasing its inventories in normal commercial channels at a price less than 5 per cent above the current loan rate plus reasonable carrying charges. When demand exceeds commercial supplies (and grower-owned supplies under loan), this provision means that purchasers must pay prices 5 to 10 per cent above the loan rate to acquire these commodities from the CCC. (Commodities under *loan* may be redeemed by the grower at any time. Ordinarily this will be advantageous whenever the market price rises even slightly above the loan rate. The more stringent price provision mentioned above applies to commodities which are *owned* by the CCC, having been turned over to the Corporation by growers in satisfaction of their nonrecourse loans.)

Special Hazards. Grain producers must place their commodities in approved types of storage facilities before they are eligible for CCC loans. During the summer of 1953 many growers were unable to find approved storage for their wheat at harvest time and took discounts of as much as 50 cents a bushel below the loan rate.

Another hazard applicable to storable crops is the possibility that growers will refuse to vote marketing quotas into effect on the subsequent crop. If this occurs, the mandatory price support level is dropped to 50 per cent of parity, which for most growers of most basic crops would be a punitive level. If this possibility is taken seriously, many growers, dealers, and storage operators will be reluctant to own and hold the commodity. The resulting pressure to sell results not only in larger quantities going under loan but also in more sales at substantial discounts below the loan rate.

Highlights on Acreage Allotments and Marketing Quotas. Acreage allotments and marketing quotas are an essential part of the price support program for basic crops. The Secretary of Agriculture is required to announce acreage allotments for most of these crops every year except under emergency conditions. The level at which acreage allotments are set depends upon the relationship of supply to expected demand for the commodity in question. When acreage allotments are in effect, the individual grower must comply with them in order to be eligible for price support. Many producers elect not to comply with acreage allotments, relying on the "umbrella effect" provided by those who do. When the market price begins to sag, eligible producers put sufficient quantities under loan to keep the market price from falling very far below the loan level. The producer who is ineligible for direct price support is enabled to sell his commodity for a few cents less than the loan rate and, at the same time, to avoid production restrictions.

When supplies of basic crops exceed certain levels, marketing quotas are invoked in addition to acreage allotments. Marketing quota legislation provides severe economic penalties for noncompliance. Thus marketing quotas are quite effective in limiting total plantings of a commodity to the desired area. They may be evaded somewhat *in spirit* by producers selecting their best land and using heavier fertilizer applications and other practices calculated to raise yields above the previous norm. But these efforts seldom offset more than a fraction of the effects of acreage reduction during the first year or two of a marketing quota program.

PROBABLE OPERATION OF PRESENT PRICE SUPPORT PROGRAM
DURING A SEVERE RECESSION [11]

It will be noted from the preceding section that a large part of the total price support activity under the present program is directed toward storable crops, particularly wheat, cotton, and feed grains. Once a fixed dollar-and-cents price support has been announced, the volume of price support activity on the forthcoming crop will depend upon variations in yield, variations in the foreign supply and demand situation, variations in domestic demand, and minor disturbing factors which are not separately measurable.

[11] The recession model described in the following pages *is not a forecast*. It is *assumed*, for illustrative purposes only.

Year-to-year fluctuations in crop yields, due mainly to weather, often overshadow the effects of year-to-year changes in consumer demand. Chart 7 summarizes variations in yields of wheat, corn, and cotton during 1901–1950. As of 1950 the zero or trend line in these

CHART 7

Variations in Adjusted Crop Yields

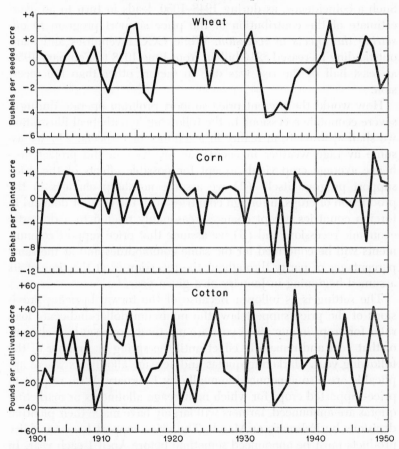

Yields adjusted roughly to 1952 conditions by averaging: (1) actual deviations from 9-year moving averages, centered and (2) percentage deviations applied to 1952 goal yields.
Source: U. S. Department of Agriculture.

charts would represent per acre yields of 14 to 15 bushels of wheat, 38 bushels of corn, and 280 pounds of cotton. The larger yield deviations for these crops exceed 10 per cent, and in a few cases 20 per cent, of the trend yield. A large part of the CCC stock build-up from June 1948 to February 1950 was due to record yields of corn and cotton in 1948, and above-average yields also in 1949. High yields have also contributed to the stock build-up currently taking place.

Sudden changes in export demand also contributed substantially to the current stock build-up and to that of 1939–1942. If such changes, or high crop yields, happen to coincide with an economic recession, there is a tendency to exaggerate the importance of the recession itself as a factor in the accumulation of price support stocks. Such a coincidence, as during 1948–1950, leads in turn to an overestimate of the contribution of the price support program *to offsetting the effects of recession.* While CCC inventories and loans outstanding increased $2½ billion from June 1948 to February 1950, at least half of the rise was due to factors other than the recession.

How would the present price support program operate during a severe economic recession? In the following hypothetical illustration we shall abstract from reality in a number of respects: (1) we assume average weather in each year involved in the projection— hence average crop yields except for possible effects of the price support program itself; (2) we assume no sharp changes in the production of crops in foreign countries or in the level of demand in foreign countries except changes reasonably related to a domestic economic recession; and (3) we assume that price support commitments will be continued for the same commodities and at the same percentages of parity throughout the recession as at the time of its assumed beginning in January of a given year.[12]

The setting is as follows: Because of the forward-pricing provisions of the price support law, the minimum dollar-and-cents loan rates for crops in any given year are mostly announced by February of that year and remain in effect until the spring or summer of the following year. Marketing quotas and acreage allotments where applicable are also announced annually by February. With respect to price-supported crops for which no acreage allotments or marketing quotas are announced, farmers will largely have made their planting decisions by February or March. The price support level for dairy products must be announced sometime before April 1 each year. In the current projection we make an assumption which is not true to fact—we assume that dairy price supports are extended at 90 per

[12] The following analysis was prepared early in 1954 and was intended to throw light on the issues confronting economists and legislators at that time. Some of the issues were at least temporarily resolved by passage of the Agricultural Act of 1954 in August of that year. However, the main features of the analysis would be unchanged if the hypothetical recession were assumed to begin in 1956 or any other year subsequent to 1954.

cent of parity, the level which applied as of January in the first recession year.[13]

Thus as of January or February, when the recession is assumed to begin, price support commitments are laid out rigidly for a period extending twelve to eighteen months into the future. Now let us consider the recession's impact on this program. The economic framework for this hypothetical recession is shown in Table 8. It is about

TABLE 8

Projections of Employment, Income, and Prices during a Hypothetical Severe Recession [a]

| | | FIRST YEAR OF RECESSION | | SECOND YEAR OF RECESSION | | THIRD YEAR OF RECESSION |
ITEM	UNIT OR BASE	January	July	January	July	January
oss national product	Bil. dol.	350	328	302	282	275
Disposable personal income	Bil. dol.	240	229	217	207	204
Disposable income per capita	Dollars	1,490	1,412	1,328	1,258	1,230
pulation [b]	Million	161.1	162.2	163.4	164.6	165.8
Labor force (civilian)	Million	63.6	64.0	64.4	64.7	65.0
Employment	Million	60.6	59.2	57.4	55.8	55.8
Unemployment	Million	3.0	4.8	7.0	8.9	9.2
dustrial production	1947–1949 = 100	125	117	109	103	100
nsumer price index	1947–1949 = 100	112	110	107	105	103
w parity index	1910–1914 = 100	274	266	260	254	251
d parity index	1910–1914 = 100	274	267	262	256	254

[a] This is not a forecast, but an assumption made for illustrative purposes. The projections are sed on a sharp decline in employment and a rise in unemployment to around 8 to 9 million rkers in the second year of recession. The workweek is shortened considerably to reflect the appearance of overtime work as well as a reduction of the standard workweek in some indus-es. Little change in output per man-hour is assumed. With reduced employment, a considerable p is projected for real output, the price level, and consumer incomes.
[b] Including armed forces overseas.

as severe a recession as seems within the range of possibility, in view of the various built-in stabilizers in the economy today and the greater readiness of government to engage in countercyclical action. *The main reason for assuming such a severe recession is to make the net influence of domestic demand factors stand out more clearly over other factors and disturbances which might largely overshadow the effects of a more moderate decline in domestic demand.* Certain key variables which influence the demand for farm products or (as in

[13] Dairy products were supported at 90 per cent of parity for two years prior to April 1, 1954. Although supports were lowered to 75 per cent of parity by the Secretary as of April 1, there was a strong drive in Congress as late as August 1954 to restore them, by law, to at least 85 per cent of parity. The 90 per cent level was assumed here because it was still in effect as of January 1954 and because it had been associated for some time, in fact and in spirit, with the 90 per cent support prices for basic crops.

the case of the prices-paid index) the level at which price supports must be set for crops in the second recession year are shown in Table 9.

We shall abstract from current reality in another respect also. We shall assume that, just before the onset of the recession, supplies and demands for all commodities are the same both with and without a price support program. For commodities eligible for direct

TABLE 9

Projections of Industrial Output, Disposable Income, and Prices Paid by Farmers during a Hypothetical Severe Recession, by Months, Eighteen-Month Period [a]

Year and Month	Industrial Production (1947–1949 = 100)	Disposable Income (billions of dollars)	Prices Paid, Including Interest, Taxes, and Wage Rates (1910–1914 = 100)	Consumer Price Index (1947–1949 = 10
First Year				
January	125	$240	274	112
February	124	238	273	111.5
March	122	236	271	111
April	121	234	270	111
May	120	232	269	110.5
June	118	231	268	110
July	117	229	266	110
August	116	227	265	109.5
September	114	225	264	109
October	113	223	263	108.5
November	111	221	262	108
December	110	219	261	108
Second year				
January	109	217	260	107
February	108	215	259	106.5
March	107	213	258	106
April	106	212	257	106
May	105	210	256	105
June	104	208	255	105

[a] This is not a forecast, but an assumption made for illustrative purposes. Figures are larg straight-line interpolations from those shown in Table 8.

price support, this means that, at the beginning of the recession, we assume supply and demand to be in balance precisely at the price support level. The purpose of this assumption is to emphasize *changes* in farm prices and incomes during the assumed recession, without regard for differences in the prerecession levels of farm prices and incomes which might have resulted from the presence or absence of price support programs.

In making the farm price, production, and income projections summarized below, I have tried to estimate for each major commodity or commodity group the prices and rates of production which would result from the assumed decline in consumer income and from the interaction of livestock and feed prices. Time lags in the adjustment of livestock and crop production were taken into account commodity by commodity. In estimating these price and production changes, statistical demand and supply relationships were extensively used, but with coefficients rounded to one or at most two significant figures. The projections as a whole are partly plastic or intuitive—they are not precisely defined by a set of structural equations, although the equations implied in the results could be written out.

The over-all results of the projections just described are shown in Table 10. The main reasons for differences with and without price supports are summarized below.

Marketings. With no supports the only change allowed for in the volume of farm marketings is a moderate increase in marketings of cattle. This reflects an expectation that cattlemen would try to move their stock and reduce their inventories more rapidly in the face of declining prices for cattle than if cattle prices remained stable. With prices of all farm products falling freely in response to declining demand, there would be little incentive to shift the pre-recession pattern of production and little opportunity to leave the farm for nonfarm employment. Total agricultural production would be maintained at about the pre-recession level.

With supports at fixed percentages of parity under storable crops and dairy products, but not under poultry, eggs, or meat animals, marketings of cattle might increase by January, second year of recession, to about the same extent and for the same reasons as they would if no other commodities were supported. In addition, the price supports for dairy products would encourage some increase in milk production as competing livestock enterprises became less and less profitable. Production and marketings of crops could not be reduced before about July of the second year of recession. The figures shown for July, second year of recession, and January, third year of recession, assume that acreages of basic crops in the second year of recession are reduced by the following percentages through the imposition of marketing quotas: wheat 10 per cent, cotton 15 per cent, tobacco 10 per cent, rice 20 per cent, and peanuts 10 per cent. It is assumed further that no attempt is made to prevent productive use

329

TABLE 10

Comparison of Farm Prices, Marketings, and Cash Receipts during a Hypothetical Severe Recession (1) with No Price Supports and (2) with Prices of Specified Commodities Supported at Fixed Percentages of Parity [a]

| DATE | MARKETINGS | | PRICES | | CASH RECEIPTS | | CASH RECEIPTS (SEASONALLY ADJUSTED ANNUAL RATES) | | |
	No Supports	"Rigid" Supports	No Supports	"Rigid" Supports [b]	No Supports	"Rigid" Supports [b]	No Supports	"Rigid" Supports [b]	Difference [b]
	(indexes, January, first year of recession = 100)						(billions of dollars)		
First year of recession									
January [c]	100.0	100.0	100.0	100.0	100.0	100.0	$30.00 [d]	$30.00 [d]	—
July	100.0	100.1	92.2	94.5	92.2	94.6	27.66	28.38	$ .72
Second year of recession									
January	100.4	100.5	85.1	89.3	85.4	89.7	25.62	26.91	1.29
July	100.4	99.4	79.3	86.9	79.6	86.4	23.88	25.92	2.04
Third year of recession									
January	100.4	98.1	78.7	87.8	79.0	86.1	23.70	25.83	2.13

[a] Aggregates built up from estimates for major commodities or groups of related commodities.

[b] Does not allow for the secondary effects reflected in Table 11. Table 11 implies that in January, third year of recession, under "rigid" supports, prices would stand at 89.3 per cent of their level in the first month of recession and cash receipts would amount to $26.28 billion, or $2.58 billion higher than with no supports.

[c] For convenience in comparing changes due to recession, it is assumed that marketings, prices, and cash receipts are the same as of January, first year of recession, with or without supports.

[d] Approximately the actual annual rate as of January 1953. Cash receipts in the 1953 calendar year totaled $30,975 million.

of acreage diverted from the basic crops. As a result, a large share of the "diverted acreage" is assumed, on the basis of past experience, to go into feed grains, oilseeds, hay, and pasture.

It is assumed that acreage allotments (but not marketing quotas) would be applied to corn in the commercial area at about the same level and with the same limited success as in recent years. Within the commercial area the acreage of corn for harvest in the first year of recession would be about 5 million acres lower than in the year before. However, much of this acreage would be expected to go into soybeans, oats, hay, and pasture, and corn acreage itself would be expected to increase somewhat outside the commercial corn area as a result of the reduction in wheat and cotton acreage. The net result would be little change in total feed grain production and marketings in the first two years of recession from levels in the year before its onset.

As of January, third year of recession, the projections under the present price support program assume cutbacks from January, first year of recession, of around 5 per cent in production and marketings of hogs, eggs, and turkeys and about 8 per cent in chickens and broilers. However, milk production in January, third year of recession, is assumed to be 5 per cent higher than two years earlier. The aggregate volume of farm marketings as of the same date is estimated to be only 2 to 2½ per cent smaller than it would have been in the absence of price supports and acreage restrictions. An additional reduction of about 1 per cent might be obtained if acreages diverted from basic crops could be kept out of currently productive uses. However, a really tight program to control diverted acres might require sizable conservation, rental, or benefit payments to the farmers affected.

Prices. With no supports, farm prices are estimated to fall 15 per cent during the first year of the recession. The bulk of this drop represents the direct effect of the assumed 10 per cent drop in disposable income upon domestic consumer demand. This effect is assumed to be somewhat augmented (1) by a weakening in commercial storage demand and in the reservation demands of farmers for storable crops and for livestock, particularly feeder cattle and cattle to maintain or augment breeding herds, and (2) by a contraction in foreign demand for our export crops. This explicitly assumes that a severe recession in the United States would have serious effects on the economies of many other countries. The further decline in disposable income during the second year of recession is estimated to result in a farm price level as of January, third year of recession, fully 20 per cent lower than that at the beginning of the recession.

With price supports at constant percentages of parity on storable crops and dairy products, a smaller, but still substantial, decline in average farm prices is indicated—between 10 and 11 per cent during the first year of recession. Up to that time, prices of meat animals, poultry and eggs, fruits and vegetables, and some other commodities not directly supported would fall much the same as if there were no price supports for other commodities. Prices of storable crops are assumed to rest more heavily on, or sag further below, their respective support prices as a result of the decline in demand. Under recession conditions it appears likely that stocks of wheat, feed grains, and possibly cotton would increase during the first crop year after the onset of the depression. For various reasons, market prices of grains sag below supports when CCC stocks are building up, although in some cases they exceed the loan levels during periods when demand is strong enough to draw supplies out of CCC ownership.

During the second recession year, some delayed effects of the price support program for feed grains begin to show up in livestock prices, as a result of cutbacks in production. As of January, third year of recession, prices of the unsupported meat animals and poultry products are estimated to average only 16 per cent below the level at the onset of the recession if feed grains are supported, as compared with 23 per cent below if feed grains are not supported.

As of January, third year of recession, the dollar-and-cents levels of price supports for the eligible commodities are 5 per cent lower than in January of the year before, reflecting the same percentage drop in the index of prices paid by farmers (the so-called "parity index"). The average drop in crop prices during the first two years of recession (including some crops not price-supported) is about 10 per cent, as contrasted with an estimated 21 or 22 per cent drop in crop prices if supports are completely absent. For farm products in the aggregate, the present price support program is estimated to hold the two-year price decline to 12 per cent, as compared with about 21 per cent in the absence of any price supports.

Cash Receipts. The cash receipts indexes are simply products of the price and marketing indexes shown in Table 10. As of January, third recession year, cash receipts are projected as down 14 per cent if the present price support program were continued as compared with a 21 per cent drop if there were no price supports.

In terms of dollars, the present price support program is shown as sustaining cash receipts at an annual rate of $1.3 billion higher in January, second recession year, and about $2.1 billion higher as of January of the next year than they would be in the absence of price supports. With production expenditures probably not much different under the two programs, the net incomes of farm families at the latter date would also be about $2 billion higher (or, more precisely, would have dropped $2 billion less from pre-recession levels) than in the absence of price supports. This difference would represent roughly 20 per cent of net farm income as of January, third recession year.

Extent of Price Support Stock Accumulations. In accomplishing this degree of income support, the price support agency would also significantly increase its outlays for, or investments in, price support stocks. Using the aggregative demand relationships described earlier, implying an elasticity of commercial utililization of farm products of —.6, the rate of total commercial movement of farm products as of January, third recession year, might be about 7 per cent lower with continued supports than in the absence of a price support program. As of the same date, however, the volume of farm marketings is estimated to be only 2.3 per cent lower than in the absence of a price support program; hence nearly 5 per cent of the volume of farm marketings at that time would be going into price support stocks. At the loan rates then existing, this would represent an accumulation of a little less than $1½ billion (annual-rate basis) during the second and third depression years.

Considering only the cutback in commercial use relative to total marketings, price support stocks might increase less than ½ billion dollars as of July, first recession year, compared with the level which would have been attained if no recession had begun. An additional billion dollars might be added to stocks out of the year's crop and as much as $1½ billion more during the next crop year. The cumulative increase in price support investments during the first two recession years might well exceed $2½ billion.

If supplies just before the beginning of an assumed recession were about average, a sizable stock pickup by the CCC might be realized as of July, first recession year. This would result from private firms' and individuals' cutting their holdings of storable commodities from a relatively easy level down to minimum working stocks. As a consequence, the net increase in price support stocks might substantially exceed the net increase in *total* stocks, price support and other combined. No allowance is made for such a shift in the present estimates because owners, fearing the burdensome surpluses already on hand, have already made this transfer. If we assumed a recession to begin at a time when commercial stocks were normal, the net shift of the storage burden from commercial to CCC hands could well amount to $1 billion.

EFFECTS OF THE PRESENT FARM PRICE SUPPORT PROGRAM ON
GENERAL ECONOMIC STABILITY DURING A SEVERE RECESSION

If we were simply interested in estimating the effects of a severe recession upon farm prices and farm income, we could, for most practical purposes, stop at this point. Obviously, a price support program of the present type affects the time path of *farm* prices and incomes during a recession. But what does a farm price support program contribute, directly or indirectly, to stability in the remainder of the economy? This is a more difficult question, to which I have never seen a well-reasoned quantitative answer.

I am not sure that I have a satisfactory answer myself. But I believe I can lay out some of the relevant considerations, and perhaps I can give a rough idea of the effect of the present farm price support program upon various economic magnitudes.

Chart 8 shows some of the major lines along which a price support program would affect other parts of the economy. The coefficient beside each arrow represents the estimated percentage change in the variable to which the arrow points that is associated with a 1 per cent change in the variable from which the arrow leads. Most of these "path coefficients" are based upon known factors, such as the weights of particular components of official index numbers, or the coefficients of statistical demand functions. Others seem reasonable to me but could be checked by empirical analysis. One coefficient assumes a "multiplier" of 2, based on studies by A. R. Smithies and others. One coefficient operates with a time lag. Values of the three coefficients marked with asterisks are pure assumptions on my part.

As indicated, the farm price support program has three immediate effects: (1) it raises the average level of prices received by farmers; (2) it reduces farm output, at least after the first twelve months of recession; and (3) it reduces the commercial utilization of farm products.

Suppose, for example, that the direct effect of a price support program is to increase farm prices by 10 per cent. If marketing margins remain constant, this will increase retail food prices about 5 per cent. Because retail food prices carry a weight of 30 per cent in the consumer price index, that index will rise 1.5 per cent.

The "influence" of the consumer price index upon wage rates is based on pure assumption. This index figures in some important wage contracts, and it is widely used as a talking point in wage disputes. The coefficient in Chart 8 implies that a 1.5 per cent increase in the consumer price index would have the effect of maintaining wage rates 1 per cent higher than they would otherwise have been. The influences of wage rates upon gross national product and

CHART 8

Lines of Influence of Present Farm Price Support Program
on Various Economic Magnitudes

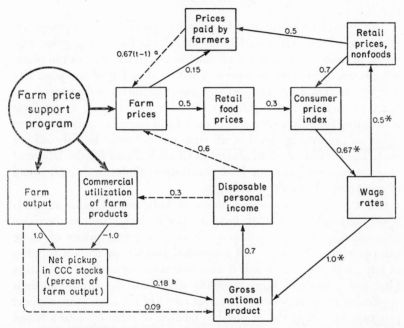

Numbers beside arrows are multipliers applicable to percentage changes in variable from which arrow leads. Those marked ✻ are assumed without empirical check.

ª Operates with time lag of one year.   ᵇ Assumes "multiplier" of 2.0

Source: U.S. Department of Agriculture.

upon the retail prices of nonfood products also rest on assumption. (The latter coefficient assumes that wages constitute about 50 per cent of value added in manufacturing and distributing processes, and that most nonfarm prices are administered in such a way that these direct wage costs are covered, even during a recession.)

Chart 8 implies that the initial or direct increase in the consumer price index generates a further increase in the same index. An increase in the consumer price index increases wage rates, which increase nonfood prices, which enter the consumer price index with a weight of 70 per cent. Hence the *total* effect upon the consumer price index of an increase in farm prices consists of the direct influence plus this "feed-back" effect.

An initial increase of 10 per cent in prices *received* by farmers leads directly, through prices of purchased livestock, feed, and food products, to something like a 1.5 per cent increase in the index of prices *paid* by farmers. There is also an indirect effect operating through the consumer price index, wage rates, and retail prices of nonfood products. This effect is only about a fourth as large as the direct one.

The dotted arrow running from "prices paid" to "farm prices" reflects use of the prices-paid index as a basis for setting price supports. Because such supports are announced in advance of the planting season, this coefficient operates with a time lag of one year. Under the present price support program the direct influence of a 1 per cent increase in the prices-paid index would apply to products accounting for only 45 per cent of cash farm income; hence the direct effect on the average level of all farm prices would be only .45 per cent. The coefficient of .67 shown in Chart 8 allows for the influence of price support levels for feed grains upon the unsupported prices of meat animals, poultry, and eggs.

Chart 8 also shows three chains of influence of price supports upon disposable personal income, particularly that of nonfarm persons. An increase in disposable income raises prices of those farm products which are not supported and whose market supplies at any given time are fixed; it also increases commercial utilization (but not prices) of farm products which are in surplus at their applicable support prices. The direct effect of the farm price support program in raising the disposable income of farm operators is not adequately allowed for in Chart 8.

The net increase in CCC stocks as a result of the price support program represents an injection of money from outside the private economy. It is equivalent to a purchase of goods by the federal government, with no simultaneous increase in government revenue. In Chart 8 we apply a multiplier of 2 to the annual rate of increase in CCC price support stocks.

The model in Chart 8 contains a number of implicit "path-multipliers." If we follow the arrow *from* farm prices through the consumer price index and back through disposable personal income *to* farm prices, we find that the initial increase in farm prices generates a secondary increase 4.2 per cent as large as the first one. The secondary increase would generate a third-order increase, and so on. Using a well-known formula for the sum of a power series, the final effect of a 1 per cent increase in farm prices along this path would be equal to

$$\frac{1}{1 - .042}$$

or 1.044 per cent.

Some minor additional effects of the same sort are found if we consider the secondary "loops" centering around the consumer price index and disposable personal income. The chain of influences from farm prices through prices paid by farmers and back again involves a similar power series, but with a time lag of one year between the change in prices paid and the next-order change in farm prices. The effects of the price support program upon farm output (by means of acreage restrictions) and upon the net increase in CCC price support stocks may be *additive* to the initial effect of the program upon farm prices and may not involve power series multipliers.

In a stationary equilibrium, eliminating the effect of the one time lag in the system, it appears that if the existing price support program initially or directly increased farm prices by 10 per cent the result would be a final level of farm prices about 12.3 per cent higher than it would have been in the absence of a price support program. (This figure depends, of course, on the coefficients in Chart 8 and would be altered if some of these coefficients were revised.)

Table 11 shows the numerical results obtained by applying the coefficients in Chart 8 to the initial price and quantity data given in Table 10 (or underlying it). The estimated decline in farm prices from January, first recession year, to January, third recession year, is only half as large as the decline experienced in the absence of price supports. As of January, third recession year, farm prices with the present support program are shown as 13 per cent higher than farm prices without support. The index of prices paid by farmers is indicated to be more than 2 per cent higher as a result of the price support program. This would mean a roughly similar increase in production expenditures and a corresponding reduction in the *net* income differences resulting from the farm prices shown. The parity ratio is shown as declining to 79 in the absence of price support, and as leveling out at 86 under the present program. The slight increase in the parity ratio with price support as of January, third recession year, reflects the delayed action of feed grain supports upon livestock production and prices. The consumer price index is shown as

2½ or 3 per cent higher with the price support program than without it.

TABLE 11

Estimated Values of Selected Economic Magnitudes during a Hypothetical Severe Recessio (1) with No Farm Price Supports and (2) with Prices of Specified Commodities Supported a Fixed Percentages of Parity a

ITEM	UNIT	1ST RECESSION YEAR January	July	2ND RECESSION YEAR January	July	3RD RECESSIO YEAR January
Prices received by farmers	(1909–1914 = 100)					
Present supports	"	252	240	226	224	225
No supports	"	252	234	214	202	199
Difference	"	0	6	12	22	26
Prices paid by farmers	(1910–1914 = 100)					
Present supports	"	274	267	262	259	257
No supports	"	274	266	260	254	251
Difference	"	0	1	2	5	6
Parity ratio b	Per cent					
Present supports	"	92	90	86	86	88
No supports	"	92	88	82	80	79
Difference	"	0	2	4	6	9
Consumer price index	(1947–1949 = 100)					
Present supports	"	112	111	108	107	106
No supports	"	112	110	107	105	103
Difference	"	0	1	1	2	3
Disposable personal income	Bil. dol.					
Present supports c	"	240	230	220	211	208
No supports	"	240	229	217	207	204
Difference c	"	0	1	3	4	4
Gross national product	Bil. dol.					
Present supports	"	350	330	305	288	281
No supports	"	350	328	302	282	275
Difference	"	0	2	3	6	6

a Projections under *present supports* are based on initial estimates in Table 10 adjusted for th assumed interaction patterns shown in Chart 8.

b Prices received by farmers as a percentage of prices paid by farmers.

c Includes rough allowance for increase in disposable income of farm operators resulting di rectly from price support program but not provided for in Chart 8.

We now come to two other magnitudes of central interest to economic forecasters. As of January, third recession year, the figures in Table 10 implied a net annual increase in CCC stocks of about $1½ billion. This effect, plus certain others indicated in Chart 8, leads to a gross national product as of January, third recession year, about

$6 billion higher with the present price support program than with no supports. While this is a substantial sum, it is only 8 per cent of the assumed total decline in GNP from peak to trough in the absence of a price support program.

Finally, as of January, third recession year, disposable income is projected as $4 billion higher with the present price support program than in the absence of price supports. This is a little more than 10 per cent of the estimated decline from January, first recession year, in the absence of price support. Of the $4 billion increase, $2 billion or more may accrue to nonfarm people, while perhaps $1½ to 2 billion probably accrues to farm operators. (In terms of net farm income *before personal taxes*, the price support program under existing legislation [14] might yield about $2 billion more at the trough of a severe recession than would result in the absence of price support.)

Although there may be several faulty coefficients in Chart 8, and some faulty lines of reasoning, I believe that Table 11 defines the net effect of the present farm price support program upon the course of an economic recession reasonably well. Under the recession pattern assumed here, the present price support program might reduce the drift in the general retail price level by as much as 30 per cent; it might reduce the decline in GNP and disposable personal income by something like 10 per cent; and it would reduce the drop in farm prices (which it is specifically set up to do) by 50 per cent relative to the level expected in the absence of a price support program.

A prolonged recession would subject the present price support program to severe stresses. A few of the problems are summarized below.

We have estimated that, as of January, third recession year, the CCC would be accumulating commodity stocks at the rate of approximately $1½ billion a year. In physical terms the CCC would be picking up nearly 5 per cent of total farm output, and the price support program might be considered out of balance to that extent.

If the economy were expected to continue at the January, third recession year, level for some time, one alternative would be a desperate attempt to reduce farm output by another 5 per cent. Possible lines of attack would include (1) reducing the national wheat acreage allotment from its present legal minimum of 55 million acres to something less than 50 million acres, (2) complete prohibition of currently productive use of acreages diverted from the basic crops, and (3) establishing marketing quotas for oilseeds.

[14] This analysis was prepared before passage of the Agricultural Act of 1954.

But these measures could hardly be expected to reduce total farm output by more than 3 per cent. The next 2 per cent reduction might require programs which have been regarded as either administratively or politically unworkable in the past, such as (1) marketing quotas for milk and butterfat and/or (2) marketing quotas for corn and perhaps other feed grains.

An alternative to these ultrarestrictive measures would be to increase consumption and discourage production by abandoning, or substantially lowering, price supports for dairy products (below the 90 per cent of parity assumed in our model). A substantial lowering of the price support level for corn and other feed grains might also be necessary. These measures would, of course, reduce the level of farm prices (perhaps about 5 per cent in the aggregate) and would have some effect on the rest of the economy as indicated in Chart 8. If price support stocks at the beginning of the recession were small, and if definite signs of economic recovery began to appear by about January, third recession year, the price support program might be able to "pull through" without resort to the tight restrictions and the support level reductions mentioned above. But if stocks were high at the beginning of the recession, as they are at this time, and/or if bumper yields should occur in the first and second recession years, not only might these two sorts of measures seem necessary, but costly and unusual surplus disposal measures might be undertaken and the whole price support program might be drastically revised.

3. Effects of Alternative Farm Programs upon General Economic Stability

Two distinct sorts of questions will be considered under this heading. In the first section we shall assume that each of a number of alternative farm programs has actually been operating for a considerable period before a recession begins and we shall inquire how each program would affect the course of events during a hypothetical recession.

The second type of question is probably of much greater interest at the time this is written (May 1954): What would be the economic repercussions of a *shift* from the present price support program to a specified alternative program (a) if the general economy remained stable and (b) if such a transition happened to coincide with an economic recession? These two questions will be dealt with in turn.

If farm price support legislation is changed in 1954, it seems most likely that the shift will be from the present program, with continuous support for specified commodities at 90 per cent of parity, to some variant of the Agricultural Act of 1949. Multiple price plans for wheat, cotton, and rice have also received considerable attention in recent months. If multiple price plans were adopted for one or more of these crops, it seems likely that prices of other products now being supported would continue to receive support either under the present program or under some variation of the Agricultural Act of 1949.

Finally, we might consider a program which has been strongly advocated by some economists and some political figures, although it has never been used on an extensive scale under peacetime conditions. This would be a program of compensatory payments on livestock products, coupled with the present type of price support program on storable crops. Compensatory payments would be made directly to livestock producers based on the difference between the actual market price of the product and some specified percentage of parity.

THE AGRICULTURAL ACT OF 1949

Contrary to some rather widespread opinions, price supports for most of the basic crops under the Agricultural Act of 1949 are not low or, in most cases, extremely flexible. A prominent visual feature of the 1949 act is a schedule of price supports, expressed as percentages of parity, which drops 1 point for every 2-point increase in the ratio of actual supplies to normal supplies. This price support schedule ranges from 90 per cent down to 75 per cent of parity. Many persons have assumed that, if the Agricultural Act of 1949 were put into effect, prices of the six basic crops would immediately fall to 75 per cent of parity and stay there. This is by no means the case.

Under the 1949 act, tobacco is to be supported at 90 per cent of parity in any year in which marketing quotas are proclaimed. And marketing quotas must be proclaimed in any year if quotas have been in effect during the preceding year. The effect is continuous support for tobacco at 90 per cent of parity. Supplies of peanuts never get very far above normal under present program operations, as excess stocks at the end of each year are generally crushed for oil and do not figure in the supply percentage for peanuts for direct edible use as nuts or peanut butter. Thus price support for peanuts would drop below 90 per cent of parity only rarely and by small percentages. In the case of cotton, even if certain special legislation not part of the 1949 act were eliminated, the price support level would rarely fall below 90 per cent of parity, and then, as a rule, by rather small amounts.

The case for wheat is different. Due to an inconsistency in the wheat legislation (which has not required correction while mandatory supports at 90 per cent of parity have been continued), wheat marketing quotas would be set at a level which, with average yields, would bring supplies in the ensuing year to a level requiring support at not less than 83 per cent of parity. If the flexible provisions of the 1949 act should go into effect, it seems likely that the present inconsistency would be eliminated in such a way that the object of wheat marketing quotas in any year would be to reduce wheat supplies to a level such that support at 90 per cent of parity would become mandatory in the following year. The provisions for corn are more nearly in accord with the popular conception of flexible price supports. However, last year's record supply of corn (1953) would have required support at not less than 82 or 83 per cent of parity.

The flexibility which might be provided by large supplies resulting from bumper yields is at least partially thwarted by the forward-pricing provision of the act. If a minimum dollar-and-cents support price for corn is announced before planting time, based on the assumption of average yields, the support price for that crop cannot subsequently be lowered to take account of favorable weather and high yields.

Hence, if we assume the Agricultural Act of 1949 to be in effect and functioning well according to its internal logic just before the onset of a recession, farm prices would fall only a little faster and a little farther than under the present program of support for basic commodities at 90 per cent of parity. Assuming that price supports for dairy products were dropped from 90 per cent down to 75 per cent of parity shortly after the recession began, the average level of farm prices under the 1949 act would fall 1 per cent below the present program results (Table 11) as of January, second recession year, and about 2 per cent as of January, third recession year. Marketing quotas and acreage allotments would likely be applied at about the same level as under the present program.

In summary, the effects of the Agricultural Act of 1949 would be very similar to those of the program under existing legislation except that the differences from "no program" would be only about four-fifths as large. For example, as of January, third recession year, the index of prices received by farmers would be estimated at about

220 under the 1949 act, compared with 225 under the present program and 199 in the absence of price supports.

Other differences would be roughly similar. As of January, third recession year, cash receipts from farm marketings might be approximately $.5 billion lower under the 1949 act than under the present program, *assuming that both programs had been in operation before the beginning of the assumed recession and that they had resulted in precisely the same average pre-recession levels of prices, marketings, and income.*

THE PRESIDENT'S FARM PROGRAM

To a large extent, the President's farm program, as transmitted to Congress on January 11, 1954, is designed to ease the transition from the program now (May 1954) in effect to the Agricultural Act of 1949. Hence, over the long run, the President's program is very similar to the 1949 act and its behavior during a recession would also be much the same.

EITHER THE PROGRAM UNDER EXISTING LEGISLATION OR THE
AGRICULTURAL ACT OF 1949 SUPPLEMENTED BY MULTIPLE
PRICE PLANS FOR WHEAT, COTTON, AND RICE

If this combination of programs were well established before the onset of a severe recession, the stability effects would be much like those of the Agricultural Act of 1949. Possibly there would be no marketing quotas on the three crops under multiple price plans; if quotas were applied, they would probably be set at higher levels than under the present program or the 1949 act. Market prices of cotton and rice might decline much as they would if no price support program were in operation. The market price of wheat, however, might change only in proportion to changes in the price of corn, which is assumed to be supported at or near 90 per cent of its parity price. Livestock prices could be a shade lower as the result of larger quantities of wheat-fed animals, but as an offset somewhat larger quantities of feed grains might be picked up by the CCC under its loan program.

The net effect of the multiple price plans would be to drop the average level of prices received by farmers about 1 per cent as of January, second recession year, and about 2 per cent as of January, third recession year. Hence if other commodities were supported as under the present program, the farm price index as of January, third recession year, might be around 220 or 221; if multiple price plans were superimposed upon the Agricultural Act of 1949 for other commodities, the farm-price-received index as of that date might be around 216, about two-thirds of the way from the "no support" level toward the level expected under the present program. However, farm output should be at least 1 per cent larger as of January, third recession year, so that the net effect of multiple price plans on the commodities specified might be to increase the drop in cash farm income during a recession about 1 per cent, or ¼ billion dollars, relative to programs which omitted the multiple price feature.

COMPENSATORY PAYMENTS ON LIVESTOCK PRODUCTS

Under this program we assume that prices of basic crops are supported directly (as under the present program) at their pre-recession level, corresponding to around 90 per cent of parity. In the case of livestock products, including milk and butterfat, we assume that no attempt will be made to interfere with market prices, but that, to the extent that market prices fall below the pre-recession percentage of parity, the government will pay the difference to livestock producers.

Under this program, farm prices would behave much as they would under the present support program through January, second recession year. As of July, second recession year, they would be about midway between the present program level and the "no support" level; in January, third recession year, they would be about one-third of the way between these two levels, but closer to the "no support" level.

Quite obviously, this program results in a higher, and hence more stable, level of cash income to farmers than any of the programs previously mentioned. As of January, third recession year, this program, including compensatory payments to producers, would return farmers nearly $4 billion more than they would receive in the absence of price supports. Alternatively, we might say that the drop in cash receipts from farm marketings *plus compensatory payments* is only four-tenths as great under this program as it would be in the absence of price supports.

However, the cost of the compensatory payments would be substantial. As of January, third recession year, these payments, on livestock products only, would be running at the rate of close to $3 billion a year. While the level of total returns maintained for livestock products would encourage a heavier consumption of feed grains and considerably reduce the CCC's pickup of feed crops, the CCC would very likely still be picking up half a billion dollars'

344

worth of other commodities (annual rate) as of January, third recession year.

The multiplier effect of compensatory payments plus net CCC stock pickups might raise GNP by around $7 billion as of January, third recession year, as compared with the "no support" level. However, the price effects upon GNP indicated in Chart 8 would amount to only $1 billion or so as of that date, so that total GNP might reach about $283 billion, compared with $281 billion under the present program and $275 billion in the absence of price supports. Disposable income might be around $210 billion as of that date, with the $2 billion increase as compared with the present program going mostly to farm operators. The consumer price index, however, might be only 1 per cent above the level which would obtain in the absence of price supports.

This would undoubtedly come closer to stabilizing the gross and net incomes of farmers than any of the other programs discussed. It would do less than the other programs to stabilize the general price level and the level of wage rates. However, prices of food would be only about 2 per cent higher at retail than they would have been in the absence of farm price supports.

The balance sheet for this program, then, shows slightly greater stability in total GNP and disposable income, and moderately less stability in prices and wage rates. However, the peak annual cost of compensatory payments, around $3 billion a year, would have serious political drawbacks if it were charged to the farm price support program as such. It might also be challenged by nonfarm people as providing farmers with a higher level of income protection than would be provided to others under the severe recession conditions we have assumed.

EFFECTS OF SHIFTING FROM THE PRESENT PROGRAM TO
ALTERNATIVE PROGRAMS AT THE PRESENT TIME (MAY 1954)

This question is the focal point of current debate over farm price support policy. Here we must step out of the "timeless" hypothetical preoccupations of the earlier part of this paper and face up to historic time.

In this area, too, there are certain misconceptions which should be set straight. The present program, involving mandatory support at 90 per cent of parity for the six basic crops, is in effect for 1954 crops. Changes in legislation will not affect the levels of price support for basic crops until the summer or fall of 1955. The level of price support for dairy products has recently been lowered from

90 to 75 per cent of parity, but this action was within the discretion of the Secretary of Agriculture under the present law. (In view of existing surpluses of dairy products, it may be argued that the language in the present law that milk and butterfat shall be supported at such levels "as will insure an adequate supply" practically required this step.)

Hence, except for a possible further sagging of market prices below loan rates during the spring and summer of 1955 in anticipation of lower support levels in the following year, the price support alternatives now under debate could have little or no effect on general economic stability before the summer of 1955.

The key elements now in controversy are as follows:

Modernized Parity. Four of the basic crops are still supported at 90 per cent of the old parity standard. At the present time, new parity prices for these crops are lower than their old parities by the following percentages: wheat 14, corn 11, cotton 3, and peanuts 19. Under present world price and domestic carry-over conditions, market prices for these crops would probably fall by very nearly these percentages if a sudden shift were made from old to new parities.

Under existing legislation the old parity formula will continue to apply to these crops until January 1, 1956. Hence the old parity standard will be used in setting loan rates for 1955 crops, but new parity will be available for use (and, so far as the letter of existing law is concerned, must be used) in setting loan rates for 1956 crops of these four commodities.

Minimum Price Support Percentages. If no new legislation is passed in 1954, the minimum price support schedules of the Agricultural Act of 1949 will be available for use with respect to 1955 crops. In view of the very large carry-overs in prospect at the beginning of the 1955 crop year, wheat prices could then be supported at as low as 75 per cent of parity, cotton prices at as low as 80 per cent, and corn prices at about 85 per cent. Hence, in spite of the fact that old parity would continue to prevail for these crops in 1955, support prices for the 1955 crops *could* be reduced by about 15, 10, and 5 per cent of parity respectively. (However, the Secretary of Agriculture would have discretionary power under the 1949 act to support prices above these minimum levels and could moderate this transition if it seemed desirable to do so.)

The combination of these possible drops in parity percentages in 1955, followed by an abrupt shift to the new parity standard in 1956, is a serious matter to producers of the commodities affected and one in which legislators concerned with the stability of both the farm and the general economy are keenly interested. This has been recognized in the President's farm program, which provides two major features intended to assure a smooth transition. The first of these is that parity prices of the four crops would be reduced by only 5 per cent a year, beginning in 1956, until the new parity level is reached. Cotton would move to the new parity standard in 1956. Corn would be practically there in 1957. Wheat would reach new parity in 1958, and peanuts in 1959.

The second major feature of the President's farm program is a $2.5 billion set-aside, including 400 to 500 million bushels of wheat, 3 to 4 million bales of cotton, and possibly certain other products. The quantities of wheat and cotton set aside would be excluded from actual supplies of these commodities in computing the supply percentages upon which minimum support prices are based. If we assume average yields of wheat and cotton in 1954, this leads to minimum support percentages for wheat of 80 to 85 per cent of parity and for cotton of 82 to 86 per cent of parity in 1955.[15] Quantities in the set-aside are to be disposed of outside of normal commercial channels if possible; they can be released into normal channels only if market prices exceed 105 per cent of parity. It is expected that the set-aside provision will also help to strengthen market prices of wheat and cotton and keep them closer to the loan rates.

However, the set-aside quantities of wheat and cotton would continue to be counted in the total supplies of these commodities for purposes of determining marketing quotas. Given average yields each year over the next three or four years, the President's farm program, as well as the program now in existence, would likely call for marketing quotas on wheat through 1957 and cotton through 1956. This would probably be true also under the Agricultural Act of 1949.

The effects of these various possible transitions can be summarized briefly. *The minimum provisions of the Agricultural Act of 1949* would reduce farm income (centering on January 1956) by about $.4 billion on the five basic cash crops (cotton, wheat, tobacco, peanuts, and rice) as compared with the program now in operation. Cash receipts from sales of corn and other feed grains might

[15] These percentages depend also upon estimated utilization of wheat and cotton during the 1954 and 1955 crop years and upon the levels of marketing quotas announced for 1955 crops.

drop slightly—probably not more than $.1 billion. The drop in corn loan rates to around 85 per cent of parity would have some slight effects on livestock production and prices later in the crop year. The net further cash income reduction in the 1956 crop year, compared with the present program including old parity, might be around $.25 billion, with another $.1 or .2 billion showing up on livestock products in 1957.

The President's farm program would result in price supports for cotton, wheat, and corn averaging perhaps 5 to 7 per cent below the present level in 1955 and perhaps 7 or 8 per cent lower than the present level in 1956. The margin is likely to average little or no greater than this in 1957 and later years. Thus, as compared with an extension of the present price support program for basic crops, the President's farm program might involve drops in farm income on the order of $.2 billion in 1955 and perhaps another $.2 billion in 1956. This level might be approximately maintained in the year or two immediately following. Compared with the effects of a severe economic recession, which in the absence of farm price supports could involve as much as $5 or 6 billion of cash farm income, the magnitudes involved in a shift from the existing program to the President's farm program are almost negligible.

It cannot be denied, however, that either the President's program or the Agricultural Act of 1949 would lead to significant reductions in the level of cash farm income from wheat. The effects on cash income from cotton and from feed grains and livestock products would be small—perhaps almost negligible.

As compared with the present program, an abrupt shift to the Agricultural Act of 1949, which is now (May 1954) on the books for application to 1955 and later crops, could result in additional successive impacts in the autumns of 1955 and 1956 of at most half a billion dollars each year. The impacts would be most severe in the specialized wheat areas and would pose serious readjustment problems for wheat producers. However, the consequences for the rest of the economy could scarcely exceed a reduction of $1 billion or thereabouts at the GNP or disposable income level.

The coincidence of such a transition with the onset of a recession might lead some lay economists to argue that the transition caused the recession. However, on the basis of the models and arguments presented here, this is a much heavier burden than a change in the farm price support program will bear. Its initial effects would do very little to aggravate a recession already under way, and its consequences, except for producers of the crops directly affected, would speedily be lost sight of if forces originating in the nonfarm sectors of the economy were sufficient to carry the recession to any considerable depth.

COMMENT

JAMES T. BONNEN, Harvard University [*]

To my knowledge, this is the first *quantitative* attempt to evaluate directly the impact of an agricultural price support program on the whole economy. It is a pioneer effort, and Fox has a significant and most thoughtful paper. In particular it is interesting methodologically. I do question, however, whether the quantitative results of the model actually support his conclusion that the present agricultural price support program would lift GNP by 8 per cent in the depths of his hypothetical depression. Fox's models are expressed in money terms with no adjustment for price level changes. It is not possible to extract a general price level index from the data, but Fox does calculate a "consumer price index." Deflating "personal disposable income" by this index brings one to the conclusion that "real" disposable income would be higher if one eliminated all agricultural price support programs (when presumably these programs are financed out of a deficit). The implication for aggregate demand and GNP are clear. To be more specific, in Table 11 of the paper, at the depth of the hypothetical depression, "total disposable personal income" was $208 billion under the present support program and $204 billion with no program, resulting in a difference of $4 billion added to demand by the support program. However, in the same table there is a consumer price index which, in the trough of the depression, is estimated at 106 under the present system of support prices and at 103 with no supports at all. Deflating the income figures by the relevant index number, one gets a "real" disposable personal income of $196.2 billion with the current support program operating, but an income of $198 billion with no support program! According to this calculation, the net effect of the present price support program was to reduce "real" disposable income by $1.8 billion. Fox will admit that this is an unexpected quantitative conclusion and will perhaps concur in the opinion that this result is due to the structural relationships which he posits and perhaps more particularly to one or two of the im-

[*] Presently assistant professor of agricultural economics at Michigan State University.

plicit "path-multipliers" which we can all admit are elusive creatures at best.

Much of Fox's *structural* data comes from work done in the old Bureau of Agricultural Economics in connection with the Inter-industry Relations Study of the Bureau of Labor Statistics. This study employs W. W. Leontief's input-output technique of general equilibrium analysis. Fox has done a good job of adapting this data for his use here, but I believe we should be under no illusions as to the limitations to a *more extensive use* of this type of analytical tool in business cycle investigations and in any specific attempt, such as we have here, to evaluate the effect of price level changes on aggregate demand. I hasten to add that Fox has not become involved in these difficulties. He has used the input-output framework in the only way in which I think it can be applied at its present state of development—that is, to provide *descriptive* and *partial* structural information which is otherwise unobtainable. Briefly, there seems to me to be three facts from which most difficulties arise. (1) The simple static model assumes a fixed input structure (the input-output equations can be said to be linear and homogeneous), which of course means that the "law of diminishing returns" does not apply (i.e. we have constant costs). (2) There is a unique or fixed demand and consumption structure given by the input-output table. There are no substitution possibilities in any realistic sense and consequently no meaningful explanation of consumption or producers' demand. Any attempt to explain changes in demand within the model would necessitate introducing "households" into the structural matrix, taking it out of the "bill of goods." If no additional changes are made, the income elasticity of demand for each commodity turns out to be unit elasticity—an unusual situation, to say the least, with the resulting calculations of induced demand becoming extremely unrealistic. Given the unreal results of the static model, if any accelerator action is added in, as it must be in the dynamic model, estimates of induced demand would likely be preposterous. It is necessary to provide leakage for the system on a fairly arbitrary and large scale before the answers become realistic. (3) The final fact is that the structure of payments for the factors of production is also fixed. Consequently, relative prices and wage rates are assumed to remain the same. It is to be noted also that the absolute level of all prices has no meaning in the system.

A dynamic model is necessary if one is to handle either a complete cycle or the phase of falling aggregate demand. In other words, one must introduce, in addition to the structure of product flows, a set of structural equations for the stocks of the economy (the inventories and fixed assets). The static model will function properly only under conditions where no problems of idle stocks or disinvestment are to be met. The use of stocks in the system introduces an accelerator action with all of the attendant difficulties of handling the necessary "leaks" and "feedbacks" so that the system will converge at a reasonable level. The usual dynamic input-output model is nonlinear in the sense of being irreversible, so that the same model cannot be used to handle the ups as well as the downs of the cycle without extensive or clumsy additional assumptions— and then I doubt if it is possible to build a model which can move *continuously* from the phase of positive accumulation to that of idle stock. Probably the most important thing to realize is that construction of a model of falling aggregate demand is far more difficult, both empirically and in theory, than building one of rising aggregate demand. Input-output analysis appears to provide no practical way of integrating a theory of money into its system; it assumes a constant interest rate and deals only in "real" terms. Even when, by operating on the system from the outside, shifts in prices are achieved, relative statements are all that can be obtained from the model, and a shift in the absolute level of one or all prices has no operational meaning.

I wish to point out again that Fox has not become involved in these difficulties. But it should be clear that any attempt to apply input-output analysis to price-demand or business cycle problems in a rigorous fashion, either as a closed-static or an open-dynamic system, is at best a dubious and difficult procedure.

Fox indicates that the farm price support program in 1953 directly involved commodities accounting for only 45 per cent of total cash receipts to agriculture. From the point of view of depression policy this is an important feature of the current support program. While it is undoubtedly true, as Fox's model indicates, that average farm income is increased by the support program, the case is not so straightforward as it might appear at first. In a situation in which, for example, a dozen commodities are selling below parity prices in a free market and only half have parity supports, the prices of the unsupported commodities might easily be adversely affected. This would seem most likely to be the case if the supported commodities have a greater elasticity of demand than the nonsupported ones. Historically, we can note that at no time have all of the commodities selling below parity been supported in the market at the same instant. Note, too, that those commodities most often supported have been products like wheat, corn, and cotton, for which demand is rather inelastic. *Conceivably*, in a general depression it might cost less per dollar of induced demand to support all farm products than to support just a limited number, as we tend to do at present.

The starting point from which comparisons of alternative models are made deserves some comment. The results of the comparisons of different policies depend not only on the nature of the policies themselves but also upon the condition of the economy or model at the time at which the policy is applied. For example, the situation in which agriculture finds itself today is quite different from that of the late twenties, preceding the Great Depression. Although real net farm income fell by about one-third between 1947 and 1953, agriculture's financial liquidity remains so much greater today than in the twenties that in all likelihood, if the same price policy had been implemented during the late twenties and were implemented at present, the reaction of the farmer and the effects on aggregate demand would be very different. Also, the fact that many of the present-day farmers experienced the depression of the thirties and still remember it quite vividly will condition the manner in which they react to various policies. All of this is related to the consideration we must give to the impact that different farm policies have upon the expectations of the various sectors of the economy. One cannot very readily introduce expectations into a model, but for policy planning purposes, where the goal is the maintenance of aggregate demand, some evaluation must be made of the effect of the policy via expectations upon demand. Forward pricing, perhaps, is a good example of how some expectations can be fairly successfully structured for planning purposes.

Let us consider the production control measures which operate under the present law and which Fox had to take into consideration in his evaluation of the price support program. Despite all of the hullabaloo over "conservation" and "production adjustments," the primary purpose of production control measures is price support. In fact, it would seem that depression conditions would be the poorest of times to attempt production adjustments. Since the demand for all products is falling, increasing the production of one commodity by reducing that of another only shifts the price support problem from one product to another. This is another reason for placing the emphasis of depression price policy upon the expansion of over-all demand and upon maintaining output in all lines of production.

Consider too that, although there is a storage program, the present price support system operates to a significant extent through raising prices and curtailing output in a severe depression, such as Fox has set up. It is difficult to know to what extent this means that the increase in farm demand for industrial production is offset by the decline in nonfarm demand due to a relative increase in the cost of living. It is reasonable to expect that the use of a different support technique, such as compensatory price payments, would have a greater impact on aggregate demand. Indeed, Fox's model indicates this, although it would increase the total cost of the support program. It was a little surprising to find the cost as high as Fox's model indicates, although he may be quite right. It would still seem to be a debatable point quantitatively.

Ultimately, in any over-all policy consideration, the economist must answer a quantitatively difficult and fundamental question not within the scope of Fox's paper. That question is: At what point will government expenditures in farm programs provide less of an increase in aggregate demand than would be returned if the expenditures were made on the nonfarm sector? Of course, economic questions as to marginal rates of return are, in actual policy planning, radically altered and also blurred by political and social factors.

An evaluation of the *long-run* impact of agricultural price support programs on the rest of the economy is outside the scope of Fox's paper. But it should be mentioned that the possible methods for ultimate financing of the price support program can have quite varied effects on the economy, and the choice should always be a serious policy consideration.

A chronically neglected problem of agriculture which none of these alternative programs ever faces is agricultural poverty. This is bad enough in periods of general prosperity, not to speak of severe depressions. None of the programs under present consideration will have any effective impact on the extremely low incomes of about 2 million American farm families.

I should like to suggest in conclusion the possibility that programs which succeed in adding to the stability of the economic system may also lower the average level at which the economy operates or retard the rate of economic progress. Also, conversely, a higher average level of activity may be gained only at the cost of greater instability. Any potential policy maker should also be aware of the well-established fact (often ignored in policy discussions) that general depressions are not caused by agricultural difficulties and that the only manner in which effective income stability and progress can be maintained in agriculture is by seeing to it that the rest of the economy is stable and economically progressive.

These comments, I believe, bring up matters which must be seriously considered in the determination of any depression policy for agriculture or the economy in general. I should like to add that Fox has presented one of the most complete models I have ever seen constructed for the purpose of analyzing the internal relationships of one sector of the economy to the total. It is a significant example of his obvious ability and long experience in handling economic statistics.

REPLY BY FOX

Early in his discussion Bonnen raises a point which, while not surprising, was certainly not brought out in my paper. When he deflates the disposable personal income figures in the last column of Table 11 by the corresponding consumer price indexes, he obtains a "real" disposable income $1.8 billion (about .9 per cent) *lower* with the price support program than without it! I would not attach much importance to the direction of this difference, as it is almost within the range of rounding errors—the consumer price index is recorded only to the nearest 1 per cent. But there are reasons for believing that the "present price support program" described in my paper may be no more than neutral in its effects on aggregate output and employment.

First, the program reduces farm output. In my model this reduction (as of January, third recession year) amounts to at least .5 billion 1954 dollars. Second, as commercial demand is less than unit elastic, domestic users pay a larger dollar amount (roughly 1 billion 1954 dollars) for a reduced supply of farm products. This, in itself, would tend to deflect some purchasing power away from nonfarm goods and services and to reduce nonfarm employment. These two effects should be approximately offset, but perhaps no more than offset, by larger purchases on the part of farm families, whose net incomes were estimated to be $2 billion higher (as of January, third recession year) with the program than without it.

The apparent neutrality of the price support program with respect to total output and employment raises a number of questions. If the program reduces the drift in nonfarm prices and wage rates, does it slow down inventory liquidation and help to maintain business investment? This seems plausible, but I believe it would be extremely difficult to quantify these effects. Second, in formulating the objectives of countercyclical policy, how much weight should be given to price stability as such, both farm and nonfarm? Price deflation increases the real burden of all obligations which were fixed in money terms before the onset of recession, and there is a widespread impression that falling prices are viewed with great concern by the business community. Certainly the severity of price dislocations and cost-price squeezes tends to increase with the speed and amplitude of general price deflation.

Perhaps it is enough that farm price supports, viewed as short-term defenses against recession, substantially increase the purchasing power of farmers even though their effects on aggregate non-farm employment may be negligible. In the absence of public intervention, agriculture responds to recession by reducing prices, and industry (to a large extent) by reducing output and employment. Public policy has been directed toward stabilizing prices in agriculture and employment in other sectors. The respective approaches have a simple and direct appeal, and it would be difficult to prove that either of them is wrong.

I should like to correct one of Bonnen's statements. I did not conclude that the present price support program "would lift GNP by 8 per cent." I said that it would, in my model, reduce the *decline* in GNP by 8 per cent. The magnitude involved, about $6 billion, is only 2 per cent of the *level* of GNP.

The argument for Bonnen's hypothesis that prices of unsupported commodities may be adversely affected by the existence of price supports on other commodities is not clear to me, perhaps because some of his assumptions are not stated. In actual practice, price supports *as such* have generally tended to raise the prices of other farm products rather than to lower them. *Acreage restrictions* on price-supported commodities, unless accompanied by tight controls over the use of the acres diverted, may lead to increased production of *unrestricted* commodities and thus to lower prices for such of these as are not supported and as do not compete in demand with price-supported commodities. But this effect is based on acreage restrictions and elasticities of supply, whereas Bonnen seems to base his argument exclusively on elasticities of demand.

The rest of Bonnen's points are well taken, in my opinion. Price support programs are not set up exclusively or even primarily as countercyclical devices. In a broader context, such programs might also be appraised in terms of their effects on the rate of technological advance in agriculture, on the efficiency of resource use within agriculture and the mobility of resources between agriculture and other sectors, on international trade and political relations, on the long-run growth of the economy, and on the short-run expansibility of agriculture to meet emergency needs. I believe that a strong and moderately flexible price support program will make a positive contribution to most of these objectives, and that some negative aspects of the present program can be better corrected by modification than by abandonment of price supports. But these questions are beyond the scope of my paper.

STABILIZATION OF
INTERNATIONAL COMMODITY PRICES

D. Gale Johnson, University of Chicago

The stabilization of international commodity prices as a means of combating depressions has attracted the interest of many able economists and has obtained the support of several well-known and highly respected ones. Keynes and the two Grahams are examples. More recently, the stabilization of international prices has been investigated as a means of preventing the spread of deflation from the presumably unstable economy of the United States to the other trading countries. The proposal is of interest to important groups in the United States, particularly agricultural producers, since many important export products of this country would be included in any such program.

This paper is restricted to a discussion of price stability of primary products—foodstuffs, other agricultural products, and minerals. Even within this group there is a considerable diversity of conditions of demand and supply. However, we can say that the typical primary product has an extremely low price elasticity of demand, a low short- and intermediate-run price elasticity of supply, and a low income elasticity of demand. The first characteristic is probably the most nearly universal of the three and obtains for one of two reasons: either because the primary product is a food and is subject to the generally low price elasticity of demand characteristic of foods, or because it is a raw material constituting only a small part of the total input in any final product and, in the short run at least, used in approximately fixed amounts per unit of output.

The low price elasticity of supply is more apparent for agricultural products than for mineral products. Most agricultural products are produced by independent proprietors who face highly inelastic supply functions for factors, while increasingly the production of minerals is undertaken by large firms or combines that can adapt their output to shifts in aggregate demand.

The low income elasticity of demand is a less widespread characteristic—iron ore, for example, has a relatively high income elasticity as do most minerals, rubber, and some textiles. Foodstuffs have low income elasticities. At first glance it might appear that a low in-

357

come elasticity of demand would be favorable to price stability in that variations in real income would have little influence upon the level of demand for the product. And this would be true if either the price elasticity of supply or that of demand, or both, were relatively high. But if these two elasticities are low, large variations in prices during a business cycle are not precluded.[1]

Effect of Price Elasticities on Price Stability

The low price elasticities of supply and demand are important in contributing to price instability because in this setting speculative activity may increase price instability at certain times, though not universally. This is not meant to constitute a condemnation of speculative activity—it does little good to condemn an activity that cannot be eliminated. Any commodity that has some degree of durability ("relatively low" cost of storage per unit of time) must be held by someone. Decisions must be made concerning the quantity of stocks and their location—it is these decisions that constitute speculative activity.

When price elasticities are low, signals that prices are "too high"

---

[1] The price behavior of primary products in response to changes in income can be readily indicated. If we assume constant price and income elasticities, with income having no effect on the quantity supplied, we have:

(1) $$q = p^{-a}Y^{\beta}$$

(2) $$q = p^{\gamma}$$

Equation 1 is the demand function. If we wish to determine the effect of changes in income on changes in price, we have $p^{\gamma} = p^{-a}Y^{\beta}$ or $p^{\gamma+a} = Y^{\beta}$ or $p = Y^{\beta}/(\gamma+a)$. The elasticity of price with respect to income is $\beta/(\gamma+a)$. Thus if the price and income elasticities are .1, the elasticity of price with respect to income is .5. If the elasticity of supply (γ) were zero in the short run, the elasticity of price with respect to income would be unity, i.e. the decline in price would be the same as the decline in income. If all three elasticities are unity, it is apparent that the elasticity of price with respect to income is .5. The influence of high elasticities of supply is immediately apparent. Assume income and price elasticities of demand equal to unity, but a price elasticity of supply equal to 5 (which is probably an underestimate for such industries as automobiles and steel for downward price adjustments); the elasticity of price with respect to income would be only 1/6.

While a large price elasticity of supply will give considerable stability to price, it does not necessarily stabilize gross income unless the income elasticity of demand is very low (appreciably less than unity). The following cases may be used for illustrative purposes, assuming a decline in income of 40 per cent: (1) Gross income would fall by 22 per cent if price and income elasticities of demand were .1 and the supply elasticity were .1; if the supply elasticity were 5.0, the decline in gross income would be 4.7 per cent. (2) If the price and income elasticities of demand were both unity, gross income would fall by 40 per cent for any value of the elasticity of supply.

or "too low" are very slow in making their appearance. If certain expectations about prices during a specified period (say, the year following the coffee harvest) have resulted in current prices that will restrict consumption during the period and create larger stocks at the end of the year than firms would be willing to hold at current prices, then an attempt will be made to reduce inventory holdings and prices may fall below the level prevailing at the beginning of the period.[2] The low price elasticity makes this type of price behavior possible since it may take several months for the small reduction in consumption to reveal itself in terms of increased inventories, especially since the data on inventories are always subject to error. If the price elasticity of demand were relatively high (say 1.0 or more), it would soon become apparent that consumption was occurring at too low a rate and price adjustments could occur rather promptly.

It should be noted that price stability for internationally traded products will not entirely insulate the level of income and employment in other countries from the effect of recession or depression in one country. As the examples in footnote 1 indicate, a decline in

[2] Let me illustrate by a hypothetical example: Assume a constant price elasticity of demand of .2 for a product at the final demand level for final use (thus excluding the demand for inventories). Total supply is 1.2 billion units for the time period. Normal working stocks (the amount held when there is no expectation of a price change during the period) are 200 million units. Something occurs that indicates demand will increase and decisions are made to increase stocks to 300 million units, thus cutting consumption by 10 per cent and increasing the price by 50 per cent. If the price rises by 50 per cent, it is not unreasonable that inventory holders will revise their expectations and attempt to increase inventories to 400 million units, thus resulting in a price approximately double the price at the beginning of the period. Assume that demand at the final consumer level has, in fact, not increased. Because of the relatively small effect on the rate of consumption, it may take one-half the time period before inventory holders realize that demand has not increased. Thus with no price change total stocks (assuming equal consumption per unit of time) would have been 700 million units at the end of one-half of the time period. With the price having doubled, stocks will be 800 million, or even less if the price rise occurred fairly evenly during the first half. If this is taken as a signal by inventory holders that final demand has not increased and an attempt is made to reduce inventories to the normal level of 200 million units, consumption will have to increase by at least 10 per cent over the rate that would have prevailed during the second half had prices remained stable during the entire period. Thus price movements during the period may be from 100 to 200 and then down to 50 by the end of the period. It is possible that as the price falls below 100, inventory holders will be willing to hold more than 200 million units as working stocks since it may be assumed that the price will return to 100 in the next period, but there is no certainty that such decisions will be made before the price falls to 50. During such a decline in price, some inventory holders will be forced to liquidate holdings because of capital impairments; others who gained liquid assets during the price rise may not purchase for inventories until they believe the price decline has been halted.

demand can have as much effect on the gross income from a product whose price is stabilized by an elastic supply function as on that from a product with highly inelastic supply and demand functions and a low income elasticity. If the income elasticity of demand is fairly high and the decline in real income large, gross income from the commodity with a stable price (highly elastic supply function) will fall sharply. Farmers' expenditures for farm machinery between 1929 and 1932 are an example of this latter type of shift. The output of farm products was unchanged, prices declined by 56 per cent, and cash receipts declined by 58 per cent. Farm machinery prices declined by 9 per cent; farmers' expenditures for farm machinery by 80 per cent. The effect of the 1937–1938 depression on the value of imports is another example. The unit value of jute imports declined by 1 per cent, the quantity of imports by 62 per cent, and the total value of imports by 63 per cent. On the other hand, the unit value of coconut oil decreased by 47 per cent, the value of imports decreased by 43 per cent, and the quantity of imports increased by 8 per cent.

While agreement on specific methods may be difficult, it is not impossible to stabilize the prices of a number of internationally traded products. In fact, if a commodity has a low income elasticity, low price elasticities of supply and demand, and relatively low costs of storage, such stabilization may not be difficult. Several examples may be given. Since 1948 the United States has gone a considerable distance in stabilizing the prices of cotton and tobacco, and the United States and Canada together have effectively stabilized wheat prices. Through various forms of internal controls and long-term contracts with the United Kingdom, New Zealand and Denmark have stabilized for the past six years the price of butter moving in international trade.

But in stabilizing prices within a fairly narrow range, the United States and Canada have not been able to stabilize export earnings. Between 1952 and 1953 the value of cotton exports declined by almost two-fifths though unit export value declined only a sixth, while United States wheat export revenues also declined by two-fifths and unit export value decreased about 7 per cent. But it should be noted that in the United States, and to a considerable degree in Canada, the gross returns received by producers were not affected to any significant extent by the decline in export returns. As a result, the purchasing power—or level of expenditures of farmers—was maintained despite the drop in export earnings.

Price Stabilization Measures

The methods that might be used to stabilize the prices of primary products that move in international trade may be classified into three general categories: [3]

1. Control of the amount moving in international trade by the use of import and export quotas, buttressed when necessary by output restrictions in the major producing countries
2. The establishment of sufficient stocks of each individual commodity to permit moderating price changes of each product
3. The establishment of a joint buffer stock operation for many commodities with the objective of stabilizing the average prices of a number of commodities, but not the price of any individual commodity

The second and third methods are related in that both rely upon variations in stocks rather than upon direct control of the amounts traded or produced. But they differ in terms of objectives and probably in terms of the appropriate institutional arrangements.

Past experience indicates that the first method has usually failed. The only important exception is the United States tobacco program in which a remarkable degree of price stabilization has been achieved by unilateral limitation of output supplemented by a storage program. With the increasing output of tobacco in other parts of the world, especially in Africa, success may bring its own undoing within the next decade. Multilateral arrangements—commodity agreements—have not had any noticeable degree of success. The 1949 International Wheat Agreement's moderate success was due more to the United States and Canadian storage program than to the Agreement itself. The difficulties of maintaining such agreements are well illustrated by the failure of the United States and the United Kingdom to reach agreement on the appropriate price range at the time of renewal.

It is reasonable, I believe, to argue that no price stabilization scheme can function without provision for the possible accumulation of relatively large stocks, and, perhaps more important, for a control of such stocks strong enough to prevent their untimely liquidation. The experience of the Federal Farm Board was evidence of the importance of stock control, while various interna-

---

[3] I will not discuss a fourth type of arrangement in which an exporter agrees to a price that is too low—a price at which there is excess demand. I suspect that some of the success of Denmark and New Zealand in stabilizing the price of butter since 1948 has been due to this kind of pricing.

tional commodity agreements failed largely because they did not provide adequate stock provisions.

It should also be noted that price stabilization achieved by control of the quantities moving in international trade does not achieve stability in the value of trade. Thus even if the first method could be operated successfully in stabilizing prices by controlling the amount traded and the amount produced, its countercyclical features would be relatively unimportant for the products with relatively high income elasticities. However, it must be noted that buffer stock operations increase in difficulty as the income elasticities of demand approach and exceed unity.

Commodity Reserves

Joint buffer stock operations that involve stabilizing the average price of a group of commodities and not the price of any one have impressive support.[4] These proposals usually take one of two forms—the use of the commodity reserves as a monetary base or as a separate operation with no direct link to national currencies.

The use of the commodity reserves as a monetary standard, in the same sense that gold has been used, seems to me to be beset with many and important difficulties with few offsetting advantages. Friedman's conclusion that a commodity reserve currency has most of the disadvantages of a gold standard while lacking its emotional appeal is difficult to refute. Compared with a fiat standard, the commodity reserve is much more expensive and would probably be no less subject to political manipulation.[5] Many requirements must be met before the commodity reserve scheme could operate as a true international standard. For example, there would have to be free trade in the commodities in the unit and the nations would have to accommodate their monetary and fiscal policies to the requirements imposed by stable exchange rates. Thus if a country were losing reserves of the commodity unit, it would have to permit a contraction of its money supply and perhaps follow a deflationary fiscal policy.

But there would be, in my opinion, no need to operate the commodity reserve as a monetary unit. Such a reserve could be operated either by an international agency or by the cooperation of a

[4] For a partial bibliography of such proposals see *Commodity Trade and Economic Development,* United Nations (E/2519), 1953, p. 35, and for a general discussion see *ibid.,* pp. 35–36 and 55–66.

[5] Milton Friedman, "Commodity-Reserve Currency," *Journal of Political Economy,* June 1951, pp. 230–232.

number of individual governments. The value of the unit could be expressed in terms of any one currency or any of a group of currencies freely convertible one to the other. The major political difficulty would be that of getting sufficient financial support to prevent the venture from collapsing at an unpropitious moment. How large the financial resources would have to be would depend upon the number of commodities included in the unit, the nature of their demand and supply functions, and the extent of changes in demand during the course of a business cycle.

But leaving the problem of finance aside, how satisfactorily would such a proposal operate? One of the first requirements for successful operation would be a self-imposed restraining ordinance by all or most members of the trading world to limit or eliminate their own price support operations. It would also be highly desirable if importing countries either allowed free trade in the commodities in the unit or maintained a constant degree of protection during the business cycle. If a country—say, the United States—had sufficiently large stocks of a commodity included in the unit, purchases of that commodity would have little or no effect on its price and if made from United States stocks would have no expansionary effects on demand. Thus price variations that would occur within the unit would be concentrated upon commodities without domestic price support programs.

If a large number of commodities were included in the unit, the degree of price instability for any one commodity would be relatively large. Price variability due to individual demand and output variability would not be eliminated. For example, the recent rise in coffee prices could not have been prevented if the commodity reserve had been in operation—nor could the subsequent fall.

But what of price variability related to the cycle? How would different commodities fare if the only source of variability were cyclical variability in demand? Three examples may help answer these questions.

In the first, it is assumed that there are only two commodities, A and B, and that they have equal importance in the commodity unit. Commodity A has a price elasticity of demand and of supply and an income elasticity equal to .1, while B has elasticities equal to 1.0.[6] Real per capita incomes fall by 30 per cent and it is desired to

---

[6] The statements concerning price and income elasticities are only approximately accurate. For ease of calculation, linear relationships were used and the elasticities relate to the prices, quantities, and incomes that prevailed prior to the decline in income.

hold the value of the unit at 100. The prices of both A and B equaled 100 before the drop in real income. Under these assumptions the price of A would rise to 112.5 and that of B would fall to 87.5. Without the commodity reserve, the prices of both commodities would have fallen to 85; thus almost all of the direct gain would have gone to the producers of commodity A.

In the second example, the characteristics of commodity A remain the same, but the supply elasticity for commodity B now is the same as for A (other characteristics as before). In this example, if the value of the unit were maintained at 100 by purchases, the price of A would be 120 and the price of B, 80. Without the program, the price of B would be about 73.

In our third example, all elasticities remain the same as in the second except that the price elasticity of demand for B is now changed to .5. After the decline in demand, the price of A would be about 134 and the price of B about 65 (instead of 50 without the program).

The above examples are not unrealistic, and I believe that groups of commodities can be found that have the characteristics of A (wheat, rye, tobacco) and the characteristics of B (the third variant is more likely than the first two because it is doubtful if any raw materials have a short-run price elasticity as high as unity). Commodities with the characteristics of B (third variant) might include rubber, jute, and perhaps cotton and wool. The first variant of B might include copper and tin, since the price elasticity can be reduced to .5 without having much effect on the results. These presumptions are admittedly made on the basis of inadequate evidence —more especially, inadequate analysis on the available data. But the absolute values of the elasticities are less important than the value of one commodity relative to that of another. If the income elasticities differ from commodity to commodity, their relative prices will be affected by additions to or deletions from the reserve.

Let us extend this exercise, using the third example as a base. Assume that, during recovery from a depression, an inflation occurs in the trading world. For a period of time, commodity units are sold at the same rate per unit of time as they were accumulated. (Real income returns to the pre-depression level, but other costs lag enough so that the average price of the unit can remain at 100 only if sales are made from the reserve.) The price of A would fall to 75, while the price of B would increase to 125. As the inflation is checked and other costs rise to reduce the demand for A and B or as the price of the unit is increased to prevent further sales, the relative prices of A and B would return to unity.

If these examples are not extreme, it is possible that the operations of the commodity reserve would introduce fairly significant variations in the prices of the commodities included in the unit. More price variability would probably occur without such a program, given a specified decline in real income. However, I can give examples which would contradict this statement.

So far as I know, none of those interested in commodity reserve proposals have discussed the problems that would arise because of differences in income elasticities and, to a lesser degree, in price elasticities of supply and demand. Such differences might present international political problems of a serious character. The major producers of many commodities similar to A are the rich countries of the world—the United States, Canada, and Australia—while some of the commodities falling in the B group come from poor areas.

There is a solution to the difficulties discussed above: each commodity in the unit might be appropriately weighted. The relative weights would have to be based upon the income elasticities of demand, but this requirement does not preclude taking into account the relative importance of the commodities in world trade or in total production. However, we may assume for the moment that all commodities would be given equal quantitative weight in the commodity reserve unit. It would then be necessary to make the weights proportional to the income elasticities of demand. Thus, if the income elasticity of demand for A were 1.0, for B, .5, and for C, .1, the reserve unit would consist of 10 units of A, 5 units of B, and only 1 unit of C. During a deflation the greater purchases of A and B relative to C would act to stabilize the prices of A, B, and C separately as well as in combination (if the supply functions did not contain a random element).

This solution has some major drawbacks: estimates of income elasticities may be unreliable; relative income elasticities may not be stable throughout the cycle; income elasticities prevailing in any one business cycle may be affected by the primary source of the decline or expansion of demand. In any case, it may be argued that, once one has modified the reserve unit in the required direction, there is much to be gained by purchasing commodities as a unit instead of separately.

Buffer Stocks for Individual Commodities

The establishment of separate buffer stock programs for each commodity (or for a group of commodities with similar income elasticities of demand) would eliminate the problem of the commodity reserve unit discussed above. But, even if several such programs were operated by a single international agency, there would be a problem of choosing the appropriate price range for individual commodity buffer stocks. How rapidly stocks can accumulate if the price is set somewhat too high can be seen from United States experience in butter, cotton, and wheat during 1951–1952 and 1952–1953. It is also evident that seemingly large stocks of an individual commodity can disappear very rapidly. Because the Department of Agriculture expected large stocks of cotton to be in existence by the fall of 1950, steps were taken in late 1949 to impose acreage limitations on cotton. Because of a small United States crop (due mainly to bad weather) combined with the expanded demand after June 1950, United States stocks declined from 6.8 million bales in August 1950 to 2.2 million in August 1951, even though the government imposed restrictive *export* quotas. It may be noted that the world supply of cotton for 1950–1951 was only 3 per cent smaller than for 1949–1950, the price of Brazilian cotton increased by 125 per cent in the nine months following June 1950, and the price of United States cotton (even with the export quota) increased 55 per cent in a year. The reduction in United States stocks was about 14 per cent of an average world crop of cotton, and the actual cotton used increased by 12.5 per cent between 1949–1950 and 1950–1951.

While it is true that individual buffer stock schemes would not tend to increase the prices of commodities with low income elasticities during a period of decline in demand, it is not certain that such schemes could reduce price variability for products with a high income elasticity and low price elasticity of demand. In other words, the size of the stocks that might be accumulated at the end of a deflationary period if prices were effectively stabilized might be beyond the limits of either the storage capacity or the financial resources of any international agency. The rise in the price of natural rubber following March 1950 may illustrate the opposite side of the problem—the size of stocks that would have been required to limit the rise in natural rubber prices during the next year or so. In 1949, natural rubber output was 1,514,000 metric tons; in 1950, output was 1,890,000 tons. In the year June 1949 through May 1950, United States output of synthetic and reclaimed rubber was 516,000 long tons; the next year output was 1,005,000 long tons. Ignoring increases in synthetic and reclaimed output elsewhere in the world, the increase in available supplies of rubber was at least 42 per cent. The price of Malayan rubber was 17.6 cents a pound in March 1949, 70.9 cents in

March 1951, and an average of 46.4 cents in the third quarter of 1951. Thus there was approximately a threefold increase in price (at one time a fourfold increase) even though output increased nearly 50 per cent in a year. If this had been a product with a very low short-run price elasticity of supply (say, .1 or less), stocks equal to a years' output of natural rubber might well have been required to have stabilized prices. And who, one might ask, would have had the foresight to have stored 1.5 million tons of natural rubber by early 1950? The output of natural rubber had increased fivefold since 1945 and still gave evidence of increasing further, while synthetic rubber output in the United States was 50 per cent below 1945. Few people really believed that the price of natural rubber would ever again go above the United States price for synthetic rubber (about 18 cents in 1949). Consequently, even if there were no problem of storage capacity or financial resources, it is hard to imagine that any buffer stock agency would have been able to prevent the rise in the price of rubber—or of cotton or wool or jute or tin or zinc—that ocurred after early or mid-1950.

Buffer stocks could have been used to prevent most of the declines in prices that occurred in 1948 and 1949. But in most cases—an exception was some foodstuffs with very low income elasticities of demand—the stocks accumulated in these two years would have been too small to have much effect upon the level of prices following June 1950. And the post-Korean decline in prices of primary products came before anyone had even hinted that the United States was in a dip, recession, or depression. In fact, the stability of primary product prices since July 1953 has been remarkable. It seems unlikely that any buffer stock agency would have tried to stem the downward movement of primary product prices that started in the second and third quarters of 1951 for several products. Given the high levels of employment and income that existed throughout the world, a decline in the prices of many primary products to pre-Korean levels seemed to many a necessary preface to longer-run equilibrium between supply and demand. And would not the United Kingdom and other Western European countries have strongly resisted stabilizing the prices of foodstuffs and raw materials at levels substantially above those of early 1950?

It should be noted that a part of the stability of primary product prices since July 1953 has been due to stock operations in the United States. These operations have been of great importance in the wheat, tobacco, and cotton markets and probably in some of the metal markets. But the stability of price of at least one product—

wheat—has been purchased at the expense of postponing a resource adjustment that appears to be inevitable.

Thus I suggest, on the basis of fairly continuous observation of storage programs in the United States and in two or three other countries, that storage programs for individual products could go some distance in providing a marked degree of price stability under certain circumstances. They could (1) reduce intra-year variations when final demand is reasonably stable; (2) prevent, where the income elasticity of demand is relatively small, significant price rises in a strong inflationary movement like that after June 1950; and (3) prevent price declines resulting from declining demand like that of 1948–1949, and probably also like that of 1937–1938, and even of 1929–1933. In a major depression large financial resources would of course be required and provision for additional storage space would be necessary.

But the degree of price stability achieved would be purchased at some cost. The cost of storage is the most direct and obvious, since direct annual storage costs (excluding interest on the value of the product) frequently amount to 8 to 12 per cent of the value of the product. Another cost can be the result of mistaken price expectations on the part of the storage agency, but this cost may be at least partly if not fully offset by the effects of greater price stability upon the allocation of resources. If one can generalize from United States experience, the introduction of greater price stability may lead to more rapid adoption of new methods of production and may induce greater emphasis upon profit maximization and less upon safety considerations in production planning.

Buffering Major United States Imports

It is obvious that the increase in expenditure by governments or an international agency for commodity reserves during a deflation would have a desirable influence upon the general level of incomes in the trading world. There would be a multiplier greater than unity, and the level of imports of areas specializing in and exporting primary products would be higher than if no such program existed.

But it must be noted that the relative importance in world income of the primary products that are relatively cheap to store is not very great, surely less than one-sixth and perhaps not more than one-tenth. The value of such products actually entering into international trade in 1950 outside the Soviet bloc, according to an estimate in *Commodity Trade and Economic Development,* was $18 billion. Thus if a storage agency had added to stocks the equivalent to the total value of world exports of some thirty-six primary products (excluding only lumber, hides, fertilizers, meat, milk, cheese, and certain oil seeds) in 1950, this amount would have been less than 7 per cent of the United States gross national product in that year.

A serious decline in world economic activity would obviously require antirecession measures of a much greater leverage. These would have to be measures carried out primarily by individual governments, operating almost wholly within their own national borders. However, if restrictions on trade were not utilized, the impact of such national measures would be felt by primary producers throughout the world. It is true that the expenditure of a dollar upon primary products for stockpiling would have more effect upon the incomes of jute producers than would the expenditure of a dollar paid out in the United Kingdom as unemployment compensation. But, in any case, the buffer stock program must be considered as only one of a number of measures required to stop a world-wide deflation, or for that matter, a world-wide inflation.

If I were a producer of a primary product, I am not certain that I would choose a countercyclical program that placed a great deal of emphasis upon stockpiling of primary products. If the price of my product is increased by adding to stocks now, the price will be decreased when stocks are reduced later. Under certain plausible circumstances it is possible for such operations to reduce the aggregate income from a product for a business cycle as a whole.

Many persons outside this country fear, not a world-wide depression, but a United States depression serious enough to create foreign exchange problems for many nations and to interrupt the flow of investment in underdeveloped areas. Since such a large share of United States merchandise imports consists of primary products, a buffer stock program operating on a relatively modest scale could insulate other parts of the world fairly effectively from declining United States demands. For example, the United States sugar program stabilizes the dollar earnings of Cuba and the Philippines from sugar exports to us, and the recently announced purchase of certain metals acts to stabilize their prices.

As a means of maintaining the demand for its exports, the United States might well consider a rather systematic buffer stock program for a number of major imports. Such programs should be worked out in cooperation with the most important exporting groups, and, in addition, the interests of competing importers should not be ignored. This program should be confined to the objective of counteracting fluctuations in dollar expenditures for primary products resulting from changes in aggregate demand in the United States.

But a proposal for a United States program of buffer stocks for durable imports certainly should be secondary to more general monetary and fiscal measures designed to minimize declines in aggregate demand. In fact, all countercyclical buffer stock schemes can at best be considered as only one element in a much more inclusive program to prevent the occurrence and spread of depressions.

COMMENT

WILFRED MALENBAUM, Massachusetts Institute of Technology

Stabilization of prices of internationally traded raw materials and agricultural products is not a very potent tool for combating recessions in the United States. This would be true even if we could assume our entire domestic agricultural price support program to be subsumed under some major international scheme. On this assumption the international scheme would have about the same leverage effects upon a downswing as would our present domestic supports. In Karl Fox's model,[1] these supports mean that gross national product falls less than it would without the support program—somewhat under 10 per cent less. This estimate takes full account of the multiplier effects of the expanded agricultural (and related service) incomes. But it is unrealistic to expect that our domestic programs would ever be handled through an international program. A scheme aimed at primary products which we export might more easily be visualized, but its role as an antirecession device would be significantly smaller. Expanded incomes from the tobacco, cotton, rice, wheat, and dried fruit exported would provide only very small stimulating effects for the United States economy. Indeed, it is hard to imagine any plan for international stabilization in these commodities which would add to the effects generated by our domestic agricultural support programs in which our export commodities are of course included.

Perhaps an international program would have more important indirect effects by stimulating exports from the United States. Thus

[1] See "The Contribution of Farm Price Support Programs to General Economic Stability," in this volume.

if a price stabilization scheme succeeded in expanding incomes in those countries where exports of primary products loom large in total incomes, purchases from the United States might be expected to increase. And the increase need not be confined only to the imports of countries directly affected by the stabilization program. These countries would also be purchasing more from third countries that might then import more from the United States. Nonetheless, the total of such expanded exports could not provide large stimulants to our economy.

On the whole, therefore, I agree with Johnson that the stabilization of international commodity prices is not an important tool for combating possible United States recessions. But a recession here may have major consequences for other countries. And some of the other devices which might well be used to counter recessions could even aggravate their "exported" effects. A curtailment of our imports can be expected to weigh more heavily upon exporters of manufactured goods, but directly and indirectly this will also affect producers of primary products. An international stabilization scheme might at least mitigate such tendencies to export our depressions.

It cannot be assumed, however, that the maintenance of United States import demand over the cycle is the basic problem with which primary exporting countries are concerned. Thus even the record levels of our national product, and our imports, through 1953 have been accompanied by growing pressures for international commodity price stabilization by important producers of raw materials entering into world trade. Year-to-year fluctuations in primary product prices would, of course, be most significant for those economies in which foreign trade is large relative to the national product and where primary goods form an important component of total international trade. With few exceptions the countries which meet these criteria are the underdeveloped countries—from Mexico, with exports at about 10 per cent of its national product and primary commodities providing about 50 per cent of exports, to Ceylon, where the foreign sector is almost 40 per cent of the national product and three primary goods constitute 90 per cent of exports.

In most underdeveloped areas there is a need for net importation of capital from abroad. In general they are countries where savings ratios simply do not permit enough investment of domestic resources under existing technological conditions to compete with the rates of population growth. Their own resources need to be supplemented from abroad if per capita income is to expand. In these countries, foreign exchange earnings are particularly important to their development programs; they need to purchase foreign products. Favorable shifts in their terms of trade (if not stabilization of export prices as such) can also provide at least a partial alternative to foreign investment, loans, and grants. Thus an interesting calculation recently made by the Department of State [2] suggests that the countries of South and Southeast Asia earned from their exports over $2 billion (1949–1950 prices) more in the period June 1950 through December 1952 simply because of the changed relationship between import and export prices after 1949–1950. (The increased earnings are $3.5 billion if account is also taken of the expanded volume of exports.) The commodities most responsible for these earnings were rubber, tin, and rice. There were similar developments for producers in other areas. The expanded incomes of the underdeveloped areas considerably enhanced their resources available for investment. Such improvements can also increase the capacity of these countries to borrow from abroad.

Our interest in some form of international commodity stabilization is thus an essential adjunct of our interest in the development of friendly nations throughout the world. This emphasis also points up the complementarity between stabilization schemes and aid. Economic development may, of course, provide some solution to the problems of instability. A frequent objective of development programs in underdeveloped areas is the diversification of the economy (less emphasis upon primary production at least for the export market and more emphasis on self-sufficiency). The same amount of instability in the prices of internationally traded commodities will have smaller effects (relatively) as this objective is achieved. This is obviously a long path to the solution, but it is probably the basic one.

It is this aspect of international commodity stabilization which makes the subject of particular importance to us, rather than any effects it may have upon cyclical fluctuations in the United States. Of course our policy of development in other lands does have great significance for long-range growth of the United States economy. The economic health of that major sector of the world's people who live in the underdeveloped areas has basic economic implications for our own future growth. One need not stress here the political implications for the United States of development in these areas.

Stabilization of What? In a recent excellent study by a United Nations group of experts, *Commodity Trade and Economic De-*

[2] "Foreign Trade Developments in South and Southeast Asia, 1950–52," unclassified *Intelligence Report* No. 6349, August 1953.

velopment, stabilization of prices usually meant the reduction of short-period fluctuations about a trend. The experts were (or tried to be) concerned with fluctuations which play an uncertain, or relatively unimportant, role in efficient resource allocation or income distribution. Such stabilization may be important, and particularly for countries with less well-organized marketing systems. Many of the underdeveloped areas fall into this last category. But, at least in my experience, this type of stabilization is only a partial concern of most of the countries seeking stabilization. With respect to prices of primary products alone, they usually seek a new trend, perhaps one that is fitted to the peaks of past fluctuations. More frequently, the new trend is one which maintains some parallelism with the trend in prices of manufactured products. This last implies some form of the parity concept, and is usually based upon the experience of a past period in which the relationship was not unfavorable to primary producers. Stabilization which results in a shift in the terms of trade will of course mean that importers of raw materials, let us say, will have to pay more for their imports than they would in the absence of a stabilization program.

Most commodity agreements imply such a transfer as of one period, with the expectation that there will be a compensating advantage to the importer at a later time, when prices in the absence of an agreement will be more favorable to the exporter. Such arrangements would seem to balance benefits over time between buyers and sellers, at least if the base period for the parity ratio was not too unrepresentative. My experience with actual commodity agreements is too limited to permit a generalization as to the degree of balancing-out that is in fact achieved. In the case of wheat, however, all transfers have to date been in only one direction. It remains to be seen whether wheat will in fact move under the present Agreement should world prices fall below the lower limit of the stipulated price range.

A stabilization scheme satisfactory to the primary producers will involve, at least initially, some transfer of resources from importing countries. Again there is some parallel with foreign assistance. Since I believe that foreign assistance is necessary in many of these countries, I have little objection to this aspect of a price stabilization program.

Presumably a country is more interested in stability of income or of foreign exchange earnings than in stability of prices. Quite obviously, high prices (however stable) accompanied by low quantities can be less advantageous under certain supply conditions than lower prices and much larger quantities. However logical it may be to concentrate upon a measure which reflects both prices and quantities, emphasis continues to remain upon stabilization of prices. This is consistent with the United States experience with parity incomes and parity prices for agricultural products. It can be explained in part by the great difficulties of administering schemes for income stabilization. Usually, however, stabilization of prices turns out to be more favorable to the producer, particularly since "stable" prices have tended to contribute to a general expansion in supply—to larger quantities.

A focus on price stability when the real objective is stability in returns prompts some concern about elasticity relationships. Johnson's discussion of this subject provides one of the most provocative sections of his paper. My disagreements with him stem largely from his use of elasticities, whether of price or income, in the form in which they are generally computed, i.e. on a national or on a total commodity basis. Neither of these is very relevant for problems of earnings from international trade. Here we are usually concerned with only one part of a nation's (or the world's) total supply of a commodity. The important variable is the volume of imports, which for many products is a difference between what is consumed and what is domestically produced (of the same or substitutable commodities). Indeed, the pertinent variable may be the volume of imports from a particular source. These residuals may well vary quite differently from total demand. Thus even though the demand for wheat is inelastic with respect both to prices and to income, and therefore the per capita consumption of wheat in France, say, varies little from year to year, there can obviously be great variations in France's demand for wheat from the United States. For a product which is produced and consumed broadly throughout the world (as is the case for most primary goods), elasticity computations for total supply and for total demand give little guidance to the price-income relationship for the exported component of the supply. This is even truer of course with respect to that component of exports going to, or coming from, a particular country. If an important United States interest in stabilization is to maintain the export earnings (or the dollar earnings) of a particular underdeveloped area, we must be concerned with the problem on an individual country (or group of countries) basis. Stabilization of prices for a commodity, or even of total payments for our imports of the commodity, will not assure this objective, whatever the over-all elasticities.

Techniques for Stabilization. On the usual proposals for price stabilization, I have little to add to the views presented in Johnson's paper. I share his general pessimism about the possibilities of achieving stabilization through export and import quotas and through buffer stock schemes either for individual or for groups of commodities. I would agree that, of all these, the buffer stock procedures for single commodities offer the most hope. Where they have been practiced in some form (and by countries willing to pay the price, like the United States), price maintenance and stability have been achieved. On an international basis there is still room for more study and more attempts toward workable arrangements. However, the nature of the problem, at least for the United States today, suggests that the greatest progress will be achieved with schemes of stabilization which come under the general heading of compensatory mechanisms.

Stabilization measures might well play a larger part in our programs of foreign aid to a particular country. There have been proposals for compensatory payments to meet marked changes in a country's foreign exchange earnings. These have usually involved more or less automatic recourse to the resources of the International Monetary Fund or the World Bank. The response to them has generally been unenthusiastic, and, at least in my opinion, appropriately so. Payments should be extended on a selective basis, and as an integral part of cooperative efforts to accelerate economic growth in particular countries. Their form might well be long-period purchase contracts for raw materials, at prices which would probably be above the market level. While this could be done by groups of purchasing countries acting together, the United States should be prepared to take steps in this direction on its own. This may of course require some form of stock-building programs by the United States, and some new arrangements relating the public program to private production, distribution, and use.

Finally, such treatment of the stabilization problem can provide a means of influencing the usage of foreign exchange earnings in the underdeveloped country. Favorable terms of trade in the past have frequently been followed by lower-priority use of the favorable exchange position in which individual countries have found themselves. Careful planning for the use of these earnings is essential if the stabilization measures are in fact to contribute to economic growth, the main focus of the United States interest in the problem.

INTERNATIONAL CURRENCY AND
RESERVE PLANS

ROBERT TRIFFIN, YALE UNIVERSITY

Introduction

The hopeful plans for currency convertibility drawn up ten years ago at the Bretton Woods Conference have long been buried under the weight of the so-called dollar shortage which accompanied postwar reconstruction, the Korean crisis, and the first years of Western rearmament. The year 1953 witnessed, at long last, a fundamental and spectacular readjustment in the world's payments pattern. From gold and dollar deficits of nearly $11 billion in 1947, foreign countries moved gradually to an actual surplus, before aid, of nearly $1 billion in 1953. Their gold and dollar holdings—including United States aid receipts—dropped by nearly $6 billion in the three years 1946–1948, but have risen since by $8 billion, of which $2.6 billion was accumulated in 1953 alone.

National and international plans for currency convertibility have thus become again, for the first time in many years, a practical policy issue. The problem was raised here, on the initiative of the United Kingdom, a little more than a year ago, but the British suggestions were received with a surprising lack of enthusiasm in this country, in continental Europe, and even in Britain. The discussion of the plan soon revealed fundamental disagreements about the very meaning of convertibility under present economic and political conditions.

The Commission on Foreign Economic Policy, under the able chairmanship of Clarence B. Randall, devoted considerable attention to the issues involved. Its report,[1] issued last January, has done much to clarify the intimate relationship between the trade and the payments aspects of international convertibility. In the meantime the British plan was discussed further in the Organization for European Economic Cooperation (OEEC) and at the Commonwealth Conference in Sidney. Important steps toward the broadening of currency transferability and the relaxation of dollar restrictions have

[1] *Report to the President and the Congress,* Commission on Foreign Economic Policy, 1954.

also been taken in recent months by a number of major countries, particularly the United Kingdom, Germany, and the Netherlands.

The United States recession and the Congressional debate on the Randall report induced a wait-and-see attitude that slowed down the adoption of even more spectacular decisions, both nationally and internationally. There is little doubt, however, that such decisions will soon be forthcoming, and that they will be vitally influenced by the long-overdue clarification of United States policies.

The 1953 British Plan and the Randall Report

The plan presented by the British last spring rested essentially on a distinction between convertibility for residents and convertibility for nonresidents. The United Kingdom proposed to restore the convertibility of sterling earned in current transactions [2] by *nonresidents of the sterling area,* but to retain the right, for the United Kingdom as well as for other sterling area countries, to impose restrictions on all foreign transactions of their own residents. These restrictions could, of course, be imposed in order to limit the foreigners' sterling earnings and the drain on the area's gold and foreign exchange reserves which might attend the conversion of such earnings into nonsterling currencies, particularly dollars. They could, moreover, be imposed on a discriminatory or even bilateral basis to restrict imports from the countries presenting "excessive" demands for conversion and to favor imports from the countries which retained their earnings in sterling or made use of them to expand their purchases from the area itself. The proposal was made conditional upon a substantial liberalization of United States trade policies and the granting of large stabilization loans or lines of credit to the United Kingdom by the International Monetary Fund and by the United States.

The major criticism leveled against the plan, both here and abroad, was that its adoption might well stimulate a new wave of trade restrictions, discrimination, and bilateralism. The Randall report agreed with this criticism and indicated that the Commission "would deplore a merely formal convertibility maintained through

[2] The exclusion of convertibility for capital transactions has become generally accepted since Bretton Woods as a permanent feature of postwar convertibility plans. The practical wisdom and feasibility of this exclusion raises very complex issues which I shall make no attempt to discuss here. It might be noted, however, that the International Monetary Fund's example was not followed by the Agreement for a European Payments Union, which applies equally to all transactions among members, whether on current or capital account.

trade restrictions. It believes that the removal of restrictions upon trade and upon payments should go hand in hand." [3]

The continental European countries were particularly fearful of the implications of the British plans for the OEEC trade liberalization program and the European Payments Union. The Randall Commission expressed a similar concern about dismantling prematurely the most effective instrument for trade liberalization and currency transferability established so far: "The Union has achieved an impressive measure of success—above all, it has shown that freeing trade and freeing payment go hand in hand—and the Commission feels that it should not sponsor any measures that might wreck the Union before there is something better to put in its place." [4]

These criticisms may spring in part from an overpessimistic view of the external position of Britain and of the world's so-called "dollar shortage." [5] In the absence of heavy balance of payments pressures, the current trend toward trade liberalization might be expected to develop even without formal commitments, and to be strengthened further by the proposed measures for currency convertibility.

Yet the possibility of renewed balance of payments difficulties— whether in Britain or in other countries—cannot be excluded. Under such circumstances formal convertibility for nonresidents, unaccompanied by parallel commitments with respect to trade policy, might force a relapse into restrictions, discrimination, and bilateralism and destroy the progress already achieved toward a multilateral system of trade and payments.

After all, the proposed sterling convertibility already exists for residents of the United States and other "American account" countries. Sterling earnings accruing to such residents are freely convertible into dollars. Any other country that wishes to is also free to refuse payment in inconvertible sterling, and to demand gold or dollar payment for its exports. Most countries are deterred from doing so by the realization that such a policy would generally expose them to tighter restrictions on their exports to sterling area countries, similar to the restrictions now applied by these countries against imports from the dollar area. Sterling convertibility for nonresidents is certainly not regarded as true convertibility by the United States exporters who already "enjoy" this status, and it is certainly not sought by other countries' exporters to whom this "privilege" is now denied.

These considerations explain the coolness with which the British

[3] *Report to the President and the Congress*, p. 73.
[4] *Ibid.*, p. 74.   [5] See below, pp. 391 ff.

plan was received in continental Europe, in the United States, and even by a large sector of British opinion. While the plan has not been formally amended, numerous indications exist that opinion is gradually shifting, in Britain and elsewhere in Europe, toward a position fairly similar to that expressed in the Randall report. To be meaningful, convertibility must apply to trade as well as payments, to residents as well as nonresidents. This implies that progress can only be gradual and must depend on the fulfillment of certain prerequisites. "The Commission does . . . wish to emphasize its view that a strong internal economy, willing and able to control its money supply and its budget as safeguards against inflation, sufficiently mobile to make the best use of its resources, and able and willing to save in order to increase its productivity and improve its competitive position in world markets, is a prerequisite to convertibility; and that the attainment over time of these conditions should be the guide as to how rapidly full convertibility could safely be approached." [6]

These "prerequisites to convertibility" constitute, indeed, an awesome list, especially if they are viewed not only as once-and-for-all prerequisites for the *restoration* of convertibility, but also as permanent prerequisites for the *maintenance* of convertibility after it has been restored. Will any future lapse from internal strength automatically spell the collapse of convertibility for the country concerned? And how will the failure of some countries to reach or maintain convertibility affect the prospects for the achievement or preservation of *international* convertibility? "The Commission believes that the decisions, the methods, the timetable, and the responsibility for introducing currency convertibility should rest on the countries concerned. It recognizes, however, that currency convertibility must be examined in the light of the policies pursued by other countries, particularly the United States." [7] The Commission thought also that the restoration of convertibility by Britain would greatly facilitate—or even be necessary for—its restoration by other countries, and would in turn be greatly eased "if some other of the major trading countries [were] able to make their currencies convertible simultaneously with sterling." [8]

The Randall report thus seems to contemplate the unilateral restoration of convertibility by each country, acting in isolation, but also recognizes the interdependence among the various countries' deci-

[6] *Report to the President and the Congress,* p. 73.
[7] *Ibid.,* pp 72–73.　　　　　　　　　　[8] *Ibid.,* p. 74.

sions and policies, particularly those of the United States, the United Kingdom, and other major trading countries. The recognition of this interdependence is in happy contrast with the naïve theory which still prevails in academic and business circles, and which long dominated the United States Treasury thinking, i.e. that convertibility merely depends on each country's "setting its own house in order" by stopping inflation, readjusting its exchange rate, abolishing trade and exchange controls, and requiring full gold or convertible currency settlement for its exports and other external transactions. Even a country as strong internally and externally as Switzerland still feels unable to adopt such a prescription and run the risk of generalized discrimination against its exports.

International currency convertibility cannot be restored and—even more important—maintained without the active participation and cooperation of the major trading countries. While this participation and cooperation could largely be taken for granted in the nineteenth century, they cannot be ensured today by mere unilateral decisions, but require at least a minimum of collective organization and mutual commitments.

Before discussing the nature of these commitments, we must clarify the meaning of currency convertibility as an international policy objective. We shall then discover that the necessary commitments are far less formidable than the "convertibility prerequisites" which are listed in the Randall report, and which, indeed, no international agreement could ever be relied upon to enforce effectively.

Toward a Definition of "Workable" Convertibility

Currency convertibility used to be defined by the maintenance of a fixed parity or exchange rate with relation to gold or gold-convertible currencies. But the modern proponents of convertibility argue in favor of flexible or "floating" exchange rates as against fixed or "pegged" rates. The reason for this shift is, of course, obvious. The fixity of exchange rates becomes largely illusory if it is preserved only through trade or exchange restrictions which control arbitrarily the access of traders to foreign exchange for each category of transactions, and may deny them the right to purchase it at any rate whatsoever. Exchange stability has little or no meaning if it is not based on exchange freedom. The latter was taken for granted in all traditional definitions of convertibility. True currency inconvertibility—as distinct from instability of exchange rates—is a relatively modern phenomenon. It might be noted, for instance, that European currencies remained convertible throughout the 1920's, even though at a fluctuating exchange rate.

Here again, the Randall report marks definite progress over previous policies, and particularly over the exaggerated emphasis placed on exchange rate stability at Bretton Woods. The Commission expressed itself as "sympathetic to the concept of a 'floating rate', which provides alternative methods of meeting trade and exchange pressures." [9]

This seems to leave us with the elimination of trade and exchange restrictions as the modern definition of convertibility. The question arises at once whether any full elimination of such restrictions is conceivable within a foreseeable future, and whether such liberalization can realistically be confined to direct, quantitative restrictions while leaving tariff restrictions to the full discretion of each individual country. There are undoubtedly very important differences between tariff restrictions and other trade or exchange restrictions. Most of these differences relate, however, to the *domestic* impact of such measures upon income and money flows. From the point of view of their *international* impact, the differences between tariffs and trade controls are not so fundamental as to justify the definition of convertibility in terms of a full elimination of the latter without any concern for the first. High and unstable tariff levels can indeed be as damaging to international trade as moderate, nondiscriminatory systems of import or exchange controls, or more so.

Shall we therefore be pushed into a definition of convertibility which equates it to the old free trade ideal of classical economists? In this case, progress will indeed have to be gradual, and full convertibility is unlikely to reward our efforts or even those of our children and grandchildren.

Clarity of thought and effectiveness of policy both require a less ambitious definition of immediate convertibility goals. Such a definition can be found in the restoration of a *multilateral system of trade and payments*, rather than in the removal of all protection for domestic production against imports from abroad. This was indeed the meaning of nineteenth-century convertibility, which accommodated itself to varying degrees of national protection. The major differences between these age-old techniques of protection and modern inconvertibility techniques lie in the fact that the former extended protection only to the national producers and only within the protecting country's boundaries, while the latter discriminate in favor

[9] *Ibid.*, p. 73.

of certain exporting countries at the expense of others, and try to protect domestic producers not only within the country's boundaries but in all foreign markets as well. Once adopted by a major country, such techniques inevitably spread from trading partner to trading partner, each country trying to secure special advantages to itself or being forced at least to defend its exporters against the discriminatory actions of others. International trade is then forced more and more into the strait jacket of bilateral negotiations, which push all considerations of price or quality competition and the underlying pattern of comparative costs and advantages into the background.

The key to "workable" convertibility is not free trade—desirable as this would be—but the maintenance of full competition in third markets. MacDougall's study of United States and United Kingdom exports in 1937 showed ample verification for the classical theory of comparative costs, but found that it depended essentially on *third market competition* rather than on direct trade between the two countries. "Before the war, American weekly wages in manufacturing were roughly double the British, and we find that, when American output per worker was more than twice the British, the United States had in general the bulk of the export market, while for the products where it was less than twice as high the bulk of the market was held by Britain. . . . But while in the normal text-book examples the exports of each country go to each other, the great bulk of the exports of the United States and the United Kingdom in 1937 went to third countries—more than 95 per cent of British exports of all our sample products but three, more than 95 per cent of American exports of all the products but six. It is true that each country was nearly always a net exporter to the other of products in which it had a comparative advantage, but this is of limited interest, since trade between them was in general a negligible proportion of their total consumption." [10]

Thus the preservation—or restoration—of traditional competitive forces in international trade depends essentially on the equal access of all foreign exporters to each national market, rather than on the elimination of all protection for domestic producers within a country's own territory. The latter objective has never been achieved, and can hardly be expected ever to be fully achieved without a political as well as economic merger among the countries concerned. Equal

---

[10] G. D. A. MacDougall, "British and American Exports: A Study Suggested by the Theory of Comparative Costs," Part I, *Economic Journal*, December 1951, pp. 697–724, particularly pp. 697–699. See also below, Table 3, col. 4.

access to third markets has always constituted the bulk and the core of international competition.

Convertibility is not incompatible, therefore, with a certain amount of protection and restrictions. The past is, in this case, a guide to the future. The restoration of convertibility depends essentially on the elimination of discrimination and bilateralism—rather than of *over-all* protection or restrictions—from the trade and payments mechanism. This implies: (1) the ability of country A to use its earnings from countries B, C, D, etc., to settle its deficits with countries X, Y, Z, etc., i.e. full currency transferability; (2) the absence of bilateral or discriminatory trade techniques designed to shift trade artificially from low cost exporters to high cost exporters, thus distorting normal competitive forces not only between domestic and foreign producers, but in all third markets as well.[11]

The two problems are largely inseparable, because payments and trade techniques reinforce one another in this respect and can often be used almost interchangeably to achieve the same result.

The weakness of the International Monetary Fund springs in large part from the artificial separation of these two problems—one of which was entrusted to the Fund, and the other to the General Agreements on Tariff and Trade—but even more from basic defects of the Fund's machinery for dealing with currency transferability. Countries may borrow from the Fund, but they cannot use the Fund to convert their earnings from one country into the currency needed to settle their deficit with another. Moreover, the Fund has in practice made little or no attempt to distinguish between exchange restrictions and discrimination. Organized discrimination against a "scarce currency" is theoretically provided for under Article VII of the Fund Agreement, but this provision has never been tested by the Fund. On the other hand, Fund members have so far retained the right to currency discrimination—against weak as well as against hard currencies—under Article XIV of the Agreement. Similar discrimination is also contemplated as a permanent feature of the Agreement under Article VIII, although its use under this article would be subject to Fund approval.

In contrast, the remarkable success achieved by the European Payments Union is largely explainable by its comprehensive approach to the problem, encompassing full multilateralism both in trade—nondiscrimination—and in payments—currency transferability. This multilateralism, however, is confined to the relationships

---

[11] This definition is very close to that proposed in *Staff Papers*, Commission on Foreign Economic Policy, 1954, pp. 467–468.

among member countries, and does not cover their trade and payments with other countries and particularly with the United States. Partial convertibility with the United States dollar is provided in EPU settlements, but each country is left free to regulate as it wishes its trade and payments with nonmember countries.[12]

Most of the difficulties which the EPU has had to meet in its four years of operation, and most of the objections raised against it, are closely related to these regional limitations of the Agreement. These were, however, unavoidable at the time the Agreement was negotiated. While they are probably unnecessary and even harmful under present conditions, their elimination might prove dangerous in the event of a renewed dollar scarcity, as it might then contribute to the unnecessary spread of deflationary forces and to an ultimate relapse into generalized bilateralism.

The Prerequisites of Convertibility

Convertibility has been defined above as the absence of discrimination, and particularly of discriminatory bilateral action, with respect to both trade and payments. While indispensable to the maintenance of international competition, such a system is also subject to a major defect. It tends to spread to the world at large any deflationary pressures arising from an economic depression or from trade restrictionism in one of the major trading centers. If each of the countries most heavily and directly affected by the decline in this center's imports adopts *nondiscriminatory* policies—internal deflation, currency devaluation, over-all trade or exchange restrictions, etc.—to restore equilibrium in its balance of payments, it will affect unfavorably the balance of payments of other countries. These may, in turn, be compelled to adopt similar policies—or to reinforce them—thus contributing to the spiraling of deflation, devaluation, or restrictions. This process will continue until the first country's surplus is ultimately eliminated, but will involve a multiple restriction of world trade—or an extensive devaluation of currencies—which might have been avoided by direct and systematic discrimination against the surplus country alone. For this alternative to be successful, however, discrimination by the deficit countries must be directed exclusively against the *over-all* creditor country, rather than against

---

[12] Payments to and from nonmember countries of the sterling area are, however, channeled through the United Kingdom's account, and are subject to the same settlement rules as are applicable among members. The same applies also to all other sterling transfers.

the countries in *bilateral* surplus with them, since such bilateral creditors may themselves be in over-all deficit rather than in over-all surplus. If discrimination is left to the discretion of each individual country, acting in isolation, it will inevitably take the form of bilateral discrimination and involve even worse distortions—and, probably, a greater contraction—of world trade.[13]

This was recognized in the "scarce currency" clause of the International Monetary Fund, but the practical implementation of such a clause would raise enormous difficulties. Public opinion in the scarce currency country is likely to pay little heed to the intricate economics of the problem and to react violently against the ganging up of other nations against its exports. The danger of retaliatory action will deter many countries from participating in systematized discrimination. This is all the more likely because such discrimination might involve the imposition of tight restrictions against essential imports from the scarce currency country while unessential imports from other countries continue to be imported freely. Countries can hardly be expected to sacrifice their own national interests in this manner for the sake of an abstract concept of international equilibrium. Certainly, the exact degree of implementation required from each participant would give rise to endless debate and controversies.

A more practical approach to the scarce currency problem lies in the extension of nondiscrimination over the widest possible area, on the basis of mutual agreements and commitments, rather than in any international quarantine of the major creditor country. The EPU experience reveals very clearly the type of commitments necessary for the effective functioning of a multilateral trading area. The creditor countries must facilitate the adoption by the debtors of *nondiscriminatory* readjustment policies:

1. By not hampering such policies through unnecessary trade or exchange restrictions over their own imports (such liberalization commitments were accepted by all EPU members, but were exceeded in practice by the surplus countries)

2. By providing fractional financing to cushion moderate deficits

[13] An abundant literature has grown up around this problem and its applicability to the so-called "dollar shortage." See, in particular:

E. M. Bernstein, "Scarce Currencies and the International Monetary Fund," *Journal of Political Economy*, March 1945, pp. 1–14

Ragnar Frisch, "On the Need for Forecasting a Multilateral Balance of Payments," *American Economic Review*, September 1947, pp. 535–551

John H. Williams, *Trade Not Aid: A Program for World Stability*, Harvard University Press, 1953 of other members with inadequate reserves, thus allowing them to ride out temporary fluctuations in their balance of payments, or to wait for the effect of more slowly acting fiscal or monetary readjustment policies

3. By avoiding retaliatory action against countries which may be compelled to restore restrictions temporarily because of heavier deficits, provided that:

    a. Such restrictions remain nondiscriminatory as among members

    b. The restricting country submits its case to full discussion by the competent organs of the OEEC, with discussion to cover not only the external measures adopted, but the whole range of monetary, fiscal, and economic policies of the country concerned

From Regional Convertibility to International Convertibility

Such a close type of cooperation is hardly feasible on a worldwide basis. It is possible only among countries which are highly interdependent (exports to the EPU area account for nearly three-fourths of member countries' exports), keenly conscious of their interdependence, and able to understand each other's problems and policies. These factors—different in degree, but not in kind, from those underlying a fuller political union—explain the success of, and justify the need for, regional cooperation in trade and payments. The maintenance of freer trade among members constitutes, of course, a form of discrimination. Such discrimination, however, rooted in mutual commitments of the type described above, may be as justified by its broad political and economic results as the discrimination against imports from abroad, and in favor of interregional imports, implicit in present boundaries between nations. The progressive elimination in the nineteenth century of internal taxes on the movement of goods between cities or provinces of the same country presents a hopeful pattern for freer movement of trade among countries ready to accept mutual trade and financial commitments limiting the untrammeled use of their economic sovereignty.

Under the inflationary strains of postwar reconstruction, the sterling area and EPU arrangements provided a practical alternative, not to a better and wider system of international convertibility, but to the infinitely worse alternative of generalized bilateralism in trade and payments. They could not, however, provide a satisfactory answer to the fundamental disequilibria then prevailing between these regions and the outside world and, particularly, to their trade and payments problems with the dollar area. In the sterling area the responsibility for handling these problems centered largely on the United Kingdom, through the administration of the dollar pool and the setting up of different types of sterling accounts—American and Canadian accounts, transferable accounts, resident sterling accounts, bilateral accounts, etc.—subject to different privileges and limitations as to their transferability in payments. In the EPU no such centralization was attempted, and each country was left free to handle its own trade and payments with nonmember countries. On the other hand—and in contrast to the exclusive use of sterling in settlement among sterling area countries—the partial gold or dollar payments involved in EPU settlements established a direct link between the positions of individual EPU countries within and outside the EPU area.

Such a system may tend to stimulate discrimination against an outside scarce currency, but also tends—contrary to a widely spread misconception—to eliminate discrimination if no such scarcity exists.

The stimulus to discrimination arises from both the payments and the trade rules governing the system. EPU creditors are forced to liberalize imports from other EPU members, but are left free to maintain—or liberalize—restrictions on imports from the outside. Since, however, they receive also partial gold or dollar payment for their EPU surpluses, they may be unable to finance large deficits with nonmembers requiring 100 per cent gold or dollar settlements. Even if their gold and dollar position enables them to do so, they may be alarmed by the continued growth of their EPU lending and adopt restrictions on outside imports, in order to force their residents to shift their purchases to EPU sources and thus reduce their rate of lending to the Union.

Debtor countries, on the other hand, will normally prefer to incur their deficits with the Union, rather than with other countries, since deficits with the Union require only partial gold and dollar payment and are, for the remainder, financed by EPU credits. These credits, however, are limited in size. When a country remains persistently in deficit with the Union, its ratio of gold to credit settlements rises steadily until the point of 100 per cent gold settlements is reached. When this occurs, the financial stimulus to discrimination disappears, and the deficit country becomes increasingly reluctant to admit freely less essential, or costlier, imports from EPU sources while continuing to restrict severely more essential or cheaper imports from the outside. On the other hand, such persistent deficits on the part of some members are reflected in persistent surpluses on the part of others. The creditors become increasingly reluctant to continue to extend larger and larger credits beyond their quotas. Since the Union, under these circumstances, is receiving 100 per cent gold settlements from the extreme debtors, its convertible resources tend to increase and to enable it to grant additional payments to the creditors either through a larger ratio of gold to credit settlements, or through some amortization of their previously accumulated claims.

The experience of the EPU so far confirms these theoretical deductions. Of the $1,350 million of EPU credits initially available to them, present members have used about $1,150 million and have therefore only about $200 million in all left available. For many months, France, Turkey, and Greece have been subject to 100 per cent gold settlements and have claimed release from their trade liberalization commitments. Restrictions were also restored by the United Kingdom as long as its quota was exhausted or remained perilously close to exhaustion, and it will be remembered that, for a while, the United Kingdom also accepted sterling payment for dollar commodities bought through London. On the creditors' side, substantial amortization payments were granted to Belgium and Portugal in June 1952, and proposals now under discussion envisage both an increase in gold settlements beyond quotas and the regular amortization of long-outstanding claims.

This normal evolution of the Union toward convertible settlements and nondiscrimination can be held in check, in the long run, only by a severe and generalized dollar scarcity. When this exists, most members will be anxious to preserve their exports against the tighter restrictions applied to dollar trade, and will recognize that this can be done only through mutual trade liberalization and the limited convertibility of intra-EPU settlements. When, however, the dollar position of a majority of members becomes more comfortable, the maintenance of discriminatory trade and payment rules is increasingly regarded not only as contrary to their own selfish interests, but also as unnecessary from the point of view of the group as a whole. It should be noted, for instance, that the EPU management has always prodded excessive debtors to readjust their deficits through monetary and fiscal policies. Exchange readjustments have sometimes been hinted at too, but with a discretion imposed by common sense as well as by the desire to avoid any conflict of jurisdiction with the International Monetary Fund. These pressures had a considerable influence on member countries' policies, particularly in the case of Germany and the Netherlands. They were reinforced in the first case by a special loan negotiated on the basis of an agreed readjustment program, but at no time has the EPU seriously entertained any proposals for further credit extensions to deficit countries which did not take adequate steps to readjust their balance of payments.

We may conclude, therefore, that while *formal* commitments to nondiscrimination and currency transferability are most likely to prove feasible on the basis of regional cooperation, such arrangements will tend *de facto* toward world-wide nondiscrimination and convertibility, except when discrimination against a "scarce currency" becomes the only alternative to the international spread of deflation or of bilateralism.

Even in the latter case the maintenance of currency transferability and nondiscrimination among member countries preserves powerful competitive pressures upon the higher cost countries. It prevents them from seeking in bilateral trade and payments agreements an escape from basic economic readjustments. They can no longer extract from their creditors bilateral import credits or discrimination in favor of their exports. Moreover, the gradual liberalization of trade restrictions among members opens each market to the competition of the lower cost producers in the area, and fundamentally influences the readjustment of national price and cost patterns, indispensable to further progress toward world-wide, rather than merely regional, convertibility. There is little doubt that full competition with Belgian, Swiss, German, and other exporters over the whole EPU area has exercised upon higher cost producers a pressure equivalent, or nearly equivalent, in most cases to that of competition from nonmember countries.

This is confirmed by the near elimination of currency discounts and gold premiums in the European free markets, and by the ease with which major steps toward trade liberalization and broader currency transferability have been absorbed in recent months. The abolition of rationing, the reopening of international commodity and gold markets in London, the merging of practically all nonresident sterling accounts—outside the dollar area—into a single transferable account system, the adoption of a similar system for Deutsche mark accounts, the liberalization of many categories of dollar imports and other transactions in Germany and the Netherlands, etc., have already narrowed considerably the gap between regional and international convertibility. There is every indication today that the remainder of the gap could be bridged if some method could be found to assuage current fears about the existence, or future resurgence, of a world-wide dollar scarcity.

International Inflation and the Dollar Shortage

A "currency scarcity" condition—i.e. the tendency for many countries to incur convergent deficits toward a single "scarce currency" country—may emerge from many different causes. A number of writers have popularized the view that a higher rate of technical advance in the United States tends to create a chronic dollar shortage. The *possibility* of such a link cannot be flatly denied on purely logical grounds. The *demonstration* of its inevitability or probability depends, however, on highly special assumptions as to the exact nature of such productivity advances, and as to their impact on prices and money wages, terms of trade, the income elasticity of import demand, etc. It would not be difficult to construct extremely plausible models of United States advances in productivity whose impact would be to reduce, rather than increase, the balance of payments surpluses of the United States, without exercising any generalized deflationary pressures on foreign prices, export levels, economic activity, or employment.

TABLE 1

Estimated Gold Reserves and Dollar Holdings of Foreign Countries

(*dollars in billions*)

					1953 AS PER CENT OF:		
	1928	1938	1948	1953	1928	1938	1948
Continental Western Europe	$4.8	$ 7.3	$ 5.8	$10.1	207%	138%	172%
France	2.0	3.0	.8	1.1	52	35	132
Switzerland	.2	.9	1.9	2.1	1,080	230	112
Other	2.6	3.4	3.1	6.9	307	177	220
Sterling area	1.4	3.9	2.9	4.0	288	104	138
Canada	.4	.4	1.2	2.4	580	610	198
Latin America	1.1	.9	2.7	3.6	320	380	132
All other foreign countries	1.0	1.3	2.3	2.9	300	225	126
International organizations	...	...	3.4	3.3			99
Total outside United States	$8.7	$13.8	$18.4	$26.4	300%	190%	143%

Details may not add to totals because of rounding.
Source: *Federal Reserve Bulletin*, March 1954, p. 245.

A dollar shortage undoubtedly tends to emerge, however, when the United States economy develops lesser inflationary pressures, or greater deflationary pressures, than the rest of the world. This timeworn doctrine still seems to me sufficient to explain the tendency of European countries to run into heavy dollar deficits during a period of intense inflationary pressures associated with war financing and the reconstruction of war damage, or in the course of a world depression marked by steeper price and income deflation in the United States than in most other industrial countries.

I find it extremely difficult, however, to discover any chronic dollar shortage in the current pattern of world payments. Foreign countries' gold reserves and dollar holdings are estimated to have increased by about $8 billion in the last five years and by $2.6 billion in the year 1953 alone. Table 1 shows that foreign gold and dollar holdings are far higher today than in any previous period. While still inferior to 1938 levels in real purchasing power, they are also probably far better distributed with relation to most countries' import levels and export instability than at any time in the recorded past.

The fears of a dollar shortage spring from the special factors underlying the present pattern of the balance of payments of the world with the United States, and particularly from:

1. The dependence of foreign countries' current dollar earnings on large and "abnormal" United States expenditures for foreign aid and military procurement overseas
2. The expected increase in their dollar needs if present restrictions and discrimination on dollar transactions were eliminated by the restoration of convertibility
3. The possible impact of a United States depression on their levels of reserves, foreign trade, and economic activity in general

THE ROLE OF "ABNORMAL" UNITED STATES EXPENDITURES ABROAD

The 1953 accumulation of gold and dollars by foreign countries far exceeds their total receipts of United States aid.[14] Even the further curtailment of United States military disbursements overseas would leave Western Europe and the Western Hemisphere in approximate gold and dollar equilibrium, but would leave the rest of the world with a deficit of about $1.7 billion (see Table 2).

Adding to this an estimated $.6 billion for stockpiling purchases, the Randall report discerns in these figures a "concealed dollar gap of some $2 billion to $3 billion annually, which would be increased if there were a change in the economic situation, such as a recession

[14] Other than so-called military-end-use items contributed in kind by the United States under military aid programs. This form of aid and the corresponding United States exports have been excluded throughout from the data presented in this paper, since there is every reason to assume that such items would not be imported in significant quantities by foreign countries under circumstances permitting the cessation of military aid programs.

TABLE 2

Gold and Dollar Transactions of Foreign Countries in 1953

(millions of dollars)

	World	Continental Western Europe	Sterling Area	Canada	Latin America	Other Countries	International Organizations
Estimated increase in gold reserves and dollar holdings	2,720	1,670	860	−20	250	−130	90
Through receipts of U.S. aid, Exclusive of Military End Items	1,770	840	400	...	20	420	90
Through all other transactions	950	840	450	−20	230	−540	...
U.S. military purchases of goods and services overseas	2,570	990	280	150	20	1,130	...
Civilian transactions	−1,620	−150	170	−170	210	−1,670	...
Net outflow of U.S. capital	590	−260	90	350	220	140	60
Government	220	−110	...	...	340	−20	...
Private	370	−150	80	350	−120	160	60
Multilateral transfers and errors and omissions	160	200	110	510	110	−730	−40
Recorded in U.S. transactions	−270	100	−220	410	130	−630	−60
Other	430	100	320	100	−20	−90	20
Current account with the U.S.	−2,370	−80	−30	−1,030	−130	−1,090	−20
Receipts	14,680	3,220	2,520	3,020	4,230	1,650	40
Expenditures	17,050	3,300	2,550	4,050	4,360	2,740	60

Source: Data are primarily derived from official estimates of the United States balance of payments, as presented by Walther Lederer on pages 22–23 of the March 1954 issue of the *Survey of Current Business* (Dept. of Commerce). Differences between total changes in estimated gold holdings as reported in the *Federal Reserve Bulletin*, March 1954, p. 240 and the United States gold sales and purchases have been entered under "other multilateral transfers" and added to the reported United States balance on foreign capital and gold to arrive at the "Estimated increase in gold reserves and dollar holdings." Unilateral transfers other than aid have been included in "current account receipts."

here or a deterioration in Western Europe's terms of trade. On the other hand, it should be recognized that major parts of our 'extraordinary' expenditures abroad are connected with our defense effort, and that the Western European countries' own defense programs affect adversely their trade position, by increasing their essential imports and by absorbing resources that would otherwise be available for expanding their exports." [15]

The constant references to Western Europe in these comments suggest that the Commission was not aware that its "concealed dollar gap" concentrates almost entirely on the Far Eastern countries—particularly Japan—whose economies have been disrupted by military events and geared to a high rate of United States military procurement. It is, of course, obvious that these countries are not now accumulating gold and dollar *surpluses* equal to whatever the United States army spends there for procurement of goods and services, plus the amounts of reconstruction or defense support aid to Korea, Nationalist China, etc. This becomes a "concealed dollar gap," however, only if one assumes that such expenditures are likely to be completely eliminated in time, without any corresponding offsets in foreign countries' dollar imports or exports.

Both assumptions would be extremely unrealistic. United States military disbursements overseas are still rising now and will at best taper off gradually, with little or no probability that they will fall to zero in the foreseeable future. Moreover, such tapering off would simultaneously release for consumption, investment, or exports the resources otherwise absorbed in the production of the goods and services contributed under these programs. This trend would be further reinforced by the decline in foreign countries' own military budgets that would be likely under such circumstances.

Absorption of these resources into civilian production will, of course, require difficult economic readjustments. For Western Europe as a whole, the problem is more likely to center on the maintenance of domestic activity and employment than on the balance of payments itself, since its current gold and dollar accumulation is already as large as the total of aid and military disbursements receipts (see Table 2 above). In the Far East, however, the readjustments will bear more heavily on the need to reduce imports or increase exports, and these readjustments might spread to other areas and recreate generalized balance of payments difficulties with the United States if the decline in United States military expendi-

[15] *Report to the President and the Congress*, p. 5.

tures were not offset in part by some increase in United States commercial imports or capital exports. Given the present rate of gold and dollar accumulation by foreign countries ($2.7 billion), however, moderate changes in United States export and import levels would be sufficient to absorb any foreseeable reduction in United States aid and military disbursements.

THE ROLE OF DOLLAR DISCRIMINATION

The removal of discrimination against dollar trade constitutes a second factor of fear and uncertainty in the progress toward convertibility. The Randall Commission *Staff Papers* report that "guesses at the magnitude of the suppressed dollar demand have ranged between $1 billion and $3 billion a year; the true figure at present is probably much closer to the former than to the latter." [16] I am inclined to reduce even further the estimates of the real quantitative impact of dollar discrimination upon the balance of payments.

First of all, we must not forget that more than half of the United States exports flow to such areas as Canada, Central America, the Caribbean Islands, the northern coast of South America, Japan, the Philippines, etc., which either have no exchange controls at all (Canada and most of Central America) or which have no reason to apply discriminatory controls against dollar goods as such.

Second, the proportion of United States and Canadian exports in total imports of the rest of the world is now already far larger than before the war. This is true not only for the world at large, but for all individual areas as well, with the single exception of the sterling area. The proportion is about one-third larger than in 1937 for Latin American and continental EPU countries, and 20 per cent larger for the countries outside the sterling area, continental EPU, and Western Hemisphere.

Third, while the elimination of dollar discrimination will tend toward an expansion of United States exports, two other factors are now acting in the opposite direction. The reduction in foreign aid eliminates some elements of discrimination *in favor of* United States shipping and commodities previously purchased under the ECA, MSA, or FOA procurement authorizations. Moreover, the recovery of production and the abatement of inflationary forces abroad reduce foreign demand for other United States goods imported in abnormal quantities in earlier years. It should be noted that the proportion of United States and Canadian goods in the

[16] *Staff Papers,* p. 18.

total imports of Western Europe and the sterling area has declined substantially over the past year, in spite of greater dollar availabilities and of the trend toward a relaxation of dollar discrimination abroad. The continuation of this trend, in a noninflationary environment, might well result primarily in price readjustments by soft currency exporters, rather than in any large diversion in the pattern of trade. This would be all the more likely if progress toward nondiscrimination were undertaken simultaneously by all major trading countries rather than by one or a few countries alone.

For all these reasons the relaxation of trade and currency discrimination against dollar goods is likely to have a much more moderate impact on the dollar position of foreign countries than is generally feared. In any case, the relatively small order of magnitude of its possible effects should be kept in mind. For instance, a 25 per cent increase in United States exports to the sterling area—where discrimination is most stringent and effective—would amount to about $375 million, and a 10 per cent increase in exports to continental Western Europe and the nondollar countries of Latin America to about $250 million and $100 million, respectively, i.e. a total of about $700 million a year.

THE INTERNATIONAL IMPACT OF A UNITED STATES RECESSION

The international impact of a United States recession could hardly be estimated in advance with any degree of precision. It may be noted, however, that the mild recession experienced since the summer of 1953 has had a far smaller impact on foreign dollar incomes than was generally expected. Gold and dollar holdings continued to rise at a rate of more than $2 billion a year throughout the period October 1953–March 1954. Current and prospective levels of foreign aid and military expenditures—at a rate of $4.3 billion a year—will continue for some time to act as a powerful stabilizing influence on foreign countries' dollar earnings. For the next two or three years at least, a United States recession might be expected primarily to slow down the current accumulation of gold and dollars abroad, but it is highly unlikely to resurrect any large surpluses in the United States balance of payments with the rest of the world.

The international impact of United States recessions, however, is not limited to direct trade between each country and the United States itself. Their major disruptive effects lie in the transmission of contractive forces from country to country, through their own mutual trade as well as through their trade with the United States. The channels through which these indirect effects are propagated are of several kinds:

1. The demand of each country for exports from other countries—and not only from the United States—may contract automatically as a consequence of the lower income levels resulting from:

   a. The loss of export earnings to the United States.

   b. Possibly, the deterioration in its terms of trade associated with a United States recession.

2. This will affect income levels in the supplying countries and react in turn on their own imports from the first, spreading the contraction from each country to the others.

3. This spiral of contractive tendencies may be broken, or on the contrary accentuated, by the economic policies adopted in each country:

   a. Some countries may succeed, through compensatory policies, in preventing a decline in national income levels and maintaining their import demand at a higher level; their balance of payments will tend to deteriorate as a consequence, reducing previous balance of payments surpluses or causing a drain on their monetary reserves.

   b. Some countries may impose currency depreciation, tariff increases, or import and exchange restrictions as either (1) the consequence of reserve losses, whether automatic or resulting from the compensatory policies above, or (2) a substitute for such compensatory policies, in order to offset through increased exports and decreased imports the effects of the recession on economic activity, incomes, and employment. Such restrictions would aggravate the difficulties of other countries.

The international propagation and intensification of a United States recession can be considerably reduced by measures which will encourage and enable countries to follow compensatory policies (3a above) rather than disruptive policies (3b above) in the course of such a recession. The difficulties of the task will be far smaller if action is taken at an early stage rather than after the recession has been permitted to spread over a wider and wider area.

The direct impact of a United States recession will be heaviest on the countries most dependent on the United States market for their exports. Canada and Latin American countries sell in the United States market about half of their total exports, while European and sterling area countries trade far more extensively with one another and sell only about 10 per cent of their total exports to the United States (see Table 3). This ratio is substantially exceeded by only a few countries outside the Western Hemisphere—mainly the Philippines, India, Indonesia, and Japan. It varies greatly, however, among individual Latin American countries, from about 25 per cent in the River Plate countries to more than 80 per cent in Mexico, Guatemala, El Salvador, and Colombia.

TABLE 3

Gold and Dollar Holdings, Total Exports, and Exports to the the United States in 1953

(*dollars in billions*)

	GOLD AND DOLLARS HOLDINGS	TOTAL EXPORTS	EXPORTS TO U.S.	PER CENT RATIO OF EXPORTS TO U.S. TO TOTAL EXPORTS	PER CENT RATIO OF GOLD AND DOLLAR HOLDINGS TO:	
					Total Exports	*Exports to U.S.*
Continental Western Europe and dependencies	$10.06	$22.2	$ 2.51	11%	45%	401%
Sterling area	4.05	18.4	1.82	10	22	222
Canada	2.42	4.6	2.52	55	52	96
Latin America	3.63	7.6	3.58	47	48	101
Other countries	2.90	6.0	1.47	24	48	197
All foreign countries	23.04	59.0	11.90	20	39	194
International organizations	3.34	. . .	. . .	. . .	. . .	. . .
Total	$26.39	$59.0	$11.90	20%	45%	222%

Sources: Gold and dollar holdings: *Federal Reserve Bulletin,* March 1954, p. 245.
Total exports: *International Financial Statistics,* April 1954, pp. 22 and 24.
Exports to the United States: *Survey of Current Business,* Dept. of Commerce, March 1954, pp. 22–23.

A 30 per cent decline in exports to the United States would therefore have a very different significance for these various countries or areas. It would correspond to only 3 per cent of over-all exports and 7.5 per cent of gold and dollar holdings for continental Western Europe, but to about 16 per cent of total exports and 31 per cent of gold and dollar holdings for Canada.

There are also very great variations in the cyclical sensitivity of different countries' exports to the United States. Sterling area exports have usually been affected far more severely and those of Canada substantially less severely, than those of other areas during past United States recessions. Exporters of wool (Australia, New Zealand, Argentina, Uruguay), minerals (Bolivia, Chile, Mexico), and raw materials in general suffer a far heavier decline than exporters of coffee, bananas (Brazil, Colombia, Central America), sugar, and other foods.

Taking into account both criteria—ratio of exports to the United States to total exports or GNP, and sensitivity of those exports to United States recessions—we should expect the most severe direct repercussions of a United States recession in some Western Hemisphere countries—particularly Canada, Mexico, Bolivia, Chile, Argentina, and Uruguay—and in Japan, the Philippines, Indonesia, and the overseas sterling area.

TABLE 4

Per Cent Changes in Exports to the United States

	1923–1924	1926–1927	1929–1932	1937–1938	1948–1949
Continental Western Europe	−6	. . .	−71	−32	−12
Sterling area	−11	−18	−79	−48	−18
Canada	−4	. . .	−65	−35	−2
Latin America	+1	−8	−68	−32	. . .
Other countries a	−8	. . .	−67	−34	−6
Total	−5	−6	−70	−35	−7

a Excluding Eastern Europe.

International policies designed to avoid or moderate the further spread and spiraling of the depression fall into two major categories: monetary policies and trade policies.

Untied loans in convertible currencies—whether from international institutions or from high reserve countries—may be necessary to relieve these countries of severe balance of payments pressures and enable them:

1. To avoid deflationary or restrictionist policies which will aggravate the depression elsewhere
2. To adopt positive compensatory domestic policies designed to sustain income levels, employment, and imports

The amount of assistance required for this purpose will depend, of course, on the level of these countries' reserves. Current ratios of gold and dollar holdings to total exports now average 40 to 50 per cent for all major regions except the sterling area (see column 5 of Table 3 above). Sterling area and EPU arrangements, however, result in a considerable economy of gold and dollar settlements in intra-area trade. As long as these arrangements continue, the need for external stabilization loans will be considerably less than it would otherwise be for Western Europe and the sterling area. The resources of the IMF in gold and United States dollars—more than $3 billion

—and in the currencies of other prospective creditors could provide all, or at least a considerable portion, of the residual assistance needed *and actually usable* to overcome the reserve deficiencies *arising from a United States recession.*

The latter qualifications, however, limit considerably the significance to be attached to international monetary cooperation as an antirecession device. Such cooperation may be more effective in preventing deflationary or restrictionist policies than in stimulating positive compensatory policies. The latter policies would prove very difficult to implement for many of the countries most severely affected by a United States recession, even if large stabilization loans relieved them of any anxiety about their reserve losses and balance of payments deficits. It is by no means easy to provide alternative employment for the men and resources left idle by the loss of export markets, especially in countries highly specialized in one or a few export products, such as tin, copper, and rubber.

Moreover, the ability of these countries to repay at a later stage the loans extended to them may very often be questioned by the prospective lenders. The lenders may take the view—rightly or wrongly—that balance of payments difficulties are aggravated during the recession, and will persist long after the end of the recession, as the result of ill-advised or irresponsible domestic policies. Disagreements on such points are likely to prove a stumbling block in many cases, especially when decisions have to be made—as is the case in the IMF—by many countries with diverse geographical, historical, and economic backgrounds. They may create far lesser difficulties in more closely knit organizations, such as the EPU and the sterling area, which group countries more highly interdependent economically, more keenly conscious of such interdependence, and more familiar with one another's problems and policies. While stabilization loans are a useful antirecession device, their limitations should be recognized and should prompt further efforts in other directions as well.

Commodity agreements and buffer stocks designed to reduce excessive instability in agricultural and raw material markets would be of far greater value to primary producing countries than monetary stabilization loans. The difficulties raised by such schemes are enormous, but so are their potentialities for economic stabilization and development.[17] One must regret, therefore, the rather cursory dismissal of this approach to the problem in the Randall Commission's report. Some of the Commission's recommendations, and

[17] See *Commodity Trade and Economic Development*, United Nations, 1953.

particularly the "avoidance of actions incidental to our own commodity control and stockpile programs that would have avoidably disruptive effects upon world prices" [18] and "continued consultation and cooperation with other nations to improve knowledge of world supply and demand for materials and food-stuffs, and to explore possible means of lessening instability," [19] are all to the good, but give little hope for concrete action in the near future. This conclusion is clearly shared by the Commission itself, which also recommends "a policy of encouragement of diversification of the economies of the countries now excessively dependent upon a small number of products." [20] The benefits of international specialization must, to this extent, be sacrificed to the objective of domestic economic stability. In practice, however, the costs and difficulties of diversification policies may well be as formidable as those of commodity stabilization, or more so.

The above measures will at best reduce, but not eliminate, the direct impact of reduced earnings from exports to the United States on the monetary reserves and economic activity of the countries affected. They should be coupled with other policy commitments designed to avoid, to the maximum extent, the adoption of beggar-my-neighbor policies of currency devaluation, tariff increases, trade and exchange controls, discrimination, and bilateralism, which are a major factor in propagating and intensifying international recessions. The cooperation of the major and stronger nations is particularly vital in this respect. The influence of their policies on other countries, and their ability to use alternative measures to fight depressive tendencies at home, are usually far greater than those of the smaller or less developed economies.

No country, however, can be expected to renounce any means to improve its own domestic activity and employment, even at the expense of others, on the basis of Platonic appeals to international cooperation. While each may realize that the cumulative effect of mutual restrictions will be damaging to all, none will feel assured that its own restraint, or lack of restraint, in this respect will decisively influence the policies of other countries. Mutual commitments, of a positive as well as of a negative nature, encompassing credit provisions together with trade provisions, remain the most promising way to promote the maximum degree of trade freedom and cooperative antirecession policies. International agreements of the International Trade Organization or GATT type deserve greater

[18] *Report to the President and the Congress*, pp. 35–36.
[19] *Ibid.*, p. 36.   [20] *Ibid.*, p. 36.

United States support than they have received in recent years. On the other hand, in this field as well as in the monetary field, regional organizations may develop a far closer degree of intimate cooperation among the participating countries than can be anticipated on a world-wide scale. The combination of trade, credit, and economic policy commitments and negotiations into a single institution can also contribute to greater success in all three fields, as the OEEC experiment has amply demonstrated during its brief span of years. We thus rejoin the conclusions reached in the previous discussion of the best means to restore and preserve convertibility in a world of national sovereignties. Regional cooperation should be viewed as a valuable adjunct, rather than a rival, of world-wide agreements.

Conclusions

The current rate of gold and dollar accumulation in Western Europe and the sterling area, together with prospective rates of United States aid and military expenditures overseas over the next few years, provide a considerable cushion against a hypothetical United States depression. We should therefore expect a continuation, and even an acceleration, of the progress already achieved in recent years and months toward currency transferability and trade liberalization.

These, however, are fair weather objectives which can be pressed forward only in an environment of high economic activity and employment. In times of depression each nation will almost inevitably resort again to trade restrictions and currency inconvertibility in an effort to insulate its own economy from external deflationary pressures. These policies cannot be successful in the end, as each country's actions tend to aggravate the difficulties of others, widening and deepening the contractionist tendencies at work. National antidepression policies of this character have always proved in the past one of the main factors in the spread and aggravation of international recessions.

This spiral can be broken only by collective arrangements giving operational meaning to the interdependence of the various countries' policies. The avoidance of disruptive action should be made both possible and attractive through adequate access to stabilization assistance in case of need and through reciprocal guarantees against all unnecessary recourse to trade and exchange restrictions. Where restrictions become unavoidable, they should be limited in scope and time, and unilateral discrimination against any country participating in the arrangements should be shunned.

International cooperation of this sort is, however, extremely difficult to negotiate and implement in practice. Moderation in its aims, hopes, and promises is indispensable to avoid later disillusionment, disaffection, and retrogression. Negotiation and implementation of world-wide arrangements are particularly slow and cumbersome, and such arrangements will necessarily remain more limited in their effective content than regional arrangements among countries which are highly interdependent, keenly aware of this interdependence, and readier to understand each other's problems and policies and to confide in the commitments and good faith of their partners.

Both types of approach should be developed and encouraged, and the potentialities of each should be as fully exploited as proves possible in practice. Much could be done today to improve the effectiveness of world-wide organizations such as GATT or the IMF. Much could be done also, under present favorable circumstances, to relax some of the regional limitations of the EPU and sterling area systems. Individual countries—particularly Britain, Germany, and the Netherlands—have recently taken important measures in this direction, but drastic revisions in the EPU Agreement to adjust it to the enormous changes which have taken place in the international pattern of trade and payments since the negotiation of the Agreement, four years ago, are now long overdue.

Major creditor nations—and especially the United States—will inevitably exercise a profound influence on the progress of other countries and of both regional and international organizations toward currency convertibility and trade liberalization. The United States has a major stake, economically and politically, in the promotion of liberal economic policies abroad and in the strengthening and development of other free nations. These objectives happily coincide with the interests of both consumers and producers in the reduction of tariff and trade barriers here, and with the need to provide increasing outlets for our exports of goods and capital.

The obvious shortcomings of the Randall Commission's report as a basic document on fundamental, long-term United States international economic policy have attracted more attention in academic circles than its very real contribution to the clarification of urgently needed, and immediately feasible, United States action in the monetary and trade field. The adoption of its major recommendations would provide the necessary spark for further and considerable advances toward the rebuilding of a workable international framework for economic growth and stability.

COMMENT

WILLIAM A. SALANT, BRANDEIS UNIVERSITY

Triffin has performed a remarkable feat by presenting a discussion of the international trade and payments problem that is at once brief, comprehensive, and fresh. His principal conclusions, as I see them, are:

1. The international payments situation is now far better balanced than at any previous time in the postwar period, and far better balanced than is often realized, especially by those of us who have become so accustomed to a state of "dollar shortage" that we have come to regard it as a permanent feature of the economic landscape.

2. The steps required to achieve an effective multilateral system of trade and payments—"workable" convertibility, as Triffin calls it—are far less formidable than those required to reach what might be called "perfect" convertibility.

3. Such a multilateral system, if attained, would be a precarious fair weather system unless supported by international commitments and facilities designed to prevent it from collapsing at the first gusts of adversity.

With these major conclusions I am in hearty agreement. My comments will represent, on the whole, not disagreements but rather elaborations or qualifications of Triffin's argument, elaborations or qualifications which, in some cases, he might well have inserted himself if time and space had permitted.

Triffin has adopted the view that convertibility, to be meaningful, must apply in some sense to the sphere of trade as well as to that of payments. He has concluded, however, that we must reconcile ourselves to some element of protection of national markets, and he is unwilling to accept the principle that tariffs are permissible while quantitative restrictions are beyond the pale. Accordingly, he has defined as his goal the elimination of discrimination and bilateralism in trade and payments alike. This approach emphasizes the elimination of discrimination in the application of import restrictions, rather than reduction of the level of those restrictions.

Now a country which restricts its "hard currency" imports more drastically than its "soft currency" imports can eliminate that discrimination in either of two ways (or by some combination of the two): it can relax the more severe restrictions, or it can tighten up the less severe ones. Either course of action will result in nondiscrimination and therefore satisfy Triffin's criterion of "workable" convertibility.

This formulation of the problem may well be open to the interpretation, certainly not intended by Triffin, that either route to nondiscrimination in trade restriction is equally desirable, or to the less extreme interpretation that "workable" convertibility, achieved through the second route, the tightening up of the less severe import restrictions, is more desirable than inconvertibility. If freedom from restrictions is regarded as desirable, the first and more extreme interpretation can be dismissed at once, but the second merits some discussion. I doubt the desirability of convertibility if it must be attained at the cost of leveling up import restrictions.

The point is not academic, as further examination will indicate. Assume a country with an inconvertible currency, which maintains severe import restrictions against countries with convertible currencies, and more liberal ones against other inconvertible countries. (This assumption describes, with varying degrees of accuracy, the actual present position of most of the EPU members and many other countries.) The country now makes its currency convertible in the sense that nonresidents who earn it through legal current transactions are permitted freely to convert their earnings into any foreign currency.[1]

At this point, if the authorities took no further action, their currency would be convertible only in the strictly financial sense; they would not have attained "workable" convertibility because they continue to discriminate against imports from other convertible countries. This situation, however, is inherently unstable, because the distinction between "hard currency" and "soft currency" imports disappears as soon as the currency becomes convertible, and the authorities therefore lose any balance of payments reason to

---

[1] For example, if the currency in question were sterling, a French wine merchant (or, alternatively, his central bank) would be permitted to convert the sterling proceeds of his exports to Great Britain into dollars or any other currency he chose. In the following paragraphs the term "convertibility" will be used in this sense, which is of course narrower than Triffin's "workable" convertibility, since it applies only to currency arrangements, not to nondiscrimination in trade restriction. Convertibility in Triffin's sense will be referred to explicitly as "workable" convertibility.

discriminate unilaterally against imports from convertible countries.[2]

The authorities of the newly convertible country can take any of three courses of action with respect to their import restrictions (or any combination of the three):

1. They can eliminate discrimination by liberalizing the restrictions against countries with convertible currencies.

2. They can eliminate discrimination by tightening up the restrictions against countries with inconvertible currencies.

3. Despite the point just made, that the balance of payments incentive to discriminate disappears when the currency becomes convertible, they may nevertheless make no change in their import restrictions; that is, they may continue to discriminate. The rationale of this possibility will be discussed below.

It is possible to offer some general observations about the circumstances in which each of these courses of action is likely to predominate. If a country makes its currency convertible at a time when it, as well as other inconvertible countries, is suffering from a "shortage" (in some relevant sense) of convertible currencies, it is entirely likely that the establishment of convertibility will be followed by a tightening of import restrictions as between the newly convertible country and the remaining inconvertible ones. Some of the relevant criteria of "dollar shortage" are (1) unsatisfactory balance of payments and reserve position, (2) lack of access to substantial international credits or reserves, and (3) high suppressed demand for dollar imports which is dammed up behind the discriminatory import restrictions. If these symptoms of dollar shortage are present, a newly convertible country which liberalized its restrictions against hard currency imports could expect its payments position to deteriorate on two counts: its hard currency imports would increase, and its exports to inconvertible countries would decline as they began to treat it as a hard currency source

---

[2] For example, an import of French wine involves a cost in convertible currency as surely as an import of Canadian wheat or American cotton. This assertion implicitly assumes the further condition that current-account balances between Great Britain and France are not settled by short-term capital movements, official or private, but rather that they are ultimately settled, whether through the action of the market or the central banks, by the transfer of some other convertible currency, such as dollars, or in gold. If this condition is realized, the statement that British imports of French wine involve a cost in convertible currency or gold is valid whether Great Britain has a deficit in its bilateral transactions with France, which permits France on balance to convert sterling into dollars or gold, or whether Great Britain has a surplus which France must settle by converting gold or dollars into sterling.

in applying their own import restrictions. In an effort to avoid this deterioration, the newly convertible country might well narrow the margin of discrimination by tightening up its restrictions on imports from inconvertible countries.

The fear of some such sequence of events as this played an important role in the reaction of some of the continental EPU countries to the proposals for convertibility advanced by the British in the spring of 1953, and, as Triffin has pointed out, led to their insistence that convertibility must not mean abandonment of the OEEC trade liberalization program. Thus it is entirely possible to conceive of a situation in which the attainment of convertibility is accompanied by agreement among a group of countries to continue to discriminate in order to avert the danger of a wave of restriction. Although currency convertibility removes the incentive for unilateral discrimination on balance of payments grounds, it still leaves room for discrimination by multilateral or bilateral agreement. (There may, of course, be additional commercial reasons for discrimination.)

The question arises whether this narrow form of currency convertibility, unaccompanied by any change in trade restrictions, would serve any useful purpose. One of the major economic gains to be derived from convertibility is a more efficient utilization of economic resources in the world. If, however, the removal of currency restrictions is not accompanied or followed by any change in trade restrictions, the flow of trade and the utilization of resources will be unaffected. It is this consideration which has led Triffin, the Randall Commission, and others to emphasize that convertibility, to be meaningful and useful, must include nondiscrimination in trade restrictions as well as in payments.

How are we to evaluate the second possibility, in which the newly convertible country eliminates discrimination by tightening its restrictions on soft currency imports, while the remaining inconvertible countries reciprocate by restricting more severely their imports from it? The chances are excellent that the flow of trade will be reduced and the utilization of resources will become less efficient (although this latter result is not inevitable). Thus when convertibility and nondiscrimination are attained through the leveling up of import restrictions, they are probably of negative value. This consideration suggests that, in the appraisal of any move toward "workable" convertibility, interest should not be confined to the elimination of discrimination, but should extend to the level of the restrictions.

The foregoing discussion suggests that, if convertibility in the technical financial sense is established under adverse conditions, either trade restrictions will remain unchanged, in which case nothing will be accomplished, or they may become more severe (although less discriminatory), which will probably represent a retrograde step. The difficulty, when import restrictions are severe, of measuring the latent demand for hard currency imports that is repressed by those restrictions adds to the risk inherent in taking large discontinuous steps toward convertibility under unfavorable conditions.[3]

In any concerted effort to move away from a restrictive trade and payments regime such as characterized the postwar period, it is probably desirable that the establishment of currency convertibility be preceded by a gradual relaxation of discriminatory restrictions against hard currency imports. In this way the margin of discrimination would be narrowed before the more drastic step of establishing currency convertibility were ventured. In recent years the trend has been precisely in this direction.

My second comment relates to the situation in which, after convertibility has been attained, a severe decline in the imports of an important trading country puts pressure on the balances of payments and income levels of other countries. The scarce currency clause of the IMF agreement was designed to meet this situation, which is usually associated with depression in the United States. Triffin doubts the practical value of the scarce currency provision and suggests an alternative approach drawn from the experience of the EPU. Yet it is not entirely clear that his alternative will really meet the situation. Some of the alternative's major elements seem to apply to a quite different problem—the problem of a single deficit country which falls into balance of payments difficulties for reasons peculiar to itself—rather than to the problem of a large number of countries in deficit because of a depression originating in a single surplus country. It would certainly be highly unfortunate if, in response to a decline in the level of economic activity and imports of one country, the rest of the world immediately and automatically applied discriminatory import restrictions against the depressed

---

[3] It was widely reported that in March 1952, when the reserve crisis of 1951–1952 was still in progress, the British government came within a "hair's breadth" of making a "dash for convertibility," in the language of the London *Economist* (November 15, 1952). Such action would presumably have been confined to the currency field, and it might well have led to measures to make sterling scarcer by tightening trade restrictions.

country. It would be far preferable, if possible, to meet the situation by nonrestrictive measures. Nevertheless, if restrictions become unavoidable, there is a strong case for the general principle that restrictions limited to imports from the surplus country are preferable to all-round restrictions. Whether the scarce currency provision is a practicable and desirable method of applying this general principle is, of course, another question.

Before we leave the subject of discriminatory trade restrictions, it is worth noting that discrimination is a usual, if not inevitable, by-product of "economic integration" of groups of countries. If two or more countries reduce the economic barriers among themselves, in connection with an agreement to coordinate their economic policies (e.g. the Benelux Union, not fully implemented) or to establish a unified market in a specified group of products (e.g. the Schuman Plan), they will probably be unwilling to extend this liberalization to the rest of the world. Such integration may well be desirable even though it implies discrimination.

In his final section Triffin refers to the tendency for dollar shortage to appear when the United States develops less inflationary pressure, or greater deflationary pressure, than the rest of the world. He appears to regard this tendency as sufficient explanation for the dollar difficulties of the postwar period. While accepting it as an extremely important element in the explanation, I should be inclined to give some weight to at least two additional factors, which might be described as nonmonetary.[4] The first is the impact of the war on European capacity to produce and to earn foreign exchange. The second is the effect of longer-term changes in the economic relations between the older industrial areas of Western Europe and the newer industrial and primary producing areas of the rest of the world. It is at least a possibility worth considering, one which can only be mentioned here without elaboration, that economic development in the rest of the world has caused changes in the conditions of international demand and supply which have been unfavorable to Western Europe, at least in part and in their initial impact, and that

[4] The distinction between "monetary" and "nonmonetary" factors is, of course, notoriously treacherous. It could be argued, for example, that the "nonmonetary" factors referred to here, although they would affect real incomes, would not give rise to balance of payments deficits or dollar stringency if inappropriate "monetary" policies did not prevent adjustment of the balance of payments. Whether or not this contention is valid, our present concern is with the factors causing the initial disequilibrium, not with the failure of the system to establish a new equilibrium instantaneously. It is not believed that the use of the term "nonmonetary" will give rise to misunderstanding in the context of the present discussion.

this unfavorable development has, for a variety of reasons, manifested itself in the form of "dollar shortage" in the postwar period. If this hypothesis has any validity, it would suggest that one of the factors that determines the stability of the present state of international balance is the extent to which the structure of world trade has been readjusted in response to these long-term developments. A familiar example of the kind of readjustment that has been required in the past in response to developments in the rest of the world is the long-sustained decline in the share of British exports represented by textiles, which began well back in the last century, and the increase in the share represented by engineering products.

Triffin calls attention to the striking improvement in both the magnitude and the distribution of the gold and dollar reserves held outside the United States. While his observation is valid in general, it should be noted that the distribution of reserves at the end of 1953 was still not as favorable to the sterling area as might be considered desirable in relation to possible needs and commitments. Nor, according to Table 1 in Triffin's paper, was it as favorable as in 1938, when the sterling area held 28 per cent of the gold reserves and dollar holdings outside the United States, as compared with 15 per cent at the end of 1953.[5] The adequacy of sterling reserves is, of course, of particular importance since current discussion of convertibility revolves around convertibility of sterling.

The Randall Commission and others have argued that the present state of world dollar balance conceals a substantial dollar gap associated with the "extraordinary" dollar expenditures of the United States government in foreign countries for defense purposes, including stockpiling, offshore procurement, construction, and the support of United States military establishments. Triffin rightly points out that, unlike aid, these disbursements are not unilateral transfers which are costless to the receiving country, since they represent payment for currently produced goods and services. As the disbursements decline (if they do), the resources producing the goods and services will be released and will become available for other purposes, including support of the balance of payments of the foreign country concerned. Although it is true that the resources will be released, it does not by any means follow that they can readily and smoothly be reabsorbed (as Triffin concedes). The

---

[5] It should be added that official gold and dollar reserves of the United Kingdom increased by a further half billion dollars between the end of 1953 and the middle of 1954, and that the share of world reserves held by the United Kingdom in the late thirties was considerably higher than in preceding periods.

problem of adjustment will be aggravated because a high proportion of the extraordinary disbursements represent payment for such services as housing and local labor supplied to United States establishments. In the case of services, it is particularly difficult to see how the resources released can be redirected in such a way as to fill the gap in the balance of payments arising from the loss of these receipts.

INDEX

incidence, 111, 121-122, 159-160, 171-172

increase in contractions, 176, 178-179, 183

progressiveness, 107-108, 109

reductions as stabilizers, 12, 13, 44, 55, 64, 73, 176, 181-182, 191-192, 203

(*see also* Budget flexibility; Corporation income tax; Government revenue as stabilizer; *and* Personal income tax)

Technical change, 9, 10

Terminals as public works, 272-274

Todd, Thomas R., 263

Toll highways and bridges, 188, 257, 259, 262-271, 280-287, 288, 292

Transfer payments, as automatic stabilizers, 12, 82, 87, 92-93, 94-95, 102, 105, 242-243 (*see also* Old age and survivors' insurance and related programs; Social security programs; *and* Unemployment compensation)

Types of business cycles, 7-12, 14-16, 21, 22-25, 103-104, 106, 243-244

(*see also* Diagnosis of contractions)

Uncertainty, 10

Undistributed profits tax, 166-169, 170

Unemployment, 13, 34, 45, 49, 59, 61, 65, 70-73, 79, 95, 101, 103, 110, 198-199, 211-213, 221, 223-225, 228, 229, 231, 234-235

Unemployment compensation, 13, 50, 92-93, 95, 110, 205-220, 234

U.S. international aid programs, 35-36, 42, 98-99, 392-395, 410-411

Wage-price relationships, 19-21, 40, 43, 51

Warranted rate of growth of investment, 66-67 (*see also* Population growth)

Weil, Ulric, 130n

Weston, J. F., 15n

Wheat agreement, 96, 361, 373

White, Anne, 198n

White, Melvin I., 198n

Williams, John H., 386n

Winnick, Louis, 242n